The Collected Works of
James M. Buchanan

VOLUME 12
Economic Inquiry and Its Logic

James M. Buchanan, Witten/Herdecke University,
Witten, Germany, October 1986

The Collected Works of

James M. Buchanan

VOLUME 12

Economic Inquiry and Its Logic

LIBERTY FUND

Indianapolis

This book is published by Liberty Fund, Inc., a foundation established to encourage study of the ideal of a society of free and responsible individuals.

The cuneiform inscription that serves as our logo and as the design motif for our endpapers is the earliest-known written appearance of the word "freedom" (*amagi*), or "liberty." It is taken from a clay document written about 2300 B.C. in the Sumerian city-state of Lagash.

04 03 02 01 00   C   5 4 3 2 1
04 03 02 01 00   P   5 4 3 2 1

Library of Congress Cataloging-in-Publication Data
Buchanan, James M.
Economic inquiry and its logic.
p.   cm. — (The collected works of James M. Buchanan ; v. 12)
Includes bibliographical references and index.
ISBN 0-86597-235-4 (hc : alk. paper). — ISBN 0-86597-236-2 (pb : alk. paper)
1. Economics.   I. Title.   II. Series: Buchanan, James M.
Works.   1999 ; v. 12.
HB71.B7792   2000
330—dc21   99-42838

LIBERTY FUND, INC.
8335 Allison Pointe Trail, Suite 300
Indianapolis, IN 46250-1684

Contents

2. Competition and Entrepreneurship

3. The Theory of Monopoly

4. Input Prices

5. Opportunity Cost and Efficient Prices

6. Increasing Returns and the Work Ethic

7. Economic Theory in a Postsocialist World

Foreword

Throughout his career James M. Buchanan has been a creative economic theorist, and he has always been interested in how we go about "doing" economics and what we presuppose as economic theorists. Moreover, in the tradition of the University of Chicago, where he took his graduate training in economics, Buchanan has also had a strong interest in microeconomic theory and its uses in explaining the pattern of economic behavior and institutional evolution. In this regard I would characterize him as an "armchair" theorist. He has never been interested in empirical research in the sense of econometric testing of hypotheses. Instead, he has sometimes been critical of such efforts, likening them to proving that "water runs downhill." Nonetheless, he has an abiding interest in the explanatory power of economic theory in the sense that such theory explains the world around us. For example, does the application of economic self-interest in a given situation lead to sensible inferences and predictions? This is the methodological consistency that Buchanan expects from economic theory, and many of the papers in this volume are written in this spirit.

With respect to this volume, which collects some of Buchanan's work in economic method and analysis, it should be stressed that many of the better-known papers in this area appear elsewhere in his Collected Works. For example, much of his work in public economics and public finance was quintessentially price-theoretic in nature. I need only mention here Buchanan's theory of clubs or his various papers on externality theory. The exceptional quality of all of this research, including the papers in this volume, is the expression of a truly creative economic theorist.

Buchanan's contributions to the discussion of economic method are, for the most part, well known. Reprinted in this volume are some of his most often cited works on methodology, including papers reflecting his emphasis on the subjective nature of opportunity costs and the implications of this subjectivity for economic analysis.

This volume also demonstrates Buchanan's continuing interest in the ideas and issues posed by economic theory. For example, we see that in recent years he has returned to the classic literature on increasing returns and made an important contribution in observing how this literature relates to ethical norms and to the work ethic in particular. And the pattern is the same across the other areas covered in this volume. The puzzle is always deep, perhaps related to an earlier classic literature on the subject. And it is basically the idea or the challenge of the idea that drives the analysis. The level of the analysis is rarely very technical in a mathematical sense, but it is always useful in terms of the level of insight applied to a difficult problem.

The volume begins in part 1 with many of Buchanan's classic papers on the methodology of economic science. The essays in part 2 consider the role of the entrepreneur in several unusual contexts. The papers in part 3 represent various contributions to the theory of monopoly pricing. The papers in part 4 consider the pricing of inputs, sometimes in novel ways. The papers in part 5 explore various points in the economic theory of efficient pricing. The papers in part 6 represent the results of Buchanan's recent return to the theory of increasing returns. As noted earlier, his papers on the work ethic are new and provocative. Finally, the papers in part 7 reflect Buchanan's views on the role of economic theory in a postsocialist world. His pessimism and feeling that economics has lost its way provide interesting reading and food for thought.

Buchanan, above all, is a creative economic theorist. He has provided us with insights across a broad range of issues, reflected in this and the other volumes of his Collected Works. The papers in this volume give us an idea of the theorist in his workshop. What is the nature of the issues that attract him? How does he deal with them? How do we profit from his efforts and insights? There are many gifts under Buchanan's tree.

Robert D. Tollison
University of Mississippi
1999

PART ONE

The Practice and Method of Economic Theory

Is Economics the Science of Choice?

... from time to time it is probably necessary to detach one's self from the technicalities of the argument and to ask quite naively what it is all about.

—F. A. Hayek, "Economics and Knowledge."

Robert Mundell commences his Preface to *Man and Economics* with the assertion: "Economics is the science of choice."[1] Most professional scholars who check off the box marked "Economist" on the Register of Scientific Personnel find no quarrel with Mundell's statement. Despite some danger of once again being called iconoclastic, I propose to examine this assertion seriously and critically. In the process, I shall not discuss what economics is or is not, should or should not be, at least in any direct sense. My question is more elementary, and its answer is obvious once it is asked. I want to ask whether a *science* of *choice* is possible at all. Are we not involved in a contradiction in terms?

There is no need to go beyond the everyday usage of the two words. I am neither competent nor interested in detailed etymological inquiry. "To choose" means "to take by preference out of all that are available," "to se-

From *Roads to Freedom—Essays in Honour of Friedrich A. von Hayek,* ed. Erich Streissler (London: Routledge & Kegan Paul, 1969), 47–64. Reprinted by permission of the publisher.

I am indebted to David B. Johnson, Roland N. McKean, Gordon Tullock, and Richard E. Wagner for helpful comments.

1. New York, 1968.

lect."[2] Choice is the "act of choosing," or "selecting." In particular, "choosing" should be distinguished from "behaving." The latter implies acting, but there is no reference to conscious selection from among alternatives. Behavior can be predetermined and, hence, predictable. Choice, by its nature, cannot be predetermined and remain choice. If we then define science in the modern sense of embodying conceptually refutable predictions, a "science of choice" becomes self-contradictory.[3]

This elementary proposition is recognized by those who accept the Mundell position. If this is the case, what are the reasons for adherence to what, at first glance, seems glaring methodological inconsistency? To the economist, choice seems to be imposed by the fact of scarcity. Given an acknowledged multiplicity of ends and a limitation on means, it becomes necessary that some selection among alternatives be made. It is in such a very general setting that economics has been classified as the study of such selection, or choice. Once this is done, replacing the word "study" with the word "science" becomes a natural extension of language. Is the science so defined devoid of predictive content? Some scholars might answer affirmatively, but surely there are many others who, at the same time that they acquiesce in Mundell's statement, busy themselves with the empirical testing of hypotheses. Are such professionals unaware of their methodological contradictions? It seems useful to try to answer these questions in some detail.

I. The Categories of Economic Theory

1. The logic of economic choice

The legitimacy of a "science of choice" may be questioned, but there should be no doubts about the usefulness of a "logic of choice." Much of orthodox economic theory is precisely this and is, therefore, concerned with choice, as such. This logical theory provides students with the "economic point of view," and it can be posed in either a normative or a positive setting. In the

---

2. *Oxford Universal Dictionary*, 1955.

3. In a wholly determinist universe, choice is purely illusory, as is discussion about choice. I do not treat this age-old issue, and I prefer to think that the subject discussed as well as the discussion itself is not illusory.

former, the logic reduces to the economic principle, the simple requirement that returns to like units of outlay or input must be equalized at the margins in order to secure a maximum of output. In this most general sense, the principle is empirically empty. It instructs the chooser, the decision-maker, on the procedures for making selections without requiring that he define either his own preference ordering of output combinations or the resource constraints within which he must operate. Empirical emptiness should not, however, be equated with uselessness. If a potential chooser is made aware of the principle in its full import, he will weigh alternatives more carefully, he will think in marginal terms, he will make evaluations of opportunity costs, and, finally, he will search more diligently for genuine alternatives. The norms for choice can be meaningfully discussed, even if the specific implementation takes place only in the internal calculus of the decision-maker. Instructing the decision-maker as to how he should choose may produce "better" choices as evaluated by his own standards.

There is a positive counterpart to the logic of choice, and this extends theory to the interaction among separate decision-makers. Commencing with the fact that choosers choose and that they do so under constraints which include the behavior of others, the economist can begin to make meaningful statements about the results that emerge from the interaction among several choosers. Certain "laws" can be deduced, even if conceptually refutable hypotheses cannot be derived. Analysis makes no attempt to specify preference orderings for particular choosers. The "law" of choice states only that the individual decision-maker will select that alternative that stands highest on his preference ordering. Defined in purely logical terms, this produces the "law of demand." In this way, trade or exchange can be explained, even in some of its most complex varieties. Characteristics of equilibrium positions can be derived, these being defined in terms of the coordination between expected and realized plans of the separate decision-takers.

In the strictest sense, the chooser is not specified in the pure logic of choice. Under the standard assumptions, the analysis applies to the individual. But the logic requires no such limitation; it applies universally. The norms for efficient choice can be treated independent of the processes through which decisions are actually made. It is not, therefore, explicitly in error to present decision-making norms for nonexistent collective entities who do not, in fact, choose. Under some conditions, it may be helpful to discuss the economizing process "as if" such entities existed, although, as we shall note in Section II, this is the source of much confusion.

In its normative variant, the logical theory of choice involves the simple principle of economizing, nothing more. This is the mathematics of maxima and minima. Much of modern economic theory is limited to various elaborations on this mathematics. By modifying the formal properties of the objective function and the constraints, interesting exercises in locating and in stating the required conditions for insuring satisfaction of the norms can be produced. Whether or not such exercises command too much of the professional investment of modern economists remains an open question.

The logical theory of interaction among many choosers may also be classified as pure mathematics. But this mathematics is not that which has attracted major interest of the professionals in that discipline, and there is some legitimacy in the economists' preemptive claim. Game theory, as one part of a general theory of interaction, owes its origin to a mathematician, but the elegant theory of competitive equilibrium was developed by economists. Major strides are being made in this purely logical theory of interaction among many choosers, some of which are aimed at relating game theory, more generally the theory of coalition formation, to the theory of competitive equilibrium. The marginal productivity of mathematically inclined economists in this area of research appears much higher than that which is aimed at working out complex variations of the simple maximization problem.

2. The abstract science of economic behavior

In the logical theory summarized, no objectives are specified. Choice remains free, and because of this, it remains choice. As we move beyond this pure logic, however, and into economic theory as more generally, if ambiguously, conceived, choice becomes circumscribed. Specific motivation is imputed to the decision-maker, and it is seldom recognized that, to the extent that this takes place, genuine "choice" is removed from the theory. What we now confront is *behavior,* not choice, behavior that is subject to conceptually predictable laws. The entity that acts, that behaves, does so in accordance with the patterns imposed by the postulates of the theoretical science.

The actor is, so to speak, programmed to behave in direct response to stimuli. The abstract science of economic behavior, as I have here classified this, has empirical content that is wholly missing in the pure logic of economic choice. This content is provided by restricting the utility function. Several degrees of restrictiveness may be imposed. Minimally, nothing more than a specification of "goods" may be introduced. From this alone, conceptually refutable hypotheses emerge. The acting-behaving unit *must* choose more of any "good" when its "price" relative to other "goods" declines.[4] Additional restrictiveness takes the form of specifying something about the internal trade-offs among "goods" in the utility function of the behaving unit. This step produces the *Homo economicus* of classical theory who must, when confronted with alternatives, select that which stands highest on his preference ranking, as evaluated in terms of a *numéraire*. The pure economic man must behave so as to take more rather than less when confronted with simple monetary alternatives. He must maximize income-wealth and minimize outlays. He must maximize profits if he plays the role of entrepreneur.

Confusion has arisen between this abstract science of economic behavior and the pure logic of choice because of ambiguities that are involved in the several means of bounding the utility functions of the acting units. In the pure logic of choice, the arguments in the utility function are not identified; "goods" and "bads" are unknown to the external observer. In any science of economic behavior, the "goods" must be classified as such. But under minimally restricted utility functions, specific trade-offs among these may remain internal to the acting units. The individual "chooses" in the sense that his selection from among several desirable alternatives remains unpredictable to the observer. What we have here is an extremely limited "science" of behavior combined with an extensive "logic" of genuine choice. We move beyond this essentially mixed framework when the trade-offs are more fully specified. Additional "laws of behavior" can then be derived; and, more importantly, predictions can be made about the results of the interaction processes. These predictions can be conceptually refuted by empirical evidence. If internal trade-offs among "goods" in utility functions are fully specified, be-

---

4. This approach may be associated with the work of A. A. Alchian and his colleagues. Cf. A. A. Alchian and W. R. Allen, *University Economics,* Belmont, Calif., 2nd edition, 1967.

havior becomes completely predictable in the abstract. Normal procedure does not, however, involve the extension to such limits.

As noted earlier, the pure logic of choice may be interpreted in either a normative or a positive sense. If choice is real, it is meaningful to refer to "better" and "worse" choices, and the simple maximizing principle can be of some assistance to the decision-taker. By relatively sharp contrast, there is no normative content in the abstract science of economic behavior. The reason is obvious. The acting unit responds to environmental stimuli in predictably unique fashion; there is no question as to the "should" of behavior. The unit responds and that is that. Failure to note this basic difference between the pure logic of choice and the pure science of behavior provides, I think, an explanation of the claim, advanced especially by Mises, that economic theory is a general theory of human action.[5] The logical theory is indeed general but empty; the scientific theory is nongeneral but operational.

At this point, it seems useful to refer to the distinction between the "subjectivist economics," espoused by both Mises and Hayek, and the "objectivist economics" which is more widely accepted, even if its limitations are seldom explicitly recognized. In the logic of choice, choosing becomes a subjective experience. The alternatives for choice as well as the evaluations placed upon them exist only in the mind of the decision-maker. Cost, which is the obstacle to choice, is purely subjective, and this consists in the chooser's evaluation of the alternative that must be sacrificed in order to attain that which is selected. This genuine opportunity cost vanishes once a decision is taken. By relatively sharp contrast with this, in the pure science of economic behavior, choice itself is illusory. In the abstract model, the behavior of the actor is predictable by an external observer. This requires that some criteria for behavior be objectively measurable, and this objectivity is supplied when the motivational postulate is plugged into the model. An actor behaves so as to maximize utility, defined in a nonempty sense. It becomes impossible, in the formal model, for an actor to "choose" less rather than more of the common denominator units, money or some *numéraire* good, when he is faced with such alternatives. Cost, in this objectivist theory, the pure science of economics, is measurable by the observer. This cost is unrelated to choice, as such, since the latter really does not exist. The opportunity cost of using a resource

5. Cf. Ludwig von Mises, *Human Action,* New Haven, 1949.

unit in one way rather than another consists in the *money* earnings of that unit in its most productive alternative use. These earnings may be objectively estimated and quantified. In this setting, the cost of a beaver is two deer, and there is no relationship between cost and sacrifice.[6] To say here that nonpecuniary elements may affect choice is to confuse the model of pure economic behavior with the model of the logic of choice. Insofar as nonpecuniary noneconomic elements actually enter the resource owner's calculus, the behavioral model is falsified.[7]

The motivational postulate, the behavior of *Homo economicus,* effectively converts the purely logical theory of choice into an abstract science of behavior. It accomplishes this by replacing the subjectivity of the logical theory by objective payoffs. Generality in explanation is and must be sacrificed in crossing this bridge. But this is replaced by predictability. The abstract science of economic behavior is the familiar world of *ceteris paribus.* This science provides the analyst with tools for discussing the complex interaction of market processes to the extent that individual participants behave economically. Equilibrium characteristics can be objectively described in terms of quantifiable, measurable relationships among variables, among prices and costs. It is this abstract theory upon which most economists rely in making rudimentary predictions about reality. When asked: "What will happen when an excise tax is placed on Product X?" the professional responds: "The price of X to consumers will rise, and less will be demanded, provided that other things remain unchanged, and provided that men behave economically." The last qualifying phrase, "provided that men behave economically," shifts the analysis into the science of behavior and enables conceptually refutable predictions to be advanced. By this qualifier, the economist states that he is preventing actors from behaving other than economically in the theoretical model that he is

---

6. For an extended discussion of the concept of cost in contrasting methodological settings, see my *Cost and Choice* (forthcoming).

7. To avoid ambiguity here, I should note that nonpecuniary "goods" can be introduced in individual utility functions in the minimally restricted limits that were discussed above. Given the specification of such "goods," conceptually refutable hypotheses about individual behavior can be derived. Nonpecuniary "goods" tend to be different for different individuals, however, and the limits of any predictive science are reached when those "goods" which are common to all persons are exhausted. This provides the basis for reliance on the strictly pecuniary motivation in the general model of the economic interaction process.

constructing. As we all recognize, many professionals do not go further than this; they do not consider it a part of their task either to examine the psychology of behavior more fully or to test empirically the predictions that the abstract science enables them to make.

Such methodological aloofness is acceptable only so long as the severe limitations of the scientist's role are appreciated. Failure to recognize these limitations leads naive professionals to claim far too much for the science and with such claims they infuriate those critics who concentrate attention on the non-economic content in human choice patterns.

3. The predictive science of economic behavior

The abstract science is restricted to the derivation of propositions or hypotheses that are conceptually refutable. The realm of predictive science is entered only when these hypotheses are subjected to empirical testing against real-world observations. One of the features of modern economic research has been its shift toward the rigorous testing of hypotheses. The pound of *ceteris paribus* no longer protects the scientist; he must, through imaginative construction of hypotheses and through exhaustive search for appropriate data, try to corroborate the predictions that the theory allows him to make. Because of empirical constraints, the range of his efforts must be more limited than that allowed to the free-floating abstract theorist. Data are difficult to come by, and even when these can be assembled, the hypotheses-tester must be prepared for frustration and failure. Data can, at best, reflect the results of genuine choices made by participants in a very complicated interaction sequence. The economic behavior implicit in these choices may be nonexistent in some cases, and swamped in effect by non-economic considerations in many others. The predictive hypotheses may be refuted at the initial levels of testing. But the scientist cannot readily use such refutation for overthrowing the general laws of behavior derived from the central structure of his theory. He must normally acknowledge his probable failure to isolate the economic from the non-economic elements of choice, and, accordingly, he must acknowledge the continuing challenge of empirical testability for his theoretically based hypotheses.

This amounts to saying that, despite his efforts, the predictive scientist remains chained to the vision of the economic universe produced in the abstract theory of economic behavior. He can, when successful, show that indeed "water runs down hill," but, with contrary results, he can rarely, if ever, refute the economic analogue to the law of gravity. At best, the predictive science is an extension of the abstract science. It must incorporate the basic motivational postulate of *Homo economicus;* indeed this provides the source for deriving the hypotheses to be tested. The paradigms are unchanged over the two subdisciplines.

There are, however, significant differences. In some strict sense, the abstract science treats only of pure economic man, unalloyed by non-economic behavioral traits. Accordingly, the theorems are simple, elegant, and aesthetically satisfying. But the real world is a grubby place, and it is this world that must be the raw source for any science that aims at operational validity. In the face of the apparent divergence of the real world from the paradigms of the abstract science, the empirical corroboration of many predictive hypotheses is perhaps surprising.

The fact that his hypotheses refer to the behavior of *many* actors greatly facilitates the predictive scientist's efforts. He need only make predictions about the behavior of average or representative participants in the processes that he observes; he need not hypothesize about the behavior of any single actor. Hence even if non-economic elements dominate the behavior of some participants, and even if these enter to some degree in the choices of all participants, given certain symmetry in the distributions of preferences, the hypotheses derived from the abstract theory may still be corroborated. For example, given comparable institutional constraints, the wage levels for plumbers and carpenters may tend toward equality even if a substantial proportion of plumbers exhibit strong non-economic preferences for their chosen occupation and even if a substantial proportion of carpenters exhibit similar preferences for their own occupation. So long as some sufficient number of persons indicates some willingness to make the occupational shift on purely economic grounds, the hypothesis about wage level equality is supported. The multiplicity of participants generates results that are identical to those predicted in the model that embodies the strict assumption that all actors behave economically.

4. The "behavioristic" science of the economy

Unless he is able to call upon the motivational postulate of the abstract science, the predictive scientist can scarcely derive the hypotheses that he seeks to test. It is folly for him to abandon this postulate deliberately in some misguided attempt at imitating the methods of the natural scientists who find it impossible to introduce comparable behavioral postulates. "Scientism" of this sort has been effectively criticized by Hayek[8] and others, and this approach need not be examined in detail here. It seems clear that with no behavioral basis from which to begin his search for uniformities and regularities in the data that he observes, the pure "behaviorist" is reduced to massive efforts at observation with very limited prospects of successful results. He confronts a universe of prices, quantities, employment levels, measures for national aggregates. He presumably remains aloof from the behavior that generates these data as results, whether this behavior be economic or not. This is not to suggest that such efforts should be wholly abandoned. It seems clear, however, that the deliberate sacrifice of the directional hypotheses provided by the paradigms of economic science should be made with great caution.

A somewhat different behaviorist approach (and one that fits the terminology considerably better) involves an attempt to specify non-economic elements that enter into the individual's choice calculus. This approach, which we may associate with the work of Herbert A. Simon and his colleagues,[9] calls upon psychological insight to assist in the development of motivational patterns that may be considerably more complex than the simple postulates of standard economic theory. Ultimately, the objective parallels those of orthodox economic science, the ability to make predictions about human behavior in the social interaction process. And, to the extent that the hypotheses of standard theory are refuted, such an approach as this offers the only avenue of advance for social science. This approach may proceed by relaxing or modifying the restrictions placed on individual utility functions, or, alternatively, the procedure may involve dropping the utilitarian framework.[10]

---

8. Cf. F. A. Hayek, *The Counter-Revolution of Science,* Glencoe, Ill., 1955.
9. Cf. H. A. Simon, *Models of Man,* New York, 1957.
10. This summary review does not do justice to the approach under discussion. For

Player B

50, 50	20, 60
60, 20	30, 30

Player
A

Figure 1

II. The Confusions of Economic Theory

Economics, as this discipline is currently interpreted, embodies elements of each of the four categories listed. The confusions arise from the failure of economists to understand the categorical distinctions. Many of the continuing and unresolved arguments over particular methodological issues can be traced more or less directly to this source.

1. THE DERIVATION OF POLICY NORMS

One of these arguments concerns the relevance of theory for deriving policy conclusions. I shall illustrate some of the confusion here through the familiar prisoners' dilemma of game theory, interpreted variously in terms of the categories of Section I. The pedagogic advantages of this construction are immense; properly employed, the dilemma allows us to introduce in a two-person interaction model many of the relevant issues of economic policy in the large.

Figure 1 presents the dilemma in a form slightly modified from its classic setting. The game depicted is positive-sum. The first term in each cell indicates the payoff to A, the player who chooses between rows. The second term shows the payoff to B, the player who chooses between columns. Each player's result depends on the behavior of the other, but, for each player, there is a dominating strategy shown by the second row and second column. The independent-behavior solution, shown in the south-east cell of the

the most part, the contributions here have been made by social scientists in disciplines other than economics. Indeed, to the extent that social "science" other than economics exists at all, it must be produced by those who adopt the approach summarized here.

matrix, depicts the dilemma; the combined payoffs are larger in the north-west cell.

With nothing more than the payoff matrix of Figure 1, something has been said about the interaction of the two players. Their choice behavior has been related to the structure of the game itself, and the possible conflict between the independent-adjustment solution and the combined-payoff potential outcome has been shown. Nonetheless, it should be noted that, to this point, nothing has been said about the nature of the payoffs. These have been treated strictly as numerical indicators of that which motivates choice behavior. In some respects, these payoffs may be thought of as being defined in utility units, so long as the purely subjective nature of utility in this context is kept in mind. In this setting, we have remained strictly in the pure logic of choice. There is absolutely no predictive content in the analysis.[11]

We move from this pure logic of choice into the abstract science of economic behavior when we define the payoffs objectively. To do this, we need only to put dollar signs in front of the numbers in the matrix illustration of Figure 1. The solution seems to remain as before, but it is now limited to those situations where players do, in fact, behave economically. There will be no convergence to the south-east cell if players in the real world should choose to behave co-operatively rather than independently. The abstract theory of economics says that they will behave economically, that the south-east cell is the "solution" to the game. This prediction may be falsified, at least conceptually.

At this level, it becomes legitimate to derive limited policy implications from the analysis. As they behave in the real world, individuals are observed to adopt the dominating strategies, as these are identified in the eyes of the observer. In the objectified payoff structure imputed to the participants, there appears to exist a conflict between the independent-adjustment outcome and the jointly desired optimal outcome. Given nothing more than the potentiality of this conflict, it becomes plausible for the political economist to consider modifications in the choice structure that would enable individual participants to eliminate such a conflict, if indeed it should exist. If ways and means can be found to remove the restrictions of the potential dilemma, if institutional re-

---

11. Cf. John C. Harsanyi, "A General Theory of Rational Behavior in Game Situations," *Econometrica* 34 (1966), 613 f.

arrangements can be made which will allow independent behavior of the participants to produce results that may be mutually more beneficial than those observed under present environmental conditions, these should, of course, be suggested. (In the strict prisoners' dilemma example, and limiting attention to the world of the two prisoners only, the introduction of communication between the two persons represents such an institutional change.) This point was recognized and well expressed by Sir Dennis Robertson when he called upon the economist to suggest ways to minimize the use of "that scarce resource Love."[12] Since Adam Smith, economists have been within the bounds of methodological propriety when they have proposed organizational-institutional arrangements that channel behavior that may be, but need not be, economically motivated in the direction of promoting what may be, but need not be, mutually desired economic objectives.

This very general policy position, which I shall call Smithean, requires minimal empirical backing along with minimal ethical content. All that is required is the conceptual possibility that payoffs relevant for individual behavior should be directionally linked with those emerging from the postulate of economic science. So long as a person may, other things equal, respond to the change in stimuli, as objectified, in the direction suggested by the central postulate of the theory, the economist is justified in his search for institutional arrangements that will remove the restrictiveness of the dilemma, should it exist. In a very general sense, this amounts to little more than opening up avenues for potential trades which participants may or may not find it advantageous to exploit. The policy prescription is, in effect, limited to suggestions for widening the range for potential choice.[13]

To the extent that the empirical testing of hypotheses supports the central behavioral postulate of the abstract theory, the productivity of Smithean institutional reforms is enhanced. But the corroboration of the behavioral postulate by empirical evidence implies much more than the *ceteris paribus* limits of the abstract theory. Such corroboration indicates that economic

---

12. D. H. Robertson, "What Does the Economist Economize?" in *Economic Commentaries*, London, 1956.

13. For an earlier and somewhat different statement of this position, see my "Positive Economics, Welfare Economics, and Political Economy," *Journal of Law and Economics* 2 (October 1959), 124–38. Reprinted in *Fiscal Theory and Political Economy*, Chapel Hill, 1960.

behavior dominates all non-economic elements of choice in the specific context examined. This offers a temptation to go much beyond the general institutional reforms implied by the Smithean position. If man can be shown to behave in some more direct relationship to an objectified payoff structure than the *ceteris paribus* potentiality implied by the abstract theory, direct manipulation of his behavior seems to become possible through the appropriate modification in the conditions for choice. It is one thing to say that when given the opportunity an individual will choose more rather than less, provided other elements affecting his choice remain unchanged. It becomes quite a different thing to say that the representative individual will choose more rather than less in terms of objectified units in the *numéraire* without regard to non-economic influences on his choice situation. Rarely will the multidimensional complexity of real-world choice allow results of such simplicity to be adduced. But, if it should do so, specific control of individual behavior through imposed changes in the payoff structures might be possible.

It is precisely at this point that a pervasive and fundamental error emerges. The false step is taken when the explicitly objectified payoff structure that is postulated for use in the abstract theory of economic behavior is translated into direct guidelines for the explicit manipulation of choice alternatives. This procedure must assume that the actual *choice-maker* in the real world *behaves* strictly as the pure economic man of the theorist's model. Markets are held to "fail" because of the dilemma-type situations that are confronted by the idealized man of the theorist's analytical model. As a follow-up to this, policy suggestions are made which incorporate this rarified behavioral postulate as reality. In a genuine sense, this whole procedure is absurd.

The point can be illustrated with the matrix of Figure 1. The abstract theory bases its elaboration of the interaction processes on the postulate that individuals behave economically in the sense that they respond to objectified and externally measurable payoffs. In this context, it is meaningful to say that, in the model, Player A selects Row 2 rather than Row 1 because of the $10 difference in payoff, regardless of what he predicts about B's behavior. It is meaningful to say that, in this model, the opportunity cost to Player A, "that which could be avoided by his not taking Row 2," is $10 in foregone payoffs. But this opportunity cost, embodied in the theoretical model for behavior, cannot then be taken as the specific basis for policy prescription aimed at manipulating A's actual choice behavior. This violates the purpose and meaning of the abstract theory and, as suggested, has little or no empirical base. Despite this, such procedure is manifest in a substantial part of modern economic policy discussion.

It is not caricature to say that modern policy discussion, which I shall call Pigovian, proceeds as follows, still within the matrix illustration of Figure 1. The economist proposes a "corrective" tax on Player A, a tax designed to make the costs that he privately confronts equivalent to those that are confronted by the collectivity in the two alternatives that are faced. The general welfare criterion becomes equality between *private* and *social* cost. To implement this result, private costs must be modified; but in order to know by how much, some assumption must be made about private payoff structures. The orthodoxy proceeds as if the purely economic man exists. The criterion calls for a tax of $10 + to be imposed on A's returns in Row 2 (or a subsidy of $10 + on his returns in Row 1). Given this change in his alternatives, Player A (similarly for Player B) will be motivated to "choose" that alternative that is jointly desired. The efficient collective outcome will be generated. The emphasis has been subtly shifted from the exploitation of potential gains-from-trade to the attaining of specifically defined results.

As the construction shows, if either A or B should behave non-economically the suggested modification of the payoff matrix may not produce the desired results. Suppose, for example, that both players value independent action highly and are willing to sacrifice economic gain to secure this objective. In this instance, the independent-adjustment solution in the south-east cell remains dominant, regardless of the imposition of the suggested corrective tax or subsidy. Some tax (or subsidy) will, of course, result in behavioral change, but the outcome may be less rather than more desirable in some "social" sense. The dilemma indicated to be present in objectified payoff structure may not exist when payoffs relevant to genuine choices are incorporated in the matrix. The artificiality of any objectified payoff structure, as conceived by the external observer, tends to be overlooked with the consequence that "dilemmas" which exist only in the mind of the observer may be imputed to actual participants in an interaction process.

The point of emphasis is clear. The costs that influence "choice" are purely subjective and these exist only within the mind of the decision-maker. The economist may, within limits, discuss this "choice," provided that he remains within what we have called the "logic of choice." He cannot, however, plug in the *Homo economicus* introduced in his abstract models of economic behavior and then use this as the basis for constructing specific choice-influencing constraints aimed at welfare improvements. Individuals choose on the basis of their own preference orderings; they may, within limits, behave as the abstract theory of economics postulates. But rarely do they behave strictly as the automatons of the analytical models. Yet this is precisely the unrecognized assumption that is implicit in most modern policy discussion.

The critical distinction to be made is that between what I have called the Smithean policy position and what I have called the Pigovian policy norms. In the former, organizational-institutional changes, modifications in the structure of property rights, require only that possible conflicts between individually adjusted behavior and mutually desired collective outcomes be recognized. Specific definition of "efficient" or "optimal" results is not needed. Such results are allowed to emerge from the choice process itself. In the Pigovian framework, by contrast, property rights are normally assumed to be fixed exogenously. Corrective measures take the form of specific modifications in the choice conditions that are confronted by individual participants. Clearly, this approach to policy requires much more knowledge about the actual preference orderings of individuals. Efficiency in outcomes is no longer defined by the observed absence of further gains-from-trade as revealed by the behavior of traders. This Smithean definition is replaced by the objectively defined set of equalities central to theoretical welfare economics.

The error extends through much of modern economics. This was at the base of the debate over the possibility of socialist calculation that took place in the 1930s. Mises and Hayek were, I think, indirectly making essentially the same point that I have tried to make here. Their arguments failed to convince their fellow economists; most economists continue to think that efficiency, at least ideally, can be produced by the enforcement of output and pricing *rules,* that these can effectively substitute for the modification in *property rights* dictated by the particular economic setting.

2. "Scientific" decision-making for the collectivity: systems analysis, operations research, cost-benefit analysis

The confusions embodied in the Pigovian norms are complemented by an even more elementary set of confusions when the economist extends his range to the "choices" of the collectivity. He tends to be trapped in the scarcity–choice maximization nexus, and it is not at all easy for him to accept the fact that a collective "decision-maker" or "chooser" is nonexistent. Failing this, he tends to conceptualize some supra-individual entity which makes effective "choices," which maximizes some objective function subject to appropriately defined constraints. This procedure allows the analyst to produce interesting and self-satisfying results. But error arises when either the analyst or his interpreters consider such results applicable to real-world issues.

Analysis of this sort is two dimensions away from real-world relevance. In the first place, the "logic of choice" for the single decision-maker is applied to a situation where no such person or entity exists. Since there is no maximizer, analysis is of questionable value when it is based on the assumption that one exists.[14] In the second place, the costs and benefits of alternative courses of action must be objectified if the analyst is to do more than present his own value orderings. This objectification runs into the same difficulty as that noted in connection with the Pigovian approach. There may be little or no relationship between the objectively defined costs and benefits and the evaluations that individuals place on alternatives in actual choice situations.

In this latter respect, the analyst has even less to fall back on than the Pigovian welfare economist. The abstract science of economic behavior with its embodiment of economic man does provide some basis for considering modifications in the conditions of choice, as faced by acting persons. For the cost-benefit analyst, however, there is no prospect of modifying the alternatives facing individual choosers. He must advance norms for choice itself. He

---

14. These comments apply only to the orthodox analyses under discussion here. It is possible to advance understanding of actual processes of group decision-making through an extension of the pure logic of choice applied to individual participants in these processes. In this approach, there need be no presumption that the collectivity, as such, maximizes anything, or indeed itself exists.

is advising the collectivity quite specifically concerning how it "should" choose. Even if the complexities of group decision-making are ignored, the subjective evaluations of individuals are of a different dimension from the objectively quantifiable measurements placed on alternatives by the analyst. And it should be emphasized here that this difficulty is not removed by allowing the careful analyst to introduce "nonquantifiable" elements into his calculus. In point of fact, the more subjective that his own calculus becomes, the *less* relevant become his efforts. At best, he may be able to place values on cost and benefit streams that would characterize the world in which all men behave economically. This calculus would be of limited, but perhaps of positive value. Once this standard drawn from the behavioral postulate of the abstract science is left behind, however, there is nothing that the analyst can provide that assists in the understanding of actual collective decision processes.

III. Conclusions

Modern economics, as practiced by professional scholars, embodies confusions that are fundamentally methodological. These have their historical foundations in the failure of economists to establish an effective synthesis between the objective and the subjective theory of value. The issues did not emerge with clarity, however, until efforts were made to extend the applicability of economic theory beyond its traditional limits. So long as the task of theory remained that of "explaining" the functioning of a market system, objective and subjective elements could exist side by side without open contradiction. During the past half-century, however, theory has been called upon to do much more than this. It has been employed to derive norms for policy aimed at making allocation more "efficient." Economists have, in other words, proceeded as if theirs were a "science of choice."

It is in such extensions that the confusions that I have stressed in this paper have emerged. The critical methodological oversight was that which Hayek emphasized, with clarity but to little avail, in several of his fundamental papers in the late 1930s and early 1940s. The failure of economists to recognize that the sense data upon which individuals actually choose in either market or political choice structures are dimensionally distinct from any data that can be objectively called upon by external observers led directly to the methodological chaos that currently exists. Economics seems unlikely to escape from this chaos for many years, if indeed it survives at all as an independent discipline. Few economists are wholly free of the confusions that I have discussed. For myself, I advance no claim that my own thinking has yet fully rid itself of the paradigms of neoclassical orthodoxy.

General Implications of
Subjectivism in Economics

I have often argued that the "Austrians" seem, somehow, to be more successful in conveying the central principle of economics to students than alternative schools, enclaves, or approaches. This theme has involved two components. First, I have argued that our most important social role is that of teaching students rather than that of serving as surrogate social engineers. Second, my hypothesis depended, of course, on a definition of just what the most important central principle in economics is. And my position is on record in this respect. *The* principle that exposure to economics *should* convey is that of the spontaneous coordination which the market achieves. The central principle of economics is not the economizing process; it is not the maximization of objective functions subject to constraints. Once we become methodologically trapped in the maximization paradigm, economics becomes applied mathematics or engineering.

In this connection, let me tell you a story. I recently talked with a prominent economist who mentioned that one of his colleagues had reported having several conversations with the then presidential candidate Jimmy Carter. This colleague passed along his view that Carter was a "good systems analyst," and my friend added, more or less as an afterthought, and "hence, a good economist." I very quickly and very emphatically put him straight, saying that nothing could be further from the "economic point of view," properly interpreted, than that of the systems analyst. Indeed this is precisely my

From *What Should Economists Do?* (Indianapolis: Liberty Fund, 1979), 81–91. Reprinted by permission of the publisher.

This chapter was initially presented as a lecture at a conference on subjectivist economics, Dallas, Texas, December 1976.

own fear about Carter, that he is, in fact, a good systems analyst without the remotest understanding of the principle of spontaneous order. I should add here that, to my friend's credit, when I pointed this out to him, he immediately took my distinction as relevant. But it is, I think, a mark of how far our whole discipline has deteriorated when we slip so readily and naturally into the simple maximization paradigm.

Or perhaps "economists" should stay in that paradigm. Argument could be made to this effect on etymological grounds. Perhaps what I should be suggesting here is that we need to be studying and promulgating something other than "economics."

But enough of general methodology, although I shall not get very far away from it anywhere. To return to "subjectivist economics" more specifically, my hypothesis is that this sort of economic theory must further a better understanding of the principle of spontaneous coordination. But I need to support this hypothesis by convincing argument. Why does the subjectivist more readily learn and accept the principle of spontaneous order than the objectivist? He does so because that which he seeks to explain and to understand is different. The subjectivist is not trying to explain, positively or normatively, the allocation of scarce resources among uses; nor is his subject matter best described as *price* theory. What he is trying to explain is exchange, conceived in its broadest sense. His is a "theory of exchange," as I have repeatedly argued, but a theory of exchange of whatever it is that persons value. The positive aspects of the theory take form in predictions about the properties of equilibrium positions, potentially observable behaviorally through the cessation of trade among parties. He also predicts, again positively, that interferences with trade or exchange must create trading opportunities that remain unconsummated, and that the existence of such opportunities must necessarily be reflected in enforcement and policing problems. The subjectivist is not likely to accept what is perhaps the most sophisticated fallacy in economic theory, the notion that because certain relationships hold in equilibrium the forced interferences designed to implement these relationships will, in fact, be desirable. In such examples of this fallacy as "equal pay for equal work," even one of the stars in the subjectivist firmament, Professor Hayek, lost his way.

But let me be clear, and fair. I am not setting up some imaginary straw creature, labeled objectivist economics, for the purpose of saying that its subject matter necessarily and certainly leads to ignorance, bewilderment, and confusion, and that the subjectivist possesses the only key to wisdom. (I could expand on this a bit. It seems to me that one of the dangers of the subjectivist approach, and particularly in its pure Austrian variant, is the tendency to form a priesthood, with the converted talking only to those who are converts, and with the deliberate withdrawal from free and open espousal of subjectivist notions to the world around.) An understanding and appreciation of the principle of spontaneous order or coordination may emerge from the very citadels of objectivism, and often does. After all, Adam Smith was no subjectivist. What I am implying is that to the extent that subjectivism tends to concentrate attention on the interaction among persons and away from the "economic problem," an understanding of the principle of order is facilitated rather than retarded. The post-Robbins maximizer must learn the principle of order in spite of rather than because of his analytical paradigm.

At this point I should restore Professor Hayek to his proper place in my overall league tables by endorsing his criticism of "scientism," a criticism also advanced by my own professor, Frank Knight. Hayek and Knight were sharply critical of any attempts to convert economics into a discipline analogous to a natural science. Economics is, or can be, scientific in a sense that is, I think, unique. The principle of spontaneous order is a scientific principle, in that it can be readily divorced from normative content. Unless we stay within the exchange paradigm, however, we lose the legitimately scientific principle and, instead, launch off into the scientistic implications that emerge directly from the maximization paradigm. Economists find themselves measuring social costs and social benefits, along with a little of everything else.

And, of course, to the extent that quantities may be measured, independent of choice behavior and hence objectively, there must exist an objectively determinate "solution" to any problem that is posed. There is some "optimal" allocation of economic resources, defined by the physical units of resource located in time and space. And let us recall here that Professor Tjalling Koopmans won a Nobel Prize in economics, not in engineering. He did so for his efforts that commenced from working out the optimal allocation of a set of tankers plying oil across the Atlantic during World War II, where the variables were ships, distances, port locations, barrels of oil, and, of course, a set of shadow prices. (To claim a bit of credit for myself here, I think I was a confirmed subjectivist long before I realized what I was because I recall thinking in 1946, when Koopmans was lecturing on this at the University of Chicago, that there seemed to be absolutely no economic content in what he was doing, at least as I then, and now, conceived our proper subject matter to be.) There must also exist an equilibrium set of prices that are objectively computable, at least conceptually, and indeed, we have observed Professor Herbert Scarf of Yale now trying to work out ways of computing equilibrium prices, which effort seems, to the subjectivist, an absurd exercise.

To the extent that there exist objectively determinate and physically describable allocations or imputations that may be evaluated by some efficiency or optimization criterion, the market is necessarily reduced to one among several institutional devices whose operations may be compared one with another. The market becomes an "analogue computing device," a "mechanism," which may or may not rank better than its alternatives in terms of the objectifiable performance criteria. At this level, the distinction between the market and the centrally planned economy is purely in comparative performance. And, at this point, there is a subtle but vitally important principle or insight that the objectivist tends to neglect. Economic performance can only be conceived in values; but how are values determined? By prices, but prices emerge only in markets. They have no meaning in a nonmarket context. Hence, the market can hardly be compared in terms of performance against a nonmarket institution. In this sense, the whole efficiency criterion as traditionally applied to socialist economies, even as idealized, is devoid of meaning.

The 1930s debate between Mises on the one hand and Lange, Lerner, and Dickinson on the other was never properly grounded. As this debate has been widely interpreted, the conceptual possibility of market socialism was made dependent on the informational potential of the central planning authority, a problem that an iterative procedure was alleged to resolve. But this is not the central issue. As I tried to discuss in my little book *Cost and Choice*,[1] the issue is not simply one of information. The central issue is the critical interdependence between market choice itself and the informational content of this process which can be revealed only as the process is allowed

---

1. *Cost and Choice: An Inquiry in Economic Theory* (Chicago: Markham Publishing Co., 1969).

to occur. Let me try to explain by an example. This seems to me to be a vitally important point, but it is one that I am not at all sure how to present here. Suppose that we consider an allocation of apples and oranges between two persons, A and B, persons who are located externally to us, say, in Timbuktu. If we know their utility functions, along with the initial endowments of the two commodities, we can define the "efficient allocation" of apples and oranges, an allocation that would, of course, be equivalent to that which would be attained as a result of voluntary exchange or trade between A and B. But we cannot, as external observers, possibly know the utility functions because such functions do not, and cannot, exist independent of the choice action of A and B in the exchange process itself. That is to say, even if we could establish perfect verbal communication with A and B, they could not "write down" their utility functions in any meaningful operational sense. We may, if we desire, postulate utility functions for the two persons, as given to us or as imagined for them, and we may then define efficiency by these postulated functions. But this would amount to empty exercise since there would be little or no relationship to the efficiency, so defined, and that which an actual exchange process might generate. (Although I cannot go into it here, there is an affinity between my criticism of orthodox procedures in economic theory and the radical Marxist-oriented criticism, by Gintis and others, centered on the assumption of invariant preferences.)

Considerations such as those outlined in the example here have led my colleague Robert Staaf to despair of even using indifference-curve analytics. I do not go quite so far, but I can recognize the pedagogical problem. Utility-function, indifference-curve constructions may be useful in depicting or illustrating the underlying rationality of the voluntary exchange process, provided that these constructions are understood in strictly subjective terms, as constructions that cannot, in their nature, be communicated to observers independent of the exchange process within which they emerge.

In one sense, it becomes misleading at the outset to say that persons "act as if they were maximizing a utility function subject to constraints," since this terminology itself tends to suggest that the utility functions exist independent of the acting-choosing process. It is better, at this level of discussion, to say simply that persons choose among alternatives as they arise, and that there is, hopefully, enough consistency in their behavior to allow us to make some predictions about changes in outcomes as a result of changes in the choice alternatives. At this point, the strict Austrians may enter into a debate with me and, more important, with those who insist on the empirical corroboration of the elementary principles of human behavior in voluntary exchange processes. Such debate has always seemed to me to be of only indirect significance. As Frank Knight used to say, most of the empirical work in economics is "proving water runs downhill," a proposition that the Austrians would scarcely question.

Indirectly, however, and in opportunity-cost terms, the empirical-nonempirical debate is of importance. The young and aspiring economist who becomes the expert empiricist has necessarily sacrificed training time in learning more about the process to which his highly polished technical tools are to be applied. These gaps in the training of modern economists are beginning to show up in many forms, not the least of which is the deadly dullness that dominates whole departments in many universities and colleges.

I should like to say something about the relationship between subjectivist economics and mathematical economics. The important and central principle that the subjectivist paradigm advances is that of spontaneous order, as I have already suggested several times. The theoretical foundations here can be readily mathematized. But the mathematics called for is not the maximization of objective functions subject to constraints. The mathematically inclined economist who seeks to put all analysis into this form is already on the wrong track, and he is likely to confuse both himself and his students. The mathematics dictated here is that of general equilibrium, properly understood, the search for the solutions of systems of simultaneous equations, solutions that emerge from the interdependence among the variables described in the whole system of equations. For this reason, I find no difficulty at all in allowing the general equilibrium theorist to do his work alongside his subjectivist, nonmathematical counterpart, provided that he does not slip into error by somehow imputing, even at some conceptual level, objective meaning into his wholly imaginary constructs.

I am perhaps even more favorable toward the sort of thinking that game theory fosters, and especially in its development of solution concepts applicable to many-person games. Almost by necessity, the game theorist is led to think about an interaction process that produces an outcome through the behavior of many participants, each one of whom acts independent of the others. Game theory takes the wrong turn, however, to the extent that the emphasis shifts to the normative problem of defining optimal strategies for particular players or coalitions of players, even for games against nature and even for the all-inclusive coalition.

I have suggested that the principle of spontaneous order is "scientific" in the sense that it embodies a logically coherent argument. But does the economist who considers his main role to be that of teaching this principle to his students necessarily plead guilty to the charge that he is imposing an ideology? In one sense the answer is yes. Adam Smith was offering an alternative vision of how an economy might work. It was necessary to provide this alternative vision before the mercantilist blinders could be removed. Smith's effort was, in this quite literal sense, subversive of the existing order and of the set of attitudes that supported this order. I see no reason why our task in 1976 is any different from that in 1776. We must offer a vision of economic process that is not natural to man's ordinary ways of thinking. And faith in the efficacy of the process of spontaneous coordination arises only from a thorough understanding which only economists are equipped to transmit.

Milton Friedman, a friend whose work I admire greatly, objects to the Austrian-subjectivist approach largely on the grounds that it implies conversion rather than gradual conviction by the weight of logical argument and empirical tests. In part, this objection is based on the observable priesthood tendencies, which I noted above. More important, however, Friedman's objection seems to be based on what I regard as a naive notion of how persons shift paradigms. Admittedly, a connection between accumulated empirical evidence and paradigm shifts must exist, but this is not nearly so direct as Friedman seems to think. But I think we all must admit that the patterns are mysterious here, and these may well vary considerably from one person to another. For my own part, I do not object to the "preaching" implications of subjectivist economics, although I can appreciate both the dangers of this and the advantages of something like the Friedman position.

Unfortunately, most modern economists have no idea of what they are doing or even of what they are ideally supposed to be doing. I challenge any of you to take any issue of any economics journal and convince yourself, and me, that a randomly chosen paper will have a social productivity greater than zero. Most modern economists are simply doing what other economists are doing while living off a form of dole that will simply not stand critical scrutiny. Beware the day for educators generally when the taxpaying public finds out that the king really has no clothes.

I think I know what I am doing, and I think that most of those who espouse a variant of Austrian-subjectivist economics know what they are doing. And I think that our efforts are socially productive, highly so. I suppose that all of this finally reduces to an admonition to keep the faith, whether we want to call this doing economics, subjectivist economics, Austrian economics, or something else. The set of ideas and attitudes that emerges from an understanding of the principle of spontaneous order can be transmitted. We can have a part to play in developing a meaningful "public philosophy," even if this amounts to little more now than playing the role of subversives of the dominating mind-set that conceives the economy as chaos independent of collective controls. But recall two things. Adam Smith had no idea that he would, in fact, work a revolution in economic thinking and in economic policy in the half-century after 1776. And the same Adam Smith memorably observed: "There's a deal of ruin in a nation." Keep the faith.

There *Is* a Science of Economics

All the sciences have a relation, greater or less, to human nature; and that, however wide any of them seem to run from it, they still return back by one passage or another. Even Mathematics, Natural Philosophy, and Natural Religion, are in some measure dependent on the science of man, since they lie under the cognisance of men, and are judged by their power and faculties.

—David Hume, *A Treatise on Human Nature*
(Oxford: Clarendon Press, 1888), xix.

The title of this chapter stems from reflection on the content of a possible introduction to a volume of Karl Brunner's nonmonetary papers. I was asked to write such an introduction, and the editor suggested concentration on the Interlaken conferences on "Analysis and Ideology." When Karl Brunner initiated this series of conferences in 1974, his stated purpose was that of introducing (exposing) European, and especially German-speaking, economists to their American counterparts who allegedly brought along analytical baggage that was more "scientific" (hard-nosed) than that which described much of the Marxist-inspired rhetoric then encountered in Europe's academies. In taking this entrepreneurial step, he was motivated by the conviction that economics does, indeed, have scientific content, analogous to, even if quite different from, that of the natural sciences. And this conviction was accompanied by the belief that genuinely scientific argument, along with the

From *Post-Socialist Political Economy: Selected Essays* (Cheltenham, U.K.: Edward Elgar, 1997): 9–19. Reprinted by permission of the publisher.

A version of this chapter was presented at the University of Texas, Dallas, Texas, March 1994.

empirical evidence that could be marshalled in support, was both necessary and sufficient to overcome the temptation of scholars to indulge in ideological romance.

My concern here is not about whether Karl Brunner succeeded in accomplishing what he sought with the Interlaken conferences. My purpose is to examine the nature of the alleged scientific content of whatever it is that economists, as professionally trained, bring to problems of social organization. How does the economist differ in this respect from the philosopher?[1] Is economics more than either a part of contractarian political philosophy or a branch of mathematics?[2]

Even if we recognize that the propositions of positive economics are scientific in the modern sense of terms here, how can we expect that demonstration of these propositions will affect the choices among institutional-organizational alternatives faced by members of a political community? What, precisely, did Karl Brunner have in mind when he predicted that a wider exposure of German social scientists to "scientific economics" would ultimately exert an impact on the direction of change in political regimes?

I suggest that we think of the role of the economist, and of economic science, in terms analogous to that of the ordinary natural scientist, and of natural science. Think then of the natural scientist not as a discoverer of new laws of nature and the universe, not as someone who is continually expanding the boundaries of what we know about the natural environment, but, instead, as a human repository of knowledge about the natural environment, as it is now known to exist. Think, that is, of the noncreative natural scientist, and of the role of such a person, and of science, in society.

What does such a scientist do? As a rough cut of an answer, consider the definition of the natural or physical feasibility space. The scientist draws the boundaries between what is and what is not feasible given the known constraints of the physical universe. Ragnar Frisch referred to these constraints as *obligative,* which he contrasted with constraints that are *facultative.*[3] The predictions of natural science tell us what we can and cannot do with the

1. Richard A. Posner, "Richard Rorty's Politics," *Critical Review* 7 (Winter 1993): 33–49.

2. Alexander Rosenberg, *Economics—Mathematical Politics or Science of Diminishing Returns?* (Chicago: University of Chicago Press, 1992).

3. Ragnar Frisch, "On Welfare Theory and Pareto Regimes," in *International Economic Papers,* vol. 9 (London: Macmillan, 1959), 39–92.

materials and potential forces that exist. The scientist does not go beyond a positive stance; no advice is offered to members of the body politic, in either private or public spheres of action, as to what should be done within the parametric limits of the feasibility space. And no critics accuse the natural scientist of committing a naturalist fallacy when the propositions of science are observed to affect the choice behaviour of nonscientists. The propositions of ordinary natural science are simply incorporated into the considerations of the choice alternatives that we face.

If economics is to be compared with natural science, economists should be able to define what can and cannot be done with the *human* materials and potential that exist. Economists, and economic science, should generate a feasibility space, fully analogous to that generated for the physical universe by natural science. But what laws of human nature become the analogues of natural laws? This question is addressed in the second section. The third section introduces the critical difference between the natural sciences and the human sciences; the difference summarized by the artifactual features of the environment within which humans confront choices and take action. The fourth section discusses the role of economic science in restricting the domain of feasible outcomes or social states. A highly abstract illustration of the whole argument is presented in the fifth section. The final section summarizes the chapter.

Human Nature

Post-medieval social philosophers—from Thomas Hobbes down to David Hume and Adam Smith—were excited about the prospects for developing the sciences of man alongside those of the natural world. The base point for this judgment was the conviction that there were uniformities in human nature that allowed for systematic inquiry. For Adam Smith, each person's drive to better his own position provided a uniform motivational element from which all understanding of economic interaction emerges. It is important to note that betterment was implicitly defined to be objectively measurable. Each person's effort to better his own position is observed as a striving to secure command and use of a larger share of goods that are commonly valued. This elementary insight is often overlooked, and it is obscured by the utilitarian rhetoric that has continued to dominate economists' thinking for two centuries. If a person's effort to better his own position is made equivalent to a person's attempt to maximize his utility, and if, in turn, utility is defined as that which is maximized, the predictive content of any genuinely economic model of human behaviour is emptied. What remains is the science of rational choice, which, although formally operational, does not perform the function previously specified. Until and unless the domain for human choice behaviour is restricted further than the minimal limits imposed by rationality criteria, the economists' enterprise warrants little respect.

The exchange relationship is, of course, central to economic interaction, but a concentration on the surface characteristics of exchange itself may add to the confusion here. At the point of trade, parties differ in their evaluation of the goods traded, and this difference motivates the trade itself. But the goods that are traded are mutually valued by both parties to exchange, and if either party could, somehow, secure more of *either* "good" without giving up some of the other, behaviour would be observed to occur along such a nontrading dimension. Trade involves giving up less-valued goods for more-valued goods, by both parties to the transaction. Both of the goods that enter into the trading process remain as positively valued arguments in the utility functions of both traders, before, during and after trade takes place.

An alternative, if somewhat more complex, way of putting the point made here is to state that each good that enters into the trading relationship embodies potential distributional conflict. No trades are observed to take place in goods that are in sufficiently abundant supply to sate all demands, or in goods that are technologically nontradeable, no matter how highly valued (for example, sunshine in Alaska in January), or in goods that meet full Samuelsonian requirements for publicness, as technologically defined.

The economist's first step towards restricting the domain of attainable positions lies in postulating that human nature is such that persons seek larger shares of those goods that are commonly and positively valued and seek smaller shares of those goods that are commonly and negatively valued. That is to say, signs need to be attached to "goods" (or "bads"). Note that this step is classificatory only; it does not require any postulate to the effect that the trade-offs among goods be identical over separate persons. The classification requires only that the set of goods that is commonly valued to be positive be identical over all potential traders. In more familiar terms, the set of arguments in individual utility or preference functions, as identified by signs of the partial derivatives, must be the same.

Human Behaviour within Rules

A categorical difference between the enterprise of the natural scientist and that of the economist emerges as the latter tries to move towards delineation of the boundaries of behavioural feasibility—a difference that makes the economist's task enormously more difficult in some relative sense. The natural scientist is able to, and indeed must, take the universe as it is found and without the overlay of a complex institutional structure that has evolved, in part constructively, and that operates to channel and to facilitate patterns of behaviour that cannot be classified to be "natural" in any primitivist sense. Furthermore, the institutional structure is not unique; distinctly different sets of rules may describe separate historical and locational settings. How can the economist, as scientist, even so much as commence to establish boundary marks between the attainable and the unattainable?

One means of reducing the task to manageable proportions is to drop any claim for generality and to introduce historical-institutional specificity. With a postulated set of structural parameters, that is, within a defined set of legal rules or facultative constraints, the economist can proceed with the basic classificatory exercise without advancing any claim to generalizability to other institutional settings. For my primary purposes in this chapter, examination and elaboration of this reduced-claim procedure is sufficient, although I shall refer briefly to the problem of generalization at a later point in the argument.

Consider, then, the basic institutional framework for the regime that facilitates the emergence and the operation of a market economy. Persons, individually or as members of organizations, are assigned enforceable rights and claims to both human and nonhuman endowments—rights that allow these endowments to be used as the assigned owners desire, within certain legal limits. Persons, again individually or as members of organizations, possess rights to enter into and complete exchanges one with another and to transfer rights on reciprocally agreed terms. As persons exercise their assigned rights by choosing and acting along the dimensions within their authority, a network of production, exchange and distributional relationships emerges, and from this network there will be generated an outcome, or patterns of outcomes, that may be described by vectors of prices, allocations of resource inputs and distributions of final outputs.

All of this summary description is, of course, familiar territory to the economist. But let me make the connection to the classificatory exercise mentioned above. Recall Adam Smith's most famous passage where he states that the butcher offers the supper's meat for sale, not from benevolence, but from his own self-interest. Economics is widely, and correctly, interpreted as providing understanding-explanation of Smith's statement. My argument here is that Smith's seemingly elementary proposition has genuine scientific content and in the following way. The imagined "social state" in which there are no persons offering meat for sale is nonfeasible, given the institutional parameters that define the rights or liberties of potential sellers and buyers and given the motivational postulate of the science. An even more romanticized alternative would be a setting in which sellers offer meat to those who desire this good, but without demanding payment in return. This result, too, may be imagined, as a social state that would be most highly preferred by meat consumers, but few would fail to incorporate the elementary elements of economics in thinking that this result could never be realized.

The principle to be emphasized is the necessity of making the distinction between those states of the world, those "social states," that can be imagined to exist and those states that can be realized, given the inclusive rules within which economic interaction must take place. The set of imagined positions is, of course, much larger than the set of potentially realizable positions, even within the limits imposed by the acknowledged natural or physical constraints. Within any given institutional structure, the difference between the set of imagined positions and the set of attainable positions stems exclusively from the operation of the motivational postulate that is central to the science of economics itself.

Restrictions on the Domain

It may be helpful to clarify the process through which the science of economics restricts the domain of outcomes or end-states of human interaction. Individual preferences are not simply taken as data. Instead, preferences are restricted by the two-part postulate to the effect that (1) persons seek their own betterment and (2) betterment is objectively measurable in goods that are defined to be commonly valued, whether positively or negatively.

Consider an individual's ordering of two social states, both of which are technologically feasible, but one of which imputes to that individual a larger quantity of a positively valued good, with the same quantities of others' goods. The individual's preferences must be such as to produce a ranking of such a state relatively higher than that accorded to the alternative. Given such an ordering, the individual cannot select the less-preferred to the more-preferred alternative if he or she is assigned rights of choices along the relevant dimension of behaviour.

In application to the last variant of the Smithian example discussed above, where sellers are imagined to offer goods without payment, such a state is to be classified as nonfeasible, so long as sellers retain rights of entry into and exit from the exchange relationship. One-sided, or nonreciprocal, "exchanges" in goods, valued by both parties, are not permissible way-stations along the road to emergent market outcomes classifiable as feasible.

This conclusion may be accepted, but the critic may immediately resort to the institutional specificity imposed initially on the whole discussion. The offer of goods without return payment, that is, trade without reciprocation, may be acknowledged to be beyond the limits of feasible economic interaction, under the standard rules of the market, in which sellers and buyers retain rights of entry to and exit from potential exchanges. But, as noted earlier, these rules are not, themselves, natural, at least in the ordinary sense. Instead, rules of the market may be considered to be artifactual, having themselves evolved historically or been constructively put in place. Is it possible, therefore, both to imagine a social state where goods are offered without a requirement of payment and to classify such a state as potentially realizable under some alternative nonmarket assignment of rights?

Consider, again, the supply-demand of meat, classified as a commonly valued good. Suppose that the rules of the market are abrogated, and that these rules are superseded by politicization-bureaucratization of this sector of the economy. Some persons are directed to produce and supply meat to those who are authorized to receive the product, and there is no reciprocal exchange. Relatively little reflection is required to suggest that the situation attained under this regime is *not* likely to be that which might have been imagined to be possible as an alternative to the market counterpart. The producer-supplier will not be observed to respond to the preferences of consumers-demanders; the product itself will not be descriptively equivalent to that traded in markets. By replacing the set of market rules, there will be, of course, a change in the set of attainable or feasible positions. But these positions will differ from those reached under in-market behaviour along many more dimensions of adjustment than economically illiterate imagination could suggest.

Nonromanticized analysis suggests that the economist's classificatory exercise is more general in scope and applicability than might initially seem to be the case. Those social states or positions that can be imagined but never realized by behaviour within the rules of the market cannot necessarily be realized under any alternative set of rules, or assignments of rights. Care must be taken to avoid the comparison of false alternatives. That which might be imagined but not realized under one regime cannot necessarily be brought into being by a shift in regime. Given a regime change, the set of imagined social states may, once again, be subjected to the economist's classificatory scrutiny, with the distinction between the feasible and nonfeasible subsets being defined.

The point to be emphasized is that many, indeed the overwhelming majority, of the technologically feasible positions cannot be behaviourally realized, *under any regime.* Most of those positions or social states that are romantically imagined to be possible are inconsistent with the motivational postulate of economics, with human nature as it exhibits its uniformities. Economics need not be the dismal science, but it can scarcely avoid being labelled as the nonromantic science. The setting in which producers-sellers offer high-quality goods for nothing while showing interests in the desires of consumers is nonfeasible in a generalized sense. There is no regime, no set of rules, no assignments of rights to choose and to act that will generate such a social state and remain consistent with the central proposition of economic science.

An Exaggerated Illustration

I can present the basic argument with an illustration (Figure 2.1) which, although it is admittedly exaggerated in some respects, conveys the counter-

B

		b_1		b_2
a_1	I	(3, 3) 3, 3	II	(4, 4) 1, 4
a_2	III	(1, 1) 4, 1	IV	(2, 2) 2, 2

A

Figure 2.1

conventional message effectively. Consider the familiar PD matrix, depicting the interaction of two players, each of whom has two available choice-action alternatives. My concern here is with the generalization properties of the interdependence rather than with particular two-person strategic aspects. Assume, first, that the two persons are assigned rights to act along the dimensions indicated. *A* chooses between rows; *B* chooses between columns. Assume, further, that the ordinal payoffs reflect objectively measurable quantities of a commonly valued good, rather than utilities.

First, note that the outcome in each cell of the matrix is a "social state," but that these states, as such, are not within the choice set of either participant. These states or positions emerge from the interaction process, given the choice of each person along the dimension assigned. To this point, nothing has been claimed about the relation of the payoffs to individual utilities. If the domain of choice is not restricted, the utility payoffs might be such as to generate any one of the four outcomes, without violating the postulates of rational choice behaviour for the players. Suppose, for example, that the ordinal utility payoffs are those indicated in the parentheses. In this case, the outcome is in Cell II. Until and unless there is some specification that relates objectified payoffs to utilities, there is no means to predict the emergent outcome or solution to the interaction.

If we generalize the model to allow for interaction among large numbers of persons, each one of whom is assigned rights to choose and to act along many separate dimensions, we can remain within the postulates of rational choice while still generating *any* outcome consistent with the obligative or technological constraints. Any social state that can be imagined may emerge, given the requirement that preference orderings over states cannot be restricted.

The economist is, however, more than a rational choice theorist. The economist, as scientist, specifies the relationships between the utility payoffs that describe human choices and the objectifiably measurable payoffs in the interdependence. In Figure 2.1, the basic economic hypothesis is that persons must act so as to maximize objective payoffs. Persons seek to get more rather than less, as measured in some denominator of common value. This proposition is central to the economist's scientific enterprise. Given this hypothesis, the economist can make falsifiable predictions about the effects of changes in facultative constraints and, in the process, classify all imagined social states into feasible and nonfeasible sets, both specifically to a given regime and generally to all regimes.

Consider, again, the simple interaction in Figure 2.1. If individuals are modelled as maximizing the payoffs indicated, the outcome in Cell IV is predicted to emerge, provided only that the participants are presumed to behave separately and independently. Given the structure of the model, no other outcome is possible.[4] If enforceable exchange contracts are possible, the Pareto-superior outcome in Cell I may be reached, but note that this result requires that the payoffs in Cells II and III be modified so as to eliminate the temptation to renege.

What my argument suggests is that the outcomes depicted in Cells II and III, those in the off-diagonal cells of the matrix, are to be classified as nonfeasible. These describe social states that can be imagined and ordinally ranked by both players, but that cannot be attained, given the rights to choose as assigned and given the central proposition of economics. These states are beyond feasibility limits, not because they are technologically impossible, but because they can never be behaviourally produced by the choices and actions of the human beings involved.

As noted in the more general discussion of the previous section, however, the assignments of rights need not be immutable. Suppose, for example, that

---

4. See Ken Binmore, *Game Theory and Social Contract*, vol. 1, *Playing Fair* (Cambridge: MIT Press, 1994).

A is the dictator. Cannot *A*, quite simply, command *B* to behave, to do b_1, so as to generate *A*'s most preferred result in Cell III? And, vice versa, with Cell II if *B* should be dictator?

This question is critical, and my argument involves the claim that it must be answered negatively, at least in any generalizable form. The behaviour of *B*, when coerced by *A*, is not equivalent to that behaviour that is voluntarily undertaken, either as an independently acting party or as a participant in an exchange relationship, in which reciprocation is forthcoming from another party or parties. At this point, attempts to formalize, mathematize and simplify the interaction process may be dangerously misleading and serve to obscure the elementary reality.

If all of the technologically possible choice alternatives can be fully specific in each and every descriptive feature, and for all actors, then the assignment of control to a single authority can coercively achieve any state. There is no behavioural space which allows any participant to adjust along any dimension. Each person, other than the single dictator, must be a total slave, and there is no *inter*action, as such. This wholly unreal setting tends to seem analytically useful, in some reductionist way, when illustrations such as that introduced here are employed. If the course of action for *B*, defined by b_1, is set out in such a form as in the matrix, it seems to follow that b_1 is b_1 is b_1, and that this course of action remains invariant whether it is voluntarily chosen by *B* or is forced upon *B* by *A*. If, however, *B* is acknowledged to retain some residual liberties from control, in any regime, then such simple illustrations must be used with caution. And, if so used, the logic through which the off-diagonal positions may be classified to be nonfeasible become convincing.[5]

A Summing Up

I am fully aware of the fact that I have restated long-familiar arguments in this chapter and that few practising economists, especially those of the Chicago tradition, will find much to criticize. In a real sense, I have done little

---

5. For elaboration of the argument of this paragraph, see James M. Buchanan, "Individual Rights, Emergent Social States, and Behavioral Feasibility," *Rationality and Society* 7 (April 1995): 141–50.

more than to repackage the economists' positive and scientific proposition to the effect that demand curves are downsloping. I should suggest, nonetheless, that packaging can on occasion matter, and that perhaps the somewhat different rhetoric of my argument will prove more convincing than the familiar postures.

In part, the manner of putting the argument in this paper stems from reconsideration of some of the analyses of social-choice theorists, who have insisted for a half-century that preferences of individuals over social states cannot and should not be restricted. I have continued to be highly critical of this research programme, both in its search for some meaning of social welfare and for its presumption that social states are possible objects of social choice. The very language of social-choice theory has, however, allowed me to develop the argument of this chapter in a manner that may prove didactically useful. Armed with such an argument, economists may just be able to man their scientific defences more adequately than heretofore.

Economists are frequently accused of committing the naturalist fallacy, the derivation of an "ought" from an "is." The approach taken in this chapter should help us avoid such a charge. If the economists can observe politically motivated action aimed quite explicitly at the achievement of results that are clearly beyond the boundaries of feasibility, given the existing regime, no norms are violated when and if they call attention to this as scientific fact.

When the economists suggest that "the market works," no normatively positive charge need be attached to such a claim. Reference is properly limited to the proposition that if persons are assigned rights of disposition over their own activities (and uses of their endowments) an outcome will emerge from the interaction that falls within the feasibility space. It may well be the case that alternative outcomes or social states may be imagined and ranked ordinally to be more desirable than those outcomes predicted to emerge from markets. But such alternatives may or may not be feasible, and it falls to the economist, as scientist, to carry out the classification that is required. And it is in this role as scientist that the economist should be able to prevent ill-fated efforts to organize political action aimed at achieving results that are beyond the boundaries of behavioural feasibility.[6]

6. The role of the economist as scientist presented in this paper is different from, but not necessarily inconsistent with, the role of the political economist sketched out in my

The discussion of minimum wage legislation offers a practical example. In a regime where firms and individuals retain rights to hire and to fire employees, the economist can make a scientific statement to the effect that an increase in the legal minimum wage must reduce employment of relatively less-skilled workers. The imagined social state in which there is a higher minimum wage accompanied by no decline in employment is nonfeasible and must be so classified. And with particular reference to such an example, we can only look with misgiving on the modern urges toward empirical verification. Statistical inquiry may reveal the existence of parallel increases in minimum wages and in employment. But to rely on such empiricism to invalidate the economists' scientific enterprise is equivalent to making the observation that Peter Pan really does fly because one's vision does not disclose the existence of the supporting wires from the rafters.

Finally, I share what I think was Karl Brunner's belief that many of the errors in political economy stem from the failure of political decision makers to separate feasible from nonfeasible states of the economy. Scientific ignorance, when combined with informed self-seeking on the part of sectional interests, has prevented the attainment of results that might have proved to be beneficial to everyone in the economic nexus. The intense 1993 opposition to NAFTA in the United States was fuelled only in part by the informed self-interests of protected groups fearing damage from any opening-up of markets. The opposition was also grounded on economic ignorance that generated a fear of imagined consequences that could never be brought into reality.

As scientists, economists have an important social role to play. There is a repository of knowledge that remains within their unique responsibility.

---

early 1959 paper. In that effort, I was concerned with how the economist, armed with the propositions of positive economics, might participate in the social discussion of policy alternatives. I suggested that the political economist's role should be that of presenting proposals as *hypotheses*, with the ultimate test being the achievement of unanimous agreement on change. In the context of the analysis here, my earlier concern was with the potential role of the political economist in the discussion of social choices among alternatives, all of which are within the set of attainable or feasible positions. See James M. Buchanan, "Positive Economics, Welfare Economics, and Political Economy," *Journal of Law and Economics* 2 (October 1959): 124–38.

They default on their role when they, too, become romantic dreamers and try to assist misguided politicians in the search for nonattainable and imaginary worlds. We can only hope that Francis Fukuyama is correct when he suggests that the demise of socialism will mark the triumph of economic science.[7]

7. Francis Fukuyama, *The End of History and the Last Man* (New York: The Free Press, 1992).

Economics as a Public Science

> For Knight, the primary role of economic theory is . . . to contribute to an understanding of how by consensus based on rational discussion we can fashion liberal society in which individual freedom is preserved and a satisfactory economic performance achieved.
>
> —George J. Stigler, "Knight, Frank Hyneman," in
> *The New Palgrave: A Dictionary of Economics,* vol. 3
> (London: Macmillan, 1987), 58.

Introduction

The editors' charge was to address the question: How should economists do economics? This opportunity allows me to develop propositions about peculiar features of economics and the implications for activity that stem therefrom. My position is essentially that imputed to my professor, Frank Knight, in the frontispiece citation from George Stigler's *Palgrave* entry. But the implications of this position require some articulation.

In a summary sense, I use the word "public" as an adjective in my title to describe what there is about "economics" that makes it distinct from other inquiries. All science is public in the familiar sense summarized in the next section. But there is a "publicness" to economics that goes well beyond the familiar, and it is this public aspect that makes those of us who claim to be professionals behave (or so should behave) quite differently from our hard

From *Foundations of Research in Economics: How Do Economists Do Economics?* ed. Steven G. Medema and Warren J. Samuels (Cheltenham, U.K.: Edward Elgar, 1996), 30–36. Reprinted by permission of the publisher.

science counterparts. In making the argument here, I call on the theory of public goods in application to the science itself.

Not surprisingly, attention must be paid to the role of teaching, which should be different (but often is not) from that which describes other scientific disciplines. Again, not surprisingly, some indirect reference must be made to the practical applications of the science.

Science as a Public Good

The knowledge component of any science is recognized to meet the classificatory definition of a public or collective "good" in the sense laid out by Paul A. Samuelson in his seminal paper.[1] Once generated, knowledge can be made available to everyone as easily as to anyone. And there are no readily available means through which persons may be denied access to knowledge that is valued.

The implications familiar from welfare theory follow directly. Because knowledge qualifies as a public good, persons, acting separately or organized as through firms, cannot be predicted to produce genuinely scientific knowledge in the amount that might be judged to be "efficient," as determined by the preferences of all members of the politically organized community. There is a publicness-externality justification for some collective subsidization of the production of basic scientific knowledge.

The generalized understanding of the working of an organized economy that is generated by the activity of economists is not different from the understanding of the physical universe generated by the activity of natural scientists. In either case, such understanding is not likely to be advanced sufficiently, either quantitatively or qualitatively, in the absence of some collective support, as appropriately institutionalized. Economists, like physicists, chemists or biologists, would be relatively unrewarded in the operation of a wholly decollectivized society.

In the United States, the sciences are institutionally subsidized, directly or indirectly, through publicly supported academic structures. In these structures, scientists are rewarded only in small part for their direct contributions

1. Paul A. Samuelson, "The Pure Theory of Public Expenditures," *Review of Economics and Statistics* 36 (1954): 387–89.

to knowledge. Instead they are recompensed for the instruction and training of others, only a small fraction of whom are themselves expected to become practicing scientists. The scientists-instructors are engaged by collectively financed institutions to provide a generalized understanding of their areas of specialized knowledge to those members of the community who are expected to be its leaders. Such understanding of science is alleged to be central to general education. In this sense, a knowledge of science, including economics, is a necessary qualification for literacy.

Economics in Public Application

It is only in the application of its scientific content that economics comes to be categorically distinct from its scientific neighbors. And it is at this point that the "public science" appellation in my title becomes relevant. With relatively few exceptions, the applications of natural science can be, and are, organized through noncollective or private institutional structures. For example, the scientific discovery of a synthetic drug is preliminary to subsequent research, testing, development, production and marketing of a final product, each stage of which may be organized by privately owned, profit-seeking firms. These stages toward the ultimate application of the scientific findings do not embody the characteristic publicness features that describe the activity of basic science. Rivalry replaces nonrivalry in potential usage, and exclusion offers a means of linking costs and promised benefits for those who place the differentially higher values on the final product.

With economics, properly defined, there is no comparable shift from "publicness" to "privateness" as the move from pure to applied science takes place. Applied physics becomes engineering, and those who do engineering, as such, command and secure compensation in the ordinary marketplace. The engineer applies the laws of physics and chemistry to enable him to instruct clients as to how to achieve whatever objective is designated to be desired. Applied economics, if interpreted analogously, would become "social engineering," but confusion emerges when it is recognized that there is no external client that dictates the objective to be sought. The "economist as social engineer" is too often placed in the roles both of the engineer as applied scientist, and the philosopher-king as the ultimate social chooser among end objectives. The professionally trained scientist who sets himself up as an "applied economist" cannot readily market his knowledge in the private sector. The reason is that the scientific knowledge, even at this level of application, remains "public" in the sense that there is no partitionable product upon which users may separately place value. Another way of putting this point is to say that access to applied economic knowledge does not provide persons with privileged claims to sources of market value.

What, then, is the "product" of economic science? If we accept the existence of a body of scientific knowledge that contributes to an understanding of the social interaction process, it is surely incumbent on us to have some idea as to how this knowledge may be applied in furtherance of some preferred objectives. It is here that the peculiar status of economics emerges onto center stage. The "product" of genuine economic science can only be described as the enactment, or repeal, of "laws" or "rules" that act to constrain or channel behaviour so as to allow persons to produce more effectively those goods and services that they themselves value. Note that this definition of the "product" of economic science is fully consistent with the Knight position summarized in the Stigler frontispiece citation and with Adam Smith's statement to the effect that political economy is the science of legislation.

There are two distinct features of the "product" here that make the publicness attribution appropriate. First of all, any general law becomes public in the Samuelsonian sense for all members of the group of persons who are subject to its application and enforcement. A law that limits the activity of one person also limits the activities of others within the relevant jurisdiction. The essential meaning of law itself is subverted if arbitrary differentiation or discrimination in application is introduced. Hence, if economic science has, as its final product, better laws, rules or institutions, the public science appellation is valid.

There is, however, quite a different sense of "publicness" that is involved here. If, indeed, we acknowledge that economic science makes possible an understanding of social interaction, why do we not defer to the scientific authority of those who are professionally trained? Why do members of the citizenry reject the efforts of economic scientists to assume roles as "engineers"?

The response is straightforward. We may acknowledge the superior understanding of the economic scientist, while, at the same time, we do not accept that this science can be decisively important in informing us about the choices we must make in choosing among the laws and rules that we are to impose upon ourselves. Differently from natural science, the applications of economics cannot be separately and independently tried out for particular persons in separated markets. With economics, the publicness feature of law guarantees that only one experiment can be conducted at a time, and an experiment that necessarily involves all members of the community as its subjects. And only on rare occasions will everyone volunteer to become a guinea pig. It is scarcely credible to think that the authority of economic science could ever be such as to command such universal assent.[2]

What to do? It is as if the application of scientific knowledge in, say, physics could not be introduced until and unless generalized public agreement is achieved. What would the physicist try to do under such circumstances? It would seem necessary to try to instruct everyone in the elementary principles of the science, thereby providing a basis for general agreement on various practical applications. Persons would need to be informed about the science, at least sufficiently to be able to know how to discriminate among authorities who claim scientific status. Needless to say, the teaching of physics would be, and should be, quite different in such a setting from that which is observed. Teaching would necessarily be extended well beyond the contributions toward minimal literacy contained in general education.

In its application, therefore, economics is public in a sense that is quite distinct from natural science. And there are profound implications to be drawn from the activity of scientists that stem directly from these differences. Teaching must involve a transmission of the basic principles of the science itself with the objective of placing the student in a potential role as a participant in the ongoing "public choice" process in which the parametric constraints for economic interaction are selected. Economists often complain about the observed fact that "everyone is his own economist," in an expression of the view that scientific counsel fails to command the deference it seems to warrant. In the absence of an effective exit option, however, everyone will continue to be, and should be, his own economist, at least to the extent of participating in the selection of constraints that are to be imposed

---

2. William H. Hutt, *Economists and the Public: A Study of Competition and Opinion* (London: Jonathan Cape, 1936).

collectively, constraints that affect the actions of everyone simultaneously.[3] The effective scientific community in economics is, therefore, necessarily inclusive in a sense that is not applicable in natural science.

"Doing economics," as the specialized activity of economists, should reflect a different emphasis on the transmission of basic knowledge relative to the discovery of new knowledge at the scientific frontiers. Because of the public features of economics noted, the activity of "doing economics" must be more akin to that observed in the behaviour of the ordinary scientist who rarely makes discoveries. In modern practice, too much talented intellectual capital is used up in searches for the solutions of stylized puzzles with little or no relevance for the ongoing, necessarily repetitive and sometimes boring, activity of "teaching" the long-accepted principles of the science.

Economics Applied in Politics

Over and beyond the generalized publicness features that make the application of economic science so different from that of natural science, the elementary logic of "democracy" intrudes to introduce an even more insurmountable barrier to the translation of scientific principles into political reality. Even if *all* participants in a community are sufficiently informed about how an economy works and, therefore, also about what changes in constraints might result in the generation of a more highly valued bundle of "goods," implementation of such changes may be impossible because the *subset* of participants who make up the dominant political majority may impose alternative changes that promise to yield higher benefits to that subset, even at the possible sacrifice of potentially higher gains for all members.

In a very real sense, the operation of majoritarian democracy acts to

3. "Exit" and "voice" are substitutes in their perceived ability to insure protection against exploitation (see Albert O. Hirschman, *Exit, Voice, and Loyalty: Responses to Decline in Firms, Organizations, and States* [Cambridge, Mass.: Harvard University Press, 1970]). If an individual has available multiple exit options, and faces relatively low cost in switching among them (as in the stylized competitive market), the exercise of voice may not be highly valued. By contrast, when exit options are nonexistent or prohibitively costly, the individual may, rightly or wrongly, perceive participation (voice) as one means of limiting collective coercion.

"undo" the publicness characteristic of applied economics by endogenously introducing discrimination between members of dominant political coalitions and those persons who remain outside. The "economist as engineer" who acts as if he is proffering advice to the inclusive membership of the polity finds no purchase for his wares. And the "economist as engineer" who proffers advice that is useful in advancing the interests of a politically dominant coalition, in part at the expense of other members of the polity, may feel uncomfortable with the conscious violation of ethical-moral neutrality.

What Is, What Might Be and What Ought to Be

As the discussion indicates, the political economist is allowed to treat the set of structural parameters (the laws or constitution) as variables and to apply the principles of the science in generating predictions about the working properties of alternative sets of constraints, both those to be observed and those to be imagined. This sets economics apart from other disciplines in which the scientist simply accepts the constraints of the universe to be invariant.

This peculiar feature of the science of political economy becomes the source of much confusion when attempts are made to extend the simpler precepts of scientific method derived from concentration on the activity of natural scientists. Consider the familiar is-ought distinction traceable to David Hume. For the natural scientist there is an "is." For the economist there is an "is," but there is, also, a whole set of "might bes" that are feasible. This sometimes fuzzy set of "might bes" is bounded by the constraints imposed by the uniformities of human nature—uniformities that are acknowledged to exist, but which are not hard-wired in any sense analogous to those encountered in the natural world. A substantial share of the economists' scientific effort is devoted to delineating the institutionally feasible constraints on behavior that may be predicted to generate generally preferred outcomes or social states.

It is this extension of economic science to the analyses of the "might bes," that seems to fuzz up the sometimes forced positive-normative distinction, so beloved by the unsophisticated methodologists. The economist may, in fact, be saying no more than that "water runs down hill" while being accused of committing the naturalistic fallacy.

That which is observed as economic reality may, indeed, be modified by changes in the rules within which human behaviour is allowed to take place. But that which is romantically imagined is no more possible in economics than in the more clearly restricted realms of the natural world. Economics, and economists, must make the categorical distinction between science fiction and potentially attainable reality. Failure to do so can produce results both exemplified by and experienced in the human tragedy of this century's failed pursuit of the impossible socialist idyll.

Ceteris Paribus
Some Notes on Methodology

At the heart of any analytical process lies simplification or abstraction, the whole purpose of which is that of making problems scientifically manageable. In the economic system we recognize, of course, that "everything depends on everything else," and also that "everything is always changing." For the requirements of analytical rigor to be met fully, we should work only with dynamic Walrasian systems. But real problems can rarely be studied in dynamic terms and almost never in true Walrasian terms.

Real problems require the construction of models, and the skill of the scientist is reflected in the predictive or explanatory value of the model chosen. We simplify reality to construct these models, but the fundamental truth of interdependence must never be forgotten. The interdependence of the economy imposes certain restrictions on any analyst, and each model stands or falls on the test of its consistency with the general equilibrium world. This paper will demonstrate that many highly sophisticated models fail this test, and for the same reason. Specifically, I shall try to show that there exists a common error in the use of the Marshallian device of *ceteris paribus*.

From *Southern Economic Journal* 24 (January 1958): 259–70. Reprinted by permission of the publisher.

An original version of this paper was delivered at the annual meeting of the Southern Economic Association in Raleigh, North Carolina on 16 November 1956. I am indebted to Jesse Markham of Princeton University for his comments on the delivered version, and to Almarin Phillips of the University of Virginia for his suggestions for revision.

Partial Equilibrium Analysis

The most familiar means through which the economist reduces the complex of reality to proportions which are scientifically manageable is provided in partial equilibrium analysis. Beginning with the world as it is, the economist takes two giant steps. First, he removes the dynamic elements by specifying certain basic data. These data, which compose the familiar trichotomy— Wants, Resources, and Technology—become parameters in the model to be constructed. Or, stating this in our terms of reference here, these are placed in the pound of *ceteris paribus*.[1] Presumably the values for these parameters may change independent of the values for the remaining variables of the model. But once this step is taken the economist is still confronted with the whole Walrasian set of interdependent variables which he presumably can organize in some set of structural relationships. But since both the data and the intellectual capacity for solving these equations simultaneously are lacking, the economist deliberately limits his task still further. He tries to choose a particular subset of relationships, and he then proceeds to *neglect* the remainder, even though he may fully recognize that certain spill-over effects are exerted on the variables which he has neglected by the changes which he imposes upon the variables chosen for closer scrutiny.

The size of the model which remains after this second step is taken depends both upon the purposes of the analysis and the structure of the system. If the purpose is purely that of mathematical manipulation, the process of partial differentiation can always be carried out upon any variable of the system, with the remaining variables treated parametrically. In other words, if the purposes of analysis are purely formal, all of the variables except two can be placed literally in *ceteris paribus*, and the relationship between these

---

1. This classification must be carefully qualified. In the real world, it seems unlikely that even these basic data are genuinely independent. An individual's taste pattern may be modified by the values of the dependent variables of the system, e.g., the structure of prices. Similar statements may be made with regard to both resources and technology. There does appear, however, to be some value in distinguishing these variables as true parameters. It is at least conceptually possible that their values remain uninfluenced by the values of the dependent variables of the system. The same statement cannot be made in reverse.

two variables traced. Presumably the economist's interests in analysis go beyond this and extend to the derivation of economically meaningful relationships. If this constraint is placed upon him, the structure of the system itself must dictate his choice among variables to be closely examined and those to be treated parametrically. If cross elasticities are high, little simplification may be achieved in this second step. Few, if any, meaningful results may be achieved by using *ceteris paribus* to eliminate the study of large numbers of variables. If such variables are closely related, they must be studied simultaneously; there is no escape route open. On the other hand, if the various subsectors of the economy exhibit substantial independence, this step may reduce the working model to reasonable proportions. Of especial significance in this respect is the size of the total system. Partial equilibrium analysis is possible only when the total number of relationships is quite large. Clearly if the total number of relationships is small and any substantial interdependence is indicated, the effects of any initial change must be traced throughout the whole system. The required damping can take place only as an initial shock spreads and becomes diffused through a sizeable web of interdependence.

It should be emphasized that this second step which consists of *neglecting* second-, third-, and fourth-order effects, even when it is analytically legitimate, is not equivalent to freezing the neglected variables in the famous pound of *ceteris paribus*. These variables are treated as parameters for the immediate purposes of the analysis, but it is recognized that their values must, in fact, be modified by the shock initially imposed. Such variables thus fall into a different classification from those genuine *ceteris paribus* variables— wants, resources, and technology—the values for which, at least conceptually, are not modified by the changes imposed on the system. The neglected variables are among the total set of interdependent variables of the system. They are treated as parameters because the analyst desires to work with a subset rather than the whole set. But subset analysis will yield economically meaningful results only if the final shifts in the values of the parameters are reasonably small.

The discussion may be more firmly anchored if we introduce the familiar problem concerning the Marshallian demand curve, perhaps the most widely used partial equilibrium tool. The methodological issues involved here have been developed at length by Milton Friedman, although in somewhat different terms.[2] When the economist is confronted with the problem of determining the influence of a price change on the quantity of a particular good demanded, the influence of such forces as money income and other prices becomes disturbing. If we exclude relationships of close complementarity and substitutability, we know that the change in one price does not affect other prices in any substantial way. Therefore, we neglect such changes as may be generated. We do not, thereby, appear to impair the predictive value of our model which is reduced to two-dimensional or blackboard size. At first glance, this neglect appears equivalent to assuming that these variables (i.e., other prices) remain unchanged in the process along with such things as tastes. If, however, the literal *ceteris paribus* restriction is placed on all such variables as other prices and money incomes, that is, if these are not allowed to change, analysis becomes impossible in the ordinary static framework. For here the analyst would be faced immediately with the logical dilemma posed by Professor Frank Knight: How can *one* price change? One price cannot, of course, change in such a setting unless offsetting changes in other variables are allowed. In equilibrium any given commodity has only one price which is consistent with the equilibrium values for all of the remaining variables of the total system. If the basic data are not presumed to change (and, since these are genuinely exogenous, useful "political economy" conclusions could hardly be expected in this fashion), a displacement must involve some relaxation of the equilibrium conditions in other sectors, that is, some release of the neglected variables from the literal confines of *ceteris paribus*.

What is required here is a modification of the literal meaning of *ceteris paribus*. If we define the restriction to mean that included variables do not change *substantially*, analysis in the usual manner becomes possible, provided always that the system is sufficiently large. Correct analysis may or may not require that the necessarily present offsetting or compensating changes in the other variables be taken explicitly into account. The method here will depend on the problem to be solved. And, for some problems which do not require the recognition of such offsetting variations, the use of the literal *ceteris paribus* terminology need not lead to erroneous results.

2. Milton Friedman, "The Marshallian Demand Curve," *Journal of Political Economy* 57 (1949): 463–95.

Look at the so-called Hicksian version of the demand curve. One price is allowed to change while money incomes and other prices are assumed unchanging. As mentioned above, and as Friedman has shown, this construction is logically inconsistent in the strict framework of comparative statics. Nevertheless, the construction provides a useful tool of analysis if the offsetting variations, *which must be present,* can be allowed to take place outside that set of variables directly influencing the behavior of the individual or the group under observation. For example, suppose that the problem is that of deriving the demand curve for cheese. As the price of cheese is allowed to change, something else must change in a compensating fashion. But conceptually at least, this compensating change can take place anywhere in the system, let us say in the price of popcorn. If the cheese demanders constitute an entirely different group from the popcorn demanders, the offsetting variations in the popcorn price need not be taken explicitly into account. Or, to vary the example, the offsetting variation may be in the price of bread, a commodity consumed by all groups. Here the relative influence of a change in the price of cheese on the behavior of the particular cheese-consuming group may be so large relative to the influence of the offsetting change in the price of bread on the behavior of the same group that the latter price change may be neglected.

In more general terms, the predictive error involved in neglecting all offsetting or compensating variations, which is equivalent to using *ceteris paribus* literally, need not be large if we remain content to analyze the behavior of one individual or some one group of individuals smaller than the total group. This provides some justification for the widespread acceptance and use of the uncompensated demand curve.

As Friedman has shown, however, erroneous results will be forthcoming from this procedure when the attempt is made to reach conclusions supposedly applicable for the totality of individuals, that is, for the whole economy, and not for a specific subsector. The dangers in the misuse of *ceteris paribus* are quite real for all cases where an attempt is made to extend conclusions reached in partial equilibrium analysis to general equilibrium problems. When the whole economy is the subject of analysis, offsets must be introduced. Suppose one price is allowed to change as before. If money income is to be held constant, other prices must be allowed to vary in some compensating manner. If the system is large, the compensating change in *any one* of the many other prices may be small enough to be neglected. But the total of such changes must completely offset the initial change imposed on the action variable. The aggregative effects of such changes must be comparable in magnitude and importance to the effects of the initial and localized variation. Friedman has shown how the oversight of this point has led to serious error in the analysis of the comparative effects of income and excise taxes.[3]

The Demand Curve for Money

The methodological error discussed here is present in some of the most important modern contributions to economic theory. The recent work by Don Patinkin may be used as a first illustration.[4] This work is selected both due to its current importance and to the clarity with which it poses the fundamental issue of this paper. Patinkin introduces a basic distinction between the aggregate demand curve for money and the market equilibrium curve relating the quantity of money and the price level. The first he derives from individual experiments, the second from the reactions of the whole market. He criticizes neo-classical writers for having failed to note the necessary differences between these two curves. I shall show that there is no distinction if the aggregate demand curve is properly derived and that Patinkin's discussion is based upon the improper usage of *ceteris paribus*.

He first conceptually derives an individual demand curve for money. This curve is constructed by confronting the individual with a change in the price level "unaccompanied by any change in the initial endowment of money."[5] The individual demand curves so derived are then summed over all individuals to produce Patinkin's aggregate demand curve for money. Although this curve is presumed to have a negative slope there is no reason why it should have the unitary elasticity property normally attributed to it by neo-classical theorists.

The second curve, which is called the market equilibrium curve, is derived

3. Milton Friedman, "The 'Welfare' Aspects of an Income Tax and an Excise Tax," *Journal of Political Economy* 60 (1952): 25–33.

4. Don Patinkin, *Money, Interest, and Prices* (Evanston: Row, Peterson and Co., 1956). I should like to thank Patinkin for his efforts to convince me that my methodological criticism is unfounded. Needless to say, he has not been successful.

5. Ibid., 42.

by changing the supply of money in the system and then examining the effects of this change on the price level. The resulting curve is shown to possess the unitary elasticity property.

From the discussions in the previous sections of this paper, it is clear that Patinkin's aggregate demand curve for money is not a methodologically legitimate construction. While it is possible to talk of an *isolated* individual experiment in which the price level is allowed to change *ceteris paribus,* this procedure cannot be used as the basis for deriving an aggregate demand curve. The price level facing an individual or group can be allowed to shift, without the supply of money changing, if we are content to examine the demand for that *individual or group only,* the necessary offsetting or compensating change taking place in the price level confronting *other* groups in the economy. But this cannot be done when we consider all individuals, or a representative one. The price level cannot be shifted, *ceteris paribus,* with any hope of deriving results which are economically meaningful. If the other variables of the economy are held constant, the price level may change only if the nominal amount of money is allowed to change. Therefore, the market equilibrium curve, which does in fact allow the price level and the nominal quantity of money to change in compensating fashion, is the only meaningful demand curve for money which may be derived for the whole economy.[6]

Perhaps the most interesting aspect of Patinkin's whole analysis is that in

6. The interdependence of supply and demand which is inherent in the Patinkin argument does not appear to be the same as that mentioned by Pigou, although the relationship is close. (See A. C. Pigou, "The Value of Money," *Quarterly Journal of Economics* [1917–18].) Reprinted in *Readings in Monetary Theory* (New York: Blakiston, 1951), 181–82. Pigou states that the demand and the supply of money are not independent as in the case of an ordinary commodity. But the interdependence he discusses stems from the effects of a possible change in supply on the "tastes" of individuals regarding the use of money. He cites Cannan to the effect that velocity would increase as the price level, *and the quantity of money,* increase. This change in tastes brought about by an increase in the money supply generates a shift in the demand curve. The difference between this sort of interdependence and that involved in the Patinkin discussion is that the Pigou-Cannan interdependence is not conceptually necessary. An independent demand curve may be drawn on the assumption that the resultant effects on habits do not materialize (see Footnote 1). In the Patinkin analysis, on the other hand, such independence between supply and demand is not even conceptually possible. The demand curve *must* shift with a shift in supply; various positions on the demand curve are not, therefore, conceptually attainable alternatives. I am indebted to E. C. Simmons for reference to the Pigou discussion.

his Mathematical Appendix[7] he rigorously explains the mathematical difference between the curve derived from individual experiments and that derived from market experiments. But at the same time he overlooks the economic meaning of this admittedly important distinction. Had he chosen to look more closely at the economic implications of his mathematical argument, he would have surely seen that the aggregate demand curve is useful only if it represents genuinely attainable alternatives. In general, demand curves are useful only because they allow some predictions to be made regarding the effects of changes in supply. Hence each point on a demand curve must represent an attainable equilibrium between demand and supply. It is extremely difficult to imagine any other possible use for a demand function. It is true, of course, that a market need not always be in equilibrium. But disequilibrium positions are *off* the relevant demand and supply curves, not on them. By Patinkin's procedure any point on the demand curve for money except one arbitrarily chosen equilibrium point must represent a position of disequilibrium, if indeed it represents a position at all.

Macro-economic Analysis

Another means through which the economist may try to simplify reality is that of moving out of partial equilibrium analysis altogether and working with a small macro-economic model. Instead of choosing to work with a single sector of the system and then extending his conclusions as appropriate, he chooses from the start to consider the whole economy. But in order that a reasonably limited set of structural relationships describe the economy, each single variable used must represent a composite of several variables and can only be attained through an aggregation process.

The system so constructed will consist of a set of structural equations. Certain variables of the system will be classified as dependent, others as independent or as parameters. And given some initial set of values for the parameters along with the functional relationships, the corresponding equilibrium values for the dependent variables of the system may be found.

The analytical process here, as in partial equilibrium, is ordinarily conceived as comparative statics. A change is imposed on one of the parameters,

7. Patinkin, *Money, Interest, and Prices,* 275–88.

with the remaining ones held in *ceteris paribus,* and the effects of the change on the values of the dependent variables are examined.

But what are the true parameters in the macro-economic model? The same economy is under observation, and, as before, wants, resources, and technology provide the only basic data which can be taken as genuinely independent. It seems clear that we do not get much that is of value if we allow only these parameters to shift about since there is little external control which can be exerted on such shifts. Perhaps it is somewhat useful to know how an economic system will react to the introduction of a new invention or a shift in liquidity preference, but since no one has yet invented a means of producing inventions or of predicting mass psychology, this knowledge will prove of relatively little value in "political economy" terms.

It is interesting to examine the standard Keynesian model in this respect. The basic data are provided in the three psychological propensities. Each implies a functional description of human behavior and each is subjected to possible shifts. In the highly simplified model the results obtained would perhaps be of little value. But once government demand is included, the "wants" part of the basic data trichotomy is subjected to external influence and control through collective action.

The quantity of money is also normally taken as a parameter in the orthodox Keynesian model. In modern economic systems it seems that the quantity of money can be taken as an independently determined parameter since government action can set a value for this independent of the values for the remaining variables of the system. Therefore, that comparative static analysis would seem useful which takes as its beginning an equilibrium position with a given money supply, changes this quantity, and then traces through the effects of this change on the values for the remaining variables of the system.

But how can the quantity of money change unless one or more of the psychological propensities shifts? Can the quantity of money be treated as independent even in an ideally simplified system? The answer to this question depends on the structure of the system. Specifically, it depends on the manner in which the so-called budget variables are introduced. If government outlay is fixed and is made equal to taxes, the quantity of money cannot vary unless "tastes" of private people vary.[8] But such an old-fashioned balanced

---

8. Assume that the government (the central bank) creates money and then purchases bonds in the open market. This use of money is a government outlay as well as that in-

budget equation is not likely to be found in any modern macro-system construction. More often we find a system which includes both government expenditures in real terms and the tax rate to be independent variables. But if these are genuinely independent, the quantity of money is no longer a parameter. Here is a source of a very common error. The money supply, government outlay, and taxes cannot be taken as three separate independent variables. The test of a genuinely independent variable is that its value remains unchanged as other values in the system are modified. But with a fixed quantity of money, clearly government outlay and taxes must be functionally related. The two sides of the budget may be treated as independent only if the quantity of money is made dependent on the resultant surplus or deficit creation.[9]

If economically meaningful results are to be produced, great care must be exercised in classifying variables, and the use of *ceteris paribus* as a tool of analysis must be approached with great caution. We may refer to Patinkin's macro-economic model for specific examples. In his attempt to reduce his analysis to two-dimensional proportions, Patinkin employs the *ceteris paribus* device loosely and inappropriately. For example, after he draws the familiar aggregate spendings diagram which relates gross expenditure and real income, he states: "It follows that, *ceteris paribus*, an increase in the price level above p_0 causes a decrease in the real value of cash balances, $M_0 p$, and a consequent downward shift in the aggregate demand curve of Figure

---

volved in the expenditure for real goods and services. It is, of course, possible that real government expenditures for goods and services can be kept constant and equal to taxes while the quantity of money is shifted.

9. The recent work of Challis A. Hall and James Tobin may be cited as an example in which this error occurs ("Income Taxation, Output, and Prices," *Economia Internazionale* 8 [1955]: 522–42). In this, Hall and Tobin specifically classify the following as independent variables: M, the quantity of money; t, the tax rate; B, government interest payments (presumably including bond retirements) in money; G/p, the expenditure of government for goods and services in real terms. They then proceed to examine the effects of a change in the tax rate while holding the other independent variables in *ceteris paribus*. They sense the difficulty here but attempt to explain it away by stating that the changes induced in the money supply by the presence of surpluses or deficits is small relative to the total money supply and also that these are dynamic changes which are not relevant for static analysis (p. 526). This explanation overlooks one basic and all-important point. The change in M induced by changes in the tax rate is of the same logical dimension for the model as the tax rate change itself.

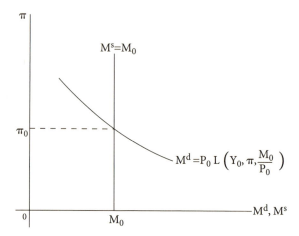

Figure 1. Patinkin's Figure 15. Reprinted by permission of MIT Press.

11. . . . ."[10] The obvious question here is the macro-economic version of the Knightian query. How does the price level change? If it shifts due to a change in spending habits, this in itself would shift the aggregate demand curve. If it shifts due to a change in M, then the real value of cash balances need not change.

One further example from Patinkin's work will suffice. I shall reproduce Patinkin's Figure 15 (p. 146) which relates the quantity of money demanded to the rate of interest. The methodological difficulty appears in the notation itself. The demand equation contains the supply of money, M_0, as a parameter. Hence the demand curve cannot possibly represent alternative positions traced by a shifting of supply. A change in M will shift the whole demand function. This circularity stems from the implicit assumption upon which the whole diagram is constructed, namely, that the rate of interest can change in some way independent of shifts in any of the other variables in the system (the price level, P_0, real income, Y_0).

Patinkin is, of course, too careful an economist to allow this methodological deficiency to distort seriously his final conclusions and thus his genuine contribution. When he considers his model in its entirety, he properly labels as parameters those variables which are independent, and as dependent

10. Patinkin, *Money, Interest, and Prices*, 133.

those variables which are not. His is an expositional deficiency which lies almost exclusively in his attempts to explain the workings of a model containing several mutually dependent variables in all of the equations. The values for these variables can only be determined simultaneously, and no amount of effort will yield a satisfactory way of showing simultaneous solution for several variables in two dimensions. In his attempt to be both rigorous and elementary, Patinkin has perhaps relied too much on the Marshallian crutch.[11]

While Patinkin has avoided the pitfall of drawing misleading and erroneous implications from his analysis, others have not been so fortunate. We may take the work of Kenneth Boulding as an example. I refer to his so-called distributional paradoxes which he advanced in his book, *The Reconstruction of Economics*.[12] There is no need to develop the Boulding construction in detail. It will be sufficient to reproduce only a few of his basic identities. We need not be concerned with the derivation of these since I shall have no quarrel with their content.

Begin with his equation (14).

$$W \equiv C_h + dQ_h - (dM_b + dK_h - dK_{h'} + D) \qquad (14)$$

This says that total wages, W, is identically equal to consumption, C_h, plus the change in the value of capital assets held by households, dQ_h, minus the items in the parenthesis. To simplify, he sets the items in the parenthesis equal to T, which he calls the transfer factor, in equation (17).

$$T \equiv dM_b + dK_h - dK_{h'} + D \qquad (17)$$

The transfer factor is identically equal to the change in business money balances, dM_b, plus the change in household debt to business, dK_h, minus the change in business debt to households, $dK_{h'}$, plus dividends, D. Any change

---

11. In the development of his analysis Patinkin follows the procedure of treating certain variables as exogenous and later incorporating these as endogenous to the system. This procedure has been held to be legitimate by Koopmans. (See Tjalling Koopmans, "When Is an Equation System Complete for Statistical Purposes," *Statistical Inference in Dynamic Economic Models* [New York: John Wiley & Sons, 1950], 394.) My main emphasis has been that of suggesting that such procedure is likely to lead to serious error.

12. New York: John Wiley & Sons, 1950.

which increases the value of the transfer factor tends to increase gross business profits and to reduce total wages.

From these equations, and the others used in their derivation, Boulding reaches his strange distributional paradoxes. He says that an increase in consumer credit, dK_h, will increase business profits. "It is clear that extending credit to households has a directly favorable effect on gross profits, and shifts the basic distribution pattern from labor to non-labor income" (p. 255). On the other hand, ". . . the greater the volume of securities sold to households, the more the distribution pattern is shifted toward wages and away from gross profits" (p. 255). Or again, ". . . the direct effect of business distribution is to increase gross profits by the same amount" (p. 256).

This is all wrong. We may accept the Boulding construction of the identities and also the simple algebra by which he reaches his conclusions. But we cannot accept the conclusions themselves. In reaching them, Boulding has fallen into the methodological trap which we have discussed. He has treated certain variables parametrically without an examination of the economic meaning of such treatment. Or, in terms of this paper, he has placed in *ceteris paribus* variables which do not belong there at all.

Look now again at his transfer identity (17). The algebra is simple. Quite clearly if consumer credit increases with the other values on the right-hand side of the equation remaining unchanged, then T must increase and thus W, wages, must decrease and gross profits increase. But the real question is: How can consumer credit increase without some of the other variables on the right side changing at the same time and in a compensating fashion? We should note that Boulding assumes a constant quantity of money (p. 254). Business cannot simply decide to expand consumer credit, and "open sesame" it is done. Any of several things may happen. An extension of consumer credit to households on the right-hand side would probably involve some business drawing down its money balances somewhere along the line. The retailer can extend credit to the consumer by increasing his indebtedness to the wholesaler. The wholesaler can, in turn, extend such credit to the retailer by increasing his indebtedness to the manufacturer. The manufacturer could conceptually meet the pressure by extending his indebtedness to production workers. But at this point business indebtedness to households, a negative factor in the transfer equation, would be increased to offset the original increase in dK_h. More realistically, of course, the manufacturer or the wholesaler or the retailer would allow the extension of consumer credit by a drawing down of money balances, dM_b, in the equation. Another alternative is a reduction in the outpayment of dividends. Or more securities could be sold to households. In each of these conceptually possible cases, there is no change in business profits merely as a result of a change in the volume of consumer credit outstanding.

The same sort of reasoning can be applied to each of the other Boulding paradoxes. Take the case in which he says that an increase in securities sold to households increases the share of income going into wages. In return for the securities, businesses receive money which builds up their money balances, or more dividends may be paid out, or consumer credit may be extended. No effect is produced by either of these changes on the value for the left side of the equation, the transfer factor, T.

At one point Boulding appears to recognize this interdependence among his variables, but he is too enamoured of his paradoxes to notice its importance. He states that he neglects "secondary interactions" for short-run fluctuations. But closer examination reveals that he does not sense the basic sort of interdependence with which we have been concerned. He says, for example, that the "most important of these (secondary interactions) is likely to be the reaction of changes in debt of dividends on the business-household balance of payments. Thus an increase in dividend payments may in part be offset by the fact that some of the money which is distributed simply remains in households without being spent" (p. 257). This statement indicates that Boulding fails to see that the money could not be distributed in the first place without some primary interaction on the other variables of the identity. We may neglect secondary interactions, but not primary ones. How could business possibly increase dividend payments without either (1) reducing money balances (2) reducing loans to individuals (3) increasing indebtedness to households? As with our other illustrative examples, this could only happen if we move outside the static framework, that is, unless we allow some of the genuinely independent variables of the system to change.

Conclusion

It has not been my purpose in this paper to criticize any particular work. The very eminence of the economist whose works have been used as illustrations indicates that the methodological error which has been discussed is important and that its use is widespread. We have been thrust too rapidly over into the greener pastures of general equilibrium without recognizing that we cannot take with us many of our partial equilibrium trappings. Many of us who have been raised on Marshall try to live on Keynes without having made the necessary methodological transformation. *Ceteris paribus* helps us to clear away a lot of jungle in partial equilibrium analysis, and partial differentiation is extremely useful in formal mathematics, but either of these devices may turn out to be a hindrance in general equilibrium economics.

This leads to a final suggestion on method. When the economist is confronted with a general equilibrium problem, that is, any problem which involves a solution for the whole economy, whether the process used be an extension of partial equilibrium, aggregative models, or generalized Walrasian systems, he must recognize the Walrasian truth of economic interdependence. And this must be taken into full account. A good dose of double-entry bookkeeping is about the best medicine one can take here. There are no independent variables on a balance sheet, and an accountant would think one foolish who proposed to change one entry with all the others left unchanged. Yet this procedure, which seems so clearly wrong when we think in terms of balance sheets, is precisely equivalent to that involved in trying to rely too much on *ceteris paribus* in general equilibrium.[13]

13. The problem discussed in this paper is related to the problem of stability in dynamic models. As Samuelson has suggested, meaningful theorems in comparative statics can only be derived upon the assumption or demonstration of the presence of certain stability properties of a system. The stability problem *per se* is concerned with the behavior of a system after some displacement has been imposed on a pre-existing equilibrium. The problem discussed here has been wholly that of defining economically meaningful displacements. However, in discussing the appropriate criteria for testing the stability of a multiple market system Samuelson appears to arrive at conclusions which may be easily translated into our *ceteris paribus* terms of reference. He says: ". . . in terms of a truly dynamic process the equilibrium must be stable for arbitrary initial conditions or displacements and for arbitrary non-singular transformations of variables, but *not* necessarily for arbitrary modifications of the dynamic equations of motion such as are involved in the Hicks procedure of holding subsets of other prices constant (by violating or relaxing true dynamical relations). In principle the Hicks procedure is clearly wrong, although in some empirical cases it may be useful to make the hypothesis that the equilibrium is stable even without the 'equilibrating' action of some variable which may be arbitrarily held constant." (Paul A. Samuelson, *Foundations of Economic Analysis* [Cambridge: Harvard, 1947], 273.)

Marshall's Mathematical Note XIX

James M. Buchanan and Charles Plott

The following note appears on page 854 of the 8th Edition of Alfred Marshall's *Principles of Economics.*

> This case corresponds, *mutatis mutandis,* to that discussed in Note XVI. If in equilibrium x' oxen annually are supplied and sold at a price $y' = \phi(x')$; and each ox yields m units of beef: and if breeders find that by modifying the breeding and feeding of oxen they can increase their meat-yielding properties to the extent of Δm units of beef (the hides and other joint products being, on the balance, unaltered), and that the extra expense of doing this is $\Delta y'$, then $\Delta y'/\Delta m$ represents the marginal supply price of beef: if this price were less than the selling price, it would be to the interest of breeders to make the change.

Marshall seems here to have strayed into error by assuming that Note XIX could be obtained by exact symmetry from Note XVI.[1] Earlier, he states that ". . . the price required to call forth the exertion necessary for producing any given amount of a commodity, may be called the *supply price* for that amount during the same time" (p. 142). In Note XIX, reproduced in full above, Marshall derives marginal supply price (in modern terminology) by taking the derivative of the cost function in a direction parallel to the coor-

From *Economic Journal* 75 (September 1965): 618–20. Copyright Royal Economic Society. Reprinted by permission of the publisher.

1. Essentially the same error is repeated by Hubert Henderson, *Supply and Demand* (University of Chicago Press, 1962), 54–55, and by Kenneth Boulding, *Economic Analysis,* rev. ed. (Harper, 1949), 708. D. H. Robertson seems to have sensed Marshall's error, but his own treatment remains ambiguous, if not wrong. See D. H. Robertson, *Lectures on Economic Principles,* vol. I (London: Staples Press, 1957), 152 ff.

dinate axis along which beef is measured. Presumably he would derive the marginal supply price of other jointly produced goods (hides, etc.) by taking similar derivatives in directions parallel to the other axes along which these goods are measured. The marginal supply prices of the component goods, derived separately in this fashion, would sum to more than the marginal cost of producing a composite unit embodying all of the goods. Therefore, insofar as there exists any marginal evaluation or marginal demand price for the remaining goods in the jointly produced unit of supply, the marginal supply price of beef is less than $\Delta y'/\Delta m$. Marginal supply price for a single good under joint production with other goods is properly defined as the derivative of the total cost function in a direction which involves an increase in all components, a directional derivative,[2] minus the marginal demand price (marginal evaluation) placed on all remaining component goods.[3] The specific direction of movement along the total cost function is determined by the locus of points indicating optimal proportions in the component "mix." At any given output level equality between the marginal rate of transformation among the component goods in production and the marginal rate of substitution among these goods in demand or consumption determines the optimal proportions in the mix.

Only in the case where joint production is not differentially efficient does the marginal cost of the composite unit of supply become the sum of the marginal supply prices of the separate component goods as defined by Marshall. There the equilibrium conditions reduce to those defined under independent or separate production.

It is interesting to speculate on why Marshall made this error. Note XVI, to which he refers at the outset of Note XIX, concerns the case of joint demand, rather than joint supply, and he derives in the earlier Note the mar-

2. For an explanation of the usefulness of directional derivatives in economic theory, see Charles Plott, "Generalized Equilibrium Conditions Under Alternative Exchange Institutions," *Research Monograph 9*, Thomas Jefferson Center for Studies in Political Economy (December 1964).

3. Both M. J. Bailey and R. H. Coase have analyzed related products, and a proper definition of marginal supply price is implicit in their discussion. However, neither of these writers relates their analysis to Marshall's, and neither explicitly defines marginal supply price. See M. J. Bailey, "Price and Output Determination by a Firm Selling Related Products," *American Economic Review* 44 (March 1954): 91; R. H. Coase, "Monopoly Pricing With Interrelated Costs and Demands," *Economica* 13 (November 1946): 278–91.

ginal demand price for hops, as an input in the production of beer, by vary-ing the amount of hops, other inputs unchanged. This procedure, which has, since Marshall, become the standard neo-classical means of measuring mar-ginal productivity, seems much less objectionable than its analogue in the joint supply analysis. While it is recognised that unless constant returns to scale are present, the payment to all inputs in accordance with marginal product will either over- or under-utilise total product, there is nothing in-herent in the logic of the model to suggest the absence of constant returns. The question becomes an empirical one, and there is no necessity for resort-ing to specific shapes of the returns curves to explain why the demand for hops is a derived demand.

The case is quite different with joint supply because Marshall's condition "(the hides and other joint products being, on the balance, unaltered)" is necessarily violated. The component goods can always be produced indepen-dently or separately, at some cost. But the jointness in supply is to be ex-plained, presumably, precisely because economies are to be found in combin-ing the several production processes. This explanation guarantees, however, that the analogue of "constant returns to scale" here is not present. Quite apart from any empirical estimation of cost functions, joint supply simply cannot be explained if the Marshallian derivation of marginal supply price is valid.

The slip here is especially surprising, since the correct definition of mar-ginal supply price when proportions of the jointly supplied commodities are variable is essentially equivalent to the definition under the assumption of fixed proportions, which, of course, we owe directly to Marshall.

The Normative Purpose of
Economic "Science"
Rediscovery of an Eighteenth Century Method

Geoffrey Brennan and James Buchanan

> . . . for governments may be so formed, or laws so framed, as will necessarily produce virtue, and make good ministers even of bad men.

> —Viscount Bolingbroke in the *Craftsman* (28 February 1730).
> As cited by Duncan Forbes, *Hume's Philosophical Politics*
> (Cambridge: Cambridge University Press, 1975), 199.

I. Introduction

The necessity of abstraction is self-evident. By its very nature, intellectual activity involves coming to terms with a chaos of observations through the imposition of an order which is itself an artifact of the mental process. In this activity, a selective strategy must be used. Irrelevances must be blotted out, where these consist of observations that tend to disprove, qualify, or overly complicate the sought-for mental picture. Any theory is abstracted from the

From *International Review of Law and Economics* 1 (December 1981): 155–66. Copyright 1981. Reprinted with permission from Elsevier Science.

This paper was originally prepared for a Liberty Fund Conference on "Science and Freedom" held in San Antonio, Texas, in March 1981. We are grateful to participants in that conference—particularly David Levy, Brian Loasby, Richard McKenzie, and Karen Vaughn—and to our colleague Bob Tollison for useful comments. Several improvements were also suggested by helpful referees. Remaining errors are our own responsibility.

reality perceived by the senses, and theory derives its potential value precisely because it *is* so abstracted. From this perspective, it follows that any theory, any model, can, and indeed must, be able to tolerate a certain amount of dissonance with perception before it loses its relative superiority over potential alternatives.

This perspective suggests that there may well be many possible mental orders or constructs that can "explain" a particular set of "facts" within the tolerated range of "error." Which particular order chosen depends on many elements, including the tastes of the analyst, intellectual habits and fashions of the times, and the extent of congruence with the reality that is perceived (congruence that embodies predictive power as an important part). We leave as basically "mysterious" the causal linkage between changes in these elements and a switching of mental orders (paradigms).

In this paper, we are interested in one particular abstraction, one that is familiar to all economists. We are concerned with the model of man that is used in economic theory—the model of man that actually takes its name from the discipline, *Homo economicus*. Our purpose is to develop a specific justification for that abstraction that has not been sufficiently recognized by our fellow practitioners. In the exposition that follows we shall argue three propositions:

1. The purpose for which a theory is to be used is itself an important consideration in choosing how it should be formulated (that is, what abstractions are acceptable);

2. The purpose for which *Homo economicus* was used in classical political economy was largely that of comparing the properties of alternative socioeconomic arrangements (constitutions) and not that of explaining "scientifically" (making predictions about) the behaviour of economizing actors;

3. There are important differences between choices that are made among alternative institutions and choices made within the structure of given institutions, differences that are relevant to the nature of the assumptions about human motivation that might be viewed as appropriate.

Our objective is to spell out these propositions in such a way as to demonstrate that, appropriately understood, they provide a justification for the usage of *Homo economicus* for comparative institutional analysis, even if the

Homo economicus behavioural postulate may be somewhat less satisfactory than possible alternatives in some predictive sense. In the discussion, we shall necessarily emphasize the differences between "constitutional choice" (that choice among institutions) and "postconstitutional or in-period choice" (the choice among alternative options within given institutions).

II. *Homo economicus* Defined in Empirical "Economic Science"

There is a necessary distinction to be drawn between the formal, but empty, economic theory that incorporates a pure "logic of choice" on the part of the actors, and the allegedly operationally scientific theory or "economic science" that embodies empirically refutable hypotheses.[1] There is a corresponding distinction between the motivational postulates attributed to the human agents in the two constructions, between man as a rational utility maximizer, with the arguments in the utility functions remaining unspecified, and man as a net wealth maximizer, which requires explicit specification of the arguments in utility functions, and the assignment of predominant weights to those arguments that may readily be transformed into monetary wealth.[2]

If we define *Homo economicus* in the second of these two senses, we have a basis for empirical scientific explanation. Man, as modelled, acts so as to maximize his own interests (or the interests of those for whom he acts) objectively defined, in his economic relationships with other persons. He need not be inherently self-interested in some personalized sense. As Wicksteed

1. See J. M. Buchanan, "Is Economics the Science of Choice?" in *Roads to Freedom,* ed. E. Streissler (Routledge and Kegan Paul, 1969), 47–64.

2. In making this two-part distinction, we are "passing over" the in-between postulate, one that involves specification of the arguments in the utility function of persons, but which does not assign weights. In this in-between setting, there remains scope for positive prediction; for example, if we know that some argument, X, is valued positively in the utility function, we can predict that more X will be chosen as the relative cost of X falls. However, note that X may be "giving to others" or anything else. In other words, we do not require net wealth maximization as a behavioural postulate in order to have a "scientific" economics. For further discussion, see J. M. Buchanan, "Professor Alchian on Economic Method," in his *Freedom in Constitutional Contract* (Texas A&M University Press, 1978).

noted, "non-tuism" is all that is required here.[3] In the interaction behaviour that is to be modelled, man is postulated to further that interest which he represents. His behaviour in the economic relationship is not influenced by ethical or moral considerations that serve to constrain his pursuit of his objectively defined interest. *Homo economicus,* by construction, is not predicted to act other than in furtherance of his interest, vis-à-vis that of his trading cohorts, as he evaluates such interest at the moment of choice. He must act so as to advance his own net wealth (or that of the party or parties that he represents in the economic interaction).

Armed with this behavioural postulate, we can test "economic theory" against real-world observations, and, as the record shows, we can explain much of what we see. There are not clearly defined limits on this model of "economic man"; there is no delineation between "economic" behaviour on the one hand and "non-economic" behaviour on the other. *Homo economicus* remains *Homo economicus.*

It may be useful to list some extreme examples in which the basic economic or economizing model of interaction is extended to behavioural settings that may not normally be classified as "economic" in nature. For example, if a judge's behaviour in his assigned occupational role is modelled strictly in *Homo economicus* terms, his decisions on the bench must be explained somehow as falling within a wealth-maximizing calculus. Similarly, for elected politicians and for bureaucrats. Parents' behaviour toward their own children may be "explained" as down-payments on reciprocal care in their dotage. Conscientiousness on the job may be interpreted in terms of the quest for promotion in a hierarchy. Honesty in business dealing is interpreted as the best policy to increase sales over the long term.

III. *Homo economicus* as Abstraction

The first point to be made is to reemphasize that the *Homo economicus* construction *is* an abstraction from reality. Its purpose is that of allowing economists to impose intellectual order on the observed chaos of human interaction, without excessive distracting detail in dimensions of the analysis that are not centrally relevant. Critics of economics may, with some legitimacy,

3. P. H. Wicksteed, *The Commonsense of Political Economy* (Macmillan, 1910).

think that economists do not recognize their own construction. There seems little doubt that there are economists, some of them influential within the profession, who do act and talk as if they think of *Homo economicus* in much more descriptive ways. There are many economists who appear to think that the rarified *Homo economicus* construction is, if not a perfect image of real man, at least sufficiently close so that no great violence is done by assuming that real man is actually *Homo economicus*. And, these economists would argue, *Homo economicus* is surely the "best" model of man that is available. In short, these economists defend the use of *Homo economicus* on empirical, "scientific" grounds.

The methodological position alluded to here has been articulated by George Stigler in his 1980 Tanner lectures at Harvard University:

> Do people possess ethical beliefs which influence their behavior in ways not dictated by, and hence in conflict with, their own long-run utility-maximizing behavior?[4] . . . The question of the existence of effective ethical value is of course an empirical question, and in principle it should be directly testable. . . . Let me predict the outcome of the systematic and comprehensive testing of behavior in situations where self-interest and ethical values with wide verbal allegiance are in conflict. Much of the time, most of the time in fact, the self-interest theory . . . will win. . . . I predict this result because it is the prevalent one found by economists not only within a wide variety of economic phenomena, but in the investigations of marital, child-bearing, criminal, religious, and other social behavior as well. We believe that man is a utility-maximizing animal . . . and to date we have not found it informative to carve out a section of his life in which he invokes a different goal of behavior. (Lecture II, pp. 23–24.)

Or, as Stigler closes the lectures, he remarks:

> . . . I arrive . . . at the thesis that flows naturally and even irresistibly from the theory of economics. Man is eternally a utility-maximizer, in his home, in his office—be it public or private—in his church, in his scientific work,

---

4. By "utility-maximizing behavior," Stigler means self-serving behaviour, with some allowance for altruism within the family and among close friends. He is careful to distinguish this usage from the purely tautological use of utility maximization as in a pure logic of choice.

in short, everywhere. He can and often does err: perhaps the calculation is too difficult, but more often his information is incomplete. He learns to correct these errors, although sometimes at heavy cost.

What we call ethics, on this approach, is a set of rules with respect to dealings with other persons, rules which in general prohibit behavior which is only myopically self-serving, or which imposes large costs on others with small gains to oneself. General observance of these rules makes not only for long-term gains to the actor but also yields some outside benefits ("externalities"), and the social approval of the ethics is a mild form of enforcement of the rules to achieve the general benefit.[5]

In Stigler's conception, *Homo economicus* literally does become a man for all seasons, and wealth-maximization becomes the only game in town. Yet there is surely much behaviour that cannot be explained, or explained without resort to fantastic mental contortions,[6] if we adhere strictly to the assumptions of the severe economic-man construction.

As many persons have noted, and as Douglass North has emphasized, the scope for "free-riding" in human interaction is so ubiquitous that if men genuinely were as economic theory depicts them, no sort of ordered society, whether market-dominated or not, would be possible. In this basic sense, the very existence of an ordered society casts doubt on the *Homo economicus* model of behaviour, if used as some all-inclusive explanatory hypothesis. For example, people vote, yet a proper income or wealth-maximizing calculus would necessarily classify the voting act as irrational in large-number electorates. Economic theory cannot "explain" voting except in the tautological terms that the act of voting is a consumption activity, and must be so because people do it. Likewise, individuals exercise courtesy and compassion in circumstances where these traits yield no apparent benefits save those inherent in the acts themselves. People volunteer to fight for their tribe, com-

---

5. G. Stigler, "The Economist as Preacher," three Tanner Lectures delivered at Harvard University, April 1980.

6. Our colleague, David Friedman, one time in conversation explained the fact that individuals marry those who love them, on the grounds that this procedure reduces monitoring costs in household production processes. This sort of explanation makes creative use of the *Homo economicus* model, but its empirical accuracy may seem questionable, and it also tends to shift the model towards a pure logic of choice, albeit in a novel manner.

munity, or country and, in so doing, take on risks of death, when it would be conspicuously more self-serving to allow others to take on defensive roles. And, more importantly for North's ultimate purposes, no satisfactory account of history—and particularly judicial history—can ignore the influence of changing views about the world and what constitutes moral behaviour in it, on the actual behaviour of those who seem to have made the decisions that influenced the course of events.

We are not, of course, calling upon our fellow economists to drop *Homo economicus* and assume, *volte face,* that persons are saints—that ethical or, generally, non-economic considerations dominate human motivations in behavioural settings that may or may not be narrowly "economic." Nor do we want to suggest that a mere demonstration that some course of action is "best" on moral grounds will be sufficient to convince persons to act in accordance with such a norm. Our plea is the more modest one that calls upon our fellow economists to recognize that *Homo economicus* has its own limits as a useful abstraction. We can only load the construction with so much, and we stand in danger of having our whole "science" collapse in an absurd heap if we push beyond the useful limits. The fact that the whole set of "non-economic" motivations are more difficult to model than the "economic" should not lead us to deny their existence.

We are not even suggesting that more-effective predictions about behaviour may be made by refining and tempering the abstraction of economic man. The loss of elegance and simplicity that would necessarily be involved in any such attempts might not be offset by marginal extensions in the accuracy of the "scientific" predictions. Our implied criticism of the over-extended usage of the *Homo economicus* abstraction in trying to explain human behaviour "scientifically" lies in our conviction that "scientific prediction," in the sense normally indicated, is *not* what our whole exercise is about and that this application is not the usage for which the abstraction was intended.

We suggest here an alternative usage of the *Homo economicus* abstraction that seems more acceptable in all respects. In one sense, we offer a *methodological,* rather than a predictive ("scientific"), defence of the whole construction. Simply put, our claim is that *Homo economicus* rightly belongs in the analytical derivation of normative propositions about appropriate institutional design. In other words, the model of human behaviour that we might properly use in choosing among alternative institutions may be different from the model that would be more appropriate in making predictions about behaviour within existing institutional structures.

At one level of analysis our claim is very simple: at another level, however, it requires a rather subtle understanding of the difference between constitutional and postconstitutional choice. Our argument is that the *Homo economicus* construction supplies a postulate about human behaviour that is in many ways uniquely suited for the comparative institutional analysis that underlies genuine constitutional choice.

IV. *Homo economicus* and Constitutional Choice

As a point of departure, let us agree that whatever model of man is to be used in evaluating alternative social orders—alternative rules of the economic/political/social game—it must be applied *uniformly* over all the possibilities to be compared. Simple requirements of methodological consistency require this. If we are to employ one set of behavioural postulates for one institution, and another set for another institution, no legitimate comparison of the two institutions can be made. The ultimate purpose of the exercise is to choose among alternative sets of rules—not among alternative "models of man." We must therefore make a prior selection of a single model of man. Otherwise it becomes analytically impossible to isolate the effects of the institutions as such; the whole analysis is muddied by the arbitrary change in behavioural assumptions mid-stream.[7]

This is a simple point, and stated in this manner seems totally unexceptionable. Yet we know that it has proved in economics to be a curiously elusive one. The model of political process implicitly assumed in most orthodox discussion of economic policy has made profoundly different assumptions about individual behaviour from the corresponding assumptions made in

---

7. We need not argue here that institutions do not affect tastes—although such an argument is implicit in much of the neoclassical tradition. Even where preferences can be shown to be endogenous (i.e., influenced by the institutional environment), the model of man upon which the institutions exercise their influences must be the same *at the outset.* In what follows, however, we ignore the question of the influence institutions may have on tastes *per se* and focus on the effects of rules on the costs and benefits to the individual of alternative courses of action.

market settings. It has only been in the last 20 years with the burgeoning of public choice that this grotesque asymmetry has been exposed, and the "benevolent despot" model of politics been seriously queried.

But what is more important, because it may be less obvious, is that the methodological requirement of uniformity in the behavioural postulate *remains* even if there is good empirical evidence and analytical presumption that behaviour may be different between different institutions. This is so because those differences in behaviour have to be *shown* to be attributable to differences in institutions; and if a different model of human behaviour is adopted for each institution at the outset, the relevant results will be simply assumed, not analytically *derived.*

A simple example may illustrate here. Suppose it is widely recognized by individual participants that the invisible hand operates in market processes to transform purely self-interested behaviour into behaviour in the interests of others. Suppose it is also recognized that no corresponding process operates in majoritarian political institutions. Then individuals may well behave in a totally self-interested manner in the market, precisely because the consequences of such behaviour are desirable, yet at the same time operate in an ostensibly more altruistic manner in the political mechanism because the consequences of contrary behaviour are much more disastrous. A rational actor who is only mildly altruistic might be predicted to behave more altruistically in the political setting than in the market: he "conserves" his altruism in the setting where it is least productive, and "spends" it in the political mechanism where it is more productive. This is the essence of the "economizing" on the scarce resource, love—which economizing, Dennis Robertson reminds us, is the prime virtue of the freely operating market order.

Suppose for the purposes of argument that this behavioural asymmetry is observed. Then it may be tempting for the "scientific observer" simply to note the fact that political agents seem more altruistic than market agents, and model behaviour in the two institutions accordingly. But this procedure precludes any proper *explanation* of why behaviour may differ—an explanation which is possible only if we maintain the methodological assumption that human motivations are the same across institutions. Moreover, the "empirical" procedure may well lead to the conclusion that people would be more altruistic if we relied more heavily on political, rather than market, institutions to coordinate individual actions, whereas, of course, no such conclusion can be drawn from the model of behavioural choice as we have given it in the preceding paragraph. On the contrary, heavier reliance on political institutions may simply destroy the incentives to behave altruistically at all.

To recapitulate, then, the requirement of a uniform model of human motivations is fundamental to proper institutional analysis, and remains so even in the face of empirical evidence that might suggest behavioural asymmetry. This requirement establishes a need for a *uniform* model of man—but not necessarily for *Homo economicus* as such. What additional arguments can we bring to bear to support the use of this *particular* model of human behaviour?

Our central argument here is simple. The question we are interested in posing about any particular social order is whether the rules by which individual actions are coordinated are such as to transform actions undertaken by participants in their own *private* interests into outcomes that are in the interests of others. We know that this curious alchemy is in fact worked by the *market*—that the invisible hand operates, under certain more or less well-defined conditions, to convert private interest into public interest. The prime task of comparative institutional analysis is to enquire whether other institutions do the same, and, if so, whether those institutions do so under more or less restrictive conditions. The only assumption required to make this task an interesting one is the assumption that some individuals behave in their narrowly defined private interest at least some of the time. Clearly, if we lived in a world in which all individuals were motivated solely by a concern for the public interest—for example, a world of pure Kantians or Benthamite utilitarians, for whom each individual's own utility counts in determining his behaviour no more and no less than anyone else's—then we should hardly be interested in whether the institutional structure served to transfer private interest into public interest or not: no distinction between private and public interest would make sense.[8] In this sense, the minimal

---

8. Of course, institutions may still be compared, but by reference to other criteria. For example, even in this world of publicly motivated individuals there is the question of how those individuals obtain the *information* necessary to enable them to act in accordance

agreement that the "invisible hand" mechanism is, *ceteris paribus,* a *virtue* in any social order is tantamount to setting aside as remote the possibility that *all* people are motivated by the public interest *all* the time. Further and more importantly for our purposes, in establishing whether any particular social order has this particular virtue, we can usefully abstract from public motivations entirely. In order to show that private interest is transformed into collective interest, we begin naturally by assuming agents to be privately motivated. If they happen to be publicly motivated *in part,* results may or may not be better: but it simply does not bear on the analysis whether they are so motivated. What is crucial is that *such privately motivated behaviour as exists is converted into public interest outcomes.* To assume that private interest is all that makes men tick is simply to focus on what is relevant for the exercise in hand.

In short, then, the question of whether *Homo economicus* is a good approximation to empirical reality determines the *significance* of the exercise of institutional comparison, but not the appropriate *method.* The invisible hand is doubtless a more spectacular virtue in a world where self-seeking behaviour is more, rather than less, prevalent. But whether institutions other than the market may exhibit an invisible hand mechanism, and under what circumstances, are matters that can only be established by examining the implications of self-seeking behaviour within those institutions: to examine the implications of nonself-seeking behaviour for such a purpose is manifestly absurd.

A simple example may help to elucidate here. Suppose you are hiring a builder to build you a house. In selecting from among available builders, you will take a number of things into account—his general competence, his conscientiousness, his honesty. The latter characteristic is important because you will not normally want to deal with a builder who you seriously believe is likely to fleece you. For empirical purposes, therefore, the assumption you will make about the said builder is that he is honest: you would not deal with

---

with their assumed norms. Interestingly enough, the market has virtues in this area as well, a point emphasized strongly by Hayek. See F. A. Hayek, "The Use of Knowledge in Society," *American Economics Review* 35 (1945): 519–30. With imperfect information, it is reasonable to expect that perceptions of the "public interest" will differ. Then one can and must distinguish between the explicit private pursuit of public interest, and the emergence of "optimal" outcomes as an "unintended consequence" of the interactions within the institutional structure.

him if you genuinely believed otherwise. But now you proceed to your law-yer's office to draw up a contract. And in this setting, the working hypothesis you make about the builder is quite different. For the contract-drawing ex-ercise, you make the assumption that the builder *is* going to fleece you, not because you believe this necessarily is his objective but because this is the contingency against which you wish to guard. The nature of the exercise leads you, in other words, to make an assumption about human motivations that you believe may be (and certainly hope will be) a poor reflection of em-pirical reality.[9]

In constitutional design, and in comparative institutional analysis more generally, one's particular beliefs about what model of man is empirically most descriptive are less relevant in precisely the same way and for much the same reason. One calls forth the *Homo economicus* assumption, not because it is necessarily the most accurate model of human behaviour but because it is the appropriate model for testing whether institutions serve to transform private interest into public. It is as simple as that.

To avoid some possible misunderstanding, we should perhaps empha-size that, in the content of constitutional design, the notion of *Homo eco-nomicus* can be broadened somewhat beyond the confines of the definition used widely in "economic science" (as described in Section II). For the pur-poses of predictive science, the elements in individual utility functions must be specified in clear, recognizable, and measurable terms. Application of the *Homo economicus* construction for empirical or predictive purposes requires something like the assumption of net wealth maximization as a surrogate for maximization of consumption more broadly conceived. For the purposes of constitutional design, however, *Homo economicus* can be seen to maximize almost anything at all, providing each individual conceives of others as op-erating without his interest in mind. That is, all that we require is that each individual, in choosing a set of rules, models the motivations of others vis-

---

9. It could of course be argued (as a referee has done) that the contract-drawing ex-ercise is based on uncertainty about the morality of alternative builders and that contract-drawing is a *cheaper* way of saving on transactions costs than acquiring additional infor-mation. Analogously, choosing the institutional structure to guard against the abuse of power may be looked on as a cheaper way of ensuring tolerable outcomes than acquiring information about which individuals are sufficiently benevolent to be entrusted with po-litical power.

à-vis himself in such a way that *excludes* their inclusion of his own interests or well-being in their utility functions. *This* version of the *Homo economicus* model in no sense rules out the possibility that each individual may be motivated by certain ethical or moral concerns, as long as we can take it that such ethical conduct on the part of anyone cannot be presumed to benefit everyone else. Burning people at the stake in order to secure for them better claims on eternal life is, for example, perfectly consistent with *Homo economicus* assumptions at the constitutional level.

For the purposes of constitutional design, then, no specification of arguments in *Homo economicus'* utility function is required: the narrowly defined *Homo economicus* of predictive science and the more open-ended construction, in which the utility function includes any arguments other than the well-being of the chooser, become *methodologically equivalent.*

An example may be helpful here. Suppose that a person is considered to be examining the working properties of an institution that would grant some other persons (say, an appointed "governor") the power to tax, with accompanying coercive enforcement. So long as the potential chooser models the behaviour of the "governor" so as to exclude his own (the chooser's) interests, the constitutional calculus remains the same whether the "governor" is modelled as using tax revenues for financing a private harem or for providing transfers to other persons in the community, or any other purpose in which the chooser expects to have no interest.

It may be useful to summarize the argument to this point. We have insisted that the model of man to be used in comparative institutional analysis, whatever its precise characteristics, must for analytic reasons be uniform across institutions. And we have insisted that such uniformity must be maintained even in the face of empirical evidence to the contrary. We have argued further that the specific model of human motivations to be used in comparative institutional analysis must emphasize private interest as the prime motivating force, because the specific issue we are interested in examining at this level is whether alternative institutional rules are such as to convert *private motivations* into publicly desired actions. To the extent that the assumption of public motivation is included in the behavioural model, we come close to simply assuming what we wish to prove. We have termed this model of man *Homo economicus,* consistent with classical usage: it is, however, somewhat less restrictive a model of man than the net-wealth-maximizing model used extensively in economic science.

This argument is, as we see it, complete. There is, however, a complementary line of reasoning that is worth mention here. It runs as follows: for the purposes of economic science, the model of man to be used is the one that gives the best "fit," the most reliable set of predictions about the effects of particular changes in parameters. What is required for such purposes is a model of the "average" or "representative" man. In constitutional choice analysis, however, we seek a model of man which is a *"weighted* average man," where the weights at stake involve the costs that various types impose on the social fabric.

Consider a simple example. Suppose we postulate a world in which half the individuals are Kantians and half are *Homines economici.* Suppose that the citizenry in this world is examining the costs and benefits of alternative restrictions on the behaviour of a dictator whose identity, and hence personality type, is presumed unknown. Clearly, a truly Kantian dictator will impose relatively little in costs upon those who are subject to his rule. A purely self-interested dictator on the other hand can be expected to impose enormously high costs on his subjects. For this reason, in any rational constitutional calculus, the model of man presumed will be much closer to the self-interest model than mere empirics might indicate. And this does not presuppose any particular risk-aversion on the part of the individual choosing constitutional restrictions. Clearly a risk-*neutral* individual will take into account the expected costs associated with dictators of different personality type; and the whole calculus will naturally be weighted towards a consideration of those cases in which most is at stake. The self-interest postulate takes on a significance in the constitutional setting, therefore, that it essentially lacks in its "scientific," or strictly predictive, setting. *Homo economicus* is alive and well, and living in the analytical foundations of constitutional choice—his natural homeland.

V. *Homo economicus* in Classical Political Economy

We consider our argument in this paper to be directly within the tradition of classical political economy. Modern economists can still learn much from the methods of the eighteenth-century philosophers, such as Mandeville, Hume, and, particularly, Adam Smith. Their reflections led them to the recognition that the peculiar alchemy of the market order allows the transformation of private interest into "public interest." Individuals with no concerns beyond their own net wealth could, by virtue of the invisible hand of the market, be induced to act as if they were furthering the interests of others than themselves. Adam Smith's butcher could be recognized to be acting in the interests of his customers without one whit of concern for their welfare. It is not required of Smith's butcher that he have no direct concern for his customers; he may well have had such concern. The significant thing is that we do *not* require him to have such a concern in his utility function; and we do not model him as having such a concern when we compare the market with alternative institutional arrangements.

It is in this cradle that *Homo economicus* was nurtured. He was a creation for a purpose—this being the demonstration of the virtues of the free market as an institutional order. Smith makes it clear that *Homo economicus* is not to be conceived as a generalized *description* of human nature. "Humanity does not desire to be great" (or, we may add, to be rich) "but to be loved."[10] And no one who has looked at the first pages of *The Theory of Moral Sentiments* can deny Smith's belief in the ubiquity of sympathy. Nonetheless, if one wishes to examine the extent to which a particular institutional order transforms private interest into public interest, it becomes entirely appropriate to focus on a model of man in which private interest predominates. To model man as publicly motivated in making such a comparison would be to assume away the problem that institutional design involves—the problem that was central to Smith's purpose.

In comparative institutional analysis, and ultimately in constitutional design, one calls forth *Homo economicus,* not for its accuracy in prediction, but for its assistance in helping to identify and to classify patterns of outcomes attributable directly to institutional differences. The central contribution of the eighteenth-century philosophers lay in their demonstration that, even under strictly *Homo economicus* assumptions about behaviour, public interest is served by the market order. No such demonstration can be made with respect to alternative arrangements.

The imputation of *Homo economicus* motivation to actors in political roles may seem to violate ordinary notions about descriptive reality more than the comparable imputation to actors in the marketplace. But this difference need not provide any justification for replacing the model used for institutional comparison. It may be that judges seek to "uphold the law"

10. A. Smith, *The Theory of Moral Sentiments* (Liberty Fund, 1976), 30.

most of the time, that most government employees try to further their own conceptions of "public interest" most of the time, and that elected politicians are genuinely concerned about promoting the "good society." But, even if this were admitted, institutional arrangements would surely be preferred which made these congruent with narrow self-interest on the part of the relevant actors. A model of human behaviour in which the natural impulse toward self-interest, narrowly defined, predominates is a highly useful artifact in helping us to identify that set of arrangements that "economize on love."

John Stuart Mill stated the point well:

> The very principle of constitutional government requires it to be assumed that political power will be abused to promote the particular purposes of the holder; not because it is always so, but because such is the natural tendency of things to guard against which is the special use of free institutions.[11]

We might add that what goes for political power goes for market power also, but this point hardly seems necessary. The *market* aspects of this truth have long since been widely recognized and accepted, which makes the continuing neglect (perhaps even denial) of the political aspects even more surprising.

VI. *Homo economicus* and Public Choice

In our recent book, *The Power to Tax*,[12] we incorporated a theory of political process in which the *Homo economicus* construction was allowed full play. Many of the modern developments in public choice theory can also be interpreted as variations on what might be called the *Homo economicus* model of politics.

In developing our approach to taxation, and particularly in attacking the benevolent despot model of politics that has for so long monopolized orthodox economic policy debates, we have been subjected to understandable criticism. The argument has been consistently made that politics is simply

11. John Stuart Mill, *On Representative Government*, in *Essays on Politics and Society*, vol. 19, *Collected Works*, 505.

12. G. Brennan and J. Buchanan, *The Power to Tax: Analytical Foundations of a Fiscal Constitution* (Cambridge University Press, 1980).

not like our models of it, that the application of the *Homo economicus* model to political processes does little more than expose our own disciplinary hubris. At the same time, some critics who are generally sympathetic to our approach have sought to defend our position on the grounds that politics is indeed "like that," like our models of it, and so, indeed, is every aspect of human behaviour. Our growing reluctance to support this latter ("Stiglerian") defence of our position has been met with some shock and sometimes resentment from some of our colleagues. But the battle over the empirical status of *Homo economicus* is *not*, in our view, the crucial issue at all. On empirical grounds, we are surely closer to Adam Smith than to our modern critics, whichever side those critics come from. We admit freely the possibility and indeed the likelihood of nonself-seeking behaviour by human agents in all institutional settings. But like Adam Smith, we believe that *Homo economicus* remains the appropriate model of behaviour in the derivation of normative propositions about the institutions themselves.

There is no inconsistency here. Nor is there any retreat from positions we have taken earlier. The appropriate use of the narrowly "economic" model depends on a prior understanding of what the model is to be used for. And although *Homo economicus* may be a more useful tool in providing a superior set of hypotheses about political behaviour—behaviour within well-defined rules—than much of traditional political science has appeared to offer, this is not to argue that it is *the* most useful model of man for such explanatory or predictive purposes, or that there is not much that such a model fails to explain. The level of discourse at which the *Homo economicus* construction seems uniquely appropriate is the constitutional level, and this may remain true even if the construction does not give precisely the "best" empirical fit.

Predictive Power and the Choice among Regimes

Geoffrey Brennan and James Buchanan

> In constraining any system of government, and fixing the several checks and controls of the constitution, every man ought to be supposed a knave, and to have no other end, in all his actions, than private interest.
>
> —David Hume, "Of the Independency of Parliament,"
> *Essays Moral, Political and Literary,* 117–18.

> The very principle of constitutional government requires it to be assumed that political power will be abused to promote the particular purposes of the holder; not because it always is so, but because such is the natural tendency of things to guard against which is the especial use of free institutions.
>
> —J. S. Mill, "Considerations on Representative Government,"
> *Essays on Politics and Society,* vol. 19 of the *Collected Works,* 505.

A basic analytic instrument in the economist's kit-bag is the model of human behaviour used—a model that, in fact, takes its name from the dismal science. In its most general (if empty) formulation, the *Homo economicus* model presumes nothing beyond the proposition that each individual acts

From *Economic Journal* 93 (March 1983): 89–105. Copyright Royal Economic Society. Reprinted by permission of the publisher.

We are indebted to James Heins, Dennis Mueller, Jonathon Pincus, and Robert Tollison and anonymous referees for helpful comments.

purposefully in pursuit of his own particular ends; for some purposes at least, the ends can remain unspecified. However, if the behavioural model is to be used to generate predictions as to the effect of changes in the underlying state of the world, or explanations as to why the world is as it is, further specification of the model becomes necessary. Standard professional practice in this regard is to formulate *Homo economicus* as a wealth-maximiser, and to justify the use of such simplification on the basis of its elegance and power.

This behavioural model in its market setting is so familiar as to be hardly worthy of comment. Its use in less traditional settings, such as in modern "public choice" theory where the methods and analytic techniques of economics are applied to the study of *political* processes, remains controversial. Most economists seem to be more comfortable with a "benevolent despot" model of government in which those who hold political power exercise it in the "public interest" (appropriately construed). Policy advice is offered on such a basis, and policy recommendations typically presuppose that this is the way in which political agents will operate. To suggest, as public choice scholars do, that those who possess discretionary power under some prevailing political order can be usefully modelled as simple wealth-maximisers apparently strikes many commentators as, at best, naïve and, at worst, biased ideologically. Such critics will typically claim that "politics is simply not like that," and call forth examples of apparently public-interested behaviour on the part of government agents. They will insist that internal moral considerations *are relevant* in constraining the behaviour of those who act in political agency roles. It is difficult to respond to such critics in a manner that is fully convincing because, descriptively, there seems to be some substance in their rejection of the *Homo economicus* model in application to political behaviour.

As the opening citations indicate, however, modern public choice scholars are in excellent company. The classical political economists insisted that political agents should be modelled on the basis of private interest—not, as Mill concedes, because such agents always behave in this way, but rather because of the nature of the particular exercise that classical political economy embodied. Our argument, in this paper and elsewhere, is that if public choice theory is interpreted to incorporate essentially the same *purposes* as classical political economy, its method is entirely appropriate and that the criticisms are fundamentally misconceived.

Classical political economy was, from its eighteenth-century origins on, largely concerned with the comparison of alternative social or institutional orders. Its main purpose was not the predicting of economic behaviour for its own sake; its purpose was, instead, that of developing appropriate models of the working of alternative institutions in order that the choice between those institutions might be better informed. Modern economics, with its orientation towards empiricism and prediction, towards positivism generally defined, seems to have moved some distance from, and in the process obscured, this classical focus. The prevailing methodology is strongly oriented towards predictive analysis of choice *within* a well-defined institutional structure (or system of constraints) rather than choice *between* alternative social institutions.

This shift in focus has important implications for the way in which analysis is conducted. One of these implications relates to the choice of models; and it does so because the model that is appropriate depends critically on the purpose for which the analysis is to be used.

Specifically, in the argument that follows, we attempt to demonstrate the following propositions:

(i) that the model of behaviour which provides the best *predictions* of market price and output levels is *not* the best model of behaviour, in general, for the purposes of comparative institutional analysis;

(ii) that the *Homo economicus* model of human behaviour may be superior in comparative institutional analysis to a more "accurate" model of human behaviour in the conventional predictive sense; and

(iii) that an attack on the use of *Homo economicus* in any institutional setting based solely on direct appeal to observation cannot be decisive, and is largely misconceived.

We shall illustrate these propositions by appeal to the simplest and most familiar institutional comparison within economics—that between monopoly and other forms of market organisation. This illustration is of some interest in its own right because it has important implications for the measurement of welfare losses from aggregated data. But our overall purpose here is much more general. We wish to argue that the monopoly illustration can be generalised to virtually all institutional forms—including, specifically, the political institutions that are the subject matter of public choice.

The central observation on which the analysis rests is that the welfare loss relevant for any institutional comparison is a convex function of the magnitude of the quantity (or price) distortion. In other words, the addition to welfare loss caused by a movement away from the efficiency ideal is *larger* the further equilibrium happens to be from that ideal. Or, equivalently, large departures from the ideal cause more than proportionately large harm. For this reason, measuring welfare losses on the basis of average or "expected" behaviour will always lead to underestimation: an adequate measure of expected welfare loss from a single behavioural model will necessarily require a model that generates outcomes somewhat further from the ideal than ordinary observation would seem to justify.

Throughout, our discussion is cast in the simplest possible diagrammatic terms. In Section I, we offer a simple monopoly example. In Section II, we provide a more general statement of the central result. In Section III, the analogy between the monopoly example and other institutional comparisons is drawn generally, and drawn in the specific context of some simple models of political process in Section IV. Section V offers the relevant conclusions.

I. A Simple Example

The proposition to be demonstrated here is that the theory of monopoly behaviour that gives the best empirical "fit" is, in general, *not* the theory of monopoly behaviour that gives the best estimate of the costs of the monopoly institution for purposes of comparison with alternative regimes.

We introduce a highly simplified hypothetical example, designed for the purpose of demonstrating our results, rather than for any suggestion as to applicability. Consider a single municipality, recently created. The citizens, directly or through elected representatives, are trying to decide on an appropriate institutional arrangement for the provision of a particular service—say garbage disposal.[1] There are two basic options: the municipality can

---

1. This choice of example is arbitrary. There is in fact some evidence that private monopoly franchises outperform municipal government in garbage disposal, but that evidence is somewhat beside the point. In fact, much of that evidence is susceptible to the

grant a monopoly franchise to some private firm (the owners of which firm are resident citizens of the municipality in question); *or*, the municipality can establish a local government instrumentality, charged with pricing the service at cost and subject to the regulatory scrutiny of a local government agency. Both sorts of arrangements are observed to be operative in neighbouring municipalities. The citizens of the new government unit would like to know which regime works "better": they need to estimate the predicted costs and benefits of each of the two arrangements in order to make an intelligent institutional choice.

In order to assist in this calculation, let us assume a professional economist (Dr H) is hired as a consultant. H gathers together a sample of two hundred municipalities—one hundred that use the monopoly franchise, one hundred that use the regulated instrumentality. The municipalities used in the sample are essentially identical (or can be normalised to be so) in all externally observable relevant respects (size, income, tastes, etc.). For each municipality, he collects information on the demand and cost conditions relating to garbage disposal, along with estimates of the current price and output policies in each case.

For the regulated instrumentalities, the outcome emerges simply for him. The consultant finds that these bodies do indeed price at marginal cost and produce the optimal output—almost without exception. However, the monitoring undertaken by the regulatory agencies is not costless—it absorbs a quantity of resources of value $A per municipality, on average. This is a fixed cost that does not bear on the optimality of pricing and output decisions for garbage disposal, but that must be reckoned with in comparing the regulated arrangement with the private franchise alternative.[2]

For the private franchised monopolists, the outcome is more complicated. The consultant is able to obtain a "best fit" on the demand and cost curves for garbage disposal, which exhibit let us say the properties shown in

---

argument made here, because it focuses on a comparison of average prices under the two institutional forms.

2. Our assumption that the municipal agencies operate efficiently and that the full costs of the regime arise from monitoring outlays independent of output is made here for expositional simplicity only. The same conclusions emerge if we allow some inefficiency in operation, but the presentation becomes messy.

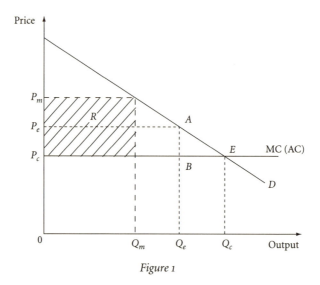

Figure 1

Fig. 1, namely linearity of the demand curve, and constant costs. Armed with these initial results, he could, of course, exploit the elementary textbook construction for the monopoly firm and derive the corresponding profit-maximising price and output.

However, H has been charged with the task of obtaining the "best fit" monopoly behaviour model. The textbook model of monopoly cannot simply be *assumed*: it must be justified empirically. As H pursues his investigations, he finds that by no means all of the monopoly firms maximise profits. Some are sales maximisers; some are "satisficers"; some—perhaps from altruistic motives, or perhaps because they fear regulation—seem to be charging a price close to marginal cost. The best *predictive* model of monopoly behaviour—the model that gives the "best fit" in the conventional sense that it minimises the variance of the observations—is one that generates an expected price-output equilibrium (P_e, Q_e) as shown in Fig. 1. For expositional convenience, suppose that this equilibrium lies half way between that predicted by the textbook monopoly analysis and the perfectly competitive outcome (the outcome under the purely "public interest" model of monopoly behaviour).

It should perhaps be emphasised that, in any explanatory sense, the model of monopoly that yields this outcome is superior to the simple textbook model. It will systematically outpredict the conventional profit-maximising model: the latter will yield predictions of price and output that are just plain wrong.

Dr H now submits his conclusions to the community residents, collects his fee, and hurries off to write up a short note for some learned journal showing how the textbook monopoly model is empirically flawed. The community residents, in turn, take the "best" monopoly model—now empirically validated—and calculate the expected net cost of monopoly organisation, as measured by the area of triangle *ABE* which, in the linear case, is equal to $\frac{1}{8}R$, where R is the maximum profit that can be derived from the franchise (the shaded area in Fig. 1). Since, by assumption, the franchise holders are also citizens of the municipalities where the franchise is exercised, their own profits are not, of course, part of "social costs" of monopoly.[3]

This cost is to be compared with that which would be expected under the regulated municipal agency, already estimated to $A. Let us suppose that A is $\frac{1}{6}R$, as defined above. Since the costs of the private franchised monopoly arrangement are smaller, this is the arrangement that the community provisionally accepts.

Suppose now, however, that there are certain consumer-oriented groups in the community who do not readily acquiesce in the provisional decision. They proceed to hire a second consultant and charge him with the task of somehow demonstrating that the decision based on the report of the first consultant is in error.

Upon careful review, the second consultant finds no errors in the empirical estimates. Nonetheless, he can report that the inferences from these estimates are totally in error, and that the proper use of cost-benefit computation suggests that the municipal agency, subject to regulation, should be installed. He does this by showing that the behavioural model derived by the first consultant will generate incorrect *estimates of welfare losses* if used di-

---

3. We shall ignore those costs that may go into securing the franchises, the rent-seeking costs. We do so, not because we think these irrelevant, but because our purpose here is not the relevance of the simple construction, but rather the methodological one of suggesting the limits of empirical estimates in institutional comparisons. For relevant papers in rent-seeking, see James M. Buchanan, Robert D. Tollison, and Gordon Tullock, eds., *Toward a Theory of the Rent-Seeking Society* (College Station: Texas A&M University Press, 1980).

rectly. The second consultant uses a different procedure for determining the expected welfare loss from monopoly. He considers the price-output equilibrium in *each* case, determines on that basis the welfare loss, and then simply adds up the welfare loss over all cases. He does not assume, as the community did in computing losses from the predicted behavioural model, that all monopolists operate precisely at the average (best estimate) price-output equilibrium. The second consultant derives a different and larger "expected" welfare loss for monopoly—the arithmetic mean of the welfare losses taken separately.

The expected welfare loss measure derived by the second consultant will be unambiguously larger than the first. We can illustrate this fact by a simple example. For analytic convenience assume that the behaviour of the firms remains constant over time periods; this assumption allows us to look only at a single period for the distribution of positions among the separate firms. Suppose that we find a very simple distribution. One-half of the firms do, indeed, operate at roughly the predicted price-output combination, at (P_e, Q_e). For the remaining fifty monopolists, however, we note that twenty-five of these operate as profit-maximising monopolists, at (P_m, Q_m). The other half, the remaining twenty-five franchisees, however, operate as if they are in fully competitive settings, at (P_c, Q_c).

Given this distribution, what is the proper measure of average welfare loss over the set for the period?

For the fifty firms operating at (P_e, Q_e), the total welfare loss is $50R/8$. For the twenty-five firms operating at (P_m, Q_m), the welfare loss is $25R/2$; for the twenty-five firms operating at the competitive equilibrium, there is no net welfare loss. The total welfare loss for the hundred monopoly arrangements is, therefore,

$$50R/8 + 25R/2 = 150R/8.$$

The average, or expected, welfare loss for the private franchise solution is therefore $\frac{3}{2}(R/8)$. Clearly, this exceeds $R/8$, the measure of excess burden calculated by the first consultant. More to the point, it also exceeds the cost of enforcing the regulatory regime, $R/6$. Consequently, the conclusion that seems to flow naturally from the first consultant's report should be reversed: the municipality should adopt the arrangement using a regulated municipal agency.

Why is there this divergence in measures of expected welfare loss? The answer is simple. As price increases from P_c, total welfare losses increase at an increasing rate. That is, marginal welfare losses increase with price increases above P_c, given our linear demand and cost constructions. From this it follows that there is an asymmetry between losses and gains as actual positions lie above and below the single best prediction of the expected position for monopoly operation (which must, of course, lie somewhere above P_c in the price dimension). That is to say, an increase in price above P_e, with the accompanying reduction in quantity, adds more to total welfare losses than an equal decrease in price below P_e subtracts from total welfare losses.[4]

II. A General Statement

The monopoly example set out in the previous section is an application of a much more general result in economics—namely that welfare losses (or "ex-

---

4. In the extensive literature on the empirical measurement of monopoly welfare losses, the general point here seems to have been either widely overlooked or left unarticulated. Dean Worcester ("New Estimates of the Welfare Losses Due to Monopoly," *Southern Economic Journal* 40 [October 1973]: 234–45) mentions that "aggregation" problems will arise in moving from finer to grosser industry definitions and that such moves will tend to bias welfare loss estimates downwards, but he does not explain how he gets this conclusion, and in any case, he believes such changes to be relatively insignificant. Keith Cowling and Dennis Mueller ("The Social Costs of Monopoly Power," *Economic Journal* 88 [December 1978]: 727–48) are immune from aggregation difficulties because they *assume* profit maximisation and calculate welfare losses directly as one-half of profit (appropriate for the linear case). However, in his seminal paper, Arnold Harberger ("Monopoly and Resource Allocation," *American Economic Review* 44 [May 1954]: 77–87), in averaging profit rates over firms in the industry to obtain an "average" price distortion, *d,* for each industry, is clearly guilty of aggregation bias. We have no way of determining how significant empirically such bias is, a matter that clearly depends on the variance of profit rates across firms in the industry. We should emphasise, however, that our concern in this paper is *not* that of making a contribution to the debate-discussion over the proper measure of welfare loss from monopoly. Our usage of this discussion is illustrative of the more general point of our emphasis.

There may, of course, be many choice situations to which the "best prediction" model is entirely appropriate. In terms of an example, suppose that, instead of some institutional comparison between regulated and unregulated monopoly, the choice is that which would face, say, a supplier of garbage bags to the municipality that had chosen to establish an unregulated monopoly in garbage disposal. The supplier may well, in this case, use the price-output prediction that best "fits" the data drawn from comparable operations. He will do so if the potential losses emergent from erroneous prediction are symmetrically related to the extent of error. The central thrust of our argument is that such symmetry in the cost of "errors" does not obtain generally in comparisons among institutions.

cess burdens" as they are more commonly called in public finance circles) are a convex function of the distortion that generates them. Generally, these welfare losses are measured by reference to Harberger triangles (or their general equilibrium equivalents, see Harberger [1971]), and a typical measure would be:

$$W = \tfrac{1}{2}Sd^2, \tag{1}$$

where W is the welfare loss, S is the slope of the demand curve, dp/dq, and d is the quantity distortion, $d = (q - q^*)$.

In fact, this formulation implicitly assumes linearity of the demand curve, and the analogous measure of welfare losses involving elasticity rather than slope assumes loglinearity. But it is entirely general that, if welfare loss is measured by the area over the relevant range under the income-compensated demand curve, then:

$$W = f(d), \tag{2}$$

where $f'' > 0$, i.e., welfare loss is such that it increases at a faster rate as d increases. This depends only on the requirement that the compensated demand curve is downward sloping (see Appendix).

In any case, we can follow professional practice and treat (1) as a totally satisfactory approximation. On this basis, the propositions that underlie the monopoly example can be conveniently depicted diagrammatically in Fig. 2. In this diagram the quantity distortion is depicted along the horizontal axis, and the welfare loss along the vertical. Consider first the proposition that the average value of W exceeds the welfare loss derived from the average distortion—that is:

$$\overline{W} > W(\overline{d}). \tag{3}$$

A simple example suffices. Let d_1 and d_2 be two values of d, and d the average of the two. In Fig. 2, the horizontal distances $d_1\overline{d}$ and $d\overline{d}_2$ are equal. The welfare losses associated with d_1 and d_2 are W_1 and W_2, and $\overline{W}$ is the average of the welfare losses—that is, $W_1\overline{W}$ equals $\overline{W}W_2$. It can be seen by inspection that $W(\overline{d})$ is less than $\overline{W}$ (as claimed in (3)).

Furthermore, it is clear that there does exist a value of the distortion, d_M, which is such that $W(d_M) = \overline{W}$. This value of d is the value that would have to emerge from a single model of the institution if that single model were

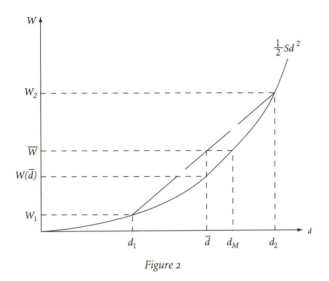

Figure 2

accurately to reflect the true expected welfare cost of that institution. Clearly, d_M exceeds $\bar{d}$, and this must always be true if the W curve is convex.

Note that the single model of monopolist's behaviour that is best for predicting price and output equilibrium is one that generates $\bar{d}$ as the predicted outcome. The single model of monopolist's behaviour that is best for predicting welfare losses—the model relevant for evaluation of monopoly as an institutional form—is one that "predicts" d_M, an outcome that is systematically worse than the average or best-predicted outcome.

Of course, this discussion does not validate the use of the textbook model of the profit-maximising monopolist, either as a means of predicting equilibrium price-output decisions or as a model for measuring welfare losses. What it does clearly suggest, however, is that, for the purposes of institutional comparison, the "best fit" or "most realistic" model does not suffice, and that a bias *towards* the profit-maximising model is required.[5]

In presenting the simple monopoly example here, we have implicitly as-

---

5. Note that we have implicitly assumed that the individual faced with the institutional choice in the example is strictly risk-neutral in the sense that he would pay at most x dollars for a 50% chance of winning $2x$ dollars. The introduction of risk-averseness will, of course, imply that the proper welfare-loss estimates will diverge even more from those derived from the best-fit empirical model of monopoly equilibrium.

sumed that the observing economist has available to him the complete set of disaggregated data from which an accurate measure of monopoly welfare costs can be derived. If, indeed, such data exist, there might seem little reason for the ordinary economist to resort to any single "best predictor" model in his estimation of welfare costs. He can measure welfare losses in each case, and derive the average of them directly. The problem emerges necessarily, however, when the economist is confronted with data that are already in aggregated form. If he has no knowledge about the distribution of observations around the expected values, there is no way in which accurate measures of welfare cost can be derived. At least in such cases, the bias towards underestimation inherent in the use of expected values can be acknowledged. A superior procedure would presumably be to "guess at" some underlying distribution of outcomes and recalculate the welfare losses on this basis. But one cannot rule out, equally, the explicit use of a model of monopoly behaviour rather closer to the profit-maximising model than the empirical evidence indicates. In other words, the use of the *Homo economicus* caricature in the monopoly context *may* be justified, even though its price-output predictions are less good than some alternative model of monopolist behaviour.

III. *Homo economicus* and Public Choice

The monopoly issue is, of course, of considerable interest to economists in its own right. It would be possible to leave the discussion at this point with a warning against careless empiricism in industrial organisation, and perhaps with a catalogue of empirical studies in which the procedures for measuring welfare losses seem to have been most inappropriate. Nothing in all this would strike the economist as particularly controversial or alarming.

But our claim here is much more general: the monopoly case is offered as an *example* of a broader proposition relating to the use of the *Homo economicus* construction in comparative institutional analysis of all types. In particular, the assumption that political agents will use any discretionary power that they possess to further their particular private interests can, we believe, be justified even where there seems to be ample empirical evidence to the contrary, on grounds essentially analogous to those for using *Homo economicus* in the monopoly context.

We begin with the proposition, probably unexceptionable to most economists and other social scientists in the classical tradition, that political institutions can be normatively justified only to the extent that they provide citizens with goods and services that those citizens value. Such goods and services may be conventional commodities, much like marketed goods and services (such as statistical data, weather reports, electricity, recreational parks, etc.) and may or may not have the properties of Samuelsonian public goods. Equally, the services provided may be rather more abstract things, such as the rule of law (without which Hobbesian anarchy would prevail) or "justice" (somehow defined). In all such cases, however, the services or goods in question are valued in essentially the same sort of way as the goods with which economists more typically deal in market settings. For all these services or goods, it is possible to conceptualise having more or less of them, and of additional units being valued more highly or less. Within this broad conceptualisation, it is possible to hypothesise a demand curve for the good or service in question; and it is reasonable to conjecture that the demand curve will exhibit conventional properties—specifically that it should reflect the principle of diminishing relative marginal utility.

Furthermore given the general state of the world—and specifically a sense of what is and is not feasible—it is possible to conceive of some output level of these politically provided goods that is "optimal," or that in some other sense represents the "public interest" outcome. If departures from this "optimal" output level occur, it is necessary only to assume that demand curves "slope downwards" in order to sustain the claim that the marginal loss imposed is larger the further the output level is from optimality, and hence that greater losses will be imposed on a society over any period of history than would be suggested by the evaluation of the "average" outcome over that period.

As we see it, the assumptions required to justify this claim are extremely weak. Yet they do establish a case *against* too ready a rejection of the *Homo economicus* assumption in analysing the workings of political institutions. The common grounds for such rejection rely on an "argument of general realism." The critic observes that many public officials seem to act to promote their versions of the "public interest"—that moral considerations do seem to constrain political agents, in at least some cases and perhaps much of the time. He concludes on this basis that the *Homo economicus* model is unrealistic, and therefore inapplicable. Our central point in response to this is that the model may well be unrealistic, but remains applicable for the comparative analysis of political institutions.

In this sense, the monopoly construct and the public choice analysis of political institutions are analogous. However, the study of market institutions differs from that of political institutions in one major respect: whereas in market contexts, one may often have access to data that permit the direct calculation of demand curves, price mark-ups, elasticities and the like, the analogous information in respect of politically provided goods is rarely available—at least directly. In the monopoly example, therefore, an obvious solution to the problem is simply to calculate welfare losses in each case separately and determine the expected welfare loss accordingly. There is simply no need to try to allow for aggregation bias by an appropriately caricatured single model of monopoly behaviour. Consequently, the basic moral to be derived from the monopoly example might be construed as being that one should measure aggregated excess burdens properly. But in the analysis of political processes, the measurement of welfare losses directly is rarely possible. Rather, the analyst is thrown back on less-refined sources of information—the broad historical record, general experience and casual observation, extrapolation from similar cases and so on. Here we cannot really "measure" excess burdens in a whole range of cases and thereby obtain some notion of the normative character of alternative political institutions. What we *can* do is to use our general understandings of the way in which excess burdens respond to deviations from "optimal" output to inform the choice of behavioural model. This is, as we see it, precisely what the classical political economists did: their choice of a *Homo economicus* model for political agents, deliberately fashioned to abstract from public interested behaviour, involved a proper procedure for the task of constitutional design in which they were involved.

IV. Some Political Examples

In order to point out the direct relevance of the monopoly example, it may be useful to examine briefly some simple models of political process in which the market analogy is most conspicuous. In each of the particular cases examined below, we consider a governmental bureau charged with providing a single good or service to citizens of the community.

(1) STANDARD BUREAUCRATIC INEFFICIENCY: PUBLIC SERVICES AT HIGH COST

Consider, first, bureaux that make no attempt to control their budgetary allocations. They provide the required service but do so (or may do so) at a cost higher than that which is "necessary" in the opportunity-cost sense. Bureaucrats may succeed in using their position to secure net rents, whether those be in the form of pecuniary or non-pecuniary benefits.

In this model, the analysis developed from the monopoly example above may be applied without substantial change. Suppose, for illustrative purposes, that one out of three such bureaux should operate at a level such that the cost presented to the community is as high as P_m in Fig. 1; a second bureau operates with cost at P_e, while a third operates at genuine opportunity cost. The best predictive model of bureaucratic behaviour involves cost, P_e, and output, Q_e. But, as the example of monopoly shows, this model is not appropriate for measuring the welfare costs of bureaucratic inefficiency.

(2) THE NISKANEN BUREAUCRACY MODEL

As a second case, consider a setting in which bureaucratic agents exercise more discretionary decision-making power. They can, by appropriate behaviour *vis-à-vis* the legislature of the community, manipulate the size of the bureau's budgetary allocation. We suppose that, half of the time (or in half the cases), these agents are constrained by internal moral considerations to pursue the "public interest," and (more heroically) that their calculation of the "public interest" outcome corresponds exactly with that which is optimal in the familiar Paretian sense. Suppose, further, that in the remaining percentage of cases, bureaucrats operate like Niskanen bureaucrats—that is, they act to maximise the size of the bureaux' budgets.[6] This "Niskanen" output level

---

6. See William Niskanen, *Bureaucracy and Representative Government* (Chicago: Aldine Press, 1971), part 3, for a full exposition of the basic model.

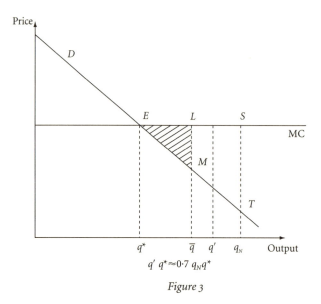

Figure 3

corresponds to that at which total net consumer surplus is zero. Expected output for a bureau will then lie exactly half way between "optimal output" and "Niskanen output." Will the measure of expected welfare loss correspond to the welfare loss at expected output? Clearly not, in general—and for precisely the same reasons analysed above.

The diagrams in this case are essentially analogous to those in Fig. 1. In Fig. 3, the curve D depicts the community demand for some publicly provided good, G. This consists, let us say, of the vertical sum of n exactly identical consumers facing a common income tax and is drawn to be linear for convenience. The optimal level of G for the community is given by q^*, the output level at E where D cuts the horizontal average (and marginal) cost schedule. This output level prevails when bureaucrats act in the public interest—which, by assumption, they do half the time.[7]

The remainder of the time, however, the bureaucrats select output at the level, q_N, which is such as to obliterate the net surplus generated by G. This output level will, in the linear case, be exactly twice the output level q^*. Ac-

---

7. This choice of probabilities is for analytic convenience only. Precisely the same general point holds for other distributions of behaviour, provided only that the variance is non-zero.

cordingly, expected output is $\bar{q}$, half way between q^* and q_N. If we were to base our normative calculus on this "expected" behaviour pattern, however, we would be systematically wrong. For the welfare loss associated with $\bar{q}$ (the triangle *ELM*, shaded in Fig. 3) is less than the expected welfare loss, which is half the area *EST*. In the linear case, *EST* is *four* times the area *ELM*. The single behavioural model which yields the appropriate measure of expected welfare loss is one which yields output q', where the ratio of q^*q_N to q^*q' is $\sqrt{2}$ (*not* 2).

As in the monopoly case, therefore, the behavioural model which yields the best estimate of *output* will not yield the best estimate of welfare loss. If our interest in modelling bureaucracy therefore issues from normative concerns of institutional comparison, the appeal to "observed" bureaucratic behaviour is misplaced. For example, suppose we are to choose whether the government "should" intervene in market processes in some case where the market is believed to fail to generate optimality. Suppose further that the allocative losses attributable to this market failure happen to be equal to one-third of the area *EST*. To make the relevant comparison of market and political institutions on the basis of average or "best predicted" bureaucratic behaviour would lead to the conclusion that intervention is justified (since $\frac{1}{3} EST > \frac{1}{4} EST$): to calculate welfare losses attributable to bureaucratic behaviour properly, however, leads to precisely the opposite conclusion (since $\frac{1}{2} EST > \frac{1}{3} EST$). If a single model of bureaucratic behaviour is required for such purposes, therefore, it will be closer to the "cynical" Niskanen model than casual observation would indicate.

(3) The generalised "political failure" model

It may be objected (and has been by some critics)[8] that both the bureaucratic inefficiency model and the Niskanen model of bureau budgetary maximisation are extreme and that professional opinion is divided (not necessarily evenly) on the question of whether the political mechanism leads either to

8. Most notably, Richard Musgrave, "Leviathan Cometh—Or Does He?" in *Tax and Expenditure Limitations,* by H. Ladd and N. Tideman (Washington: Urban Institute Press, 1981), 77–117.

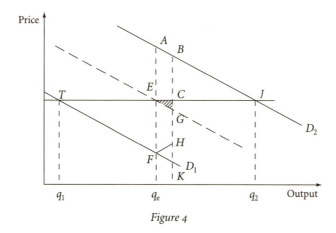

Figure 4

grossly higher costs or to over-expanded budgets,[9] and that any conclusion drawn from these models is tainted with a certain ideological "bias."

We should, therefore, emphasise that the force of the general argument does not depend in any way on the particular models—merely on the inherent convexity of the situation. Suppose, for example, one were to take the view that, over the whole range of public outputs supplied through particular bureaux, the likelihood of over-expansion is about as great as the likelihood of under-expansion in any given case. Ideologically, this is surely an even-handed position, and seems consistent with an acknowledgement of the theoretical arguments on both sides. To be more specific, suppose, as depicted in Fig. 4, that q_e is the observed output of the publicly provided good, G, and that there is an equal chance that the true demand curve for G is either D_1 or D_2—that is, an equal chance that q_1 or q_2 is the "optimal" output. Can we now conclude that the best estimate of public sector outcomes is that they are optimal?

9. As a counterpoise to the over-expansion result in the Niskanen model, or the same result reached by the different model outlined by James M. Buchanan and Gordon Tullock (*The Calculus of Consent: Logical Foundations of Constitutional Democracy* [Ann Arbor: University of Michigan Press, 1962]), see Anthony Downs, "Why the Government Is Too Small in a Democracy," *World Politics* 13 (1960): 541–63, or the more journalistic claims of John Galbraith. Ryan Amacher, Robert Tollison and T. Willett ("Budget Size in a Democracy: A Review of the Arguments," *Public Finance Quarterly* 3 [1975]: 99–120) provide a survey of the relevant literature.

For certain purposes, the answer is clearly *yes*. If, for example, we wish to calculate the efficiency effects of changes in output, the appropriate assumption is precisely that q_e is optimal. That is, in our linear demand case, the expected welfare loss of an expansion (or contraction) of output is equal to the welfare loss when q_e is known to be optimal.[10] The expected welfare loss of an expansion of output from q_e to q'_e is

$$E(W) = \tfrac{1}{2}(\text{welfare gain when } D_2 \text{ applies})$$
$$- \tfrac{1}{2}(\text{welfare loss when } D_1 \text{ applies})$$
$$= \tfrac{1}{2}ABCE - \tfrac{1}{2}ECFK.$$

Let point H be such that $BC = CH$. Since EF equals EA, then $ABCE$ equals $EFHC$. So $E(W) = \tfrac{1}{2}FHK = ECG$.

But for comparative institutional analysis, the assumption that the public sector will generate optimal outcomes is totally unacceptable. The expected welfare loss associated with the institution is not that generated by some sort of general "best predicted" bureaucratic behaviour. For we know that the expected welfare loss from bureaucratic provision is the area EAJ (or equally TEF) and not *zero*. In this particular case, it does not matter which of the under- or over-expansion models we use to estimate welfare loss. Either will do. But the procedure of making institutional comparisons on the basis of the "best-fit" model of the political mechanism will yield a measure of welfare losses of zero; the procedure therefore generates systematically wrong results, just as in the other models.

V. Conclusions

Modern public choice theorists have followed classical political economists in modelling individuals in their political roles in terms of the same "private interest" models of human behaviour that are commonly used in market settings. This procedure is frequently criticised on the grounds that it pays no attention to the obvious relevance of moral considerations in constraining the behaviour of individuals in political contexts.

---

10. This point is made in another context by Geoffrey Brennan and Thomas G. McGuire ("Optimal Policy Choice under Uncertainty," *Journal of Public Economics* 4 [February 1975]: 205–9).

But even if the empirical claim is valid, this line of criticism is not by any means decisive *provided that* the purpose of public choice analysis is seen as being the comparative evaluation of alternative institutions rather than the development of purely predictive theories of political behaviour. Our claim here is that the model of human behaviour appropriate for comparative institutional analysis will generally be one that generates worse outcomes (i.e., outcomes further from some conceptual optimum) than the empirical record would justify. For this reason, it may be appropriate to use the *Homo economicus* construction precisely *because* it indicates worse outcomes (in both political and market settings) than would seem likely on average. We have attempted to indicate the *nature* of our general reasoning first by appeal to an extremely simple and familiar case—the question of the choice between non-regulated monopoly and regulated monopoly. Our argument in this context suggests that there may be a case for retaining something like the textbook profit-maximising model, even where the empirical evidence in favour of satisficing and sales maximisation seems strong, *if the purpose of the analysis is to assist in the evaluation of monopoly as an institutional form.* Even though the profit-maximising model is an abstraction that does much violence to "predictive" reality, it may still produce better results in measuring welfare losses than the genuinely "realistic" model of positive predictive science. We have extended the results drawn from the simple monopoly example to several cases of bureaucratic supply of public goods.

Our more general argument, one that we believe would be entirely congenial to classical "political economists," is that the general characteristics of the monopoly example apply commonly in the whole range of political/ social contexts, and specifically that there *is* a generalised analogue to the downward-sloping demand-curve embedded in political and social institutions. To deny this, seems to deny the notion that politicians-bureaucrats serve as suppliers of services that are valued by the citizenry. The evaluation of these public services, even if they are not directly priced, is not essentially different from the evaluation of services purchased in markets. If, therefore, we take any defined "public interest" model of behaviour as an idealised benchmark, and conceptualise the output of services generated by such behaviour, it becomes apparent that restrictions (or expansions) of valued output from that idealised benchmark will involve increasing marginal welfare losses to the citizens.

Once this view of things is accepted, it follows that, for purposes of constitutional dialogue, the model which embodies self-serving behaviour on the part of *all* politicians may be superior to that which accurately predicts behaviour in the conventional probabilistic sense.

There is one final observation to be made. *Homo economicus* by no means represents the worst imaginable character for the social drama. The natural monopolist whose predilection towards the "small is beautiful" philosophy leads him to produce *less* output than would-be profit-maximising; such a monopolist inflicts yet larger marginal losses on the community than his rapacious wealth-maximising counterpart. The political zealot who works with self-sacrificing conscientiousness to pursue some ideological goal—such as the purification of the race, or securing the world for Islam—can cause much greater harm than the mere budget-maximiser. It may be that this budget-maximiser is somewhat "worse" than the average or representative politico-economic agent; but, as we have tried to show, this may be a *virtue* of our disciplinary method—not a weakness.

Appendix

The reader should be alerted to the fact that this condition is sufficient to ensure that f in equation (2) is convex (i.e., $f'' > 0$) only in the case where welfare loss is expressed as a function of *quantity* distortion. If instead we express welfare loss as a function of *price* distortion, then the assumption that the compensated demand curve is negatively sloped is *not* sufficient to ensure that welfare loss increases at a faster rate the larger the distortion.

To see this, consider without loss of generality the case in which quantity distortion is positive. Then $d^+ = q - q^* > 0$ and

$$\frac{dd^+}{dq} = 1. \tag{i}$$

Then $W = f(d)$ will be convex in d if $W = f(q)$ is convex in q. Note that

$$W = -\left[\int_{q^*}^{q} g(q) - \int_{q^*}^{q} c'(q) \right] dq, \tag{ii}$$

where $g(q)$ is the compensated demand curve and $c(q)$ is the cost function, and for convenience is assumed linear.

$$\frac{dW}{dq} = [g(q^*) - c'(q^*)] - [g(q) - c'(q)]. \tag{iii}$$

Since q^* defines optimality, the first bracketed term on the right hand side is zero, and $c'(q)$ is a constant. Hence:

$$\frac{d^2W}{dq^2} = -g'(q) > 0 \text{ if } g'(q) < 0 \text{ and q.e.d.}$$

Suppose instead that we define welfare loss as a function of *price* distortion, i.e.,

$$W = h(v), \tag{iv}$$

where

$$v = p - p^*. \tag{v}$$

Is the fact that $W = f(d)$ is convex sufficient to ensure that h is convex? Clearly not, for:

$$W = h(v) = f[k(v)] \tag{vi}$$

where

$$d = k(v)$$

and

$$h' = f'[k(v)]k' \tag{vii}$$

and

$$h'' = f''[k(v)](k')^2 + k''f'[k(v)]. \tag{viii}$$

Now, in (viii), we know that f'', $(k')^2$, $f' > 0$. But the sign of k' is indeterminate. Note that k' is $-dq/dp$ and k'' is $-d^2q/dp^2$. So if d^2q/dp^2 is positive and sufficiently large, (viii) *may* conceivably be negative.

One might conjecture that the cases in which the demand curve is sufficiently concave (from above) to ensure that h'' is negative are so rare as to be ignorable: that is, there is a strong *presumption* that doubling the price distortion will more than double the welfare loss. And this conclusion seems reasonable. But a presumption is not a certainty, and plausible possible formulations of the demand curve exist for which the presumption is violated.

(We are grateful to David Austen-Smith for bringing some examples to our attention.)

To avoid such caveats in the text, we have defined distortion exclusively in *quantity* terms. Then pure logic generates the conclusions from standard demand theory.

Of course, in the empirical literature on the estimation of welfare losses, some form of linearity is assumed—in which case, k'' is zero and h'' is positive. Linearity is also assumed whenever one uses average price and average quantity data to determine benchmarks for welfare loss estimation: in general, $(\overline{p}, \overline{q})$ will not lie on the demand curve. To assume that it does implies linearity.

The Economizing Element in
Knight's Ethical Critique of
Capitalist Order

With this conference, we honor the centenary of Frank Knight's birth. It is a measure of the man that we feel compelled to criticize rather than to praise his work. As I have noted elsewhere,[1] there is so much of Knight embedded deeply in my own thought processes that any criticism may amount to removing cobwebs of my own. My respect for Knight prompts the question as to whether or not any ambiguity that I might allegedly expose is only that in the "Buchanan understanding" rather than in the source.

With this statement as prologue, I shall advance the thesis that Frank Knight's work is flawed by a methodological ambiguity that he shares with the overwhelming majority of those who now profess membership in the academy of professional economics. Knight's intellectual honesty forced him to the very edges of a shift in vision, but he was never able to escape the maximizing paradigm which his own early work, in part, helped to impose on the whole discipline. I shall not, in this paper, develop any full-fledged methodological analysis of Knight's works. I shall, instead, limit discussion largely to the influence of the economizing-*maximizing element* on the clas-

From *Ethics* 98 (October 1987): 61–75. Copyright 1987 by The University of Chicago. All rights reserved. Reprinted by permission of the University of Chicago Press, publisher.

I am indebted to my colleagues David Levy and Robert Tollison for helpful comments. This paper was originally delivered at the conference "Frank H. Knight (1885–1972): A Reappraisal of His Intellectual Contributions" (Chicago, November 7–9, 1985).

1. See my foreword to Frank H. Knight, *Freedom and Reform* (Indianapolis: Liberty Fund, 1982).

sic Knightian evaluation of competitive order.[2] How might this critique have been different if Knight had been able to escape from the maximizing paradigm? Specifically, how and to what extent does a substitution of a *catallactic* for a *maximizing* perspective on economic interaction mitigate the Knightian listing of the limits to any measured ethical defense of market organization?

In the second section, I shall, by selected citation, demonstrate that Knight remained always within the standard maximization paradigm, and I shall criticize the normative implication of this methodology. In the third section, I discuss briefly the difference between these two paradigms, and I shall criticize the normative implication of this methodology. In the third section, I discuss briefly the difference between these two paradigms, and I sketch the content of the second. In the fourth section, I survey the Knightian criticisms in some detail, and in so doing I shall demonstrate that several of them depend on the acceptance of a maximizing vision. The fifth section summarizes the whole Knightian exercise. Finally, in the last section, I attempt to show that the ethical implication of Knight's criticism can be modified under a shift in methodological perspective. I shall concentrate attention on the arguments advanced in *The Ethics of Competition,*[3] although, where necessary, I shall make reference to other of Knight's writings.

Economic Interaction and a Social Value Scale

> An organized system must operate in accordance with a *social* standard. This standard will of course be related in some way to the values of the individuals making up the society, but it cannot be merely identical with them; it presupposes some process of organizing the various individual interests, weighing them against each other and adjudicating conflicts among them. [p. 42]

2. For a more general discussion, see R. A. Gonce, "Frank H. Knight on Social Control and the Scope and Method of Economics," *Southern Economic Journal* 36 (1972): 547–58; see also Mark Casson, "Frank Knight and the Theory of Society" (Reading, Pa.: University of Reading, 1985, mimeographed).

3. Frank Knight, *The Ethics of Competition* (London: George Allen & Unwin, Ltd., 1935). Page numbers given in parentheses in text refer to this volume.

It is impossible to form any concept of "social efficiency" in the absence of some general measure of value. [p. 42]

There is no more important function of the first course in economics than to make the student see that the whole problem of social management is a *value* problem. [p. 43]

The commonly recognized function of economic organization is to utilize the limited resources at the command of the social group in bringing about the largest possible satisfaction of the wants of its members. [p. 102]

It [the first function] is the function of setting standards, of establishing a scale of values, or the function of social choice.[4]

Statements such as those above may be found scattered throughout Knight's writings. They now seem commonplace only because his explicit formulation became a model for elementary textbook exposition. The Knightian classification of the five functions of an economic system (no matter how organized) offers what initially seems to be a useful way to get a handle on the whole disciplinary subject matter. Considered noncritically, the first function, that of (1) establishing a value scale, seems in balance with the others, (2) organizing production, (3) distributing product, (4) providing for progress, and (5) adjusting consumption to production in the short period.

The whole Knightian exercise may be criticized in these respects, on what we may call Hayekian grounds, by suggesting that an economic system as such does not really exist and that it is confusing to discuss "functions" to be performed or carried out by nonexistent entities. I shall not elaborate such a criticism here; even if the entity to which functions are assigned does not exist there may be some usefulness in proceeding as if it did, and, indeed, most of us resort to such terms in both everyday and scholarly discourse.[5] I shall, therefore, take as given that we may discuss the functions of an economic system and that the second, third, fourth, and fifth of those listed in the clas-

---

4. Frank Knight, "The Economic Organization" (Chicago: University of Chicago, 1933, mimeographed), 8.

5. See David Levy, "The Impossibility of a Methodological Individualist: Reduction When Knowledge Is Imperfect," *Economics and Philosophy* (1985): 101–8.

sification create no special problems. My concern is centered exclusively on the first function, that of the establishment of a value scale.

The economic system does, indeed, establish a value scale, and in this sense it performs a function comparable to the other four in the classic Knightian listing. But, as the selected citations above suggest, the establishment of a value scale is different from the other functions in that Knight adds a *normative* implication as a more or less natural extension. A value scale or standard, once established, allows overall performance to be evaluated or measured. Economic outcomes may be arrayed in terms of the units on the scale. "Better" and "worse" descriptions may be assigned to specific allocations. The objective of *maximizing* the value of the criterion so derived emerges almost as a matter of course. It becomes quite natural to define as optimally or ideally efficient that allocation of resources which maximizes the value of the criterion and to classify as inefficient or nonoptimal all allocations that fall short of this target. From this stage of conceptualization, it is but a small step to the next which assigns to the economic system, by inference if not directly, the function of "improving efficiency" in resource usage.

This efficiency-enhancing "function" is, however, categorically different from that which stops merely at the establishment of a value scale. The establishment of the scale, in itself, need not imply the normative objective of maximization. It seems clear that Knight did not fully understand this point, as the citations indicate.

I have asserted that the establishment of a value scale or standard, as such, does not carry with it any implication to the effect that "the system," "the society," or "the government" *should* maximize the criterion defined by such a scalar or that the working of "the system" be normatively assessed in such terms. That is to say, the value scale so established is not, in any necessary sense, a *social* value scale.

Consider an analogy. If we weigh apples and oranges we need something other than physical units to make the items comparable. We introduce pounds, a common scale that allows us to combine and aggregate differing quantities of apples and oranges and to generate a single meaningful total—weight—that may be useful for some purposes. The use of the standard of measurement does not carry any normative implication relating to maximization or minimization. The standard has served its purpose in allowing us to reduce the dimensionality of the initial set of heterogeneous items in the bundle.

Consider now the scale or standard that is established in the complex interaction that we call the market. Prices emerge in the process, and these prices have the effect of reducing the dimensionality of the bundle of initially heterogeneous goods and services. Prices establish a common denominator of value akin to the common denominator of weight that the use of pounds establishes in the earlier example. At this level, there is no necessary normative implication that the value of the bundle is to be maximized or minimized, any more than weight, temperature, or volume should be in other examples. The function of the system is completed when the scale is established.

But does a maximization inference emerge when we look more closely at the purposes of the economic value scale? It is here that the critical mistake is likely to be made. For the individual, the activity of choosing among alternatives under conditions of scarcity is necessarily a process of *evaluation* through which internal rates of trade-off are settled. The individual who acts so as to place a higher value on an orange than on an apple is, in the very process of evaluation itself, *economizing* in the allocation of that which is scarce. It is, therefore, appropriate to attach a normative implication directly to the individual's own choice behavior in setting up his internal value scale. It is entirely acceptable to model the behavior of the economizing individual as the maximization of that which he values, whether this be called utility, satisfaction, or simply X. It is inappropriate to transfer this subjectively defined maximization norm of the individual (any individual) to the system of interaction, the society, or the state. The common value scale, confronted by each participant and represented by the vector of prices that emerges from the interaction of many persons, does not carry any maximizing implication or inference. That which is maximized in the idealized market is the internal value of each person subject to the constraints defined by his initial endowments and the value scale reflected in the price vector. Prices serve a function for the individual that is analogous to the use of a standard of weight in the earlier example. Prices, as confronted, allow the individual to reduce to a single value dimension the set of diverse opportunities among which he must choose. Prices of ten cents on an orange and five cents on an apple offer the individual the external terms at which these heterogeneous items may be exchanged. He maximizes his internally determined subjective value by adjusting behavior until the internal trade-offs match the external.

In the idealized market there is only one set of prices that will allow all participants to achieve maxima of their internally derived scales of values, subject to the separate constraints that each faces. To refer to this "solution" as "socially efficient" or "optimal," however, is without meaning. And it is precisely with such usage of terms that critical error is made. The linkage is clear. If the value scale established in the market does, indeed, provide a criterion for the measurement of "social efficiency," it follows naturally that a supplementary function of the economic organization or system is one of achieving some sort of maximum as defined on this scalar. It is but a small step from this sort of discussion to conceptualization of the system as the economizing unit and to thinking of a "society's economic problem," with better or worse solutions, as measured by the value scale. The seeds of the social welfare–function absurdities of the middle decades of this century are to be found in Knight's writings as well as in those of his peers.

Economics as Catallaxy

I suggested in the first section that Knight came to the very edges of escape from the maximization paradigm, and those of us who recall his expressions of frustration at the "bright young men" who seemed to think that maximization was the be-all and end-all of economics must credit him with some sense of limits in these respects. Consider the following statement: "The organization as a whole has no value in itself or purpose of its own . . . but exists solely to promote the interests of its members."[6] This statement simply cannot be reconciled with the selected citations at the start of the preceding section.

In this statement, Knight's view of economic organization may be placed squarely within a perspective that has been called catallactics, one that describes the discipline as "the science of exchange."[7] This alternative perspec-

---

6. Knight, "The Economic Organization," 23–24.

7. See James M. Buchanan, "What Should Economists Do?" *Southern Economic Journal* 30 (1964): 213–22, reprinted as the title essay in my book *What Should Economists Do?* (Indianapolis: Liberty Fund, 1979).

tive (paradigm, research program, vision) separates our disciplinary subject matter from that of the other social sciences quite differently from the maximizing perspective. That is, the two "cuts" divide the human sciences along quite different planes.

The maximizing-economizing paradigm allows the economist to claim domain over all rational behavior, as Knight stressed, over all behavior that involves the usage of means to achieve ends. That which is extra-economic is limited to the nonrational or the irrational. Knight himself was instrumental in emphasizing the limits of the economizing model in explaining and predicting human behavior patterns, but he held fast to the notion that, within such limits, economizing is what economics is all about. And, of course, etymologically, he was correct.

Exchange can, of course, be brought within the maximization framework readily; individual actors can be modeled as seeking out and exploiting exchange opportunities as instrumental to the furtherance of ends. In this context, exchange is conceptually equivalent to production, as Knight often stressed; both processes are aimed at enhancing value. Exchange activity is grounded in the individual's rational adaptation of available, but scarce, means to ends. Crusoe models, in which the isolated individual "exchanges" fish for coconuts by reallocating his scarce resource, time, analyze behavior that seems conceptually equivalent to that examined in models in which persons exchange money for goods in a market nexus. Nor are the market models different in this respect from those in which some persons use their decision-making authority over others to make value-enhancing "exchanges," for example, through a reassignment of tasks to members of a working party.

It is easy to understand Knight's expressed concern about the limits of economic explanation once his methodological ambiguity is clarified. If, indeed, a "social" value scale is established in the economy, and if rationality dictates using scarce resources to maximize value, Knight's worry about there being no room left for an independent ethics seems fully justified. If, however, a catallactic perspective is taken and inquiry is focused on the exchange process per se and on behavior in that process, there is a natural barrier to the extension of the rationality norm. Within a prospective exchange a trader may, of course, treat others as instruments or means toward furtherance of his own purposes. He does so, however, in the knowledge that others are behaving reciprocally toward him. Rationality norms apply only to the attempts to satisfy each individual trader's *own* purposes, constrained by the behavior of other traders. Such norms cannot be extended upward, so to speak, to evaluate the outcomes or results of trade, as such.

As previously stressed, there is no social value scale, as such, established in market exchange. The price vector that does emerge becomes a commonly shared constraint to which all persons adjust independently in their efforts to maximize their own subjectively determined scales of value. It is conceptually meaningless to think of "the economy" as "economizing" on the use of resources. Only individuals "economize," given their resource endowments and the constraints that they face, constraints that embody the economizing-maximizing behavior of other participants in the whole exchange nexus.

Knight's Ethical Critique of Market Order

Consider the statement "A freely competitive organization of society tends to place every productive resource in that position in the productive system where it can make the greatest possible addition to the total social dividend as measured in price terms, and tends to reward every participant in production by giving it the increase in the social dividend that its cooperation makes possible. In the writer's opinion, such a proposition is entirely sound; but it is not a statement of a sound ethical social ideal" (p. 48). If criticized from the catallactic perspective, the proposition would have to be characterized as "entirely meaningless" since there is no "social dividend," as such. On the other hand, the catallactic stance does permit us to revise the statement in such a way as to suggest a possibly differing ethical implication. Consider the following revision: "A freely competitive organization of society tends to place every productive resource in that position in the productive system such that each participant in that system is enabled to maximize his own values subject to the constraints of the initial distribution of endowments among persons and to the preferences of others than himself. Such a proposition is entirely sound." Note that in the suggested revision I have deliberately left off the ethical implication appended to the initial Knight statement. I do so because this implication is the basic subject matter of my whole inquiry in this paper. Shortly after making the statement cited, Knight went on to list twelve separate criticisms of the competitive economic order; these were presented in apparent support of his ethical conclusion. I want to examine each of these criticisms in the light of the modified methodological position that the revised statement above reflects. How many of the twelve criticisms of the competitive order stand up under a catallactic perspective which concentrates attention on processes of exchange rather than on allocative end states or outcomes?

I shall follow the numbered order in which Knight listed his criticisms (pp. 49–55). Several of the items may be discussed quite briefly. The summaries are my own translations of Knight's more extensive discussions.

1. How do we define the appropriate set of individuals who make contractual exchanges? How do we treat children, incompetents, and those who subject themselves to domination by others?

This criticism is not affected by the choice between the contrasting paradigms. These questions remain thorny ones for any methodological or normative individualist.

2. The individual is, at least in part, a product of the economic and social system and cannot, therefore, be treated as a *datum*. The competitive economic order need not tend to form character that exhibits desirable properties.

More or less the same comments apply here as with the first criticism. The individualist must acknowledge that any system that allows all persons to retain liberty of choice may allow some persons to survive and even to prosper who do not possess character traits deemed desirable by some or even a large number of their fellows.

3. Effective competition calls for perfect divisibility of goods entering into exchange.

It is difficult for me to understand just what Knight was getting at in the short paragraph devoted to this criticism. He may have been expressing a fear that increasing returns to scale are more pervasive than empirical observation has suggested. Even if, however, increasing returns are widespread over relevant output ranges, it is inappropriate to compare the operation of an economy in such a setting with that of an idealized and imaginary economy in which increasing returns are not present. As a criticism of the competitive order, therefore, this criticism seems to be without foundation in either of the paradigms that are compared here.

4. Perfect competition requires perfect knowledge of all exchange opportunities.

This criticism totally collapses in any process paradigm of economic interaction. It is advanced only by those who conceptualize some ideally efficient allocation of resources that exists and can be defined independent of the trading process through which the competitive allocation emerges. It is, in retrospect, surprising that Knight advanced this as a serious argument.

5. Competition requires accurate knowledge on the part of buyers as to the ability of goods and services to satisfy wants.

Once again, this criticism is difficult to understand. Knight seems to be making an illegitimate comparison between human fallibility and idealized infallibility. There is no sense of comparative institutional analysis, despite the stated purpose of the whole exercise.[8] As with criticism 3 above, the analytical framework does not matter; the criticism is without foundation in either of the two paradigms.

6. The results of intelligent action will be ethically ideal only if the ends or purposes of such action are themselves "true values."

This criticism can be interpreted in two ways. Most straightforward, Knight seems to suggest here that there exists some set of true values that can be ascertained either by reason or revelation and that the market order will promote these true values only if the individual participants commonly share them. In other words, there must be a correspondence between individuals' values as reflected in market exchange and the values that the philosopher can judge to be "true" or "good." One inference of this interpretation would be that if objectively measurable wealth (the social dividend) is at

8. David Levy has suggested that my criticism is unfair to Knight here, in that Knight was working within the orthodox moral theorist's perspective that allows an idealized order to be described for evaluative purposes, independent of its possible existence. While I acknowledge that deep philosophical issues beyond my competence arise here, I think we should recognize fantasy, whether in art or morals, and beware of using it as the basis of criticizing that which is or can be.

least one true value, the market order which does tend to maximize this value may be partially absolved of criticism. But, to the extent that other and possibly conflicting true values exist, this order falls short of some ideally operating institutional alternative.

In a lengthy footnote that accompanies this criticism, Knight seems to be saying something different. He suggests that because individual wants are to a large extent shaped by the process of interaction in which they are expressed the process may, in the case of market exchange, create distortions such that revealed preferences in the marketplace are different from individuals' "true" preferences. In this interpretation, there need be no inference that some externally definable set of true values exists independent of individual sources.

The first interpretation makes sense only in some inclusively defined maximizing paradigm in which the performance of the market order can be evaluated in terms of its relative success or failure in achieving those ends that exist independent of the process, that is, only if there does in fact exist a social welfare function. There is no content in this criticism, under this first interpretation, in a catallactic or process model of market interaction, which is grounded on the presupposition that no such function exists.

The second interpretation creates some difficulty, even within the catallactic model. The individual participants are taken as givens, and there is no criterion that enables any evaluation of values or preferences. The process of exchange is the only object of possible evaluation. If, however, the market order tends to promote efforts to subvert what might be called the "natural exchange" process through some effort to distort and conceal effective alternatives from participants, there is a basis for criticism akin to that which might be brought against overt fraud. As in some of the other criticisms, however, this one can become meaningful only if there might exist some alternative institutional arrangements that would be predicted to eliminate this tendency.

7. The competitive order requires freedom of entry to insure against the tendency toward monopolization. Such freedom of entry is not automatically guaranteed by the workings of competition itself.

This criticism should be taken as directed toward those advocates of market order who do not accept the necessity that there be an appropriately designed legal framework without which the order cannot be expected to function. This requirement was clearly understood by Adam Smith and the other classical economists. It is not a criticism of the competitive order but, rather, of a genuine laissez-faire structure that embodies no recognition of the importance of the legal framework.

8. The competitive market order does not internalize all Pareto-relevant externalities.

This criticism is valid in either the maximizing or the catallactic paradigm, but the test for failure is quite different in the two cases. In the maximizing paradigm, where a genuine social value scale is presumed to exist, the presence of relevant externalities is conceptually identified by the shortfall in total value between the market result or outcome and that which might be generated with idealized correction. In the catallactic paradigm, by contrast, the presence of relevant externalities is identified, quite simply, by the existence of potential gains-from-trade in institutional change that will effectively internalize the spillovers. Careful examination of Knight's rather brief discussion of this criticism suggests that he clearly worked within the first of the paradigms and that he thought of relevant externalities as elements that reduced social value.

9. The competitive order cannot work effectively without predictability in the value of the monetary unit.

It is not properly a criticism of market organization but, rather, of laissez-faire arrangements that make inadequate provision for an institutional-constitutional framework that will generate monetary stability. The observed historical record suggests that governments have rarely fulfilled this responsibility, but the criticism should be directed at the political process rather than the organization of the economy.

10. The competitive market order need not make appropriate provision for progress, since aggregate results depend on separate individual decisions to invest rather than to consume.

By comparison with several of the other criticisms, Knight's discussion here is surprisingly tempered. He recognizes that his strictures apply equally to almost any institutional structure. On the other hand, the statement of the criticism in itself suggests that there exists some external basis for making an evaluation.

11. Individual behavior in the market order need not reflect rational response to the necessary presence of genuine uncertainty.

As with number 10, Knight's discussion of this point recognizes that any structure may prove deficient in this respect and that the criticism is not directed at market organization as such. It remains clear, however, that Knight was basing this criticism on the presumed existence of some determinate scale of evaluation.

12. In a competitive system, resource payments reflect marginal productivities, and productive contribution is not an ethical measure of desert.

This criticism is aimed at the wrong target. The target should be the pre-market distribution of endowments among persons rather than the market as such, which simply takes the former as given and tends to maximize values of the separate parties subject to the constraints defined by the endowments distribution and the preferences of the participants. Interpreted in this way, Knight's distributional critique is appropriately directed at the legal and political framework and becomes analogous to the criticisms discussed under 7 and 9 above.

This redirection of the distributional criticism is perhaps less evident than was the case with monopoly and money. It may possibly be claimed that only through some institutional alternative to the market could any ethically justified distribution of claims to final product be secured. That is to say, the only corrective institutional process might be alleged to be that in which economic interaction takes place. In this context, the economic nexus becomes the instrument for implementing political-legal objectives and cannot be treated independently. There is no prospect for evaluating the competitive order, as such. The whole exercise, both that attempted by Knight and my own reexamination, becomes impossible. If, on the other hand, the exercise is to remain meaningful, there must be a separation between the attribution of justice or injustice to the pre-market distribution of endowments and the attribution of justice or injustice to the exchange process that is based on whatever distribution of endowments is fed into it. In this context, it is quite plausible to suggest that the exchange or market process might be deemed to have desirable ethical properties even if the underlying distribution of endowments might be generally judged to be unjust. The market may, in this case, be absolved of responsibility for the distributional ills of the whole complex political-legal-economic-social order.

The Knightian Criticisms Summarized

The criticisms listed and discussed briefly above were explicitly advanced by Knight as his reasons "why individualism and competition cannot bring about an ideal utilization of social resources" (p. 54). From our perspective six decades after publication of *The Ethics of Competition,* these criticisms make up a peculiarly mixed bag. It will be useful to sort them out and to determine how many of the criticisms hold up from the modified methodological perspective.

As noted, numbers 7, 9, and 12 do not seem to be criticisms of the market process as such but are, instead, more general criticisms of the political-legal order. Those criticisms numbered 6, 10, and 11 do not seem to be directed at any particular organizational process; any institutional system may fail to promote "true" values, to make "sufficient" provision for progress, or to insure that individuals make "rational" responses to uncertainty. There is no sense of comparative institutional performance in the Knightian discussion even if the implicit presumption of the existence of some external criteria for truth, sufficiency, and rationality is ignored. Criticisms 3, 4, and 5, those which suggest that the efficacy of competition depends on divisibility, full knowledge, and accuracy in prediction, seem misguided if a catallactic perspective is taken. These criticisms make sense only in some comparison between the workings of a potentially observable market process and an idealized imaginary construction.

There remain only the criticisms 1, 2, and 8, which I have acknowledged to remain relevant. The ultimate ethical argument for a free society, more inclusively defined than any reference to economic organization alone, rests squarely on the presupposition that persons are competent to determine their own interests or, at least, that they are more competent than any designated guardians. This position is scarcely sustainable when children and idiots are included within the definition of persons. Acknowledgment of the problems that arise in defining the limits of membership in the effectively free society should not, however, imply ethical negation of the basic structural principle. The necessity for making carefully discriminating judgment in application and extension of the principle is not at all the same as judging the principle to be inapplicable.

Knight's second criticism should be similarly acknowledged. The person whose preferences are reflected in the market process need not match anyone's set of ideals. But should the process itself be judged to fail on ethical grounds if the participants in it do not match up to externally defined standards? There is ethical content in this criticism only if it might be demonstrated that the process in itself exerts predictable effects on the character of participants, effects that are generally deemed to operate to make persons worse than they would be under some plausible institutional alternative. Even if this judgment should be shared, however, the negative effects here would have to be weighed against the positive ethical content of any system that allows liberty for persons to choose as they wish.

The third criticism that warrants mention in this summary treatment is the eighth, that which calls attention to the failure of the market exchange process to deal adequately with third party or external effects. In one sense, this criticism might be handled like 7, 9, and 12, that is, as a criticism of the political-legal framework which has not defined properly the rights which persons possess when they initially enter the trading process. Nonetheless, it seems preferable in this respect to acknowledge that "competitive organization," as this term is usually understood, does not embody correctives for all externalities and that there may be limits to the extension of this organizational form when there are spillover effects that are not readily priced. As with criticism I discussed above, however, the acknowledgment of limits should not be taken to negate the ethical principle upon which the structure rests. Recognizing the necessity for discrimination in application is quite different from rejection of the whole organizational norm.[9]

***

9. George Stigler has reexamined the set of Knightian criticisms for a somewhat different purpose than my own (*The Economist as Preacher* [Chicago: University of Chicago Press, 1982], 18–19).

Can an Amended Economics Restore Ethical
Content to Competitive Order?

Recall the statement cited at the beginning of the fourth section concerning the operation of the freely competitive organization of society, and recall that Knight ended the statement with "but it is not a statement of a sound ethical social ideal." Following the citation from Knight, I suggested a catallactic revision, which I repeat here:

> A freely competitive organization of society tends to place every productive resource in that position in the productive system such that each participant in that system is enabled to maximize his own values subject to the constraints of the initial distribution of endowments among persons and to the preferences of others than himself. Such a proposition is entirely sound. (Furthermore, within the limits defined and on the recognition that the organization of economic interaction is only one element in overall social order, there is positive ethical weight to be assigned to competitive organization on the fundamental liberal supposition that individuals are the only ultimate sources of value.)

Recall that in the first statement of the revision I did not include the ethical implication contained in the sentence enclosed by parentheses. The stated purpose of the fifth section was to examine whether or not Knight's several criticisms would apply with force sufficient to deny the validity of any such ethical inference.

The catallactic perspective does not allow us to advance critical argument based on the failure of any organizational form to attain maximum levels measured on some social value scale. "Social value," as such, carries no ethical weight. A system must be ethically judged, if at all, exclusively in terms of its ability to allow individuals to further their own values, whatever these may be. And interpreted in this way, the ethical inference appended to the revised statement above seems to be justifiable.

The limits of the ethical inference should be stressed. There is no implication to be drawn to the effect that the market order will internalize all externalities, that it will, in itself, generate the evolution of the "public goods" associated with the services of the minimal or protective state, including the monetary framework, or that it will generate distributional results that will satisfy some externally defined criteria of justice. Furthermore, there is no implication to be drawn concerning the correspondence between the preferences reflected in the marketplace and those that might be deemed aesthetically or ethically "best" by some set of would-be arbiters. In the marketplace, a pushpin is as good as poetry, for the quite simple reason that both goods rise or fall from favor in accordance with the operations of the same evaluative process.

In the catallactic perspective, individual liberty to initiate voluntary exchanges, along with the availability of exchange alternatives, assumes central ethical significance. Coercion is not as good as liberty. In this sense, an ethical scalar does indeed emerge. The scalar here is, however, that which is embodied in the philosophical presuppositions of individualism itself. Those who seek to evaluate the market order in ethical terms cannot be allowed to have it both ways. They cannot, at the same time, be genuine individualists and seek to criticize the market in terms of a nonindividualistic value scale.

Frank Knight would not have objected to the position outlined immediately above. As I suggested earlier, he seemed on the very edge of a shift from the methodological stance that I have subjected to scrutiny. Especially in his later writings, Knight seemed fully to recognize the positive ethical content of market organization while at the same time he made little or no reference to the meaningfulness of a social value scale. Consider the following statements from his 1950 presidential address to the American Economic Association:

> Economic principles are simply the more general implications of the principle of . . . free association. . . . The free association in question is exchange in markets.[10]

> The only agreement called for in market relations is acceptance of the one essentially negative *ethical principle,* that the units are not to prey upon one another through coercion and fraud.[11] [Italics added]

---

10. Frank Knight, "The Role of Principles in Economics and Politics," in his *On the History and Method of Economics* (Chicago: University of Chicago Press, 1956), 257–58.
    11. Ibid., 267.

The society pictured by the . . . idealized market economy is . . . one held together by the *single moral principle* just stated. This is entirely proper . . . at a certain stage of abstraction.[12] [Italics added]

In this address, in particular, Knight stressed the limits of any single principle, and his earlier ethical critique of market organization can perhaps best be interpreted as a reaction against the pronouncements of those who may have placed excessive emphasis on the moral virtues of the free market. The readily discernible shift in Knight's writings over the decades is explained, in part, by the general drift of academic-intellectual opinion. In the early 1920s, Knight, the eternal critic, felt it necessary to attack the strident defenders of laissez-faire. By the 1950s, the appropriate targets had become those who refused to appreciate the moral principle of free association itself.

My central argument in this paper, however, is that Knight never wholly escaped from the straitjacket that his conception of economics imposed upon his thought. It is, of course, possible that it was precisely the methodological ambiguity that created the tension in Knight's analysis and that it is this tension that allows us to remain fascinated with his works. The early conversion to a full-fledged catallactic perspective would have removed much of the content from Knight's classical ethical criticism of capitalism. In so doing, it also would have reduced the influence of Knight on his peers in economics, in his time and our own, an influence that must surely be judged to have been positive. This judgment is based on the observation that, from the 1920s through the 1980s, the overwhelming majority of those who claim membership in the academy of economists have exhibited much more rigid adherence to the maximization paradigm than Knight himself.

This paper has been very Knightian in spirit. I follow Knight in holding that the main purpose of examining classical writers is to profit from their error, confusion, and ambiguity. I know that Frank Knight would not have objected to my purpose, and I like to think that he might, himself, have written some such paper as this. Perhaps the most important single principle we learned from Knight is that nothing is to be held sacrosanct, least of all our own words.

12. Ibid., 268.

Professor Alchian
on Economic Method

In chapter two I argued that economists have failed to distinguish their methodological categories. Specifically, I distinguished among (1) a logic of economic choice, (2) an abstract science of economic behavior, and (3) a predictive science of economic behavior. In the first of these categories, no attempt is made to incorporate empirical reality; no identification of "goods" is made; no predictive hypotheses emerge. What we get is a *general* theory of human action, or choice, as Mises argues, but because it is general it must remain nonoperational and empirically empty. In the second category, which I call the "abstract science of economic behavior" and which I, personally, associate with the thinking of Frank Knight, we move beyond strict logical limits. Here we do plug in some aspects of reality and by so doing we ensure that actors behave, not *choose,* and that they do so in a directed fashion. Here *Homo economicus* comes into his own, and economic motivation serves as the driving behavioral force. At an abstract level, hypotheses derived are conceptually refutable. If men behave economically, predictions can be falsified. But we know that economic motivation is not pervasive over all human behavior. We know that men do choose. Hence, Knight was willing to draw limits on the explanatory potential of economic theory, limits that are short of empirical falsification. My third category, the "predictive science of economic behavior," involves a shift beyond Knight's limits, a shift to the development of hypotheses that are empirically testable.

From *What Should Economists Do?* (Indianapolis: Liberty Fund, 1979), 65–79. Reprinted by permission of the publisher.

This chapter was initially developed for a seminar presentation at the University of California, Los Angeles, in November 1969. For obvious reasons, I used some of Professor Alchian's work as a target for a more generalized criticism of economic method.

I am not going to repeat here the argument of chapter two. I do propose to call into question one aspect of my categorization. In that discussion, I placed what might be called the "Alchian approach" squarely within the science of behavior, one or the other of the last two categories mentioned above. I am now wondering whether or not it belongs there or in the first category, the pure logic of choice. To put matters dramatically, let me pose the question, Is the Alchian approach empirically empty? Is there any positive content in it?

Let me first specify what I understand by the Alchian approach, which may not, of course, square with what Professor Alchian himself believes it to be. Alchian appears to go beyond any mere logic of choice by his apparent identification of "goods." He seems to commence analysis with an identification of goods in the individual's utility function. He specifically warns, however, that these goods are not to be constrained to that set which might be construed as narrowly "economic." The utility function of the actor is extended to include such things as "prestige, power, friends, love, respect, self-expression, talent, liberty, knowledge, good looks, leisure . . . the welfare of other people."[1] But what are the effective limits to such an extension? I may be misinterpreting him here, but Professor Alchian seems to leave his utility functions open-ended, so to speak, to allow almost any argument to be included so long as it qualifies as a good. But how does he define a good? The answer here is not clear, but he seems to do so by observing human behavior and by labeling a good anything upon which men are generally observed to place value; that is, as anything for which men demonstrate a willingness to pay a price, anything for which men seem willing to bear a cost in terms of sacrificed alternatives. Having so defined goods, Alchian then proceeds to develop the law of demand, or Postulate No. 5 in *University Economics,* which Alchian and Allen declare to be "an extremely powerful proposition." I wonder! It now seems to me that Alchian comes perilously close to defining a good as that for which the first law of demand applies and then holds up the latter as an extremely powerful proposition.

---

1. A. A. Alchian and W. R. Allen, *University Economics,* 2d ed. (Belmont, Calif.: Wadsworth Press, 1968), 16. Perhaps my critique and discussion should be directed at the Alchian-Allen approach. I limit discussion to Alchian here because I attribute to him the relevant methodology subjected to criticism here.

Let me acknowledge my own confusion here, but let me try to indicate some of my worries. Suppose that I am observed to place dimes in the apple machine and get apples in return. Does this observation alone indicate that apples are a good in my utility function? Is it not possible that my observed actions merely represent the disposal of "bads," in this case, dimes, not the securing of goods. Both apples and dimes may be bads to me, and the only means of disposing of one bad may be to take on another one. The observed behavior at this level of treatment would be identical in the two cases. We must have something other than this observation to make our identification of goods. The additional requirement may be the observation that more apples are taken when the prices are reduced. When you observe that I take more apples per week when the price per apple falls from a dime to a nickel, this does, in fact, tell you that both apples and dimes are goods in my utility function. If they were bads, I should be observed to do just the opposite.

It seems to me clear that in order to make the law of demand into the powerful proposition that Alchian wants it to be, he must introduce, at some point in his construction, *external* criteria of identification or definition for goods. He cannot rely on subjectively generated criteria to make the identification of goods which are then employed to derive predictive hypotheses about behavior. The external source in *Homo economicus* is apparently straightforward (at least on the producing or supply side; things are much more fuzzy on the consuming or demand side). Alchian, however, along with many other economists, does not really want to work within the constraints imposed by the *Homo economicus* assumptions about human motivation. He seeks to explain behavior that remains outside the explanatory potential of the limited set of hypotheses derivable from the behavior of simple economic man. He apparently accomplishes his objective by allowing the set of goods to be expanded to include many things vulgarly classified as "noneconomic." No objection can be raised to this procedure at all so long as precise identification is made and so long as it is clear that this identification is made on the basis of criteria other than the behavior that is to be predicted or explained in the first place.

This step need not necessarily be difficult in particular applications. Most men do value pretty secretaries, and "prettiness" can be objectively measured. Hence, the famous Alchian prediction that nonprofit institutions will be observed to employ relatively more pretty secretaries can be falsified. But just what hypothesis is being tested? That men place value on pretty secretaries? What is there about the law of demand that adds anything to this? If men value something, the so-called law of demand seems redundant; it is excess baggage, so to speak. Is this what Frank Knight really meant when he talked about economists' proving that water runs downhill?

Let us suppose, however, that these minor quibbles are neglected and that we are able, successfully, to identify externally the set of goods in individuals' utility functions. So long as our observations indicate that men seek the good and shun the bad, so identified, can we then say they are behaving economically? What content is there left in the term *economic behavior* here?

Let me tell you how I got into all this. Consider the following example. Suppose that a person has finished his picnic lunch on a public beach and that he has some refuse or garbage to dump somewhere. He knows that a refuse bin is a half-mile down the beach. He also knows that no overt sanctions will be imposed on him if he litters the beach by simply dumping the refuse nearby. Can economic theory help us in providing an explanatory hypothesis about his behavior? Both an unlittered beach and time may be goods in the individual's utility function. But we cannot say anything at all about which alternative he values more highly, anything at all about his subjective rate of trade-off between the two goods. We can, however, introduce apparent operational content by allowing the trade-off that he confronts to be modified and by observing his change in behavior. Suppose, now, that the refuse bin is removed to one mile down the beach. We can then hypothesize that relatively more litter will be dumped on the sand and less in the refuse bin. This behavior may, it seems, be plausibly classified as "economic."

To this point there should be no quarrel. However, we should note that we have implicitly accepted a somewhat strange usage of the word *economic* to describe behavior here. We are not necessarily observing the old Adam that is *Homo economicus*. Interestingly, to me at least, a person who, in his every act, behaves in strict accordance with the Kantian generalization principle would also behave "economically" in this context. So long as *both* the unlittered beach and time are goods in his utility function, he will obey the law of demand in his behavior. The pure Kantian will, at some point, dump refuse on the sand rather than walk to the refuse bin, even when he generalizes his behavior to all members of the community. This suggests that we are unable, as economic theorists, to develop hypotheses that will allow us to distinguish by behavioral observation between those persons who act according to their own narrow self-interest and those that behave in accordance with the ethical principles laid down by Kant.

This has extremely important implications for the discussion of policy. If men do, in fact, behave in accordance with some version of the Kantian imperative, potential externalities, in the normal usage of this term, will tend to be internalized within the calculus of the actors. Individuals will tend to take into account the effects of their own actions on the situation of others than themselves. Hence, in such a world there can be no need for corrective collective or governmental intervention in the private decision processes. It becomes impossible to observe "market failure" in the standard sense. We simply have no means of determining the extent to which men as they are actually behaving are internalizing potential externalities.

I doubt that any objections can be raised at this point, but it does seem plausible to hope for a somewhat more restrictive economic theory, one that might allow a distinction between "economic" and "noneconomic" behavior, between narrow self-interest and enlightened self-interest. To do this we must move outside and beyond the Alchian limits. We must do something more than identify "goods" in the utility function. We must say something specifically about the subjective trade-offs among such "goods." We should, somehow, like to be able to say that the person behaves *economically* when he is observed to dump the litter on the sand and to say that he behaves *noneconomically* when he walks all the way to the refuse bin. But this step is a difficult one to take. Just how much need the payoffs vary to enable us to say where "economic" behavior stops and "socially responsible" behavior begins? And vice versa? Once we plug in some numbers, even if we could do so, we are already perhaps beyond the limits of absurdity.

Some of this can be illustrated by numbers in the familiar prisoners' dilemma setting, discussed in chapter two. Consider the matrix below. As shown, the matrix has no empirical content at all, since the numbers that represent positive payoffs to A and to B from actions 1 and 2 can be in "utils." We must plug in some external meaning to the payoffs. Suppose we put dollar signs in front of the numbers. This allows us to make positive and quite specific predictions about behavior. Both A and B will follow strategy 2; if they do not, the hypothesis predicting strict economic behavior is falsified. So long as the payoff to an individual from one course of action exceeds that

	B	
	1	2
A		
1	50, 50	20, 60
2	60, 20	30, 30

expected from another course of action, we predict that he will adopt that course of action. He will select the *highest* payoff. This is simple, direct, operational. This is *Homo economicus.* Despite the fact that in the matrix illustration both 1 and 2 yield expected goods in both A's and B's utility functions, the conversion of these into numerical value indicators allows us to make specific predictions that can be tested against observations. If Kantian rules of behavior should prevail, the hypothesis is falsified. The economist's predictive science breaks down.

Something of this nature seems to have been in the minds of those who have criticized economic theory and economic science. As economists, I think that we may have been too defensive and defensive in the wrong way. We have been too prone to respond to the Carlyle-Ruskin criticism by saying that our behavioral assumptions are much less restrictive than the naive criticism implies. We retreat from the attack by saying that, after all, we can explain behavior regarding such goods as the well-being of others, cultural and social relationships, etc. As we have moved defensively in this direction, I think that we have often lost sight of the drainage of predictive content from our science. Would it not have been better to adopt the Frank Knight defense? That is, to admit, openly and directly, that economic behavior is only one aspect of man's reality; to accept the limits of our science; and to accept the role of scientific isolationists rather than that of scientific imperialists.

In the more restricted domain of *Homo economicus,* we can define market failure. Indeed, markets *necessarily* fail when the joint or social maximum exceeds the sum of private maxima, as externally objectified and measured. The prisoners necessarily confess. The political economist's role is clear; he identifies instances of market failure. He sorts out the various sorts of externalities. And, much more than this, he can lay down directions of adjustment that are required to produce efficiency. He can make quite specific proposals for correction. The firm with the smoking chimney can be assessed for the damages caused to the laundries of the neighborhood housewives. And this is all there is to it. The answers fall out readily from the model, and systematic correction for pervasive market failure requires only the turning of a few relevant cranks in the machine of economic theory.

The obvious difficulty in all this is that the modern welfare economist has been all too ready to do just what I have suggested, almost in caricature, without having bothered at all to inform himself about the implicit motivational assumptions of his model. He must adopt *Homo economicus* in a very strictly defined sense. And, if men behave this way in market interactions, what basis is there for presuming that they behave differently in nonmarket interactions, and specifically those that will be required for carrying out the corrections for market failure. Empirical evidence drawn from the observations of "economic" behavior in the general and noneconomic Alchian methodological world provides no basis for judgment about the usefulness of the market failure models which are based on normally restrictive economic motivational assumptions.

It seems to me that rather early in the game a conflict emerges between the use and the abuse of economic theory in a *predictive scientific* sense, and its use in what we may call an *explanatory* sense. If I may speak loosely here, we may think of a tradition stemming from the classical economists and running through Marshall to Friedman and the other modern positivists, a tradition that is essentially predictive. On the other hand, and by comparison and contrast, we can think of a tradition with some classical roots also but extending directly from the Austrians, and notably through Wicksteed, Knight, Hayek, and Mises, in which tradition the role of economic theory is largely if not wholly *explanatory.* The main point of this paper is to raise the question, Where does Professor Alchian fit in all this? His position, if I interpret him correctly, seems to face both ways. He appears to seek directly testable implications of his theory, and in this sense he seems to stress predictive content. Yet, as I have indicated, he extends the motivational hypotheses so broadly as to make effective refutation of hypotheses extremely difficult if not impossible.

The whole discussion could, however, be treated as an essay in my own confusion. I find myself simultaneously being pulled in both directions, and I suspect that critics may classify some of my works as falling within one camp and some as falling within the other. On the one hand, I can appreciate the merit in restricting utility functions so that market failure becomes a meaningful prediction in some objectively measurable sense. The whole theory of externality does tell us something about markets, something that should allow us to make predictions. At the same time, however, this same theory should also be extended to tell us something about government failure. And the theory of political externality should enable us to make predictions about the behavior of individuals in nonmarket settings. We should not be allowed to have it both ways, as seems to have been characteristic of many modern welfare economists. We should not be allowed to restrict the utility function of individual actors in the market setting, including those interactions that embody externalities, and then treat the utility function of these same actors as completely open-ended when they are placed in political decision-making roles. The diagnosticians of market failure seem to me to be duty-bound to diagnose political or governmental failure.

On the other hand, I can appreciate the explanatory power that is forthcoming when we allow utility functions to incorporate as goods almost anything that might motivate persons to act. There is a genuine aesthetic satisfaction in being able to say that the tools of economic theory remain applicable over noneconomic ranges of human behavior, to be able to respond to those critics who charge us with purveying crass materialism that exploits and isolates the worst motives in the human breast. And the explanatory potential is, I think, real. Men require a vision of the social order in which they live, and the "economic point of view" can be instrumental in providing persons with a vision of social order that is not chaotic, uncontrolled, and unplanned. This suggests, of course, that economic science or economic theory serves a didactic purpose, as we all must recognize. And in one sense, modern welfare economics represents a shift from the didactic theory of classical and neoclassical economics. It is therefore understandable that this modern attack on the classical paradigms finds its roots in Marshallian economic science, translated most directly through Pigou and all of the post-Pigovians, which science includes most of us in one form or another.

We can expand the explanatory potential of economic theory, however, only at a cost. Let me take the economics of charity or income redistribution as an example. There is now considerable research work, both theoretical and empirical, devoted to the economic theory of income transfers, private and public. Almost all of the scholars working in this field commence with an attack on the neoclassical dichotomy between resource allocation and income distribution. They point out that charitable motives are present in human beings, and that utility functions can readily be expanded to include arguments for the income levels of others (in money or in kind, or in utility levels themselves). From this, they proceed to set up plausible models that allow equilibrium conditions to be defined, that allow institutional structures to be examined, and predictions about institutional changes to be made. As suggested, this sort of discussion is helpfully explanatory. It is satisfying to be able to *understand* charity, with the tools of simple economic theory.

The cost of this extension is not so evident, but it must be recognized nonetheless. We can "explain" charity by an extension of the economist's model, and we can remain in predictive limits when we "explain" the market's failure to provide the "public good." But we cannot, as a next step, also explain the governmental redistribution that we observe to take place as reflecting the revealed preferences of persons for income redistribution and then, in turn, use this for either normative or predictive purposes. If the economist extends his own professional tools to explain this behavior, to produce an understanding of this behavior, the same economist cannot then use these tools as instruments of control, even in the most indirect sense. (The error here is pervasive in many areas of economics. It is often made by students of socialist planning, as pointed out by Craig Roberts, when they try to derive the objective function from the revealed behavior of the planners and then, in turn, use the objective function so derived for making statements that are thought to take the form of normatively meaningful advice.)

For the economist who utilizes *Homo economicus,* who can identify market failure, I have suggested above that he is under an obligation to identify government or political failure. For the economist who drops *Homo economicus* in favor of an open-ended utility function, no failure can be recognized. He cannot identify market failure, but neither can he identify government or political failure. It is as much of a sin for Mises or his followers to decry government failure on the basis of their empirically empty model as it is for Bator to neglect governmental failure in his extremely restricted model.

I feel much of the same ambivalence toward the explicit introduction of transactions costs into the body of economic theory. There is much explan-atory potential in the transactions-costs notion, and it helps us to *understand* aspects of observed economic reality. Just as with the extended utility func-tions, however, the additional understanding comes at a cost. Scientific pre-dictive content in the theory is reduced; the whole structure of analysis be-comes less discriminating in the predictions it can make. If men behave economically, and if transactions costs can be neglected, our tools enable us to predict that prices paid by all buyers in a market for a physically homo-geneous commodity will be equivalent. If we allow our actors to behave dif-ferently, to consider nonpecuniary aspects of the buying relationship, for ex-ample, the prettiness of the salesgirls, or if we allow transactions costs to make retrading inefficient, this central theorem of price equivalence cannot be tested. When we observe the absence of price uniformity, should we re-treat into the generalized escape routes or should we simply admit the limi-tations of our science? As I have indicated, I do not think that the arguments are all on one side here.

I am reminded of George Stigler's early paper on built-in flexibility and average cost curves. He explained, you will recall, how profit-maximizing firms which face demand and output uncertainties may find it advantageous to build plants so that they will remain tolerably efficient at many levels of output rather than optimally efficient over much narrower ranges. The anal-ogy with economic science seems close. We do increase, and substantially so, the explanatory flexibility of economic science when we incorporate such things as open-ended utility functions, transactions costs, threshold-sensitive behavior. But in the process of adding this flexibility, efficiency in making pre-cise predictions is lost. Properly extended, economic theory can, of course, ex-plain everything, but this is familiarly equivalent to saying that it predicts nothing.

My own prejudices, no doubt apparent from my own work, suggest that economic theory may be extended somewhat differently. My preferred ap-proach is one of holding onto the predictive power provided by *Homo eco-nomicus* while moving beyond the market relationship strictly defined. As the predictive power of this central motivational assumption is progres-sively weakened as we shift further from the simple exchange interaction, we should forthrightly acknowledge the limits of our science.

In practice, of course, the difference between the approach that I have here associated with Alchian and my own becomes minimal. When my purpose is didactic, I am quite willing to fall back on the extended utility function or transactions costs to assist me in explanation. And when Alchian's purpose is policy oriented, he is quite willing to talk about one set of property rights as being more likely to produce desirable results than another. Indeed, his whole interest in property rights and institutional arrangements would be difficult to explain were it not for the fact that Professor Alchian does, implicitly perhaps, adopt his own version of *Homo economicus.*

PART TWO

Competition and Entrepreneurship

Cognition, Choice, and Entrepreneurship

James M. Buchanan and Alberto di Pierro

I. Introduction

This paper is aimed at clarification of ambiguities in the treatment of the relationship between uncertainty and choice, and with special attention to this relationship as it impacts on entrepreneurial choice. Much of the received doctrine in the theory of choice-under-uncertainty seems to reflect a fundamental neglect of the distinction between cognition and choice itself, a distinction partially reflected in our title.

In Section II, we return to the classic work of Frank H. Knight, and we summarize his conclusions while emphasizing the setting within which the whole analysis was conducted. Section III compares and contrasts Knight's analysis with that of G. L. S. Shackle, with reference to their quite different conceptions of uncertainty. In Section IV, the role of information in reducing cognitive uncertainty is discussed. Section V examines individual choice within structures that embody cognitive certainty. In this section, the longest in the paper, we offer a criticism of the standard utility analysis of choice behavior under Knightian risk. In Section VI, we shift attention to individual choice behavior with structures that embody cognitive uncertainty, and with particular reference to entrepreneurial choice. In Section VII, we offer some general conclusions of the analysis.

From *Southern Economic Journal* 46 (January 1980): 693–701. Reprinted by permission of the publisher.

II. Risk, Uncertainty, and Profit in Neoclassical Competitive Structures

The remembered contribution from Knight's *Risk, Uncertainty, and Profit*[1] is the categorical distinction between risk and uncertainty. Knight defined risk to be the nonpredictable element in outcomes that might be generated from an experiment or structure in which the pattern of outcomes over a sequence or over a whole population of events is objectively known in some probabilistic sense, or at least may be conceptually determined. He defined uncertainty as the unpredictable element in outcomes that might be generated from a structure or process in which no such probabilistic features apply. It is important to understand the intellectual setting which offered the background for Knight's distinction and, in particular, to understand the problem that he conceived his distinction to resolve.

Knight thought of his work as offering a critique of the then-orthodox neoclassical economic theory and, notably, as represented in the works of Alfred Marshall, works that exercised a dominating influence in English-language scholarship. *Risk, Uncertainty, and Profit* was conceived as a tidying up, a filling in of what seemed to be logical gaps in the structure of analysis. In particular, Knight tried to explain the logical place of profits and to distinguish profits categorically from factor returns. He sensed the confusion involved in lumping together the wages of management, the interest returns on investment, and the payments for risk-bearing (all of which can be considered factor returns, and thereby subject to determination in a competitive process) along with the rewards (positive or negative) to those who bear uncertainty, rewards that are not equilibrated in any working of competition.

Risk and uncertainty are alternative *properties of structures* that have differing implications for the theory of the competitive economic process. These properties are not directly related to a theory or analysis, normative or positive, of individual *choice* or decision. Knight did not think of himself as making a contribution to the theory of choice, and he did not really raise the issue as to whether or not his risk-uncertainty distinction had any relevance for such a theory. It is only later, after the development of the models of for-

---

1. Frank H. Knight, *Risk, Uncertainty, and Profit* (New York: Houghton Mifflin, 1921).

mal choice theory, that individual choice behavior under uncertainty came to be an object of scholarly attention.

III. G. L. S. Shackle and Choice-under-Uncertainty

By contrast with the work of Frank Knight, that of G. L. S. Shackle has been largely devoted to the theory of individual choice or decision, as indeed the titles of some of his books suggest (*Decision, Order, and Time* and *Epistemics and Economics*[2]). Shackle ties choice directly to uncertainty, and he argues that without uncertainty choice does not take place in any meaningful sense. With certainty, the individual cannot be said to "choose" at all. In the Shackle perspective, the Knightian distinction between risk and uncertainty vanishes at the level of individual choice. The word "uncertainty" refers to different things in the two perspectives because the objects of analysis are different. To Knight, as noted, uncertainty is a property or descriptive characteristic of a structure or system. To Shackle, uncertainty is a property of an individual decision setting. Hence, an individual's choice alternatives may be "uncertain" even in a structure of interaction, in an experiment, that may be described as embodying risk rather than uncertainty in the Knightian sense. Consider a person who is allowed only one draw from an urn that is known to contain x red balls and y black balls. To the chooser, "red" and "black" are rival hypotheses. Choice between these two alternatives is necessarily made under uncertainty regardless of the information content of the experiment and regardless of the characteristics of the structure.

More formal theorists have been, like Shackle, concerned with individual choice behavior, and, also like Shackle, they have tended to combine situations embodying Knightian risk with those embodying uncertainty. The central problem discussed has been the degree and manner of applying a probability calculus, in either a positive or a normative sense, to the individual choice process.[3] Shackle's life-long debate has been with those who, in his view, inappropriately use such a calculus.

2. G. L. S. Shackle, *Decision, Order, and Time* (Cambridge: Cambridge University Press, 1961); *Epistemics and Economics* (Cambridge: Cambridge University Press, 1972).

3. For a critical review of the literature, see the first essay in Kenneth Arrow, *Essays in the Theory of Risk-Bearing* (Amsterdam: North Holland, 1971).

IV. Information and Structural Cognition

Quite clearly, Knight uses the word "uncertainty" to refer to something different from those discussed later by Shackle and by most of the modern choice theorists. It is perhaps not surprising that ambiguities have appeared. Our purpose in this section is to clarify the issues. We do so, first, by making the basic distinction already alluded to, namely that between *properties of structure* and *properties of choice*. By structure, we refer to the whole set of possible outcomes that might be generated by the "rules" of the "game," along with the "rules" themselves. As noted above, the Knightian distinction applies to properties of structure, and he classifies these in two mutually exclusive sets, those embodying risk and those embodying uncertainty.

The distinction here may be clarified if we introduce the role of information in the potential classification process. Consider, first, an "experiment" or "game" in which there do exist objective probabilities that are potentially assignable to outcomes, that is, a structure that embodies Knightian risk. This is idealized, of course, in the familiar ball-and-urn or fair-coin example. Individuals who are evaluating such a structure of experiment may not, however, know what the objective probabilities are. They may not possess full and complete information about the descriptive characteristics of the structure. In this setting, information acts to bring the *cognition* of the observing-evaluating person toward the objective realities of the experiment itself. This conclusion holds whether the information is obtained through an observation of a sequence of outcomes, through some exchange of results with other persons, or through some analytical modelling of the observed structure, independent of the outcomes.

We may, if desired, discuss this evaluative convergence in terms of subjective and objective probabilities. To the extent that a person evaluates a structure without complete information as to its predicted working properties or descriptive characteristics, his evaluation (which must be subjective in all cases) may, of course, be different from that evaluation that he would make if he should possess such complete information. As the information content of his evaluative behavior is increased, his subjective probabilities assigned to the structure will tend to converge toward those that are objectively determinate. At the limit, when information is complete in the relevant sense, there is no difference between the subjective probability assignment of the evaluator and the objective probabilities assignable by the structure itself, by "God" as it were.[4]

We designate structures that meet these requirements as embodying *potential cognitive certainty*.

Now consider a structure of interaction, a game, in which there do not exist objective probabilities that can be potentially assignable to the pattern of outcomes, even by some omniscient being external to the operation of the structure itself. Such a structure embodies Knightian uncertainty rather than risk. In this setting, information plays a wholly different role. The accumulation of information cannot, even in some conceptually limiting or extreme idealization, produce cognitive certainty about the operation of the structure, about the predicted pattern of outcomes in some objectively probabilistic sense.

We designate structures that meet these requirements as embodying *cognitive uncertainty*.

Note, however, that to this point we have said nothing at all about *choice* or the *properties of a choice setting* that an individual finds himself in. Whether the structure embodies cognitive certainty or cognitive uncertainty, the choice behavior of the individual must take place under uncertainty as to the prospect or outcome of a necessarily unique decision or selection. It would appear to be evident that, if the basic structure embodies cognitive uncertainty, there would be no reason to expect or to predict that any two persons, faced with the same choice alternatives, would choose similarly. Since, by definition, there exists no stochastically determinate pattern that can describe the structure, the individual's choice among alternatives for single decisions within such a structure cannot be brought within any expected value calculus.

V. Individual Choice in Structures Characterized by Potential Cognitive Certainty

The issues here become considerably more complex when we shift attention to individual choice within structures that embody cognitive certainty. Here

---

4. It is in this setting that the argument to the effect that subjective probabilities approach objective probabilities as information accumulates applies. It is also in this setting that the Aumann discussion of information exchange becomes relevant and important. See Robert J. Aumann, "Agreeing to Disagree," *The Annals of Statistics* 4 (1976): 1236–39.

the stochastic character of the pattern of outcomes is potentially knowable. Consider the urn example, and assume that a potential chooser has sufficient information to enable him to assign a prior of one-half on drawing a red ball on any one round. That is to say, his subjective probabilities are equivalent to the objective probabilities in reality. But this equivalence applies only to the individual's cognition of the structure. Assume that he is put into the position where he must actually choose *red* or *black* on a single round of play, and further assume that the consequences of his choice involve measurable opportunity cost. By construction, the individual cannot choose both colors and assign a one-half probability coefficient to each. He must select one option or the other in a mutually exclusive set.

A second person, placed in the same situation, would be expected to possess cognition about the structure that is equivalent to that possessed by the first person. The two would agree cognitively. It is, however, improper to infer from such cognitive agreement that they would make the same choice on any particular draw or that they would be *indifferent* as between the two prospects, between *red* and *black* in the urn example.

The theory of individual utility-maximization under risk is confused at this point when it suggests that individuals would accept fair gambles only if (1) they enjoy gaming, as such, or (2) they are risk lovers.[5] If the individual, faced with a single choice within a structure embodying cognitive certainty, is not indifferent as among the choice alternatives offered in reflection of the objective characteristics of the structure itself, it would be possible to rearrange the odds such that indifference would emerge at some offer of alternatives that would make the expected value of the choice prospect negative, that would make the gamble unfair. Suppose, for example, that there are actually 50 red balls and 50 black balls in the urn, and that this is known by everyone, including the person who is to make the single draw. Further, the drawing or selection process itself is known to be random. When forced to choose, however, a person selects *red*, and indicates that he is not indifferent

5. See J. Hirshleifer, "Investment Decision under Uncertainty—Choice Theoretic Approaches," *Quarterly Journal of Economics* 79 (November 1965): 509–39, for a summary of the prevailing theory. In his second paper, "Investment Decision under Uncertainty—Applications of the State Preference Approach," *Quarterly Journal of Economics* 80 (May 1966): 252–77, Hirshleifer acknowledges the relevance of "playing hunches" in explanations of gambling. He attributes little importance to this element, however.

as between *red* and *black*. Observing this, some other observer may offer a gamble that involves, say, a 49 per cent prospect of *black* emerging from the single draw. Consistency would require that the chooser accept the bet (or some appropriately scaled one that is analogous), even when he recognizes, at some cognitive level, that the expected value of the offer is negative.

To accept similar offers or bets over a whole sequence of draws would indeed seem irrational, given the choice setting and the constraints as specified. But, in the example, there is only one round of play, only one draw, and there are only two possible outcomes, *red* and *black*. As Shackle says, these are mutually exclusive and rival hypotheses. In the cognitive sense, we have postulated that the chooser knows the objective possibilities. But he also knows that any observed pattern of outcomes or results maps into these objective probabilities only over a sequence of draws. It is highly confusing in this case to say that unless the chooser indicates indifference as between the two prospects his subjective probabilities differ from the objective probabilities. At the cognitive level, and as applied to the structure of the experiment or game, we have postulated the equivalence between the chooser's subjective probabilities and the objective probabilities. But this does not imply anything at all about the attitude toward the choice alternatives on a single draw or round of play.

Note that, if the chooser should exhibit indifference as among the prospects in a single draw or round, this result would imply *anonymity* in the choice alternatives, and this anonymity would, in its turn, remove choice from the picture. Structures do exist which embody such anonymity. Many lotteries are of this type. Persons invest in tickets; they do not *choose* specific colors or numbers. The difference between lotteries of this type and those that allow participants to choose among numbers is directly relevant to our discussion. In the anonymous prospect setting, the orthodox choice-theoretic argument concerning the motivation for gambling, for risk taking, seems fully correct. A person will voluntarily enter such a game for a single draw only if he prefers risk, or if he enjoys gaming, as such. As we move beyond this setting, however, as soon as we allow the choice among the alternatives to be real, as they are in the selection of a number, a color, or a side of a coin, the motivational setting may become quite different. There are, in effect, two steps in the choice process; the player chooses to enter or not to enter the game itself, and, further, he chooses the particular option or prospect within the set of alternatives presented. His evaluation of a particular prospect, *red* or *black* in the urn example, may dominate his choice behavior to the extent that he might enter a game that is explicitly unfair in some objective sense, even when he places no explicit value on gaming, as such, and even if he is risk neutral.

By saying that a person may, in such games, evaluate the particular outcome or prospect differently from the objective probabilities computable from the characteristics of the structure of the rules, we are not implying that his utility function exhibits a "taste" or "preference" for such outcomes or prospects, for *red* or *black,* in some aesthetic sense that could, under one usage of the term, be deemed "irrational." Our explanation is much more simple. A person may enter the single round of play, the single draw, *because he expects to win.* He may remain strictly risk neutral; he may place neither positive nor negative value on gaming as such; he may have no "taste" for particular outcomes. But he may act from a subjectively sensed precognition of the outcome for the single round.

As we have already suggested, there is a conceptual test of our hypothesis readily available. If a person is observed to enter a gaming situation in which the odds confronting him reflect a fair gamble, as determined by the structural characteristics of the experiment, and if when presented with an opportunity to do so, he refuses to change his selected prospect for some proffered compensation greater than zero, we have clear and definitive evidence that such person is acting from some motive *other* than risk preference and/or love of gaming. In the case at hand, there is evidence that the chooser is "playing his hunches" in the simple anticipation of gain.

We have deliberately restricted discussion in this section to situations that remain within the Knightian structural classification of risk. Once we move beyond these highly formalized experimental examples, the explanatory failures of the standard models of choice-under-uncertainty become more evident. Consider a case, introduced by Shackle, that falls between the formalized examples and the relevant economic decision-taking by entrepreneurs. A person is to observe a race between two horses. He has available all of the information on past performances. The pari-mutuel machines will assure him that the track will offer odds that reflect the composite attitudes of all other bettors. The person may have no personal preference for either horse. But, given the odds, he will select horse A and bet $2 on his winning the race. If he is asked to exchange his $2 ticket on A for a $2 ticket on B after he has made his bet but prior to the race itself, there would be little prospect that the bettor would agree to the exchange. He will not exhibit indifference as among the alternatives. The horse player here is estimating the probabilities differently from those with whom he bets. The odds do not sum to unity, in the sense relevant for informing the choices of the participants in the game.[6]

We do not propose to discuss the concept of "rationality" in detail here. But it will be useful to examine briefly the problem of testability. Is a chooser necessarily irrational when, in the face of full information concerning the structural properties of the experiment or game, he engages in an "unfair" gamble, or in a "fair" gamble when he does not prefer risk or enjoy gaming? Let us return to the urn example, and assume that the chooser selects *red* and bets 51 cents against the offer of 49 cents that *black* will emerge on the single draw. Can we judge such behavior to be irrational in terms of *ex post* observation of error? Suppose that, after the wager, *black* does, in fact, emerge. But this result does not, in any way, corroborate the hypothesis that error was made in the choice *ex ante*. Even if the chooser could have found someone willing to wager 60 cents on *black* as against 40 cents on *red* he might also have lost the wager. *Ex post* results in situations of unique choices among prospects, where one of rival results must emerge, cannot be used to refute or to corroborate hypotheses of error in choice itself.[7]

VI. Individual Choice in Structures Characterized by Cognitive Uncertainty

In Section V, we examined individual choice under situations or structures where, at the level of cognition, persons might attain cognitive certainty

---

6. At the cognitive level, the priors of the participants in the game may converge, as suggested above, in which case the additivity property would hold. But even in this limit, such additivity need not carry over, analogously as it were, to the selection of the choice alternatives, to the actual choices made by participants. If there should be the equivalent to convergence in this respect, no bets could be made; no exchanges of wagers could be mutually advantageous.

7. "Previsions are not predictions and so there is no point in comparing the previsions with the results in order to discuss whether the former have been 'confirmed' or 'contradicted' as if it made sense, being 'wise after the event,' to ask whether they were 'right' or 'wrong' " (Bruno de Finetti, *Theory of Probability,* vol. 1 [New York: John Wiley, 1974], 207). See also Mario Rizzo, "Uncertainty, Subjectivity, and the Economic Analysis of Law" (New York University, 1978, mimeographed paper 78-02), 8, 22.

about patterns of outcomes, provided that they secure full information. Even in such structures, choice takes place under "uncertainty" in the sense advanced by Shackle. For particular choice events, for specific rounds of play, there need be no convergence in potential choice behavior as among several possible choosers or participants. Shackle's criticisms of formalized theories of choice-under-uncertainty have been primarily interpreted as applicable to choices made within structures that we have designated as embodying potential cognitive certainty.

Since, to Shackle himself, the distinction we have developed is irrelevant to his purposes, his critics have interpreted his target to be choice made in situations where the alternative outcomes of an experiment are known, and where, at some extreme cognitive level, there does exist an objective probability distribution among such alternatives over a sequence of events. To this known set of alternatives, a potential chooser is presumed able to assign, first, a set of payoffs or utilities, and, second, a set of probability coefficients. Discussion in formal models of the probability calculus and in decision theory have almost all been concentrated on the two assignment problems noted.

Shackle's critique does indeed apply to these highly structured and formal models of choice-making. But it also applies, and in a more persuasive sense, to those situations where choice is made in settings that embody genuine Knightian uncertainty. Despite his continued emphasis in the act of creativity that is necessarily involved in choice itself, Shackle does not seem to have sensed that the properties of the structural setting within which choice is made may exert significant influences on what we might call the "psychology of choice" itself.

Our distinction between structures embodying potential cognitive certainty and those embodying cognitive uncertainty seems important in this respect. With entrepreneurial choice, as in many other choices confronted by individuals, the alternative outcomes, the possibles, cannot be fully known at the time of choice itself. There exists basic uncertainty, at the cognitive level, about the set of possibles that might be realized upon choice or consequent to choice. In a very real sense, the entrepreneur creates his own opportunity set and the act of choice enters a new world that unfolds with choice itself. When this point is recognized, formal theories of probability have little or no contribution to make to our understanding of entrepreneurial choice.[8]

---

8. For a recent example of an attempt to force the formal model of choice-under-

At this point it is useful to refer to the modern Austrian theory of entrepreneurship, and notably as developed by Israel Kirzner.[9] The paradigm for
entrepreneurial choice becomes economic arbitrage, rather than the balls-
and-urns probabilistic calculus. Arbitrage opportunities arise when prices
differ between locations by more than transfer-transactions costs. Generalization of this notion suggests that profit-seeking entrepreneurs create
their own opportunities by sensing the cross-location, cross-style, cross-
material, cross-input, cross-technology, cross-output, cross-domain relationships which offer potential gains to all parties and which do not come
into being, do not exist, without entrepreneurial action. Kirzner's own example of the sore-footed caveman who saw a piece of cowhide and "created"
the possibility of shoes makes the point emphatically.

In entrepreneurial choice (or, more broadly, choice within structure that
embodies cognitive uncertainty), the role of precognition is enormously increased over that which it plays or might play in choices within structures
that embody cognitive certainty, at least potentially. As we have emphasized
above, the individual chooser may not be indifferent as among the separate
prospects offered in reflection of the objectively determined characteristics
of a contrived experiment. He may sense that a red ball will come up on the
next draw. When we consider individual choice behavior in the context of
Knightian uncertainty, where the set of outcomes is not and cannot be determinate, either in a definitional or in a stochastic sense, the very notion of
a strict calculus that involves expected value maximization under some subjective probability distribution becomes ambiguous and misleading.

The entrepreneur chooses a particular action because he thinks he can
make profits. "Playing one's hunches," calling on one's sensory precognition
about the potential profitability of then-nonexistent opportunities, dominates any calculus-computation of expected values. Indeed, there could
probably be no entrepreneurship at all if all choices were made on the basis
of expected values. On the average, net private returns to entrepreneurship
are probably negative,[10] and potential entrepreneurs do not necessarily prefer

---

uncertainty to apply to entrepreneurial decision, see B. Stigum, "Entrepreneurial Choice
over Time under Conditions of Uncertainty," *International Economic Review* 10 (1969):
427–42.

9. Israel Kirzner, *Competition and Entrepreneurship* (Chicago: University of Chicago
Press, 1973).

10. Net private returns to entrepreneurial activity may be negative, zero, or positive

to live dangerously. Instead, each entrepreneur confronts a unique situation, and he thinks he can see opportunities, can create opportunities, to make profits. He acts quite simply because he thinks he can win.

VII. Conclusions

This paper should not be interpreted as a critique of formalism, as such. It may be interpreted as a critique of the misapplication of formal theories of probability to choice, both in a positive and in a normative sense. Almost all of the formal theory of subjective probability retains direct relevance for the analysis of properties of structures that embody stochastically determinate patterns of outcomes. The role of information and information exchange in generating a convergence of priors, the role of experience and observation in modifying subjective estimates of predicted patterns, the whole of the Bayesian logic—these can be applied directly to the analysis of the individual's (any individual's) *cognition* of the structure within which he might or might not be required to or attracted to choose among alternative outcomes.

To extend this analysis, either in some positive, predictive sense or in some normative sense, to the individual's *choice* among the separate prospects once he is in the "game" represents a major intellectual leap that has not been adequately recognized. Cognitive knowledge about the structure of the experiment or game within which the individual choice is to be made will, of course, affect choice behavior. The person who knows that there are, in fact, 50 red balls and 50 black balls in the urn is in a "better" position, informationally, than someone who does not have this knowledge. But the presumption that he has such cognitive knowledge tells us nothing at all about his choice among a set of alternatives bounded within some limits. The informed player may refuse to enter certain "unfair" games that might not deter the ignorant player, despite a possible precognition of a particular outcome. However, within the relevant set of "reasonable" offers, there is no presumption that the player who is fully informed about the structure of the game will do better in choosing than the player who remains ignorant in this

---

while "social" returns remain positive. A divergence between private and social returns need not reflect "market failure," however, unless the divergence exists as the appropriately defined "margin" of activity.

cognitive sense. Cognitive knowledge may be of little value in the development of a "skill" or "sense" of emergent outcomes.

If this argument can be accepted even for the contrived ball-and-urn examples, its importance in extensions to individual choice made under any residual cognitive uncertainty should be evident. Entrepreneurial talent may not be readily amenable to analysis by the tools of modern decision theory. If this be the case, the direction of emphasis should be clear. We should drop attempts to apply irrelevant theory rather than to force incompatible material into a received analytical orthodoxy. It may or may not be possible to "model" entrepreneurial choice in a manner that is aesthetically satisfying to the formal theorist. But any modelling that leaves no room for the creative and imaginative elements in such choice lends confusion rather than enlightenment to our understanding of the well springs of economic progress.

Resource Allocation and Entrepreneurship

I. An Elementary Statement of the Coase Theorem

Persons trade when the relative evaluations of the units traded differ. When trade ceases, the traded units are held by those persons who place relatively higher value on such units than other persons. When there are no impediments to trade, all valued units are allocated to their highest valued uses, with values being settled at the moment of trade.

The elementary statements made above can be interpreted as one version of the now-classic Coase Theorem on the allocation of resources. But, as stated here, the question immediately suggested is, Why would anyone have thought differently? We can, I think, point to some reasons for the modern oversight of the quite elementary propositions that the Coase Theorem embodies. If we look, not at the *trading process,* but at the results, or end-states, of trade, and, further, if we look at the characteristics of equilibrium end-states, and implicitly make the assumption that all traded items are divisible into small units, the elementary statements made above do not hold. In equi-

From The Arne Ryde Symposium on the Economic Theory of Institutions, *Statsvetenskaplig Tidskrift* (The Swedish Journal of Political Science) 5 (1980): 285–92. Reprinted by permission of the publisher.

The author is indebted to Roger Faith for helpful discussion.

The critique developed in this paper involves the neglect of the entrepreneurship role in the theory of the resource allocation process of the economy. My critique is similar to and related to that advanced by Israel Kirzner in his book *Competition and Entrepreneurship* (Chicago, 1974). It also has close affinities with the classic work of Joseph Schumpeter, whose book *Theory of Economic Development* was published in its first version as early as 1911.

librium, all persons place the *same* relative evaluation on any unit of any traded item or commodity. Conversely, separate units have the *same* value in each use. The possible differential evaluations placed on inframarginal units of potential use become irrelevant in equilibrium adjustment. The relative evaluations placed on the inframarginal units will, of course, determine where the margins are located; that is, the evaluations over the inframarginal ranges will determine the final allocation of the total stock of any given traded item among separate traders, or among all projected uses or employments. In the simplest of trading examples, that of two-person trade in two goods (A and B trade apples and oranges), with given initial endowments, we cannot predict how many apples and how many oranges each person will have acquired when equilibrium is reached until and unless we know something about the evaluations over the inframarginal ranges of anticipated usage. We can say, however, that for the quantity of any item purchased in unimpeded trade, the purchaser will place a higher relative value on such quantity than anyone else. This statement holds even if, for a marginal unit (and any unit if marginal), relative valuations are identical as over all persons.

To this point, I have done nothing more than restate some of the most elementary principles of economics. I want, however, to use this restatement for a purpose. I want to examine some of the implications of the proposition that the stock of traded items is allocated among all potential purchasers or users so as to insure possession or ownership by those of the group who place the relatively highest value on all units of the stock. To my knowledge, the implications of this elementary proposition have not been fully explored.

II. The Allocation of Final Goods

Initially and by way of introduction, we may restrict analysis to trade in final goods, or consumption end-items. We can say, almost tautologically, that unimpeded trade will generate an allocation of a fixed stock of such a good among persons such that "utility," evaluated in some numeraire good, is higher than that achieved in any other conceivable allocation. Since, however, "utility" is not interpersonally comparable, this statement really adds nothing at all to understanding. There is no way of getting at the question, Why does Mr. A value the bundle of oranges that he retains in full-trading equilibrium more than Mr. B? To answer such a question, we should have to get "inside" Mr. A's utility function itself, something that economists have been reluctant to attempt.

Until and unless we could begin to answer such questions, however, there is no predictive content in economic theory at this level. By our unwillingness and/or inability to measure "utility," we insure that there is no empirical, "objective" content in analysis. There is no way that the economist can lay down presumably objective conditions or standards, which might be empirically checked, in order to guarantee efficiency (highest value) in the use of a final good. By his own methodological constraints, the economist is forced to search for his efficiency criteria by an examination of the trading process rather than by any examination or testing of the end results. The economic theory of the exchange economy, with initial endowments of final goods, must be beyond the pale for "positive economics" in the modern sense.

III. The Allocation of Intermediate Goods

The initial consideration of the proposition with respect to trade in final goods is useful for purposes of contrast and comparison with the implications for intermediate goods, those goods, resources, assets, or services that do not enter directly as end-items in the individual's utility function. These goods are traded, but they (or their services) are not consumed directly (transformed into utility). These goods are indirectly consumed via a productive process that involves their transformation into final goods and, through time, into "utility."

The characteristics of the trading process are unchanged. Such items or goods are allocated to their most highly valued uses to the extent that trade is unimpeded. But, if these items do not yield direct utility to their purchasers-users, why should they be valued *differently* by different persons? Complexities arise at this point if we remain within the certainty paradigm of much modern theory. If the "capacity to produce" is something inherent in a unit of intermediate good, and if this "capacity" is known with measurably objective certainty, and by all persons, it follows that all persons will value such a unit at precisely the *same* amount. In this case, we should observe no trade to take place. To rationalize or to "explain" trade in nonfinal or intermediate goods, therefore, we must introduce differences among potential traders in their subjective assessments of the potential "capacity" embodied in units of such goods. In general, a purchaser does not buy a fork-lift truck because he has a "taste" for this equipment. The prospective buyer must somehow think that a unit of an intermediate good or service has a higher capacity to produce final goods, and hence utility, in some ultimate sense, than does the person who might enter as a prospective seller on the other side of a trade.

Let me go through some elementary economics by way of getting to some of my main argument. Consider an example, that of a potential owner-operator of a warehouse who enters the market for fork-lift trucks. In the familiar diagram of Figure 1, we can depict his "demand" for units of the good, and, given the fixed supply price, he will purchase, illustratively, seventeen units. This quantity will maximize the purchaser's rental value of the complementary resource inputs (labor, pallets, space), as shown by the "buyer's surplus" triangle, S. We can think of this same owner-operator as entering the market for each one of these complementary inputs, and we might depict his surplus-maximizing solution in the same manner as that shown for fork-lift trucks in Figure 1. We can model his decision process as

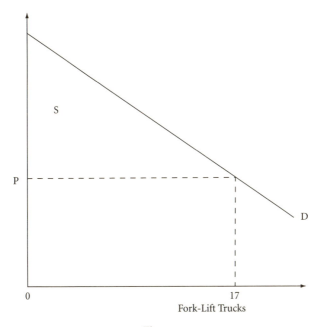

Figure 1

one of simultaneous determination of the surplus-maximizing rates of purchase (or hire or lease) in all of the input markets.

In full competitive equilibrium, the payment for all inputs will just equal revenues derived from the sale of the goods or services produced; there will be no economic profits. In his decisions, however, the owner-operator of the warehouse must seek, and he must expect to find, positive profits. He will try to maximize net surplus or net rents. If he has no anticipation of securing profits, over and beyond the required outlays on the resource inputs purchased, he will not, of course, organize production. That is, he will not "trade" with the suppliers of these inputs, since, by assumption, he has no "taste" for the inputs, as such.

IV. The Circulation or Evenly Rotating Equilibrium in the Stationary Economy

I get confused, however, when I try to think out the full implications of this elementary account of the behavior of the entrepreneur in a competitive environment. In full competitive equilibrium, as noted, we cannot allow for returns to pure entrepreneurship over and beyond the opportunity costs of the resource inputs actually used. But does this fact alone not suggest that an equilibrium becomes *logically* impossible? There seems to be nothing in the system to "make the wheels go round," so to speak. Schumpeter speaks about the circular flow in full stationary equilibrium, where all economic agents find that their expectations are fulfilled, and where they repeat the same behavior period after period, given no change in the exogenous parameters of the system (wants, resources, technology).

I can model such a circular flow process, the evenly rotating stationary state, under the assumptions of a pure exchange economy, in which each participant commences with an endowment of end-products, the same each period and received in some "manna-from-heaven" distribution. In such a setting, each person would repeat the same behavior in each period; he would trade the same units of his initial endowment for the more highly valued end-items in order to maximize his utility. Failure to behave in this fashion would mean lower utility attainment. The same prices will be reestablished in each period; the same final allocation of goods to persons will be consumed.

In a similar way, I have no difficulty with a production economy when each person is assumed to be endowed with a capacity to produce a single end-item, and where the use of this capacity is also an argument (a bad) in each person's utility function. Nor is there any difficulty in relaxing this restriction to allow that productive capacity may be used in producing several consumption goods, so long as we describe the utility function to include arguments for each use of the inputs. In both of these models of a production economy, the individual's utility maximization behavior will, just as in the pure exchange economy, lead to the same allocation of capacities in each period, the same set of prices, the same final allocation of consumption among persons.

The reason for the constant repetition of the equilibrium allocation, period after period, is found in the fact that each person, by behaving any differently, will be in a worse position. There must be differential advantages to be gained from behaving so as to generate the repeatable equilibrium solution, even if these advantages be infinitesimal at the appropriate behavioral margins.

Consider the case of a person who can produce either gidgets or widgets with his talents. Why would he spend two hours on gidgets and six on widgets each and every day? He would do so only because any different behavior would reduce his utility. Hence, producers' surplus serves the self-same allocation purpose as consumers' surplus in the allocation of final end-items.

As normally stated, however, producers' surplus, scarcity rents, profits, are not supposed present in the abstracted general equilibrium of the fully competitive economy. Owners of resource inputs are presumed to be confronted with alternative employments, each one of which yields the same return, and, further, these resource owners are presumed to be indifferent as among the separate potential uses. In such a setting, however, why will the equilibrium allocation be repeated period-by-period? Clearly, there is nothing unique in the solution if rents are wholly absent, even for a single, solitary unit of input.

I offer no answer to my own puzzle here. I leave this to the so-called "economic theorists," but you can see how this puzzle relates directly to my interest in entrepreneurship and its role in the allocative process. If rents or profits are allowed as possible, or even if they are only thought to be possible, entrepreneurial activity will "drive the system," and, of course, competitive entry will always put pressure on observed profits and rents such as to erode these. I ask only whether or not we have modelled an internally contradictory structure that leaves no room for producers' surplus, profits, or rents, and whether or not such a modelling has inadvertently modified the mindset of the economists who then come to think of idealized allocations without allocators.

Should we drop the very notion of general equilibrium, even as a logical construction, once we recognize the contradiction? Or should we try to reconstruct it so as to allow universalized producers' surplus? Note that if we allow entrepreneurs in the model, we do get a solution to the allocation problem, *ex ante*. All resource units flow necessarily to the most highly valued uses, as viewed by the entrepreneurs who implement and carry forward the input combinations and who organize production.

V. Optimistic Entrepreneurs

The potential producer, the entrepreneur, must be relatively "optimistic" about his ability to combine resources so as to achieve a positive rent or surplus. He places a higher expected value on the bundle of resource inputs that he decides to purchase than anyone else in the economy or trading network. What does this statement imply about realized values, about realized rents, surplus, or profits? As noted above, at the moment of entrepreneurial choice, expected returns, expected profits, must be positive. In competitive equilibrium, however, profits will disappear. To the extent that unimpeded trade, including freedom of entry and exit into and from all markets, generates any adjustment toward equilibrium, even if such a state is never attained, realized rents will tend to fall below expected profits. From this it follows that the entrepreneurs, as a group, or in some representative sense, must be *disappointed*. This result must hold despite the possible presence of individual cases in which realized rents might exceed expected rents. Realized rents or profits may range the spectrum from higher-than-expected levels at the one extreme to large negative values at the other. Entrepreneurs in the first group, that is, those whose initial optimism pays off beyond expectations, need not be disappointed. But, by necessity, these entrepreneurs represent only the tail of the distribution that we may assume to be symmetric in some fashion.

The tendency of the market process to insure that resources come into the usage and ownership of those persons who are most optimistic about their productivity, who place the relatively highest value of these resources *ex ante*, is, at the same time, reflected in the mirror image of ubiquitous entrepreneurial disappointment. Plans are not realized, and, on average, rents fall short of those anticipated. The disappointment of entrepreneurs has several important implications. Because plans do not live up to expectations, entrepreneurs will be led to turn over assets, to modify their projects, to change their rates of purchase of resource units more frequently than that rate that might be predicted under the standard assumptions that are imbedded in economic theory. Under the latter assumptions, error leading to negative profits may be made, leading to corrective adjustments on the part of entrepreneurs. When the generality of entrepreneurial disappointment is reckoned on, however, it becomes clear that entrepreneurs will tend to modify plans and to shift among separate projects even when realized profits may be positive, possibly strongly so.

For illustration, consider two separate projects undertaken by two separate entrepreneurs, projects that are not directly related, one to the other. Each of the two entrepreneurs expects to secure, say, $1000 in net profits when he makes the decision to organize production and proceeds to purchase the inputs required. (Note that we cannot define expected profits in terms of a "rate of return" on anything.) Both are typical, or representative, entrepreneurs, and, hence, are disappointed to find that realized profits, or surplus, amount to only $500 in each, each still positive but not so high as anticipated. Each entrepreneur, viewing the alternative project to his own, may now consider switching his efforts, despite the presence of an observed profit level that is no greater than that realized. It is quite possible to get such a switching among projects without any change in the total of profits realized. This result could not emerge under the standard assumptions of economic theory, which would suggest, in this example, that both of the entrepreneurs would remain in production of the projects initially commenced.

This tendency to shift resource combinations, to change projects, will, of course, be dampened to the extent that specificity is a necessary component of project choice. If an entrepreneur, in organizing production for an initial project, finds it advantageous to convert transformable units of resources into forms that are specific to the project, the differential between realized quasi-rents and the scrap or disposal values of assets may seriously inhibit the switching of production or production technique.

VI. Managerial Rotation[1]

One direct implication of this analysis of entrepreneurial disappointment involves the rate of turnover or rotation of managers of enterprises. Entrepreneurs hire managers to supervise production; managers are among the resource units purchased. But, by definition, managers "manage"; that is, they are expected to exercise discretion in the supervision of other input usage. Managerial talents tend to be readily transferable as among alternative employments. These qualities of management, combined with the ubiquity of entrepreneurial disappointment, suggest that managers will be quite vulnerable to discharge and rotation, and quite independent of any problem in the internal incentive structure that may affect the behavior of managers themselves. In other terms, the effect described here would occur even in the extreme case where managers behaved, in each and every instance, as if their own interest should be identical with that of the entrepreneur.

Professional sports enterprises offer an excellent real-world illustration of the argument here. Owners-entrepreneurs are optimistic about the prospects of franchises, and they tend to assign expected values to franchises in excess of any values that might be realized. They hire managers, and they tend to be disappointed with managerial performance, quite independent of any measure of the actual quality of managerial decisions. Frustrated when results do not match up to anticipations, owners fire managers and hire new ones, for the most part from the pool of available persons who have, themselves, been fired by other owners-entrepreneurs and for the same reason. We observe a high rate of managerial turnover without noticeable changes in the relative fortunes of the separate franchises.

VII. Entrepreneurship and Risk-Taking

Entrepreneurs act because they expect to make profits. Their action has no relationship to the bearing of risk or uncertainty, as such. An entrepreneur

1. The discussion in this section is due to a suggestion by Roger Faith.

may exhibit risk preference, risk neutrality, or risk averseness. To the extent that he is risk averse, the expected profit from any project necessary to bring him over the threshold of positive action will be greater than that which would be necessary under risk neutrality or risk preference. The risk-averse entrepreneur would never undertake a project that promises a marginally positive expected surplus, if there is risk or uncertainty involved.

It may be argued, further, that since each entrepreneurial choice is unique, genuine uncertainty must be present. As Shackle has stressed, since the properties of the whole experiment, which may embody Knightian risk rather than Knightian uncertainty, cannot be relevant to the unique choice that must be made, entrepreneurs must choose among actions that are necessarily uncertain as to outcomes. This argument may be, indeed must be, granted, but there remains the possibility of arraying, at least conceptually, the entrepreneurial choice situations in terms of their uncertainty characteristics. In the one extreme, an entrepreneur may be "relatively certain" that the outcome he predicts will, in fact, occur consequent to his action. The entrepreneur who buys wheat in one market and sells it simultaneously in another, and for a different price, is acting under conditions of "relative certainty." When we examine entrepreneurial choice under conditions of relative certainty somewhat more carefully, we can show that profits, the residual rewards to entrepreneurship, are not properly described or defined as a reward for risk or uncertainty bearing on an economy. Consider the entrepreneur-arbitrageur who buys wheat in one market and sells it simultaneously in another. There is little or no risk or uncertainty involved, and such an entrepreneur may be highly risk averse. The profit that he makes rewards him for his ability to "see" the profit opportunity and to act upon it. He is rewarded for "creating" value by sensing the differentials in price. Without such a prospect of reward the value would not, in fact, exist or come into being at all.

In most conditions for entrepreneurial choice, of course, decisions must be made under uncertainty, and entrepreneurs must, in one sense, accept such uncertainty bearing as a necessary characteristic of their choice situation. But a willingness to bear uncertainty is surely not a sufficient condition for entrepreneurship. There may exist many persons, who are genuinely risk-loving, and who will gladly take on the uncertainty of investments in projects that are presented to them. Such persons may, however, wholly lack any ability to see profit opportunities, to invent in their mind's eye new arrangements, new technology, new resource combinations. There may be no correlation at all between personal talents in this respect and personal proclivities to take risks.

VIII. Entrepreneurship and Time

To this point, I have done little more than recast slightly, and with the somewhat interesting managerial implications, the theory of entrepreneurship presented by Kirzner. I want now, however, to diverge from Kirzner's conception in one important respect, namely in his emphasis on the absence of any necessary relationship between ownership and entrepreneurship. I can appreciate Kirzner's purpose; he sought to divorce or to separate the economic function or role played by the owners of capital assets from the role or function of the entrepreneur. I have no quarrel with such separation, which is essential for logical clarity. As Kirzner emphasized, the pure entrepreneur need hold no assets at all. His idealization is the instantaneous arbitrageur, who simultaneously enters separate markets on differing sides, seeking profit in the process.

This idealization is a biased one, however, and is best described as an extreme end of a possible spectrum of models for entrepreneurship, and in no way "representative" of the sort of entrepreneurs Kirzner seeks to place in his motivating roles in a competitive economy. Almost universally, entrepreneurs seek their profits by holding, or owning, assets *through time* rather than the instantaneous arbitraging modelled by Kirzner. I do not suggest that they hold capital assets "as capitalists," that is, in order to secure a rate of return of the ordinary sort. Quite the contrary, and Kirzner is quite correct in stressing the difference here. My point is rather that, in order to engage in entrepreneurial arbitrage, defined in the large, most "traders" must work in time. They do not "hedge" as if they are the classic-case flour millers. Most entrepreneurs buy in one market *now*, and expect to sell in another market *later*, or vice versa, or at least I should argue that this is a more representative model of entrepreneurial activity than Kirzner's instantaneous or simultaneous model.

This model suggests that confusion about the pure entrepreneurial role is especially likely to emerge, since the temporal aspects suggest the risk or uncertainty-bearing function previously discussed as well as the capitalist or pure ownership function associated with the productivity of capital itself. The pure entrepreneur, however, sublimates as inessential or inconsequential *both* the risk-bearing and the ownership role, which he may, nonetheless, be required to occupy in order to take advantage of the profitable opportunity that he thinks he sees before him. The pure entrepreneur may, of course, borrow sufficient funds to finance the required outlay on the assets to be transferred to his ownership, and the rates at which he borrows may be even higher than any nominally computed "return" on the value of these assets. In this setting, the entrepreneur is not at all a "capitalist" in any net-asset or net-wealth sense. He may be, and probably is, more normally in a net debtor than a net creditor position. But nonetheless, the entrepreneur must secure, and hold, title to the particular asset, or asset bundle, that he purchases in order to secure for himself the anticipated profits from later resale at a higher price. This "arbitrage-through-time" model of entrepreneurship can incorporate examples extending from ordinary speculation in real estate through the organization of production of final goods and services.

IX. Entrepreneurship and Inflation

Unless the temporal setting within which entrepreneurial action takes place is recognized, the effects of anticipated inflation upon entrepreneurship, and, through this, on the dynamics of the economic process, tend to be obscured. Implicitly, or by presumption, the role of the entrepreneur, and of entrepreneurship, discussed in preceding sections of this paper is carried out in the context of an economy described by monetary stability, at least within limits of tolerance. That is to say, the individual entrepreneur, who purchases resource units for the purpose of exploiting a profit opportunity that is not universally seen by all participants in the economy, acts in the expectation of being able to create *real value,* as measured by the response of market participants when confronted with the opportunities that he constructs. Although individual entrepreneurs are not conscious of such unintended consequences, their action, in net, is generative of increases in real product value in the economy. Resources are reallocated via entrepreneurial creativity in such fashion as to increase overall value productivity.

Let us superimpose upon this dynamic model of economic process governmentally generated, continuous, and anticipated inflation. The predicted effects are clear. Opportunities for entrepreneurial profits emerge that do not necessarily generate increases in real value. Anticipated inflation opens up generalized opportunities for arbitrage-through-time rather than the specialized opportunities open to ordinary entrepreneurship in conditions of monetary stability. Attempted exploitation of the generalized opportunities here will drive up the prices of real-valued assets that are durable relative to prices of either nondurable goods or of claims to nominal-valued assets. The specialized opportunities for genuinely creative entrepreneurship will, of course, continue to exist, potentially, in the inflationary setting. However, exploitation of these opportunities is made more difficult by the relative bias introduced in the structure of temporally designated prices of goods. To take advantage of a genuine opportunity, an entrepreneur must secure title to real-valued assets. In order to do so, he must assume a fixed-value liability; he must issue "bonds," denominated in nominal yields. If the purchaser of such "bonds" (the seller of the real asset) and the entrepreneur place the same expected value on the anticipated rate of inflation, and, further, if this rate is universally expected by *all* persons in the economy, the effects that have been suggested here need not arise.

If, however, we allow the more plausible realistic model in which *some* but not *all* persons in the economy fully anticipate the inflation, the relative price bias note must emerge. This point is worth developing in some detail.

Assume that the government is committed to maintain a specific rate of continuing inflation. Assume, further, that the full effects of this policy are predicted by only *some* of the economy's participants (facetiously, we may call these "the economists"). Members of the latter group will see the arbitrage opportunities available to them as a result of their superior knowledge about the effects of the government's announced behavior. These persons (the "new entrepreneurs") will, therefore, reduce current holdings of money and nominal claims ("bonds") and increase current holdings of durable assets that are expected to appreciate in value over time. Prices of the latter assets will rise; prices of "bonds" will fall.

There is, however, no necessary intersection between the set of "true entrepreneurs" and that set of "new entrepreneurs" attracted to invest in real assets solely because of the anticipated inflation. For members of the former set who are not, simultaneously, members of the latter set, the terms-of-trade will have shifted dramatically against them. Potential profit opportunities which might exist in monetary stability vanish in the *ex ante* sense, and no entrepreneurial reallocation of resource toward generating higher real values takes place. The dynamic development of the economy is dampened.

The effect on economic process generated by this dampening of entrepreneurial activity is not inconsistent with *ex post* findings that, as a group, entrepreneurs secure relative gains from inflation. We get the somewhat paradoxical result that while inflation may substantially reduce the number of entrepreneurial projects, among those introduced there will be relatively few failures or bankruptcies. Entrepreneurs may gain, *ex post*, from inflation due largely to the net monetary debtor status or, what amounts to about the same thing, to entrepreneurs' necessary role in the temporal arbitrage process. To the extent, however, that the set of "new entrepreneurs," created by the inflationary expectations, and the "true entrepreneurs" do not match precisely, inflation must have the effect of preventing some resources from those employments or usages where they are most highly valued, in the *ex ante* sense. A land parcel held for potential inflationary gains by a "new entrepreneur" may not be worth the asking price to a "true entrepreneur," who may envisage genuine development prospects but who may not fully anticipate the inflationary effects of government policy. As a result, the economy produces lower real value than otherwise might have been produced.

Resources flow, via the activity of entrepreneurs, to those uses that promise the highest value, as estimated by entrepreneurs at the moment of market exchange. The introduction of inflation does not modify this basic proposition. But inflation does have the effect of distorting the prospective values estimated by entrepreneurs. In this context, it is worth keeping in mind that the "highest valued uses" do not exist independent of entrepreneurial estimates. "Highest valued uses" for resources are "created" in the imagination of entrepreneurs, and any distortion introduced into entrepreneurial estimates may destroy potential value never to be replaced.

As noted earlier, the effects of anticipated inflation discussed here take place only so long as some potential entrepreneurs fail to incorporate the correct inflationary anticipations in their own estimates. If and when *all* potential entrepreneurs come to act upon the same anticipated rate of inflation, along with all other participants in the economy, the distortions will, of course, disappear. Critical errors may be made, however, in the failure to distinguish between an inflation anticipated by *some* persons in the economy and an inflation anticipated by *all* persons in the economy. The state of "equilibrium expectations" describing the latter situation may not be reached until the end of an extremely long temporal sequence.

X. Conclusions

This paper has developed no central "theme" or "principle." It should perhaps have been entitled "Notes on Entrepreneurship." In writing this paper, in two versions separated by several months, I have had the feeling that many other implications than those discussed here would emerge. To this point, no others have dramatically appeared. I become more convinced, however, that a "breaking out" of the intellectual constraints imposed on so many of us by the equilibrium constructions of neoclassical economic theory is necessary if we are to understand the economic process properly, and through some such understanding, begin to get some handles on how the dynamic potential of the market order might, once again, be harnessed.

Entrepreneurship and the Internalization of Externalities

James M. Buchanan and Roger L. Faith

I. Introduction

In an idealized setting for the operation of markets, it becomes artificial and redundant to interpret the production-trade process itself as involving the internalization of potentially relevant externalities. Nonetheless, it may be useful to think of the ordinary operation of the market in these terms when we want to move beyond the economists' idealized construction to settings where "externalities," defined in the orthodox sense, may exist. In such settings, trade becomes only one among several institutional arrangements for "internalizing externalities." In this paper, we suggest that for the particular types of economic interaction consequent upon the inauguration of entrepreneurial ventures the internalization embodied in a well-functioning legal structure may be superior to either trade or overt political arrangements. Our purpose is to compare alternative means of "internalizing" potential externalities in terms of the effects on the activity of entrepreneurs, and, through such activity, on the pace of economic development.

Consider the two-party example made familiar by R. H. Coase in his now-classic paper on social cost.[1] At an elementary level of analysis, the interac-

Journal of Law and Economics (April 1981): 95–111. Reprinted by permission of the publisher.

We are especially indebted to our colleague Robert Staaf, whose combined law and economics expertise has, we are sure, kept us from some egregious blunders. But he cannot be held responsible for those that may remain.

1. R. H. Coase, "The Problem of Social Cost," *Journal of Law and Economics* 3 (1960): 1.

tion between the cattle rancher and the wheat farmer is not different from that between any two ordinary traders; indeed, this point was the fundamental one in Coase's argument. To the extent that the "externality" is Pareto-relevant, exchange will tend to take place, hence "internalizing" the effect and guaranteeing an efficient outcome.[2] Although much of his discussion was posed in terms of "liability for damages," the implicit model for Coase's analysis is one that assumes all property rights to be well defined and enforced and, hence, tradable.[3] In Calabresi-Melamed terms, the basic Coasian analysis presumes that entitlements are protected by a *property rule,* insuring that, absent transaction costs, the operation of the market will effectively internalize a potential externality.[4] We propose initially to compare and contrast the operation of a property rule with that of a *liability rule,*[5] both assumed to be operative in a regime that does not involve explicitly collectivized efforts at "internalization."[6]

Our concern is not with the comparative allocative results of alternative assignments of entitlements or rights, the question that is central for most of the Coase-theorem analysis. Instead, we concentrate on alternative results

2. For the basic definition of Pareto-relevant externality, see James M. Buchanan and William Craig Stubblebine, "Externality," *Economica* 29 (n.s. 1962): 371.

3. Compare H. E. Frech III, "The Extended Coase Theorem and Long-Run Equilibrium: The Nonequivalence of Liability Rules and Property Rights," *Economic Inquiry* 17 (1979): 254–68. See also James M. Buchanan, "The Coase Theorem and the Theory of the State," *Natural Resources Journal* 13 (1973): 579.

4. "An entitlement is protected by a property rule to the extent that someone who wishes to remove the entitlement from its holder must buy it from him in a voluntary transaction in which the value of the entitlement is agreed upon by the seller" (Guido Calabresi and A. Douglas Melamed, "Property Rules, Liability Rules, and Inalienability: One View of the Cathedral," *Harvard Law Review* 85 [1972]: 1089, 1092).

5. "Whenever someone may destroy the initial entitlement if he is willing to pay an objectively determined value for it, an entitlement is protected by a liability rule" (Ibid.). For a similar distinction that does not introduce the terms "property rule" or "liability rule," see James M. Buchanan, "The Institutional Structure of Externality," *Public Choice* 14 (Spring 1973): 69.

6. A. Mitchell Polinsky has comparatively analyzed the property rule, the liability rule, and tax-subsidy schemes. His emphasis is on static efficiency properties, degree of protection for entitlements, and the consequences of information, none of which is central to our analysis here. See A. Mitchell Polinsky, "Controlling Externalities and Protecting Entitlements: Property Right, Liability Rule, and Tax-Subsidy Approaches," *Journal of Legal Studies* 8 (1979): 1, and "On the Choice between Property Rules and Liability Rules," October 1978, National Bureau of Economic Research Working Paper 286.

under the differing institutional arrangements through which a specific assignment of rights is protected or enforced. In this respect the first part of our analysis is an extension of the Calabresi-Melamed discussion rather than that of Coase. Nor are we directly concerned with the static efficiency properties of the two arrangements, which was central to the analysis of Frech and, to a large extent, that of Polinsky. In the more-inclusive sense, we are interested in the "dynamic efficiency" properties of the alternatives examined.

We are also concerned primarily with lumpy projects or ventures rather than with marginal extensions of already-existing activities. We concentrate attention on the anticipated gains and anticipated damages consequent to the commencement of a new entrepreneurial venture. While some predictions as to the "rate of production" within the project, once started, must inform any estimates of gains or losses to the venture as a whole, the internal margin of adjustment (which has been the central focus of attention in almost all the analysis of externalities) is not of direct relevance for our purposes. The appropriate margin for our analysis is that between commencing and not commencing an entrepreneurial venture.

Comparisons that have been made of the effects of the property rule and the liability rule have concentrated on the differences in the strategic setting faced by the participants under the alternative means of protecting nominal entitlements. Under a property rule, where the permission of the party who may be potentially damaged must be purchased *in advance,* the bargaining position of the damaged party is much stronger than it is under liability-rule protection, where the potentially damaged party can file enforceable claims *ex post,* claims that will be settled by some third-party adjudicator. This differential in bargaining strength under the two rules will be present even if all parties, those inside as well as those outside the interaction, predict the same level of damages consequent on the inauguration of the entrepreneurial venture.

Our emphasis in this paper, however, is not directly on such *strategic* effects on behavior and on the predicted influences of such effects on results. Our emphasis is on the *subjective* aspects, and in particular on possible predictable differences between potentially estimated and realized damages.[7] We

---

7. R. Staaf and W. Wares emphasize the subjectivity of costs and benefits in externality relationships as a means of distinguishing tort law and contracts as alternative guarantors

shall argue that these aspects alone generate a predictable difference between the effects of the property rule and the liability rule under certain restricted conditions.[8] The effects that we stress here tend to reinforce and perhaps to overwhelm in importance those that may be traceable to the effects stemming from strategic influences on behavior in the two idealized legal settings.

Our comparison of legal arrangements will provide the basis for an analysis and examination of collective alternatives. As the institutional "internalization of externalities" shifts from that situation best described by the operation of law to one that is described by general collectivization of decisions on development, we can predict a dampening of entrepreneurial innovation, a closing off of opportunities for the implementation of optimistic expectations, a stifling of hope in the sense of continuing or accelerated growth based on technological advance.

II. The Costs and Benefits of Alternative Stylized Legal Arrangements for the Internalization of Externalities

We propose now to examine in more detail the costs and benefits that might be associated with the two stylized legal arrangements. We defer until Section III discussion of the actual operation of legal institutions. In Section IV we introduce explicit collectivization of the internalization process.

Return to the Coase example and assume that the wheat grower, himself a former entrepreneur, holds an entitlement to his crops that is protected by a strict property rule. No one can damage this entitlement without first securing the farmer's permission. Or, if someone indicated such an intent, the farmer could seek, and expect to be granted, an injunction that would effectively prohibit the enjoined activity. Suppose, now, that a new entrepreneur,

---

of efficiency in allocative results. They do not, however, extend their discussion to the dynamic effects that we examine here. See R. Staaf and W. Wares, "Individual Choice, Social Choice, and Common Law Efficiency" (University of Miami, December 1979, unpublished paper).

8. In a totally different context, we have demonstrated that differences in subjective estimates of the working properties of alternative institutions can exert predictable effects on joint decisions. See James M. Buchanan and Roger Faith, "Subjective Elements in Rawlsian Contractual Agreement on Distributional Rules," *Economic Inquiry* 18 (1980): 23.

a rancher, proposes to graze cattle on lands adjacent to the wheat, but that there is the prospect for straying and destroying crops. There is no reason for assuming that the two parties place the same anticipated value on the genuinely uncertain prospects for crop damage. Let us assume that the rancher estimates anticipated damages optimistically, at a low value, while the farmer estimates damages pessimistically, at a high value. The relatively more optimistic rancher thinks that his operation will be profitable within broad ranges of his damage estimates, but not if he is required to make payments at the level of damages estimated by the farmer. Under the strict property rule the rancher will be required to purchase grazing rights *before* any cattle are pastured. In the situation indicated, no bargains can be struck. No cattle will be grazed on the lands adjacent to the growing wheat.

If the wheat grower should estimate damages at a lower value than the entrepreneur-rancher, the strict property rule would not inhibit the commencement of the grazing operation since the permission of the farmer could be purchased at anticipated "bargain prices." In general, however, we should expect that entrepreneurs tend toward optimism, both with respect to the internal profit potential emergent on the productive activity and to the value of possible spillover damage. In any case, the strict property rule will prevent some projects from being undertaken.

Let us now assume that the wheat grower's entitlement in his crops is protected by a strict liability rule rather than a property rule. In this case, the rancher will put cattle on the lands if he thinks the operation profitable, even when he reckons on making damage payments. The farmer cannot prevent such entrepreneurial action. Under the liability rule, if the rancher's expectations prove correct, "development" will take place and will be validated *ex post.* The total product of the economy will be higher under the liability than under the property rule. On the other hand, if the entrepreneurial estimates are overly optimistic, the new venture will be unable to cover costs, and product value in the economy may be lower under the liability rule than the property rule. The costs of error, however, are borne by the entrepreneur, not by those who might suffer damages. In the net, the differential effects on total product value under the two rules cannot be predicted. But the differential effects on the development of new projects are clear; *more* projects will be carried forward under the liability rule than under the property rule.

We should stress that our comparison of the two legal arrangements is restricted to the effects on entrepreneurial decisions to begin new projects. We assume that "entrepreneurial vision" is limited to the profit potential in particular activities. This assumption allows us to rule out the merger option that would realize potential gains-from-trade emergent upon any difference in subjective estimates of spillover damage. In our example, if the rancher-entrepreneur estimates damages to be less than those estimated by the wheat grower, and if direct purchases of permissions to allow cattle to graze do not seem profitable under a property rule, the rancher might be able to buy out the wheat-growing operation with the prospect of managing the combined or merged activities.[9] This result requires, however, the presumption that the entrepreneurial talents of the rancher extend to farming as well. The assumption of entrepreneurial specialization is designed to rule out such merger options.[10]

For purposes of discussion here, we want also to rule out the prospects for contingency contracts which might serve partially to exploit the mutual gains to be had as a result of the differing evaluations placed on the uncertainty involved in the interdependence of the two activities. The rancher could offer the farmer a contract that commits him to pay full damages, as measured by a third party, *plus* some premium. The farmer may accept if he considers third-party adjudication reasonably accurate. In this way, some of the slow-down effects of a property rule may be mitigated, although the direction of effect remains. In the presence of transaction costs, the working out of such contingency contracts may prove difficult. Quite apart from transaction costs of the ordinary sort, the bankruptcy potential may inhibit the implementation of contingency contracts in situations where the value of the interdependence looms large relative to the value of the direct production.[11]

9. As Frech notes, much of the Coase theorem discussion has proceeded on the assumption that the merger option is ruled out by transaction-cost differentials. Polinsky, for example, tends to ignore the merger option.

10. Failure to recognize the mutuality of advantage from merger, under the restrictive assumptions of the Coase-theorem analysis, led Greenwood and Ingene to argue that the basic Coasian proposition on resource allocation is incorrect under differing attitudes toward uncertainty. See Peter Greenwood and Charles Ingene, "Uncertain Externalities, Liability Rules, and Resource Allocation," *American Economic Review* 68 (1978): 300.

11. We should also note that, given the property rights assignment assumed in our ex-

Calabresi and Melamed suggest that a liability rule may be more desirable in certain situations because of the holdout power that a strict property rule grants to the holders of existing entitlements. As noted above, our argument reinforces the Calabresi-Melamed support of liability rules by our introduction of the predicted difference in subjective estimates of damage, a difference that becomes important precisely in those situations where entrepreneurs tend to be relatively more optimistic about the profitability of new resource combinations than holders of existing property rights. In a stationary economy, where by definition entrepreneurial activity does not exist, there could be little argument for a liability rule in preference to a property rule in the protection of entitlements.[12] The value of a well-defined property right to the use of a resource unit, the productivity of which is known, will be higher if this right is protected by a strict property rule. Since this applies to all units of resources, total value will be higher in an economy with a universalized property rule than it will be in an economy that allows a liability rule for the protection of any or all entitlements.

The case for a liability rule arises only when the dynamic properties of the economic process are recognized. Whereas the value of existing resources will tend to be higher under a generalized regime of property rules, the rate of increase in this value through time will tend to be larger than a regime that offers only liability-rule protection of established entitlements against new and untried intrusions that may be minimal requisites for any development at all.

The economy could scarcely be characterized by growth and development while nominal entitlements are all protected by strict property rules. Such legal arrangements would tend to insure that little change from an existing

---

ample (the farmer has full rights in his crops), there is no scope for insurance contracts of the ordinary sort to emerge. Since the farmer's crops are fully protected by the strict property rule, he will never need to pay for insurance against potential damage from straying cattle. Such an insurance contract between the farmer and rancher will emerge only if the farmer, who anticipates more damages than the rancher, is protected *neither* by a property nor a liability rule.

12. This conclusion requires the presumption that the "bundle of allowable activities" to be protected by either alternative is defined in some plausibly efficient manner. If a generalized property rule is applied to a definition or assignment of rights that is overly restrictive, liability-rule protection might be desired, even in a stationary setting.

status quo is possible. The potential for the profitability-productivity of new resource combinations can first be imagined only in the minds of entrepreneurs. Others in the economy cannot share such visions.[13] Further, any activation of such entrepreneurial projects must necessarily involve uncertainty about their total effects. And there seems to be no grounds for assuming that such effects can be contained (internalized) within the strictly defined entitlements under the responsibility-accountability of the entrepreneurs. Spillover effects, or externalities, will almost necessarily accompany any development or change from the existing *status quo*.

To the extent that the entrepreneurs anticipate such effects, and are liable for possible damages under a liability rule, they can proceed without generating net "social damage," measured in some *ex post* sense. They suffer the consequences of their action. If their vision errs on the side of overoptimism, they pay the full costs, save in the case where bankruptcy proceedings allow them to escape.

III. Law and Externalities

The law has necessarily evolved in the dynamic economy of the real world. It is not, therefore, surprising that the law does not precisely mirror the stylized distinctions that would emerge from economic analysis. But the degree to which legal arrangements have operated to further the "dynamic efficiency" of the economy seems worthy of notice. Within broad limits, the common law has tended to treat negative externalities by what is essentially a liability rule rather than a property rule.[14] Interpretations of the law of nuisances

13. Our conception of the entrepreneur will be recognized as similar to the views of Schumpeter and Kirzner, which, although differing in detail, can be generically related. See J. A. Schumpeter, "Theory of Economic Development" (Redvera Opie trans. 1934), and Israel M. Kirzner, *Competition and Entrepreneurship* (1973).

14. The law of nuisance and of negligence has not, in some situations, been extended to the limits that an economic interpretation of a liability rule, defined in Calabresi-Melamed terms, would require. Persons whose entitlements suffer physical damage, inclusively defined, may not be able to file enforceable claims if the acting party can demonstrate "reasonableness" in any of several dimensions. Courts may "balance hardships" rather than seek to protect nominally defined entitlements. A possible logical basis for some departure from applying a strict liability rule in the law of nuisance may be found

seem to have incorporated the recognition that restrictiveness akin to a strict property rule would stifle technological development. Entrepreneurs have not generally been required to purchase "rights to generate spillover damages" prior to the undertaking of new ventures. And especially when the promised gains more than overbalance the spillover damages imposed, courts have been reluctant to go beyond the requirement that damages be paid. The tendency seems to have been to grant injunctive relief only in settings where the damages are large relative to the gain.[15]

The restrictive limit of the liability rule that seems to be operative in law is perhaps more interesting for economists.[16] The protective umbrella of the liability rule has been extended more or less in accordance with the economists' efficiency criterion. Liability for damages tends to be restricted to "physical" damage, broadly defined, and this liability has not been normally extended to cover damages transmitted through market prices for inputs and outputs. In this respect, the legal boundaries for actionable claims seem to follow, to a very rough first approximation, that between "technological" and "pecuniary" ("price" or "exchange") externalities, the distinction which has been the traditional criterion used in theoretical welfare economics for suggesting corrective measures.[17] Although the analytical treatment of the precise differentiation between technological and pecuniary (or price) externalities remains unsatisfactory,[18] the thrust of the orthodox economic argument for generalized policy neglect of the latter is located in the notion that

---

in the inherent or "natural" fuzziness or ambiguity of entitlements in precisely those situations where negative externalities (nuisances) seem most likely to arise.

15. See, in particular, the opinion of the majority of the New York Court of Appeals in *Boomer v. Atlantic Cement Co.*, 26 N.Y. 2d 219 (1970).

16. The liability rule is, of course, subject to abuse through overextension by legal zealots. Artificially contrived and orchestrated extensions of damage claims beyond those traditionally legitimatized, along with increasingly costly litigation, might convert a liability rule into an instrument that would match a property rule in its restrictiveness on potential entrepreneurship.

17. The precise relationship between the treatment of externalities in the law and in normative economic analysis has not, to our knowledge, been examined. This seems to be a project of some interest.

18. There is surprisingly little explicit discussion or analysis of this distinction in the economics literature, perhaps due to the inherent difficulties. For what remains one of the best treatments, see Roland N. McKean, *Efficiency in Government through Systems Analysis* (1958).

market forces operate to insure that potential gains exceed potential losses. It should be evident that a comprehensive property rule for the protection of nominal entitlements could not possibly make the distinction between the two types of spillover damages. There will, of course, be pecuniary gains to offset purely pecuniary losses, but those third parties who have prospective opportunities to secure the gains could have no standing in the legal interaction between the directly acting party and the parties threatened with damages. But, even within liability-rule protection, what remains interesting, and somewhat surprising to us, is the fact that the law, which has evolved in terms of individual rights, should have drawn the liability-for-damages line at roughly the technological-pecuniary limits, obviously independent of any "macro" or "systemwide" consideration of total effects. Pecuniary externalities imposed on an individual or firm via exogenous changes in demand prices or supply prices engender "suffering" and "damage" that is indistinguishable in a personal sense from those damages that do become legitimate bases for claims against perpetrators. What is the origin of the limits of the law in its failure to protect such "rights"? We can, given our dynamic efficiency perspective here, be pleasantly surprised that the law, as it has evolved, has not incorporated even liability-rule protection for pecuniary or market-transmitted externalities. In a legal order that attempted to embody such cumbersome definitions of "rights" eligible for protection, the scope and range for entrepreneurial activity would be exceedingly narrow, and in the presence of such an order, we might have remained in the "dark ages" of economic development.

IV. The Collective Institutionalization of Property Rules

The comparison of alternative legal arrangements in the two preceding sections is not presented as an exhaustive analysis for what seems surely to be a subject worth more extensive explorations, both by economists and by legal scholars. Despite its length here, it is intended only to serve as a lead-in to our discussion of explicitly collective or governmental instruments of internalization.

Let us suppose that some proximate equivalent of a liability rule has historically existed with respect to the hazy areas where spillover damages may occur, where well-defined rights, defendable by something akin to a property rule, cannot have come into being prior to the emergence of the relevant interdependencies. In this situation, persons and groups who think that they may be potentially damaged, either physically or financially, by development projects may seek and succeed to secure the overt collectivization of the internalization process, effectively bypassing the ordinary operations of the law. Political economists have emphasized the significance of shifts between the market and the collective sector, but little attention seems to have been given to the accompanying shift from law to politics as means of resolving conflicts. Basic institutional change of the sort here discussed seems descriptive of the movement toward collectivized regulatory controls in the 1960s and 1970s, controls over many aspects of the environment, whether of the workplace, the quality and range of products, or the more general "atmosphere" for living. Well-defined property rights could never exist in such things as occupational or product safety, quality of air and water, and "silence." An awakened emphasis on observed deterioration in the environment, defined generally, led to the establishment of direct control agencies rather than to the more efficacious extension and application of traditional legal remedies.[19] Essentially the results embody the collectivized analogue to a very strict property rule with the effects on entrepreneurial development prospects that are predicted by our analysis.

Direct control institutions make no clear distinction between technological and pecuniary externalities.[20] By contrast and as noted earlier, the law has always been discriminatory in this respect. Legal protection of "entitlements" has never been extended to include capital values, as such. The franchisee of the local McDonald's could hardly expect the law of nuisance to protect his capital value against the potential loss from the nearby opening of a Burger King. But if the internalization of externalities comes to be institutionalized in an explicitly political manner, there is no distinction to be

---

19. It is interesting to speculate on why the traditional legal remedies were deemed to be failing and, if such judgments were correct, on what adjustments and extension in law might have been required for correction.

20. The relationship between exchange or "price" externalities and political attempts aimed at protecting values of existing entitlements was discussed by Kenneth Goldin, "Price Externalities Influence Public Policy," *Public Choice* 23 (1975): 1. Goldin did not, however, relate his analysis to the legal setting in the absence of political action.

drawn between sources of potential damages. The private costs consequent on a shift in the "market environment" (a shift in demand price or supply price) are indistinguishable from those costs consequent on a shift in the "physical environment." The motivation for an attempted response by potentially affected individuals or firms is equivalent in the two cases. The firm is threatened with capital loss in either case and it will seek to influence political outcomes.

Consider a familiar setting. Assume initially that there is no zoning ordinance in a municipality. Entrepreneurs may develop parcels of land as they see fit under what amounts to an operative liability rule. Physical damages to properties that may result from the development become the basis for legitimate claims. Assume now, however, that owners of properties in the municipality seek to maintain the capitalized market values of their rights by the enactment of a zoning regulation. They collectively appoint a zoning administrator, whose approval is to be required, *in advance,* before the development of any project that involves any departure from known patterns of activity.

Suppose that, subsequent to this institutional change, an entrepreneur sees prospects for a development that will possibly exert some spillover or external damages on adjacent owners. These potential damages may take two forms: (1) those that affect production functions or the utility functions of persons or firms in the neighborhood, and (2) those that affect the demand prices or the supply prices of outputs or inputs for neighborhood producers and/or consumers, but which do not affect production or utility functions directly. As noted earlier, in the absence of politicization, the law of nuisance might be anticipated to operate so as to insure the payment of claims for the first of these types of damage. Assume that the entrepreneur, the developer, fully reckons on the first sort of spillover damages and considers these to be a part of the cost of his project, as estimated subjectively prior to onset of development itself. He then seeks the approval of the zoning administrator, who, we now assume, acts strictly as agent for the set of potentially damaged parties. In this role, the zoning administrator will make no distinction at all between the two types of anticipated external damage.

The role of the administrator might be expanded somewhat by allowing him to act as agent for all parties other than the entrepreneur-developer, those who are to be potentially damaged and those who are to be potential spillover beneficiaries. If the latter are included, their prospective gains will offset market-transmitted losses in the administrator's decision calculus. He will be sensitive only to the spillover damages that are not offset by spillover benefits. There seems, however, to be a categorical difference between the interests of potentially damaged parties and the interests of potentially benefited parties. The former are threatened with losses in existing capital values, whether these be generated through prices or through nonpecuniary channels. The latter are prospective recipients of now nonexisting increments to capital values; as such these parties seem highly unlikely to exert an influence on political agents that is comparable to that exerted by those who are potentially damaged.

In any plausible setting where the agent does not take the interests of the entrepreneur into account, it seems clear that the results are *even more* inhibitory toward positive development than would be the operation of a strict property rule in the absence of politicization. Under the latter, the developer could, at some price, "purchase" rights to impose the anticipated damages, even if this price would have to reflect the subjective estimates of both pecuniary and nonpecuniary damages to the owners of existing entitlements. Inefficiencies would tend to emerge under the property-rule protection because of the inclusion of market-transmitted effects and also because of differences in subjective estimates. In the case where the approval of an administrative official, acting as agent for the potentially damaged parties, is required in advance, however, inefficiencies are even greater. The entrepreneur is not allowed to purchase, *at any price,* "rights" to impose possibly anticipated damages, provided we assume there is no overt corruption or bribery. Regardless of the potential profitability of a project, as envisaged by the entrepreneur, there is no way that a part of this expected profitability can be readily transferred as a "purchase price" for rights to impose external damages to those who may be affected. There is no scope for contractual or bargained "agreement" in the standard sense. Under normal institutional arrangements, the zoning administrator cannot act strictly as a bargaining agent for the potentially damaged parties. He cannot merely act as a conduit between the entrepreneur and his "clients," at least directly. Under these conditions, the zoning administrator will tend to prohibit the development of any project that will impose even minimal anticipated spillover effects, whether nonpecuniary or pecuniary, and even when it is understood by everyone that claims for physical damages may be actionable in the courts.

We may modify this severely restricted result if we assume that the zoning administrator acts as agent "for the whole community," including the entrepreneur, and not simply as agent for other parties. The plausibility of such a genuine "public interest" administrator may be questioned, but it will be useful to examine the logical implications of such a model. If the administrator assigns equal weights to dollars of costs and benefits, by whomever these might be borne or received, he will try to estimate whether a proposed project is or is not beneficial in net terms. He will tend to be somewhat more pessimistic than the entrepreneur who proposes to develop the project, by the simple fact that the latter is the entrepreneur and not the administrator. But the difference may not be large, and the effects on the rate of development in the community, by comparison with a liability rule without zoning, may be relatively limited. The direction of effect will, however, remain as before. In effect, the "public interest" agent becomes the institutional equivalent of a modified "property rule," with the assignment of all entitlements other than those of the entrepreneur to himself for purposes of decision. If he estimates that net benefits of a project exceed net costs, this calculus produces results fully analogous to the "purchase" of rights under a property rule, the only difference being the difference in decision makers and, of course, in the incentive structure. Such a "public interest" calculus will offset the positive expected values for entrepreneurial profits and specialized resource rents against the negative expected values for pecuniary rents on existing entitlements and anticipated physical damages. If the net sign is positive, the project will be approved.

The differentially restrictive effects of political internalization of potential externalities would tend to be eliminated only in the setting where the political agent or administrator acts for the potential entrepreneurs rather than for the potentially damaged parties or for the "public." In such a "capture" setting, where the zoning administrator acts for developers, the advance approval requirement becomes perfunctory, and the liability rule effectively operates.

V. From Single-Party to Multi-party Decision Making

The differential restrictiveness of the prior approval requirement may be increased or decreased when the decision-making authority for the collectivity is lodged, not in a single person, but in a committee or board operating under a specified decision rule. Consider a five-person board empowered to act by simple majority voting rules. A coalition of three members of the board must be secured before the approval of any proposed development project is forthcoming.

There are at least two effects that warrant note here. In the consideration of any project, a majority-rule requirement places decisive power in the hands of that board or committee member who is *median* along an "optimism-pessimism" scale. We can presume that the entrepreneur who proposes a new development project will be more optimistic about its prospects than any zoning-board member. But board members may themselves be arrayed in some optimism-pessimism dimension, at least by project.[21] To the extent that the median member acts in the "public interest," as defined above, the majority-rule result will tend to be equivalent to that produced by a strict property rule, with such a median member acting as if he might have been the owner of the entitlements, although without, of course, any direct financial incentive to consider alternatives carefully. The median member of such a board or committee may be more or less optimistic than any single administrator.

In the composition of a board or committee, however, there is surely less plausibility in a "public interest" model for individual behavior than in the single-person model. We should normally expect members of such boards

---

21. If members of a collective decision-making group, a committee or board, can be characterized generally in terms of their relative optimism or pessimism over a whole set or sequence of decisions, predictions may be made about the set of outcomes under simple majority voting, independent of knowledge about particular preferences. Interestingly, this setting offers several analogues to the more familiar voting-theory problems that arise when the choice options extend beyond the Yes-No alternatives. See Roger L. Faith and James M. Buchanan, "Towards a Theory of Yes-No Voting," *Public Choice* (forthcoming).

to consider themselves to be representative of particular constituencies, ranging from the entrepreneurs themselves on the one hand to the holders and protectors of existing entitlements on the other. In such settings as those for a board or committee of zoning appeals, a "capture" theory of bureaucracy or regulatory agency would suggest that potential developers-entrepreneurs might have concentrated interests in and be successful in securing effective control. On the other hand, in settings where the potential impact is diversified so as to affect many industries, as with environmental control boards, the bias in representation may well be toward constituencies that seek primarily to inhibit change.

To the extent that more than a simple majority of a board or committee is required for advance or prior approval of projects, whether such an inclusive rule be formal or informal, the shift of decision power toward the relatively pessimistic end of the scale is enhanced. In the limit, if unanimous agreement is stipulated, the power of determining the pace of development rests with the most pessimistic member.

VI. Unanimity, Majority, and Individual Action

Our analysis suggests that any overt politicization of the internalization of externalities tends to reduce, perhaps dramatically, the scope and range for entrepreneurial activity generally, with the growth-inhibiting effects becoming most severe when something akin to a unanimity rule is allowed to operate, either for the whole set of persons in a community, or for the subset of representatives chosen to act on behalf of defined constituencies which, in turn, encompass the whole community. In effect, a unanimity rule allows the *status quo* values of all existing entitlements to be preserved against any unpredictable possible intrusions from the spillover effects of new and untried ventures, with no distinction between physical (technological) and financial (pecuniary) effects.[22]

---

22. Striking empirical support of our hypothesis is provided by the relative absence of fencing of grazing lands on the Navajo Indian reservation. Although fencing costs are borne by the government, few fences are built because of the requirement that the unanimous consent of all neighboring herders must be secured prior to such action, along with the consent of all others who might be affected. See Gary D. Libecap and Ronald N. John-

Such a characteristic of a unanimity rule has been stressed, in the general setting of political theory, in the critiques developed by Douglas Rae, James Fishkin, and others.[23] Quite apart from the acknowledged costs of attaining unanimous agreement, which may make a unanimity rule "inefficient" in the sense that it would rarely, if ever, be chosen constitutionally,[24] Rae and Fishkin criticize the rule even as an idealized benchmark for political decision making. They argue that while a unanimity rule may effectively prevent the collectivity from undertaking action that will damage individual interests, from "sins of commission," the rule will also prevent the collectivity from taking action that might prove, in the net, beneficial, due to the recalcitrance of some stubborn pessimists, who will, effectively, hold decisive power. Note that this argument is *not* equivalent to that based on the possibly prohibitive decisions costs (transactions costs) of securing unanimous agreement. Even in the total absence of such costs, the pessimist's preferences tend to be satisfied.

This paper is clearly not the appropriate vehicle for an examination of the Rae-Fishkin argument in the context of normative political theory. We would suggest only that the whole analysis, both normative and positive, of "political externalities" must be categorically separated from the more narrowly circumscribed "economic externalities" which are, of course, always restricted within the confines of a legal order. Our concern here is with the limited set of issues that involve potential "economic" externalities and alternative processes of internalization. As we have already noted, essentially the same argument, even if somewhat less emphatically, can be made against the use of majority-rule decision making. The dividing line for our analysis is that between overtly political attempts at internalization (whether through an administrative bureaucracy, through boards or committees that act on majority rule, or through effective unanimity rules) and the internalization of emergent externalities that will be predicted to take place through the law of liability. We have suggested that any politicization tends to generate results akin to a severely restrictive property rule.

---

son, "Legislating Commons: The Navajo Tribal Council and the Navajo Range," *Economic Inquiry* 18 (1980): 69.

23. See Douglas Rae, "The Limits of Consensual Decision," *American Political Science Review* 69 (1975): 1270; James S. Fishkin, *Tyranny and Legitimacy: A Critique of Political Theories* (1979), especially at 67–72.

24. Compare James M. Buchanan and Gordon Tullock, *The Calculus of Consent* (1962).

We should note that these conclusions follow regardless of the control mechanisms that may be used. Economists, generally, tend to support corrective taxes and subsidies as opposed to more direct schemes for controlling externalities, especially in large-number settings. The argument is based on the notion that, with appropriately set rates, private decision makers can adjust optimally to measures of "true" social costs and benefits. However, the whole argument about alternative control devices presumes that the potential spillover or external costs or benefits of economic activities are fully predictable in advance. There is no recognition of the elementary fact that new ventures will necessarily be unpredictable, both with respect to their internal profitability and to their spillover effects. Any political setting of corrective rates of tax would tend to embody the predictions of the politician-bureaucrat-administrator who would necessarily tend to be relatively more pessimistic than the entrepreneur who alone has the vision and imagination for the new resource combination that a project represents. The same conclusions will, of course, apply to more direct control measures such as the setting of standards or limits. Further, and perhaps more significantly, the whole of the economists' argument must presume that the political decision concerning the distinction between "correctable" and "noncorrectable" spillover effects has been made, or will be made, correctly.

The thrust of our argument suggests that individual entrepreneurial action, rather than political action carried forward by administrative agency, by majority voting, or by unanimity, should be unimpeded except by the *ex post* adjustments that are required in tort law, where those who generate physical damages to others stand liable. When the potentially damaged parties are numerous, cost thresholds may prevent the individualized origination of claims. Recognition of this prospect justifies some institutional arrangements for class-action suits.

Many economists seem to have overlooked the elementary fact that many Pareto-relevant externalities are internalized by the operation of the law itself. With respect to negative externalities, our argument becomes what might be called the "legal" supplement to Coase's "economic" one. Although he surely did not neglect the operation of the law itself, Coase has been largely interpreted by economists as suggesting that, given freedom of contract and absent prohibitive transaction costs, the market or exchange process will effectively internalize potential externalities that are Pareto-relevant. We suggest here that for those areas where rights remain ill-defined or where, for any reason, contractual processes break down or do not come into being, if litigation is not prohibitively costly, the law itself provides for *ex post* internalization, at least for negative externalities.

As Staaf and Wares point out, the law of torts does not extend to cover positive externalities or external economies. Here the legal institution for internalization is limited to the law of contract. For our purposes, however, the legal asymmetry is not significant since it is the processes of internalizing negative externalities that assume dominant importance in our "dynamic efficiency" framework. Entrepreneurial activity, the primary source of economic growth and development, seems to be much more likely to be adversely affected by legal and/or political protections against possible external diseconomies than it is to be thwarted by the failure of entrepreneurs to collect payments for the possible spillover benefits that their activities confer on others.

Our argument should not be interpreted as suggesting that "Texas-style" entrepreneurs be unloosed and allowed free rein to invade or otherwise intrude upon any and all entitlements, subject only to the enforcement of a liability rule. Entrepreneurial activity is instrumental to economic development or growth, but such growth is, of course, only one among several objectives for viable social order. "Security of person and property" is surely of equal importance, and for whole classes of entitlements, this objective can only be achieved with an enforceable property rule or its equivalent. Our argument suggests only that on the legal-economic interfaces created by technological advance, where new and necessarily uncertain "invasions," "spillovers," or "harmful effects" may take place, liability-rule protection offers a legal climate within which economic growth can proceed, whereas property-rule protection of all claimed entitlements will surely retard such growth. In particular, the opportunity costs of the attempted extension of "rights" under the protection of the politicized equivalent of a property rule should be recognized.

PART THREE

The Theory of Monopoly

The Theory of Monopolistic
Quantity Discounts

The derivation of a single-valued function between the variables, quantity demanded and price, requires, in addition to the usual *ceteris paribus* assumptions, that the buyer conceptually be faced with alternative supply functions in each of which price is invariant. If the buyer exerts any control over price, no demand curve can be derived, since quantity demanded then depends on the whole market offer, not on price alone. The marginal value product curve, for example, does not constitute a demand curve for a productive service when the purchaser is a monopsonist. This point has been recognised in the analysis of the firm, but has received relatively little attention in the analysis of the behaviour of the buyers of final products in spite of the fact that there are significant theoretical differences in the two cases. The analysis of the behaviour of buyers faced with down-sloping supply functions has been especially neglected. Professor Weintraub has examined the behaviour of consumers faced with up-sloping curves; he has done little more than mention the down-sloping case.[1]

From *Review of Economic Studies* 20 (June 1953): 199–208. Reprinted by permission of the Review of Economic Studies Ltd.

I am greatly indebted to Professor Milton Friedman, of the University of Chicago, for pointing out to me errors and omissions in an earlier draft of this paper. Helpful suggestions have also been made by my colleagues Professors Clark Allen and Marshall Colberg, but I am solely responsible for all errors that may remain.

1. Sidney Weintraub, *Price Theory* (New York: Pitman Publishing Corp., 1949), 251–56; "The Theory of Consumer Monopsony," *Review of Economic Studies* 18 (1949–50): 168–78.

The decreasing supply-price case is mentioned by Bain, Boulding, Robinson, and Scitovsky, but no thorough analysis is presented. See Joe S. Bain, *Price Theory* (New York:

This paper has two purposes: (1) to provide a rigorous analysis of the behaviour of the buyer of final products faced with down-sloping supply curves, and (2) to draw from this analysis some inferences concerning the effects of monopolistically imposed quantity discounts on the welfare of the buyer. The consideration of the welfare aspects will be limited to those cases where the quantity discounts are introduced as sales promotion devices by monopolistic sellers.[2] This excludes only those cost-reflecting quantity discounts that may be found in purely competitive markets.[3]

II.

The market offer made to an individual buyer may be illustrated in Fig. 1. The curve *s* indicates the various average supply prices at which various quantities may be purchased from a monopolistic seller.[4] The price elasticity of this curve must be greater than unity at all points, since no seller would offer to sell a larger quantity for a smaller total expenditure (except in the

---

Henry Holt & Co., 1952), 387 f.; Kenneth Boulding, *Economic Analysis*, revised edition (New York: Harper & Brothers, 1948), 539–42; Joan Robinson, *The Economics of Imperfect Competition* (London: Macmillan & Co., 1933), 221 f.; Tibor Scitovsky, *Welfare and Competition* (Chicago: Richard D. Irwin, 1951), 410–13.

2. The decreasing supply-price case, when discussed at all in economic analysis, has normally been included under the general topic of "monopsony" (Scitovsky and Boulding are exceptions). It is implied that the market power of the buyer is instrumental in forcing sellers to lower supply prices for larger orders. The word "monopsony" connotes buyer control arising from the fewness of numbers. Monopsony power is not, however, a necessary condition for the phenomenon of declining supply price over quantity. This type of market offer, which is widespread in consumer markets, is more likely to stem from the power of the seller.

3. There would appear to be little reason why a monopolist should introduce quantity discounts reflecting precisely the rate of change in cost, even for quantities in excess of that which might be marketed at a uniform monopoly price. But even if this should be the case, the analysis of this paper still holds. No monopolist would ever introduce cost-reflecting quantity discount offers over all quantities, provided that alternative offers exist.

4. It makes no difference for this analysis whether all units or only the marginal ones are offered at lower prices as greater amounts are purchased. A lowered price on additional units is equivalent to a lowered average price on all units. This particular characteristic of the market offer will exert influence on the buyer's behaviour only if such behaviour is irrational. If rational, the buyer will consider the marginal supply price, whether stated directly or as a lowered average price.

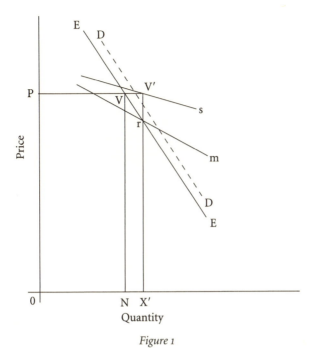

Figure 1

extreme case where marginal costs are negative). The curve *m* is drawn marginal to the *s* curve, and may be called the curve of marginal supply price. It
represents the rate of change in the buyer's outlay as the quantity purchased
is varied.

The usual indifference curve approach will be utilised and may be illustrated in Fig. 2. All other goods (whose money prices are assumed constant)
are summed up as money and represented on the *Y* axis; the commodity under consideration is represented on the *X* axis. A market offer similar to that
shown in Fig. 1 is transformed into an opportunity curve which declines in
slope as more units are purchased. Various points on this opportunity curve
represent alternative possible combinations of money income retained and
units of commodity purchased within the restraint of a given money income.
The slope of this opportunity curve at any point indicates the rate at which
the buyer's outlay changes, or the marginal supply price. It does not represent the average price, which under a quantity discount offer always will exceed the marginal supply price. Thus, the opportunity curve is not a price
curve as is the normal case when price is uniform over quantity.

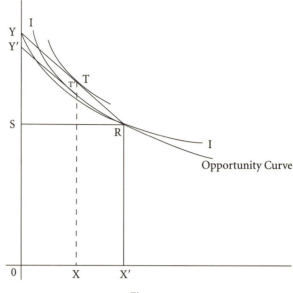

Figure 2

The buyer will move to a position shown by the point of tangency, *R*, between an indifference curve and the opportunity curve. The average supply price may be found by dividing the money given up, *YS*, by the number of units purchased, $0X'$ or *SR*.

It may be seen from Fig. 2 that the introduction of uniform pricing in the place of the quantity discount offer will both reduce the equilibrium amount of the commodity purchased and allow the buyer to move to a preferred position. If the buyer is offered the commodity at a uniform price equal to the average supply price prevailing under the quantity discount, his new position of equilibrium will be indicated by *T*, the new opportunity curve now being the price line *YR*. He will purchase only $0X$ units and will have reached a higher preference level than at *R*. This conclusion depends for its validity only upon the existence of a diminishing marginal rate of substitution between money and the commodity under consideration.

The income compensation (negative) which would be required to keep the buyer on the same preference level as before the change may be shown as *YY'* in Fig. 2. With money income reduced by *YY'* to compensate for the introduction of uniform pricing, the compensated equilibrium position may be shown at T'. If the commodity is a superior (inferior) good, T' will lie to the left (right) of T. T' will always lie to the left of R, as will T.

III.

The above analysis provides a means of deriving a particular position of equilibrium, given the tastes and opportunities of the buyer. It does not provide a means of deriving a unique relationship between various market offers and quantities taken. By the use of the orthodox indifference-opportunity analysis, successive positions of equilibria are traced as opportunities (prices) are changed; thus, the laws of consumer choice are derived. The buyer's price-consumption curve is derived and is then transformed on to the Marshallian co-ordinate axes as the individual buyer's demand curve. No such procedure is possible here; for by merely changing the conditions of the market offer, differing equilibrium quantities will be taken at the same marginal supply price, and conversely, the same quantity will be taken at different marginal supply prices. No price-consumption function or demand function may be derived.

Some such relation is needed however; it is not sufficient that each market offer determine a demand point. The monopolist has no supply curve, and the monopsonistic purchaser of productive services has no demand curve, but the monopolist's marginal cost curve and the monopsonist's marginal value product curve may be employed. These functions are single-valued relations between price and quantity and allow the usual Marshallian co-ordinates to be employed. For the buyer faced with quantity discount offers, there is needed something analogous to the marginal value product curve of the monopsonistic purchaser of productive services. Some sort of curve of marginal evaluation must be derived which is independent of the conditions of the market offer.

Weintraub, in recognising this need, has attempted to derive such a curve which he calls the "monopsony demand" or "marginal demand" curve.[5] The

---

5. Weintraub, *Price Theory*, 254 f.; "The Theory of Consumer Monopsony," 171 ff. Bain discusses the problem in terms of a "marginal benefit" schedule, but apparently does not recognise the difficulties involved in deriving such a schedule since he does not distinguish between factor and product buyers (Bain, *Price Theory*, 280–82). Boulding utilises

curve which he derives is essentially the same as Hicks' "marginal valuation" curve.[6] It is derived by taking as ordinates the slopes of the separate indifference curves at the points at which they cut the given opportunity curve. The "marginal demand" curve represents the successive amounts of money the buyer is willing to give up for additional units of the commodity once he has acquired previous units at the prices indicated by the slopes of the opportunity curve at various points. As Weintraub admits, this curve is not similar to the orthodox demand curve since it does not represent alternative quantities taken at all possible prices. Rather, each point is tied to every other point on the curve since it is drawn on the assumption of seriatim purchase.

The Weintraub curve seems to be of questionable usefulness. For in order to derive the curve at all, Weintraub specifically states that the conditions of supply cannot be allowed to change.[7] Although the Weintraub curve is derived in a manner similar to those of Hicks, the latter are used for the purpose of tracing changing positions of equilibria as supply conditions do change.[8] For Hicks, however, a change in supply conditions is equivalent merely to a change in a single price, since he is concerned only with buyers faced with perfectly elastic supply functions. In both Weintraub's analysis and that of this paper, a change in supply conditions means an adjustment of the whole market offer. But unless these conditions are somehow allowed to change, the "monopsony demand" curve tells us no more about the behaviour of the buyer than we knew before.

Weintraub is unable to allow the conditions of supply to vary because he is restricted by the assumptions of the orthodox demand curve. With money income and other prices assumed fixed, the Weintraub curve is the only curve of marginal evaluation which can be derived. If, however, these restrictions are relaxed, and money income is allowed to vary, while introducing the substitute restriction of constant real income, a more meaningful and

---

the normal demand schedule in his analysis of the problem without pointing out the contradictions involved (Boulding, *Economic Analysis*, 542).

6. J. R. Hicks, "The Four Consumer Surpluses," *Review of Economic Studies* 11 (1943): 31–42.

7. Weintraub, "The Theory of Consumer Monopsony," 171 f.

8. Hicks, "The Four Consumer Surpluses," 41.

perhaps more useful curve of marginal evaluation may be constructed which does allow the conditions of the market offer to be varied.

IV.

This curve of marginal evaluation may be derived without difficulty. If real income is to be held constant under all market offers, the buyer will remain on the same indifference level, which may be represented by a single indifference curve. For each marginal supply price there is only one quantity which will be taken, for there is only one point at which the slope of the fixed indifference curve will equal the given marginal supply price.[9] As the market offer is changed, the shifting opportunity curves "cradle" the fixed indifference curve; a single opportunity curve being tangent to the indifference curve at only one point.[10] The single indifference curve may, however, be tangent to several opportunity curves at the same point. It will be tangent to the whole subset of opportunity curves passing through the point which have the same slope.

By taking the slope of the fixed indifference curve at various quantities as ordinates, a single-valued functional relationship between marginal supply price and quantity is derived. This may be transformed on to the Marshallian co-ordinate axes. It is drawn as the curve *EE* in Fig. 1. This function does not, however, define a similar unique relation between average supply price and quantity. For the rate of the discount determines the difference between av-

---

9. It is assumed that the conditions of the market offer do not cause changes in the indifference map of the buyer. This is, of course, the assumption normally employed in the derivation of the laws of consumer choice from the indifference curve analysis. It seems likely, however, that such an assumption should be questioned even more in this analysis than in the usual case.

10. The fact that a buyer purchases a determinate quantity of the commodity is sufficient evidence that the convexity of the indifference curve exceeds the convexity of the opportunity curves. If this were not true, the buyer could reach his highest indifference level by purchasing none of the commodity at all. If an opportunity curve were of precisely the same degree of convexity as the indifference curve the behaviour of the buyer would be completely erratic. This correspondence of the opportunity curve with the indifference curve of the consumer may be considered the limit to the form of the quantity discount offer.

erage and marginal supply price; the same marginal supply price may represent several average supply prices under differing rates of discount. In order to maintain the constancy in real income that is required, a change in the rate of discount must be offset by changes in money income even though the same marginal supply price is retained.

This curve of marginal evaluation, when derived as indicated, is not a "demand" curve in the orthodox or Hicksian sense. On the latter curve, money income is held constant at all points; on the marginal evaluation curve, money income varies from point to point, and even a single point may represent different levels of money income. Therefore, little that is useful may be gained from an examination of the relative positions of this curve and the orthodox demand curve. This relationship will depend solely upon the real income position assumed to begin with. If the commodity is a superior good, and the real income level is to be held constant at the level represented by the indifference curve II in Fig. 2, the slope of the opportunity curve at R may be taken as an ordinate on both curves. On the orthodox demand curve other prices and money income are adjusted so that the real income indicated by the indifference curve passing through R is attained. The orthodox demand curve and the marginal evaluation curve must intersect at the price so chosen. On the marginal evaluation curve money income varies in a compensating fashion as marginal (or average) supply price changes.[11] As this increases, positive money income compensations are required to keep real income constant. Thus, for all prices higher than that represented by the slope of the initial opportunity curve at R, the marginal evaluation curve will lie above the orthodox demand curve. For all prices below this, the demand curve will lie above the marginal evaluation curve.

The fact that different types of compensating variation are required for these two curves reduces the usefulness of a comparison of their respective positions. A much more meaningful comparison of this nature may be made if the meaning of the demand curve is changed in accordance with the suggestions advanced by Professor Friedman.[12] His construction and interpre-

11. The compensations required must be in money income and not other prices, since quantities are to be related to absolute not relative prices. See Milton Friedman, "The Marshallian Demand Curve," *Journal of Political Economy* 57 (December 1949): 468.

12. Milton Friedman, ibid. This construction is also supported by Professor F. H.

tation of the Marshallian demand curve make it similar to the curve of marginal evaluation developed here. Real income is held constant at all points, and compensating variations are introduced in the prices of other goods (not closely related) and/or in money incomes. Accepting this meaning of the demand curve, the comparison of positions on it with those on the marginal evaluation curve becomes easier. If the same real income level is assumed, the Friedman demand curve becomes the same as the marginal evaluation curve.[13] This assumption of the same real income is of little use, however, since it requires that money income compensations of precisely the necessary amounts take place when uniform pricing and quantity discounts are substituted for each other, and when the rate of quantity discount is changed. If such compensations do indeed take place, the fact that the same quantity would be purchased at the same prices regardless of the nature of the market offer is neither surprising nor revealing. In addition, even if it is legitimate to introduce the necessary income compensations as a methodological tool, the comparison of quantities taken under a quantity discount offer and under a uniform price equal to the marginal supply price is not the correct one. In selling at a quantity discount, the seller lowers marginal supply price below average supply price in order to promote sales volume; he would never offer the commodity at a uniform price equal to the lowered marginal price.[14] A much more realistic alternative to the buyer is uniform pricing at a level equal to the average supply price under the quantity discount offer. In reference to Fig. 1, the initial position of the buyer under the discount offer is shown at r. With uniform pricing substituted for the discount offer at the same average supply price ($0P$), the new position of the buyer is shown at V. This indicates the same result shown above at T' in Fig. 2. Even if fully compensated so as to retain the same real income level, the substitution of the quantity discount offer for a uniform price offer while maintaining the

---

Knight; see his "Realism and Relevance in the Theory of Demand," *Journal of Political Economy* 52 (1944): 299.

13. Assuming that the compensating variations are in income, not other prices.

14. A difference between this case and that of the up-sloping supply curve should be noted here. If the buyer is faced with an up-sloping supply curve, marginal supply price exceeds average supply price. Here it might be more useful to compare the behaviour of the buyer with that in the situation where price is uniform at the marginal price. This is the procedure followed by Weintraub. ("The Theory of Consumer Monopsony," 173.)

same average price will always result in a greater quantity taken (from $0N$ to $0X'$ in Fig. 1).[15] Thus, the effect of this type of market offer is clearly that of forcing the buyer to purchase the commodity at a price in excess of the marginal contribution to his "satisfaction" provided by a unit of the commodity.[16]

A more useful comparison is that between the buyer in the quantity discount position and the uniform price position without compensation. The introduction of a quantity discount offer reduces the real income of the buyer unless the average supply price is lowered. These two positions are shown by T and R in Fig. 2. For this case, the marginal evaluation curve will lie to the left of the Friedman demand curve at all points. But, even if uncompensated, the buyer will purchase a greater amount under the quantity discount than under the uniform supply price. Therefore, the Friedman demand curve, shown approximately by DD in Fig. 1, must cut the line PVV' between the points V and V'.[17]

V.

The introduction of the type of quantity discounts examined here is equivalent to a reduction in the real income of the buyers and an increase in the real income of the sellers. The use of the Marshallian co-ordinates allows this real income transfer to be represented readily. This is illustrated in Fig. 3. It is assumed that a monopolist sells his product in a market composed of many identical purchasers. This assumption allows the inter-buyer discrimination problem to be eliminated. The curve Dd represents the demand curve for one

15. It should be noted that the movement from r to V in Fig. 1 requires an income compensation just the reverse of that normally required in moving upward along a Friedman demand curve. To maintain constancy in real income movement upward normally requires that the buyer be compensated positively. In this example, the movement from r to V requires a negative compensation.

16. A similar analysis for purchasers of productive services has been provided by M. Bronfenbrenner. He shows that under certain offers of labour services of an all-or-none nature, the employer may be forced to pay a wage rate in excess of marginal revenue product. (M. Bronfenbrenner, "Wages in Excess of Marginal Revenue Product," *Southern Economic Journal* 16 [January 1950]: 297–310.) See, also, in this connection, William Fellner, *Competition Among the Few* (New York: Alfred A. Knopf, 1949), 277 f.

17. It should be recognised that different rates of quantity discount affect the level of the buyer's real income differently, and consequently the relation between the marginal evaluation curve and a Friedman demand curve.

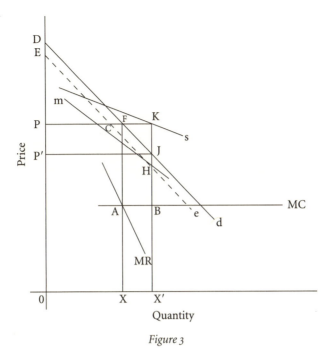

Figure 3

of these buyers (drawn under the Friedman interpretation), and the corresponding marginal revenue curve is shown as *MR*. The marginal cost curve of the monopolist is drawn horizontally as *MC*. If uniform pricing is to be followed, the profit-maximising price is $0P$ and the quantity sold to this buyer is $0X$. Now suppose that the monopolist tries to retain the same average price ($0P$), but to increase his sales by the introduction of a quantity discount offer. He makes the offer represented by the curves, *s* and *m*. This quantity discount offer reduces the real income of the buyer; therefore, the marginal evaluation curve appropriate for the locating of his equilibrium purchase will lie slightly below *Dd*. This may be shown by the dotted line *Ee*. The buyer will purchase $0X'$ units at the same average supply price $0P$. The monopolist's profits are increased by the amount shown by the rectangle *ABKF*.

A money measure of the reduction in the welfare of the buyer may be shown by the rectangle *PP'JK*. In the initial equilibrium position the buyer purchased $0X$ units at a price $0P$; under the new offer he purchases $0X'$ units at an unchanged average price. In order to produce the additional amount XX', the monopolist will find it necessary to bid resources away from the production of other commodities. This will reduce the supplies of other commodities which would tend to increase their prices. In order to prevent these compensating price increases, money income must be reduced sufficiently to keep demands in relation to the reduced supplies. Thus, the compensating effects are precisely the same as those which would take place under a normal movement along a Friedman demand curve (i.e., from F to J in Fig. 3). With these compensations taking place, the buyer would have to be offered the amount $0X'$ at an average price $0P'$ in order that his real income position remain unchanged. But he is forced to pay a price higher by PP'. Thus, the net reduction in real income as a result of the introduction of the quantity discount must be represented by the rectangle $PP'JK$.

This money equivalent of the reduction in real income of the buyer need not be equal to the money increase in the monopolist's profits. Since the buyer spends more for the monopolist's product, less will be available for expenditure on other commodities. This will reduce profits and payments to productive factors in other industries. If the monopolist is also a buyer from other industries, his additional purchases may completely offset the reduced purchases of his buyers. Spillover effects may be present, however, tending either to increase the monopolist's profits more or less than the money reduction in buyers' income. The shape of the cost function will also tend to affect the degree of correspondence between the increase in the monopolist's profits and the decrease in buyers' money incomes. If average cost is increasing, a portion of the money transferred from consumers will be absorbed as increased costs, and will not become monopoly profits. If average cost is decreasing over the relevant range, the monopolist's profits will be increased more than the incomes of the buyers are reduced, providing that the spillover effects are not significantly important.

Uniform pricing may not exist as a true alternative offer to the buyer. In order for the monopolist to secure enough total revenue to cover costs, the introduction of a quantity discount offer may be necessary. In such cases, the analysis above concerning the effects on the real income of the buyer does not fully apply. The real income of the buyer is still reduced below that which would prevail under uniform pricing were this possible, but it is presumably increased by the chance to purchase the commodity rather than do without it.

VI.

There remains to be considered the question of determining the profit-maximising quantity discount for the seller. Monopoly profits are increased by the offer shown in Fig. 3, but not necessarily maximised. The profit-maximising quantity discount must be one which transfers as much income as possible from buyer to seller, which secures for the monopolist as much "consumer's surplus" as is possible. The total area under a Friedman demand curve may be taken as the total amount that the buyer is willing to give up for the commodity rather than go without it.[18] Thus, in reference to Fig. 3, the consumer would be willing to give up the amount represented by the area $0DJX'$ for the quantity $0X'$, provided that his real income remains the same as the initial position at F. Any more than this amount would reduce his real income; any less than this amount given up would serve to increase his real income. But the quantity discount has reduced the real income of the buyer, in the manner shown above. At the reduced real income the amount the buyer would be willing to give for the amount $0X'$ rather than go without it is shown by the area $0EHX'$. Through the means of the quantity discount he is actually being forced to give up an amount indicated by the area $0PKX'$. All of the area $0PKX'$ is included in the area $0EHX'$ except the triangle CKH. All of the area $0EHX'$ is included in the area $0PKX'$ except the triangle PEC. If the triangle PEC is larger than the triangle CKH, then the quantity discount is not optional from the point of view of the monopolist. A still greater transfer of income from the buyer may be effected by an alteration in the rate of the quantity discount.

The profit-maximising rate of quantity discount may be illustrated in Fig. 4. The demand curve and the marginal cost curve are the same as for Fig. 3. Thus the initial equilibrium position for uniform price profit maximisation is again shown at point F. The profit-maximising quantity discount offer is shown approximately by the curve m'. It may be seen that the marginal evaluation curve $E'e'$ represents the limiting slope of the curve of declining marginal supply price. If the curve of marginal supply price is allowed to fall at the same rate as the marginal evaluation curve, it will cut the marginal cost curve at H'. At this point the following equality holds and represents the de-

---

18. Friedman, "Marshallian Demand Curve," 478.

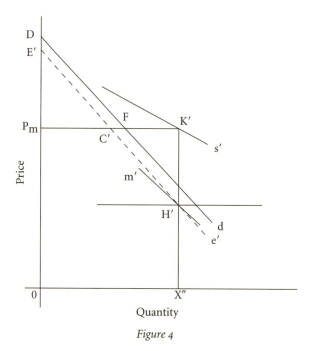

Figure 4

sired position for the monopolist: marginal cost = marginal supply price = marginal evaluation. It may be shown that this equality insures that the quantity discount is profit maximising. The area of the triangle $P_m E' C'$ is approximately equal to that of the triangle $C' K' H'$.[19] This means that at the reduced level of real income caused by the introduction of the discount offer the buyer is now being forced to give up the maximum amount that he would be willing to give up for the commodity rather than do without it. He is securing no "consumer surplus" from the purchase of $0X''$ units at an average supply price of $0P_m$. The marginal evaluation curve has become the seller's marginal revenue curve in this case of quantity discounts; therefore, the above-mentioned equality is the necessary condition for profit maximisation. The profit-maximising quantity discount is thus a particular case of perfect price discrimination.[20] Or rather, it is a means whereby perfect discrimination in selling to one buyer may be approached.

19. This is proved by the fact that $P_m C'$ must be equal to $C' K'$ and $P_m E'$ equal to $K' H'$ since $E' e'$ is marginal to s'.

20. See Bain, *Price Theory*, 416–25, for an excellent treatment of the general case of perfect discrimination.

The actual limits to buyer exploitation via the mechanism of quantity discounts are set by forces similar to those limiting the exercise of other forms of price discrimination. The rate of quantity discount cannot be so great that significant resale and repurchase among buyers of differing quantities is promoted. Although not considered in this paper, the corollary purpose of quantity discounts is that of discriminating among buyers of different size. The underlying criterion for this motivation for quantity discounts must be that the demand schedule of small buyers is more inelastic over the relevant price range than that of large buyers. The analysis of this paper has shown that even if this criterion is not met, i.e., even if elasticities of demand over the relevant price ranges are roughly equivalent for all buyers, the introduction of quantity discounts is still likely to prove profitable.

The sales promotion effects of quantity discounts will be limited to those commodities and services normally purchased by a sizeable number of purchasers in blocks of several units. For example, the monopolist would gain little by offering to sell electric refrigerators at a quantity discount. "Buying clubs" might thereby be promoted, but each individual member would, in such a case, be motivated by the average price ("his share"), not the marginal price. Among final products, therefore, quantity discounts appear largely among grocery and drug items. The effects are to encourage buyers to purchase greater quantities than would be purchased with the items priced uniformly at the same average price.

A final point: the analysis of this paper applies only to the behaviour of the buyer in a single instant of time. If longer periods are taken into account, the effects of quantity discounts may not be as significant. While the buyer will clearly purchase more at "any one time" as a result of this type of offer, the effects of this upon his consumption and hence his purchase "over time" do not appear precisely determinate. A major effect of widespread quantity discount offers may be an increase in the average length of the period between purchase and consumption accompanied by an increase in consumer inventories.

The "Dead Hand" of Monopoly

James M. Buchanan and Gordon Tullock

Introduction

There is apparently some sort of common agreement, one presumably based on observation, that firms possessing and exercising monopoly power in varying degrees do in fact exist in many local, regional, national, and international markets. And by analytical definition the exercise of such monopoly power violates the necessary conditions for optimum "efficiency" or, more technically, for "Pareto-optimality" in resource use. By inference, then, there must necessarily exist some unexploited "gains-from-trade" between the monopolist, on the one hand, and his consumers-customers, actual and potential, on the other. Why, then, do we not also observe, especially in localized markets, more efforts on the part of consumer-organized "cooperatives" to secure control of the monopoly firms through ordinary market purchase or acquisition? Casual observation suggests that such attempts are rare indeed.[1]

This set of circumstances can be "explained," of course, on either one of two familiar grounds. It can be argued, first, that the pervasiveness of "emerging competition" is such that monopoly power, where it exists, is *always on the way to being dissipated.* Thus, in this view, the dynamics of the competitive

From *Antitrust Law and Economics Review* 1 (Summer 1968): 85–96. Copyright by *Antitrust Law and Economics Review.* Reprinted by permission of the copyright holder.

1. See John S. McGee, "Patent Exploitation: Some Economic and Legal Problems," *Journal of Law and Economics* 9 (October 1966): 148: "It *is* true that intelligent, self-coerced consumer organizations, if created at low cost—or [by] the state acting in their behalf—could outbid the monopolist, producing net benefits and yet paying off the inventor. But little has been said of this possibility in the reform literature."

process itself are such that monopoly is not really a serious problem at all, and the absence of consumer-cooperative attempts at market control is merely evidence of this fact.

A second line of reasoning partially contradicts and partially supplements that first one. Monopoly power can, it is admitted here, be a serious problem, and major inefficiencies can and do exist because of those monopoly restrictions. However, consumers cannot be expected to organize to exploit the resulting gains-from-trade because of the *cost of organization*. Consumers of the monopoly firm's product are likely to be many, and any attempt on their part to secure joint action would run into prohibitively high cost barriers. Thus, even in the presence of a significant degree of monopoly exploitation, it still might not be feasible for consumers to organize themselves, or to submit to the activities of entrepreneurs seeking to organize them, and enter into market-like negotiations to buy out the monopolist.

Monopoly Profits

There is doubtless some measure of validity in both of these familiar arguments. But they nonetheless tend to gloss over and conceal an important aspect of the whole monopoly issue, namely, the fact that the *current* owners of monopoly firms may not in fact be earning more than a competitive return on *their* investment, that all present and future monopoly profits may have already been "capitalized" and removed by former owners of the firm. Thus we might still fail to observe such units being formed even in the presence of what seem to be really serious cases of monopoly power and even if the *costs* of organizing such effective consumers' cooperatives were absent or, say, fully subsidized from federal funds. In one sense, however, our analysis here can be incorporated into the "cost" argument, since we also demonstrate why individual consumers would be reluctant to enter into such arrangements.

The Welfare Triangle

Consumer gain — social gain

Consider a single consumer of a monopolist's product, as, for example, the one depicted in Figure 1. For the sake of simplicity, assume that all of the

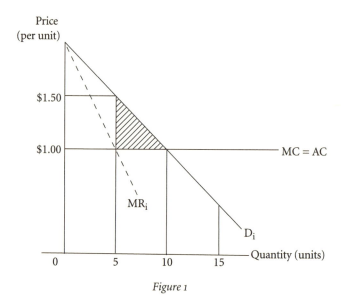

Figure 1

many consumers of this product are identical and that the monopolist himself is secured in his position, i.e., freed from the threat of entry by potential
competitors by, say, patent rights. The costs of producing the good, including a normal rate of return on market-valued assets, are known to be $1 per
unit and these are constant over a wide quantity range. The price charged
by the monopolist is $1.50 per unit, at which price each of his consumers-
customers purchases 5 units per period, for a total outlay of $7.50. At a price
of $1 (the normal or "competitive" price), the consumer would purchase 10
units, for a total expenditure of $10. The measure of the gain that would ac-
crue *to this consumer* by abolition of the monopoly is shown by the familiar
triangle, shaded in Figure 1, *and* the profit rectangle to its left. Arithmetically,
this amounts to $3.75 in this example and, of course, $2.50 of this is a pure
"transfer." *The measure of the welfare gain to society would be $1.25 per buyer,*
i.e., $1.25 multiplied by the number of consumers of the product (all of whom
are assumed to be identical).

RECAPTURING THE "WELFARE TRIANGLE"

This simplified example suggests that the consumer should, rationally, stand
willing to offer *up to $3.75* ($2.50 plus $1.25) for the privilege of being allowed

to purchase freely at a normal or competitive price of $1. The monopolist should, on the other side of such a potential exchange, stand willing to provide the consumer with this privilege *at any sum over and above $2.50.*

Note that, if we confine the discussion to one customer, there seems to be no reason, at least in the conventional economic analysis of this problem, why the monopolist and the customer should not in fact make a mutually profitable arrangement here. The monopolist himself, for example, could form a "discount club," one selling the right to buy the commodity for $1.00 to all customers willing to pay the present value of an income stream of, say, $2.90 per year. This would *recapture the welfare triangle* ($1.25) and thus benefit *both* the monopolist and the customers. (Under monopoly pricing, *neither* gets it.) And this opportunity for mutual profit would not appear, at least at first glance, to be confined to abstract models. If we consider only the traditional arguments, we should also expect such bargains to be struck in the real world, as can be readily demonstrated if we consider the problems of the real monopolist who wishes to maximize the *present* value of his *future* income stream. Clearly he could not sell the right to buy unlimited quantities at the competitive price, but putting limits on the quantities purchased should not pose any major problems for him. The prices charged for entry into the "discount club" could be a simple multiple of the number of units purchased in the year before it was organized.[2]

CAPITALIZED VALUE OF MONOPOLY FIRM

This scheme, it will be seen, immediately obviates one of the major reasons normally given for the absence of such efforts by customers to buy out monopolists. There is no need here for agreement among all the customers, although we might well expect all of them to buy into the discount club and hence eliminate the monopoly altogether. The real question, then, as noted, is the reason for the extreme shortage of such arrangements in the real world. (Dr. Ferdinand Levy has suggested that the sale of "repair warranty" contracts by manufacturers of consumer durables, e.g., automobiles, may be

2. Note that there is no effort here to obtain the "consumer's surplus" above the original monopoly price. Further, there is no need to get *all* of the customers to join the discount club. Membership could be offered on a non-discriminatory basis to anyone who wanted to pay for it.

an example.) For this purpose, let us return to our earlier model, one in which each of the customers is equal, and consider the bargaining situation when a sequence of time periods is explicitly taken into account. Protected by a patent monopoly in this example, our monopolist will sell his right to exploit any customer for any sum above [$2.50/r], where r is the appropriate rate of "discount" (corrected to reflect risk premiums). Assuming consumers estimate the monopolist's risks to be the same as he estimates them, they should then be willing to pay for the whole operation any sum up to a maximum total of [$3.75/r]. Gains-from-trade continue to exist in terms of capitalized values.

Capitalized value of "consumers' surplus"

Consider, however, the position of the single consumer who may be asked to buy into this permanent discount club. Suppose that the monopolist has set a selling price of [$3.00/r] for membership. If the consumer expects his individual demand for the good to remain stable for a sufficiently long period of time, a subjective capitalization of prospective consumer's surplus in subsequent periods may yield meaningfully high present values and the consumer may, in this case, express a willingness to buy. Rarely, however, will the individual consumer actually expect his demand to remain stable over such long periods of time and, even if this should be the case, the limitation on life spans would doubtless interfere to prevent the full capitalization of the consumer's surplus the above computation suggests.

This failure of the individual to capitalize fully his prospective consumer's surplus on his own account may not prevent his joining the club under certain conditions, however. Even if he expects his personal demand to be highly unstable and acts on the basis of a very limited time horizon, he may nevertheless express a willingness to buy in if, in exchange for his investment, he can secure a readily *marketable,* transferable asset. In the prospective exchange between the monopolist and the consumer, however, there is an asymmetry in that, for his part, the monopolist secures a currently liquid asset, while the consumer, on his part, secures the present value of an "expectation" only, his own expected consumer's surplus, an intangible that cannot so readily be transformed into current liquid assets.

Suppose, for example, that an exchange is made on the terms suggested and that, after a few time periods have elapsed, the consumer seeks to market his membership. It is possible, of course, to imagine several institutional arrangements that could make such a marketing of individual shares reasonably efficient, but these arrangements would in every case be costly in themselves. The individual who either enters the market or leaves it entirely can probably be taken care of without too much difficulty, but it is hard to see how the consumer who wishes to reduce his consumption (perhaps as a result of a change in technology) could get his capital back. If, for example, individual consumers (and/or the monopolist) could yearly buy and sell the right to purchase one unit, then the real cost per unit to the individual purchaser would return to what it was before the discount club was organized. The best alternative would probably be to sell the original memberships at a price that not only discounts the monopolist's view of changes in his market, but the individual consumer's view as to whether or not he will remain a part of that market. New customers could buy in, but old customers could not sell out; they would simply lose their capital when they moved out of the market. This would of course sharply reduce the desirability of entering the club in the first place, however, thus suggesting that the individual, as a consumer, might well be reluctant to capitalize his prospective consumer's surplus in such a highly uncertain world.

Monopoly Profits, "Deadweight" Debt, and "Future Generations"

THE "TIME-DIMENSION" PROBLEM

The difficulty in organizing exchanges where consumers can secure fully marketable assets stems, in turn, from the more fundamental problem raised by the *time dimensions* of the exchanges, a problem that is almost wholly ignored in orthodox analysis. The welfare gains that might possibly be secured from the elimination of monopoly output restrictions accrue largely to consumers in periods of time *subsequent* to that in which an institutional exchange of the sort discussed above might take place. Consumers in any *current* period may be reluctant to enter into such purchase agreements because of this feature alone, a fact that immediately suggests the analogy with the retirement of "deadweight" public debt. In this latter situation, current tax-payers may be very reluctant to retire outstanding issues of deadweight public debt for the simple reason that the *beneficiaries* of this action will be tax-payers living in time periods *subsequent* to the retirement operation, i.e., "future generations." Only to the extent that they, themselves, expect to be members of such future taxpaying groups will current taxpayers willingly retire such deadweight public debt, and there are perhaps very few who will be sufficiently Ricardian in their outlook to carry out the full capitalization required to make such a decision wholly rational.[3]

"Burden" of monopoly

The suggestion here is that the "burden" of existing monopoly restrictions is similar to that involved in carrying public debt of this type. The latter consists in the *interest charges* on the debt and, within any single period of time, these charges may be small relative to some appropriate national output measure, e.g., gross national product (GNP). Similarly, the "burden" of monopoly, a loss approximated by the welfare triangle, may be small relative to GNP in any single period, as indeed recent attempts at empirical measurement have tended to suggest.[4] Neither of these conclusions should imply, however, that major public benefits would not be produced by the elimination of the burden-producing debt instruments and monopolistic institutions. Effective retirement of outstanding deadweight debt would produce definite *present-value* benefits, the magnitude of these being measured by the capitalized annual interest charges. And elimination of monopoly restrictions would also produce substantial *present-value* benefits, the size of these being measured by the capitalized current welfare losses (approximated by the welfare triangle in Figure 1). It is these present-value *benefits* that must be

3. For the theory of public debt upon which this discussion is based, see James M. Buchanan, *Public Principles of Public Debt* (Homewood, Ill.: Richard D. Irwin, 1958); for subsequent discussions by both supporters and opponents, see James Ferguson, ed., *Public Debt and Future Generations* (Chapel Hill: University of North Carolina Press, 1964).

4. See A. C. Harberger, "Monopoly and Resource Allocation," *American Economic Review* 44 (May 1954), 77–87.

placed alongside the *costs* of taking such action in any rational cost-benefit calculus.

Monopoly-creation "models"

The analogy with deadweight public debt can be applied also to the *creation* of monopoly. The monopolization of an industry previously competitive in structure is, in the absence of technological change, analogous in effect to the issuance of public debt to finance *wholly worthless* public outlays. The net *wealth of the community is reduced* in either case, with wealth being properly measured to include present values for future tax liabilities, in the one case, and present values of foregone consumers' surplus, in the other.

As an alternative model, consider a monopoly that emerges coincident with a technological innovation, say, through a conferred patent right. The wealth of the community may well increase, and the monopolist's valuation of his patent right should be included in any measurement of national wealth. In addition, some consumers' surplus may also be produced, despite the prospects of monopoly restriction. (This is represented, in Figure 1, by the *upper* triangle above the monopoly-profits area.) And conceptually, at least, the present value of *this* stream of prospective consumers' surplus should also be included in any measurement procedure. This latter monopoly model thus becomes partially analogous to an issue of public debt to finance a public project that is *more than marginally productive*. Here, net *national wealth is in fact increased* to some extent. The claims that public creditors, internal or external, have against the community in the form of the debt instruments is thus in some respects similar to the "claim" of the monopolist, as measured by his valuation of his patent right. The differences between the two cases here stem from the different *locations* of the wealth-creating activity. In the monopoly case, new wealth is presumably brought into being by the monopolist, this act of creation justifying or validating his "right" to a claim against the community. In the debt-issue case, new wealth is also presumably brought into being, but by an act of the community as a whole. The net worth of the creditors who lend funds for the activation of the new project is not changed; instead, the increase in net worth is distributed over all citizens in accordance with their expectations of "beneficiaries' surplus." Aside from this essentially distributional difference, the two cases differ also in that the proper valuation of the debt-financed project will include a full measure of prospective "beneficiaries' surplus," the whole of the area under the "demand curve," with no expected monopoly restriction. In other words, the welfare triangle will be included in this measure.

A third model of monopoly-creation lies somewhere between these first two. The introduction of a technological innovation, for example, even if it causes or allows a previously competitive industry to become monopolized in the process, might well leave the country's net *national wealth unchanged.* In this instance, the monopoly output restriction might do no more than *just offset* the technological gains introduced. Hence the appropriate analogy in this case would be that of a public-debt issue employed to finance a project that is *just marginally productive.*

Monopoly profits "capitalized" at "moment of creation"

Attention to the various analogies between monopoly-creation and public-debt issue produces what should be an obvious conclusion but one that, in our view, has not been sufficiently emphasized before. *The benefits of monopoly tend to be capitalized at the moment of creation,* at least to the extent that marketable assets (e.g., stocks) are brought into being. And insofar as such capitalization does in fact take place, "future generations," in the aggregate, must bear the monopoly burden in terms of the offsetting losses in consumers' surplus.

Suppose that, in some "base" year t_0, an individual is granted a monopoly right to produce the good depicted in Figure 1. The present-value of this right, over and above the market value of the assets used to produce it, is measured at [\$3.00 n/r]. This is a marketable asset, and the individual monopolist enters this on the left-hand side of his balance sheet, offsetting it with a similar increase in net worth on the right-hand side. On the national balance sheet, therefore, there will appear an increment to or increase in the wealth of the economy. We assume that the capitalized value of consumers' surplus, measured by the upper triangle, is not computed.

Suppose now that, in a later period t_1, the individual who owns the monopoly right sells out to a purchaser at a price approximated by [\$3.00 n/r].

To the purchaser, this investment must be roughly equal in yield to his alternative investment prospects. And, to the seller, competition among prospective purchasers will insure that the yield is equal to that on alternative investments of roughly the same risk. The purchaser of his monopoly right, in t_1, thus writes up this asset on his balance sheet and writes down some other asset. His net worth remains unchanged, save for the possibility of marginal adjustments. Having acquired the monopoly right, however, the net worth of the new owner *now depends on the continuation of the existing and expected monopoly output restrictions.* If through governmental action or otherwise, his monopoly "right" is now eliminated, he suffers a capital loss. *His* net worth is reduced, while the *net worth of the original monopolizer remains unchanged.* To make our example dramatic, we can allow the latter to die between t_1 and t_2, with the monopoly restriction eliminated only in the latter period, after his death.

No monopoly profits for current owners

Thus it may be quite literally true that existing monopoly restrictions do not differentially benefit *current* owners of monopoly firms, save in some opportunity-cost sense, but, rather, that these benefits have long since been capitalized by monopoly entrepreneurs of generations past. The "evil of monopoly" lies in the period of creation, and the "ill-gotten gains" may now be enjoyed by third-generation playboys who cruise the Riviera and live off gilt-edge coupons, quite beyond the reach of any antitrust order. These gains thus remain untouched by any efforts to break up and eliminate the monopolies existing at any particular moment in time, leaving the unfortunate current owners of the monopoly rights as the ones singled out for "unjust" public treatment.

It is of course widely recognized that monopoly restrictions do not necessarily imply monopoly profits. It is perhaps less widely acknowledged that the existence of monopoly profits, in the ordinary sense, do not imply that any current owner of a monopoly firm earns more than a normal rate of return on his own *personal* investment. The *physical* assets of the firm will be employed in such a way as to yield more than a normal return but the current owner, in *purchasing* these assets, may have transferred to the *former* owners the fully capitalized value of all expected *future* monopoly returns.

Implications for Public Policy

The monopoly problem is thus seen here as a blend of simple capitalization theory, simple accounting, and a recognition of the analogy with the problem of "deadweight" public debt. Once these separate elements of the analysis are seen, the general conclusions are fairly self-evident. Mention might be made here, however, of a number of practical policy suggestions presented by this analysis.

"PREVENTION" VERSUS "CURE"

Both equity and casual observation of the collective or political decision-making process suggests the importance of concentrating on the *prevention* of monopoly, rather than upon its elimination after it has already been created. The social "evil" of monopoly tends to be *concentrated in the moment of creation* and, once this "original sin" is committed, the effects are capitalized or "frozen" into the system. And while it is of course true that monopoly-creation can be, and probably is in many cases, a continuous process that grows over time, the more instantaneous phenomenon is nonetheless sufficiently real to warrant a shift of emphasis toward the prevention rather than the attempted cure of monopoly problems.

"COMPENSATION" FOR CURRENT MONOPOLY-OWNERS?

Equity considerations alone suggest the desirability of providing appropriate *compensation* to current stockholders when long-existing monopoly restrictions are eliminated by express governmental action. These restrictions having probably been long since capitalized by former owners, the *current* owners may well be realizing, as noted, no more than the normally expected gains from their individual investments. Simple norms of justice would thus suggest that those current owners of shares in monopoly firms be considered no more "guilty" than non-owners and hence that any monopoly-elimination without compensation would amount, in such cases, to a particularly discriminatory "tax" on current shareholders, one that, if placed on that group openly, might well fail to win legislative approval or even constitutional sanction by the judiciary.

"POLITICAL" BARRIERS TO "COMPENSATION"?

Despite these acknowledged equity considerations, however, even cursory attention to democratic decision-making processes suggests that public policy would rarely attempt to eliminate any existing monopoly positions if compensation *was* in fact tied to the elimination measures. To pay compensation requires an outlay of public funds, and it would doubtless be very difficult to persuade current-period taxpayers (as represented in legislative assemblies) that *they* should support such outlays today when the prospective beneficiaries of their sacrifice would be consumers of *future* periods. The policy solution is almost implied. The appropriate *method of financing* such compensation would be one involving the use of special issues of public debt instruments, a solution that would of course allow for an appropriate balancing-off, in a temporal sense, of anticipated costs and anticipated benefits, making the suggested outcome plausible for a rational democratic choice while at the same time securing reasonable equity in results.

Thus at least two specific applications of these principles come immediately to mind. First, if a collective decision should be made to shift a long-standing private monopoly to public or national ownership for the purpose of eliminating its monopoly output restrictions, this analysis clearly suggests that the funds to be used for compensating existing owners should be financed by debt issue, not by taxation.

PATENT POLICY — FREE LICENSING

Perhaps a more important practical application, however, lies in the realm of patent policy. If the award of monopoly rights is considered essential to insure the continuation of adequate incentives for invention, research, and development, this analysis suggests that many of the undesirable side-effects of patent monopolies could be eliminated by a combination of the institutional devices noted here. Thus an individual or firm could be granted full patent rights on new products but, once those rights were established at market values, public purchase (financed by debt issue) could be undertaken, accompanied by an arrangement for *free licensing,* a solution that would allow public purchase of the patent right without implying public purchase or ownership of producing assets.

On Monopoly Price

Geoffrey Brennan, James Buchanan,
and Dwight Lee

I. Introduction

In this paper we shall argue that the orthodox theory of monopoly price is incomplete and, in some respects at least, misleading. The standard criterion for profit-maximization, the equality between marginal cost and marginal revenue, is, in general, invalid, unless the criterion is interpreted in such a way as to make it empty of normative content. Under the static demand and cost conditions that are implicit in orthodox textbook formulations, the monopolist's profit-maximizing price will normally be *above* that price-quantity combination that equates long-run marginal cost and long-run marginal revenue.

Our emendation to the basic theory here incorporates the recognition that buyer adjustment to price change takes time. The simple proposition that the price elasticity of demand is typically lower in the short run than in the long run is, of course, widely accepted, and it has empirical as well as analytical support. If demonstration is required, perhaps the most straightforward procedure would be to consider consumer behavior in "household production function" terms, associated with the work of Becker, Becker and

From *Kyklos* 36, Fasc. 4 (1983): 531–47. Copyright by Helbing and Lichtenhahn. Reprinted by permission of the publisher.

Center for Study of Public Choice, George Mason University, Fairfax, Va., U.S.A. We are grateful to David Levy and participants in the Public Choice Center's Seminar Series for helpful comments. This topic came to our attention because of certain similarities to the question of tax revenue maximization in discussions of the Laffer curve. See James Buchanan and Dwight Lee, "Politics, Time, and the Laffer Curve," *Journal of Political Economy* 90 (1982): 816–19, for a somewhat related argument on the Laffer curve question.

Michael, and Stigler and Becker.[1] In this approach, consumers acquire human capital in transforming purchased goods, the X's, into the underlying Z goods that enter into the relevant utility functions. Such human capital cannot be instantly acquired or accumulated or costlessly destroyed; it takes *time* fully to adjust the level of such capital to that which is optimal or efficient in the light of any changed vector of prices for the X goods. We should, accordingly, predict that quantity adjustments made in response to any given change in product prices will be smaller in the short run than in the long run. Even if the Becker approach is not adopted, it is evident that many products that are purchased have durable goods complements and/or substitutes. For example, even if there is some instantaneous reduction in miles traveled in response to an increase in gasoline price, complete adjustment to the higher price is delayed by the size of existing automobiles. Full adjustment to the price increase will occur only after the sizes of the engines have been reduced through replacement of the initially existing stock of vehicles. In all such cases, short-run consumer-purchaser response to price changes will be "sticky" in the short run relative to the long run.

The implications of this simple, and unchallenged, proposition for the theory of monopoly price are straightforward, even if devastating in certain respects. We find it surprising that these implications have not, at least to our knowledge, been long since incorporated into orthodox analysis.

In this paper, we shall trace out these implications in the simplest possible analytical setting. In Section II, we discuss the implicit assumptions about temporal dimensionality that are required in order to work within the orthodox monopoly model. In Section III, we set out the basic analytic ingredients of our alternative model. In Section IV, we present a simple linear model in which the familiar "long-run marginal revenue equals long-run marginal cost" criterion *is* a necessary condition for profit maximization, and we indicate the particular circumstances that are critically required for this solution. We then proceed to derive, still using linear examples, several other propositions that are generalized in Section V. In both Sections IV and V,

1. Gary S. Becker, "A Theory of the Allocation of Time" (1965), in *The Economic Approach to Human Behavior* (Chicago, 1976); Gary S. Becker and Robert T. Michael, "On the New Theory of Consumer Behavior" (1973), in ibid.; and George J. Stigler and Gary S. Becker, "De Gustibus Non Est Disputandum," *American Economic Review* 67 (1977): 76–90.

we focus entirely on the single price solution to the monopolist's profit-maximizing problem. In Section VI, the possible efficacy of an oscillating pricing strategy is explored. In Section VII, we introduce buyer expectations, and indirectly demonstrate the applicability of the single-price constraint. In Section VIII, we draw relevant conclusions.

II. Temporal Dimensionality in the Conventional Textbook Monopoly Case

Conventional monopoly theory takes as its point of departure the simple, single, down-sloping demand curve for the product of the monopoly seller. The model is presented without reference to the time dimension. But what time frame is implicitly assumed? At first glance, it would not seem necessary to be specific as to time dimension: it may seem possible to select any "period of consumer adjustment" desired or appropriate for the analysis purposes at hand.

Such an inference would, however, be totally wrong. In fact, the single demand-curve construction necessarily implies a long-run perspective because only under the assumption that *all* relevant consumer adjustment has taken place in response to price changes is it possible to postulate a unique relationship between price and quantity demanded. The location of any demand curve that is constructed to reflect buyer adjustments short of the completion of the sequence must necessarily depend on the position from which the adjustment commenced.

To put this point more generally, there exists for any initial price-quantity equilibrium on the long-run (full adjustment) demand curve an entire family of demand curves issuing from that equilibrium position, each one of which reflects a different adjustment period. In Figure 1, for example, suppose that the initial position is that shown at $E(p_1, q_1)$ on the long-run demand curve for product X, labeled D_{LR}. A price increase from p_1 to p_2 will induce a quantity reduction that will depend on the length of time allowed for buyers to adjust to the change, say to q_2 after one month, to q_3 after a quarter, to q_4 after one year, and finally to q_5 on the long-run demand curve. Given any other starting position along D_{LR}, it is possible to construct another precisely analogous set of short- and intermediate-run demand curves, as shown for position F in Figure 1. There is only one curve that represents

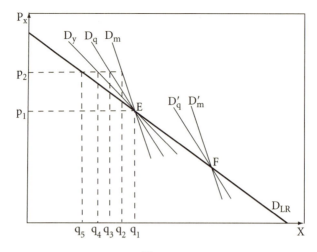

Figure 1

a unique, ahistorical demand relationship between price and quantity demanded—the long-run demand curve. No other curve can be drawn without reference to the particular price history.

III. The Model

For the purposes of our discussion here, we shall collapse all considerations of time into the simple "short-run/long-run" distinction: to analyze the adjustment process in terms of continuous time would be formidable technically and probably serve only to obscure the central points. The "long run" is defined as the length of time it takes for *full* consumer adjustment to price change. We define the "short run" to be exactly one half of the long run. On this basis, we can define a "period" to last the length of the short run, and thereby simplify the matter of discounting.

We shall abstract entirely from costs: total, average and marginal costs are assumed to be zero. That is, we are dealing with Cournot's classic mineral spring: the single profit-maximizing monopolist owns a unique non-depreciating resource that costlessly produces a continuous flow of homogeneous, directly consumable, non-storable output units, at a level more than sufficient to meet aggregate demand at any non-negative price in any period.

The long-run demand curve for the monopolist's product is depicted by

$$q = f(p), \tag{1}$$

where $f'(p) < 0$. The short-run demand curve is given by

$$q = g(p, p_0), \tag{2}$$

where p is the price in the current period and p_0 is the price to which behavior has been adjusted prior to the current price change. We note that

$$0 > g_1 > g_2[= f'(p)],$$

where g_i is the partial derivative of g with respect to the ith argument.

Because of the zero-cost assumption, profit is the product of price and output. Profit in the long run is

$$\Pi_L = p \cdot f(p). \tag{3}$$

This is maximized at the price-output combination (p^*, q^*)—that is, where long-run marginal revenue equals long-run marginal cost (here zero). In other words, we define p^* such that

$$\frac{d\Pi_L}{dp}(p^*) = 0 \tag{4}$$

and hence,

$$p^* = \frac{f(p^*)}{-f'(p^*)}. \tag{5}$$

This is the orthodox profit-maximizing solution. Short-run profit is

$$\Pi_s = p \cdot g(p, p_0), \tag{6}$$

which is maximized at the price-output combination (p_s, q_s) where

$$\frac{\partial \Pi_s}{\partial p}(p_s) = 0. \tag{7}$$

The p_s so defined will be a function of p_0, and can be written

$$p_s = \frac{g(p_s, p_0)}{g'(p_s, p_0)}. \tag{8}$$

The monopolist aims to maximize the present discounted value of the profit stream from his assets, the discount rate used being necessarily equal to the market rate of return since his monopoly right is taken to be a fully marketable asset in which he owns a costlessly enforceable property right.

The monopolist's maximand is thus

$$PV_\Pi = \Pi_s + \frac{\Pi_L}{r}, \tag{9}$$

where r is the market rate of return. Initially we shall deal with this problem *as if* the solution involved choosing a single best price to prevail in all periods. Subsequently, we shall relax the single-price requirement to explore alternative price strategies. However, as we shall argue, the single-price model may be a fair approximation to the profit-maximizing strategy once the complication of consumer price expectations is included in the analysis. Unless otherwise stated, we shall adopt the "Cournot" assumption that consumers always act as if the current price will prevail forever.

IV. A Preliminary Example

We commence with a highly simplified linear example. We first present a case in which the orthodox "long-run marginal-revenue/marginal-cost" equation is valid and then proceed to isolate the conditions under which—in the context of this linear example—the orthodox rule fails.

Suppose that the monopolist, "Cournot," stumbles across his mineral spring while wandering one day in an obscure corner of the wilderness. No one has ever sampled mineral water before: there is no competitive source of supply. In this case, the initially prevailing output is necessarily zero. The demand curve for mineral water which "Cournot" faces in the first period is the short-run demand curve depicted as D_S in Figure 2. The characteristic feature of D_S is that it intersects the long-run demand curve, D_L, at the *zero output* level—or at what we might term the "choke" price, $\overline{p}$. Both D_L and D_S are taken to be linear for the purposes of the discussion of this section.

We further suppose that "Cournot" is seeking a *single* price, to be set currently and to prevail over an indefinite future in which demand conditions are constant and are known to be as depicted in Figure 2. What price will maximize the present discounted value of the profit stream? Recall that "Cournot" is seeking to maximize

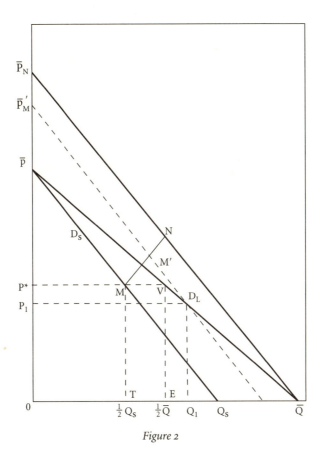

Figure 2

$$PV_\Pi = \Pi_s + \frac{\Pi_L}{r}.$$

In this case, the price that maximizes Π_s is also the price that maximizes Π_L. Hence, that price, p*, will maximize PV_Π. This can be seen most easily perhaps by appeal to Figure 2. From a familiar theorem, we know that with linear demand curves that intersect along the ordinate, price elasticity is constant along any horizontal line. It follows that the unitary price elasticity point on D_S and D_L involves the same price—a price that is exactly half the "choke" price, $\bar{p}$.[2] Hence, the price that maximizes the present value of the

2. We can depict the short run demand curve as

profit stream is that where long-run marginal revenue equals long-run marginal cost (of zero): the familiar result emerges unscathed.

It should be emphasized, however, that there is nothing "natural" or intrinsically compelling about starting from the zero output "equilibrium." It is every bit as natural to suppose that "Cournot" receives his monopoly position by acquiring an enforceable property right to a natural resource that had long since been widely used as a free good. Or, we might suppose that he has "bought out" his competitors in the mineral spring business (possibly at zero price). In either of these cases, we would begin from a *zero* price (or competitive marginal cost) equilibrium. Alternatively, "Cournot" may have inherited his monopoly franchise from a gallery of ancestors who had dutifully read the formal analysis of the monopoly price problem and set price accordingly at p^*. In none of these quite plausible cases is zero output the starting point. Yet the zero output starting point is, in our example, crucial to the orthodox result.

To see this, note that the price, p_s, that maximizes short-run profit will, in the linear case, always be one half of the short-run "choke" price (where the short-run demand curve cuts the vertical axis). For *any* starting point on D_L other than $(\overline{p}, 0)$, this short-run "choke" price exceeds $\frac{1}{2}\overline{p}$ and hence exceeds p^*. For example, if the initial equilibrium had been at (p_1, q_1) on D_L, the short-run "choke" price would be $\overline{p}'_M$ and the short-run profit maximum at M'. More generally, the locus of short-run profit maxima, as the initially prevailing equilibrium price falls from $\overline{p}$ to zero, is the line segment MN, a segment of the ray from the origin through M.

Now, since p_s exceeds p^* for all starting points other than $(\overline{p}, 0)$, it follows that

$$\frac{d\Pi_s}{dp}(p^*) > 0. \tag{10}$$

$D_S = b(\overline{p} - p)$, and hence $\Pi_s = b(\overline{p} - p) \cdot p$,

which is maximized at $p_s = \frac{1}{2}\overline{p}$. The long-run demand curve is

$D_L = a(\overline{p} - p) \ (a > b)$ and $\Pi_L = a(\overline{p} - p) \cdot p$,

which is maximized at $p^* = \frac{1}{2}\overline{p}$.

Hence,

$$\frac{dPV_\Pi}{dp}(p^*) = \frac{d\Pi_s}{dp}(p^*) + \frac{1}{r} \cdot \frac{d\Pi_L}{dp}(p^*) > 0, \qquad (11)$$

since $d\Pi_L/dp(p^*) = 0$ by definition.

We have therefore shown that the profit-maximizing monopolist, in this simple linear example, will set a price *greater than* p^*, except where the initially prevailing equilibrium involves zero output. In general, the "long-run-marginal-revenue-equals-zero" rule is wrong.[3]

V. The General Case

In this section, we discard the linearity assumptions of our simple example in Section IV. Our aim is to prove a set of general propositions about the pricing strategy of the profit-maximizing monopolist, retaining the assumption that a single price is to be set that will prevail for the indefinite future.

Proposition 1

$$\frac{\partial PV_\Pi(p^*, p_0)}{\partial p} > 0 \; \forall \; p_0 \leq p^*$$

Proof

$$PV_\Pi(p, p_0) = pg(p, p_0) + \frac{1}{r}pf(p),$$

so

$$\frac{\partial PV_\Pi}{\partial p} = pg_1(p, p_0) + g(p, p_0) + \frac{1}{r}[pf'(p) + f(p)]. \qquad (12)$$

When evaluated at $p = p^*$, the bracketed term on the right vanishes by virtue of equation (5), and

$$\frac{\partial PV_n(P^*, P_0)}{\partial P} = pg_1(p^*, p_0) + g(p^*, p_0) > pf'(p^*) + f(p^*) = 0. \qquad (13)$$

3. It can be shown that in this linear case, the price that maximizes PV_Π is a weighted average of p_s and p^*, with the weights depending on the discount rate, r, and the short-run and long-run elasticities.

The inequality in (13) follows from the fact that $g_1(p^*, p_0) > f'(p^*)$ (the short-run response to a given price can never be as large in absolute value as the long-run response) and $g(p^*, p_0) \geq f(p^*) \; \forall \; p_0 \leq p^*$, with the equality holding only when $p_0 = p^*$.

Proposition 1 is sufficient to discredit the familiar Cournot result. Assuming nothing more than downward-sloping demand curves, and that short-run elasticities are smaller than long-run, the profit-maximizing price exceeds p^* for any initial equilibrium price less than or equal to p^* (and, by normal continuity assumptions, for some initial price above p^*). In particular, if the Cournot price, p^*, prevails, there will always be a rational incentive to increase price above that level: if "Cournot" prices his mineral water according to the Cournot rule, he can expect to be bought out by an entrepreneur who will charge a higher price.

Proposition 2

$$\frac{\partial PV_{\Pi}}{\partial p_0}(\hat{p}) < 0,$$

where $\hat{p}$ is the price that maximizes PV_{Π}.

Proof. The price, $\hat{p}$, that maximizes PV_{Π} depends on the initially prevailing price, p_0. If we set (12) at zero, therefore, we implicitly define $\hat{p}$ as a continuously differentiable function of p_0 (assuming second-order conditions to be satisfied):

$$\hat{p} = h(p_0).$$

Taking the total derivative of maximum profit with respect to p_0, yields

$$\frac{dPV_{\Pi}(\hat{p})}{dp_0} = [\hat{p} \cdot g_1 + g + \frac{1}{r}(p \cdot f' + f)] \frac{d\hat{p}}{dp_0} + \hat{p} \cdot g_2, \qquad (14)$$

and we note that this first term on the right-hand side of (14) is zero, so

$$\frac{dPV_{\Pi}(\hat{p})}{dp_0} = \hat{p} \cdot g_2 < 0.$$

What *Proposition 2* reminds us is that the value of the monopoly right depends crucially on the *price history:* an entrepreneur will pay more for "Cournot's" mineral spring the *lower* the price that "Cournot" has been charging. The spring that "Cournot" discovers ab initio is worth less than if that identical spring had long since been enjoyed at zero price.

Proposition 3

$$\frac{d\hat{p}}{dp_0} < 0 \text{ unless } g_2(\hat{p}, p_0) + \hat{p} \cdot g_{12}(\hat{p}, p_0) > 0$$

Proof. Setting (12) at zero defines $\hat{p}$ as a function of p_0, $\hat{p} = h(p_0)$.
Taking the total derivatives of $PV_\Pi(\hat{p})$ with respect to p_0, yields

$$\left[\hat{p}g_{11} + 2g_1 + \frac{1}{r}(pf'' + 2f')\right]\frac{d\hat{p}}{dp_0} + g_2 + \hat{p}g_{12} = 0,$$

or

$$\frac{d\hat{p}}{dp_0} = \frac{-(g_2 + \hat{p}g_{12})}{\left[\hat{p}g_{11} + 2g_1 + \frac{1}{r}(pf'' + 2f')\right]}. \tag{15}$$

Satisfaction of the sufficiency conditions implies the denominator of (14) is negative. Therefore

$$\frac{d\hat{p}}{dp_0} \text{ has the same sign as } (g_2 + \hat{p}g_{12}).$$

This proposition needs some interpreting. We know that

$$g_2(\hat{p}, p_0) < 0.$$

Hence, $g_2 + \hat{p}g_{12}$ can be non-negative only if $g_{12}(\hat{p}, p_0) > 0$. This requires that as we move up the long-run demand curve from $(0, \overline{Q})$, the short-run demand curve become steeper. Now, if short-run demand curves were to *intersect*, we would seem to have a totally perverse case. Setting that possibility aside clearly sets limits on how much greater than zero g_{12} can be. On this basis, it seems reasonable to expect that the lower is the initially prevailing equilibrium price p_0, the higher will be the profit-maximizing price, $\hat{p}$.

Taken together, these propositions are sufficient to demonstrate two more general claims:

first, that the "long-run-marginal-revenue-equals-zero" rule will not, in general, yield the true profit-maximizing price; second, that the previous price history is a crucial determinant of both monopoly price and monopoly profit and that, in this sense, here at least, bygones are not bygones.

These propositions do, however, depend on the assumption that the monopolist sets a single price to prevail over an indefinite future. Whether this is a reasonable assumption or not is a question to which we now turn.

VI. Oscillating Price and Unfolding History

It is surely tempting, on simple inspection of the profit-maximizing problem as depicted in equation (9), to query whether the setting of a *single* price can be any sort of profit-maximizing strategy. Why not set a price that maximizes short-run profit in the current period and then set the price that maximizes long-run profit thereafter?

Clearly, the answer to this question, on reflection, is that the "long run" never comes. The maximization of the present value of profits at *any* point in time includes an inescapable short-run dimension. And as we have indicated, the "long-run" profit-maximizing price p* is not generally a "best" price. Consequently, although the price that maximizes the present value of profits will change with time as the price history changes, it will not "settle down" to the long-run profit-maximizing price. We know this because if price did happen to settle on p*, a price increase would raise the present value of the profit stream. So, even if a completely dynamic solution to the monopoly pricing problem was developed, it is clear that any convergent price path (assuming one exists) would converge to a price higher than p*. We leave it to others to investigate the relevant dynamics here.

There exists the possibility, of course, that the price path does not converge and a truly dynamic solution will call for price to oscillate explosively. Because of this there remains an important question of how the case of explosive oscillation is to be interpreted. Purely economic considerations will occasionally set bounds on mathematically unbounded outcomes. Suppose, for example, we rule out negative prices and negative quantities. Then the explosive case simply reverts to that in which the monopolist oscillates between a zero price and the price that maximizes short-run profit based on a starting price p_0 of zero. Then price will oscillate "explosively" only if the profit stream thereby generated exceeds the profit stream generated by a single profit-maximizing price.

We can easily establish conditions under which this is so. Suppose, for example, we start at the zero price. Then when a single uniform price is charged,

$$PV_\Pi = p[\overline{Q} - bp] + \frac{1}{r}[\overline{Q} - ap]p,$$

which is maximized for p_s^0 where

$$p_s^0 = \frac{(1 + r)\overline{Q}}{2a + 2br},$$

and PV_Π becomes

$$PV_\Pi(p_s^0) = \frac{(1 + r)^2}{4r} \cdot \frac{\overline{Q}^2}{a + br}.$$

If the solution is "explosive," then we oscillate between

(i) a zero price, and hence a zero profit; and
(ii) the short-run profit-maximizing price and associated profit based on p_0 being zero. The profit in this case is

$$p_0^*(\overline{Q} - bp_0^*),$$

where

$$p_0^* = \frac{\overline{Q}}{2b}[\text{found by maximizing } p_0^*(\overline{Q} - bp_0^*)].$$

Consequently, the present value of profits in this oscillating case is

$$PV_\Pi(\text{osc.}) = p_0^*(\overline{Q} - bp_0^*) + \frac{p_0^*(\overline{Q} - bp_0^*)}{(1 + r)^2} + \cdots = \frac{(1 + r)^2\overline{Q}^2}{4r \cdot (2 + r)b}.$$

The oscillating equilibrium will dominate if and only if

$$\frac{1}{(2 + r)b} > \frac{1}{a + rb} \quad \text{i.e., } a > 2b.$$

VII. Expectations Introduced

In both the single-price and the oscillating-price models analyzed above, we have implicitly assumed that buyers of the monopolist's product expect the price that prevails in any period to be maintained indefinitely. This expectation is, of course, rational in the single-price setting, but only because the single-price requirement was directly imposed on the monopolist's pricing strategy. As the analysis of Section VI suggests, if buyers always expect the current-period price to be permanent, the monopolist can exploit his profit opportunities by adopting a pricing strategy in which prices move up and down through time. In such a setting, it would scarcely be rational for buyers to maintain any expectation of price uniformity. Rather, buyers should both learn from price experience and recognize their own potential vulnerability to a price-oscillation strategy.

If we model the buyers' expectations so as to incorporate a recognition of the monopolist's proclivity to adopt a non-uniform pricing strategy, the single-price model becomes considerably less arbitrary. In the face of a set of potential buyers, all of whom are rational in their expectations, the profit-maximizing monopolist may well select a single price and leave this price unchanged over the whole sequence of periods.

Consider a single potential buyer, in the setting where he observes the monopolization of a previously competitive industry, and where he predicts that the monopoly rights will be permanent. New entrants will not emerge to erode the monopoly position. This buyer will recognize the short-run profits available to the newly established monopolist during the period of adjustment from the previous level of competitive price. He will reckon that the monopolist can move to exploit these short-run opportunities. He will also predict, however, that, having once exploited these adjustment-period gains, the monopolist may have an incentive to drop price dramatically in order to create later opportunities for comparable short-run gains. The buyer will not, however, respond to the short-run increases or decreases in price that the monopolist makes in the post-adjustment periods in a manner that the non-expectational models of earlier sections imply.

There are at least two ways that the consumer can adjust his short-run consumption response to price changes that are expected to be temporary. Both types of adjustment reduce the profitability of an oscillating-price policy relative to the profitability of a single-price policy. First, adjustments in consumption-related capital will be motivated by oscillating prices that increase the elasticity of the short-run demand curves. For example, in response to oscillations in the price of gasoline the consumer may situate himself more conveniently to public transportation which can be immediately utilized when gas price is increased. Secondly, the earlier assumption of nonstorability becomes more restrictive once we consider the possibility of oscillating prices. The product that is not economically storable (the cost of storage exceeds the benefit) when a steady supply is available at a constant price may become economically storable when price oscillates. If, as is likely, the consumer responds to price oscillations by investing in storage facilities, the effect will again be to increase the elasticity of the short-run demand curve.

Faced with the possibility of these consumer adjustments, the monopolist may find that profit maximization requires pursuing a credible single-price policy rather than attempting to gain a series of short-run advantages by varying price over time. The analytics of Section VI provides some analytical support for this conclusion. Ruling out explosive price oscillations that will eventually find price moving from plus to minus infinity, the choice is between bounded oscillations of the type previously analyzed, and a single price. As indicated in the previous section, the more elastic is the short-run demand curve relative to the long-run demand curve, the more profitable the single-price policy relative to the oscillating-price policy. So the assumption that the monopolist picks a single price and maintains it may not be overly restrictive once it is recognized that the monopolist will not be able to confront the consumer with strategic pricing behavior without motivating a strategic response.

On this basis, we advance the analysis of the single-price monopolist, set out in the earlier sections, as an interesting and potentially relevant case.

VIII. Conclusions

We suggested at the outset of this paper that the received theory of monopoly price is incomplete and that our aim was that of filling in the gaps. We do not claim that our emendations are paradigm-shaking in any quantitative sense. Given relatively low real rates of return on capital in an economy, the monopolist who strictly adopts the profit-maximizing precepts of our models, when and if such opportunities emerge, need not behave in a manner that is dramatically different from the monopolist who follows the precepts of Cournot. There will, however, be a qualitative difference in behavior here, a difference that should be analytically recognized.[4]

We should not expect that the textbook orthodoxy on monopoly price would be greatly modified in the light of our emendations to the theory. We should, however, expect textbook authors and instructors to make the simple transference of the short-run–long-run elasticity distinction found in the demand-theory chapters to the chapter on monopoly price. And, more importantly, we should expect that more attention would be paid to the relevance of the *history of prices,* both in deriving pricing strategies and in computing the capital values of monopoly enterprises.

Summary

A fundamental proposition from elementary price theory is that monopoly profits are maximized at the price that equates the marginal revenue derived from the long-run demand curve to the marginal cost of production. An equally well known proposition is that demand elasticities are greater in the long run than the short run. It is shown in the present paper that the former proposition is qualified in important ways when the latter proposition is incorporated into the analysis of the monopoly problem. In general, the monopoly profit-maximizing price will be higher than the one derived from the conventional analysis. This will not be true in the special case of linear short- and long-run demand curves with an initial price that chokes off all demand. In this case the profit-maximizing monopoly price will be identical to that

---

4. An aspect of the theory of monopoly behavior that is closely analogous to that which we emphasize here has been widely recognized. If we drop the assumption made throughout our analysis that the monopolist is protected and allow for entry, no one would question the proposition that profit-seeking behavior would involve the attempt to capture short-run profits. The difference between this familiar model and our own lies in the fact that in our construction the exploitation of short-run profits involves costs in present value of long-run profits, whereas, in the case of potential entry, long-run profits will be eroded quite independent of the monopolist's short-period behavior.

obtained from the standard approach. As this suggests, and as we show, price history is an important consideration when choosing the profit-maximizing price. The lower the price in the past, the higher, in general, will be the price that maximizes the present value of future profits, and the greater this present value will be.

A Regional Countermeasure to National Wage Standardization

James M. Buchanan and John E. Moes

Economists have, almost without exception, discussed policy questions from the point of view of national governments. Political reality indicates that even within a single government's over-all policy program internally conflicting and offsetting measures are often encountered. Even more likely is it that, when two or more independently organized and overlapping governmental units enact economic policy measures simultaneously over the domain of the same economy, the separate governmental units may have sharply conflicting policy objectives as well as different constitutionally determined powers of action. In political federalism, conflicts between the national government and the state or regional government units seem certain to occur. In such a political setting, the economist's tools may be quite helpful in suggesting ways and means through which a separate governmental unit may take action to offset or negate the effects of policy measures taken by an overlapping jurisdiction. The possibility that action taken by the separate states may serve to offset national government policy which is contrary to the interest of the national economy has not been adequately considered. This paper attempts to examine a particular case of this sort.

We assume a closed economy extending over a wide geographical area. The economic order is competitive, and the legal structure includes institutions which effectively enforce competitive norms except where specific exemption is granted. The national government also enforces the employment

From *American Economic Review* 50 (June 1960): 434–38. Reprinted by permission of the publisher.

of a common currency unit throughout the economy. Suppose now that the national government imposes a legal minimum wage, higher than the lowest wage that would otherwise prevail. This wage is standardized for the whole economy, and its coverage extends over a significant number of the employed workers, but not over all workers. No account is taken of differing labor-market conditions in the separate regions. We also assume specifically that there is a national policy of exempting labor organizations from the legal sanctions against restraint of trade. Labor organizations are encouraged to bargain collectively to obtain favorable wage contracts. These contracts are assumed to include standardized wage rates for similar jobs in different geographic regions of the economy.

Within this single national economy there are a number of regional governmental units possessing residual political powers. These states are prohibited by the Constitution from interfering directly with the flow of resources, goods, and services across state boundary lines. The states retain financial independence. They are empowered to tax individuals directly and indirectly to secure revenue for the performance of independent governmental functions or to provide transfers.

The states are classified into two groups, the difference between which is defined in terms of the ratios of the productive factors. The origins of these differences in factor ratios need not concern us; they may be due to historical development, a different natural resource base, or to any other reason. The first group contains large amounts of unskilled and semiskilled labor relative to capital and skilled labor. The second group contains large amounts of capital and skilled labor relative to unskilled and semiskilled labor. We shall call the first group the "labor-surplus" states, and the second group the "capital-surplus" states, although the relative nature of the surplus in each case should be kept clearly in mind.

In this setting, it is clear that the effects of the two specific national policy measures mentioned, standardized minimum wages and standardized union-enforced wage rates, will cause real wages in covered industries in the labor-surplus states to be too high from the point of view of the usual market criteria for maximum efficiency. If the minimum wage is at all effective, some qualified workers in the labor-surplus states will not be able to find employment at the wage rates prevailing in the industries covered by the legislation. These workers will be forced to remain unemployed or to find employment in those occupational and industrial groupings not covered by either standardized wage contracts or minimum wage restrictions; or, perhaps more realistically, these workers will be forced to remain employed ("underemployed") in the uncovered areas of the regional economy. It follows that wages in the occupations and industries not covered by either the minimum wage legislation or by standardized union contracts will be lower than those that would prevail in the absence of the national policy measures outlined.

Workers unable to find employment in the covered or standardized industries in the labor-surplus states will find it advantageous to migrate to the capital-surplus states to the extent that labor can be absorbed there. Since the policies discussed are national in scope, the employers in covered industries in the capital-surplus states cannot hire workers below the nationally set wage levels. Migration of capital and skilled labor from the capital-surplus to the labor-surplus states will also take place to some extent, but this migration may be impeded by the wage standardization policies.

We now seek specifically to answer the question, Is there any action that the individual states may take which will effectively offset the central government policy of enforced wage standardization? It is evident that only the labor-surplus states will be directly interested in such action.

If offsetting action by the individual labor-surplus state is to be effective, it must result in a lowering of real labor costs for the unskilled and semiskilled categories in those industries covered by the standardization, where the relative surplus is assumed to exist. We propose a policy of state taxation of employees' wages coupled with the subsidization of all employers in proportion to their wage bills. This policy measure seems clearly to fall within the limits of state constitutional powers as outlined in the policy model. The tax would be generally imposed on all payrolls; it would not be discriminatory. The proceeds would be returned directly to employers of labor in proportion to their total payrolls.

The policy proposal suggested is deceptively simple, so much so that some further analysis of its effects seems warranted. The employer would be authorized to deduct the proportional state tax from the paychecks of the individual wage and salary earners. What would be the incidence of this tax? It is necessary here to distinguish quite sharply between those categories of labor which are in "surplus" and those which are "scarce." In our model, we have assumed that the labor-surplus areas are characterized by a relatively large number of unskilled and semiskilled laborers, but by a relatively small number of skilled workers. For the surplus laborers employed in covered or standardized industries, the tax would fall squarely on the wage earner. Because of the large supply of labor that is able and willing to work at the standardized wage rate, even after payment of the tax, the employer would not find it necessary to increase wages or salaries to offset the tax. The effect of the tax will clearly be to reduce labor costs to the covered industry employer for those categories of labor in surplus. In the case of the labor that is scarce, however, the tax-subsidy scheme will immediately cause employers to bid up the prices of these laborers. The tax will quickly be passed along to the employers who also receive the offsetting subsidy. On these groups, therefore, the tax-subsidy plan is fully neutralizing. There will be no incentive provided for those members of the labor force which are in the greatest demand to migrate to the capital-surplus states because of the fiscal action.[1]

In the uncovered industries, wages are assumed to be determined competitively prior to any action. The result of the tax-subsidy scheme will be to increase the demand for labor in the covered occupations, leading to the transfer of labor from the uncovered to the covered industries where labor productivity is greater. If universally applied as this model assumes, the tax-subsidy plan would produce a full equalization of wage levels for comparable quality laborers in the covered and the uncovered industries. For laborers remaining in the uncovered industries, the net result of the proposed measure would be an increase in real wages after taxes. For society as a whole, the

---

1. If we assume that the supply of the scarce labor (skilled labor in our model) is fixed, the effects of the tax-subsidy scheme can be easily traced. The effect of the subsidy is to shift the demand curve for this category of labor upward so that the price increases by the full amount of the tax. This, of course, is a first approximation. To the extent that skilled laborers are substitutes for unskilled and semiskilled laborers in production in the relevant industries, skilled labor's wages will rise by less than the full amount of the tax. To the extent that the opposite or complementary relationship holds, skilled labor's wage rate will be increased by more than the tax.

This assumption as to the supply curve of the scarce labor may be contrasted with that of the surplus labor. In the latter case, our model assumes that the supply curve is horizontal at the going wage level. Thus, the subsidy-induced shifting in the demand curve has the effect of increasing employment without increasing wage rates. The incidence of the tax must remain with the wage earners.

shifting of economic resources from less productive to more productive employments would clearly increase over-all efficiency, as this is normally measured.

Before the policy action, the primary burden of attaining some ultimate resource equilibrium necessarily rests on migration. After the action, there will be less incentive for those who are underemployed in the surplus-labor states to migrate to the capital-surplus states. Some semiskilled and unskilled workers employed in covered industries before the tax might be induced to migrate to the capital-surplus region to escape tax liability. However, by stimulating the inflow of capital investment into the labor-surplus states the proposed measure would, in the long run, tend to reduce the postulated difference in labor incomes between the two regions.

One of the most interesting features of the simple proposal of wage-bill subsidization from gross payroll taxes is its self-correcting or neutralizing aspects. As implied already in the analysis of the scarce labor sector above, the proposal cannot interfere with the "efficient" working of the market mechanism. It can only correct "inefficiencies," which it does by acting as a substitute for wage flexibility. This feature insures that the proposal could not become a means whereby interstate competition could reduce national real income, as measured by efficiency criteria.

A capital-surplus state, where, by assumption, both unskilled and semiskilled labor are scarce, can never compete with the labor-surplus states by enacting the same policy measures. For, as we have seen, when the resource is scarce, the effects of the tax and the subsidy are completely neutralizing, and nothing could be gained from implementing such measures. There is no federal government policy to be negated here.[2] By the same reasoning, once the relative labor surplus is eliminated in those states which we have called labor-surplus states, the policy ceases to be effective.

It must, of course, be recognized that the policy proposal presented here does not represent the best of all possible worlds for residents of the labor-surplus states. Broadly speaking, the effects of the policy outlined are similar

---

2. If in fact national government policy should include the fixing of rates of return to nonlabor resource units, the analysis presented here is fully applicable. For example, a national minimum land rental policy could be offset by the "land-surplus" states.

to those that would result from a change in national policy which produces competition in the labor markets. State offsetting policy must be within the realm of the second-best, but it is important to recognize that it does provide a substitute for national policy changes with respect to minimum wage restrictions and union wage standardization.

Alternative policy measures taken at the state level may also be developed to deal with substantially the same problem. For instance, a policy which might generate more political support in the labor-surplus states would be one which extends the subsidies to only new enterprises. Many variants on policies of this sort are to be found in the real-world attempts of governmental units to attract new industry. Given the national policy as fact, there are many possibilities for independent action by smaller political units. These are worthy of further exploration and research.

PART FOUR

Input Prices

Saving and the Rate of Interest
A Comment

In his recent highly provocative paper, Martin J. Bailey has attempted to apply the demand-curve methodology developed by Milton Friedman, and elaborated by Bailey himself, to the problem of predicting the response of saving to interest-rate changes.[1] His procedure is that of separating the income or wealth effect of an interest-rate change from the substitution effect, followed by the construction of a model in which the substitution effect alone remains. In such a model, which embodies constancy in real resources (or opportunities), Bailey's argument purports to prove that saving must be positively related to changes in the interest rate.

This note challenges Bailey's conclusion, even within the confines of the "pure substitution" model. My argument is neither directed to, nor is it relevant for, other aspects of Bailey's paper. The argument which follows may be summarized: the generalized commodity demand curve which is derived on the assumption of constancy in real resources must be negatively sloped, but no restrictions are placed on the absolute value of the elasticity coefficient.

From *Journal of Political Economy* 67 (February 1959): 79–82. Copyright 1959 by The University of Chicago. All rights reserved. Reprinted by permission of the University of Chicago Press, publisher.

I am indebted to Warren Nutter, Procter Thomson, and Leland Yeager for helpful discussion of the issues raised in this note. I have also benefited from correspondence with Martin J. Bailey. In particular, Section IV has been revised as a result of his comments on an earlier draft.

1. Martin J. Bailey, "Saving and the Rate of Interest," *Journal of Political Economy* 65 (1957): 279–305.

The basic Friedman paper is "The Marshallian Demand Curve," *Journal of Political Economy* 57 (1949): 463–95. Bailey's discussion of this is contained in "The Marshallian Demand Curve," *Journal of Political Economy* 62 (1954): 255–61.

Bailey's particular extension of this analysis to the interest-rate-saving problem suggests that all constant real resource demand curves are price elastic at all points. Since this implication is not acceptable, the particular analysis of the saving problem must be in error. Examination reveals that Bailey has incorporated the effect of the compensating income variation along with the effect of the interest-rate change in reaching his conclusions. This procedure does not seem appropriate. The elasticity of demand for future income remains the relevant consideration in determining whether or not saving increases or decreases as a result of a fully compensated interest-rate change.

I. The Constant Real Resources Demand Curve

Bailey's earlier contribution to demand theory may be reviewed briefly. If over-all fixity in resource supply is to be maintained along with fixed technology, the community must remain within the limits indicated by some fixed production-possibility frontier. If the usual assumptions about convexity in individual indifference curves are accepted, the demand curve for any commodity must be negatively sloped. Conceptually, this demand curve is derived by taking as prices the slopes of successive "representative" individual indifference curves at the points at which these cut the single "representative" individual production possibility curve.[2] "Income" effects are not entirely eliminated in the sense that consumers do shift to different levels of preference as they move along the fixed production-possibility frontier, but an operational relationship between price and quantity demanded is produced which is fully consistent with the stationary conditions imposed on the analysis.

Nothing is suggested or implied concerning the elasticity of the demand curve for a particular commodity derived in this way. The elasticity property is designed to place additional restrictions on the shapes of particular demand functions, that is, to describe more fully the characteristics of consumer preference functions.

The concept of price elasticity has developed, however, almost exclusively

---

2. Actually, since consumer preference maps are not "revealed" to the observer, the demand curve is derived through the procedure of stabilizing a quantity index weighted by some arbitrary set of base prices.

in application to uncompensated demand curves. Here an elasticity coefficient less than unity suggests that as price is lowered more units of a commodity are normally purchased but that less total expenditure is made. Some purchasing power is freed for the purchase of other commodities, and, since no compensating changes occur, more units of other commodities are purchased. Clearly, these results cannot apply to compensated or constant resource demand curves. The fact that goods are substitutes in production imposes on the analysis from the outset the requirement that the consumer gets more of one commodity only by giving up some of others. A simultaneous increase in the consumption of all goods is impossible.[3]

This does not suggest that the elasticity of the fully compensated demand curve is necessarily greater than unity. The consumer may still spend less upon more units of the commodity which has been reduced in price and more on those which have been subjected to compensating price increases.

II. A Crusoe Model

As Bailey correctly suggests, the interest-rate-saving problem is a particular example of the allocation of income among competing uses. To emphasize this similarity, I shall consider first a highly simplified model. I assume a closed economy, populated by Crusoe and Friday alone. There are only two goods, coconuts and apples. For simplicity in exposition, constant returns are assumed to prevail throughout the range of production possibilities. The introduction of diminishing returns will not modify the conclusions. Crusoe is assumed to know Friday's choice pattern fully, and, further, Crusoe is assumed to be willing to allow Friday to make all production and consumption decisions for both individuals. Crusoe retains, however, full and complete sovereignty; he is the "government."

The initial position of this community is shown in Figure 1 at point α, with the production possibility line as *CA*. Now assume that Crusoe decides, as an experiment, to introduce an arbitrary change in the relative prices of the two goods. He places a subsidy directly on the consumption of apples. Friday's initial reaction when the subsidy is announced will be that the economy's

---

3. Similar conclusions apply to the constant real income demand curve proposed by Friedman.

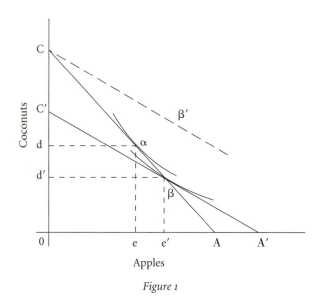

Figure 1

production possibilities have somehow improved, and he will think that β' is a position possible of attainment. But, since actual production possibilities have not shifted, Crusoe, in order to finance the subsidy, must place a lump-sum tax on the "income" of the group. He does this in such a way that Friday considers the tax obligation to be unaffected by his behavior. In choosing the magnitude of the tax, Crusoe must, of course, know and act upon his knowledge of Friday's choice pattern. Friday will, when confronted with his more realistic prospects, view the apparent production possibility line as $C'A'$.[4] He will shift to point β, a new equilibrium position.

What are the implications of this model for the elasticity of demand for apples? Since more coconuts are given up in the final position and more apples are consumed, the price elasticity of demand for apples would seem to be both negative and *greater than unity* in absolute value. In order to show

---

4. Friday cannot consider the previous position, α, to be attainable under his new opportunities. Bailey, in his slightly more complex model, makes an error at this point ("Saving and the Rate of Interest," 283). The reverse is true in the Bailey demand curve construction, that is, the new position was available, but not chosen, *under the previous opportunities*. The relevant difference between the Friedman and the Bailey demand-curve constructions is precisely this one.

that this holds true only in a very peculiar sense, we may trace carefully the derivation of the demand curve for apples. The price of apples in terms of coconuts in the initial position is *OC/OA*; in the final position price is *OC'/OA'*. Quantity is taken directly off Figure 1; 0*e* in the initial position; 0*e'* finally. A demand curve relating these prices and quantities is drawn to scale in Figure 2. In general, it would now appear that nothing can be concluded about the absolute value of the elasticity coefficient. The demand curve must slope downward; but, since price and quantity move in opposing directions, nothing can be stated, a priori, concerning the amount of total expenditure on the commodity. As Figure 1 and Figure 2 are drawn, the elasticity between the two prices is less than unity.

Bailey's implied suggestion that all such demand curves are price elastic is not difficult to explain. In the final position more coconuts are given up to secure apples. To move directly from this statement of fact to any suggestion, explicit or by implication, that demand elasticity is greater than unity fails to take into account that Friday, in making his decision, operates on the basis of the apparent production-possibility curve, *C'A'*, rather than on the actual curve, *CA*. The actual number of coconuts given up to attain 0*e'* apples is *Cd'*, which is larger than *Cd*. But this actual outlay is made up of *two* component parts which must be carefully distinguished. There is, first, the *expen-*

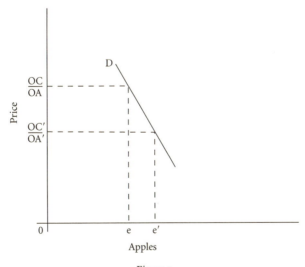

Figure 2

diture, $C'd'$, explicitly considered as such. Second, there is the *compensating tax, CC'*. The derivation of a meaningful demand curve is based on only one of these—the amount of expenditure on the commodity in question. The expenditure $C'd'$ may be greater than, equal to, or less than, the initial expenditure, Cd. The restrictions of the model require only that more apples be purchased at the fully compensated lower price.

III. The Crusoe Saving Model

The model may be easily changed to apply to the saving problem. Instead of coconuts and apples, let the x-axis measure units of future goods, in real terms, and the y-axis measure units of present goods. Again assume that in order to make future goods arbitrarily cheaper the government (Crusoe) decides to impose a subsidy on interest receipts, financing this subsidy from the proceeds of a tax which is imposed in such a way that the amount paid will not be considered by Friday to be influenced by his behavior. Friday will again move from α to β. He will purchase more units of future goods and retain fewer units of present goods. Friday's *explicit* and *voluntary* outlay on future goods is $C'd'$. This may or may not be greater than Cd. The fact that real consumption is reduced does not suggest that saving has been increased in this model. For the community as a whole the amount of present goods *given up* has been increased. But a portion of this increase is due to the *coercive* levy of the compensating lump-sum tax, not to any decisions on the part of the individuals to save.

The tax must be levied in such a way that individual choice is not affected. This being true, the apparent production-possibility curve, $C'A'$, must assume real significance for the decision maker. From his *disposable* income he saves $C'd'$, not Cd'.

Bailey's error lies in his attempt to make the compensating tax or subsidy do double duty. He defines the compensating fiscal operation as one in which the compensating variation is not affected significantly by the behavior of the individual in changing his assets. This can mean only that the subsidy (Bailey's model is the reverse of the simpler one used here) must be of the lump-sum variety. By this device, the impact of the relative price change can be isolated, *provided* that the lump-sum amount is appropriately chosen. This amount must be so adjusted to individual behavior that the final equilibrium position lies on the fixed production-possibility curve. But individual behavior must itself be based on a different and new production-possibility curve, one which cuts the old one only at the new position of equilibrium. To be sure, this point is the only relevant one in the sense that it is the only point on the new curve which is attainable. But the individual, in moving to this point, cannot consider his production possibilities to be unchanged. If this were true, quite obviously his behavior would not be modified, and no conceptual experiment would be possible. If the consumer fully appreciates the illusion involved, no compensated change can occur. To the decision maker, production possibilities, as they affect his behavior, are modified, and, on the basis of his new prospects, he may voluntarily choose to spend more, less, or the same amount. Variations in the lump-sum tax or subsidy will keep the individual from making choices which are inconsistent with the over-all possibilities for the economy. But the individual cannot be allowed to recognize, in advance, that his share of the compensating tax or subsidy will depend on his decision.

IV. The Definition of Real Saving

Implicit in the analysis of the preceding sections has been a definition of real saving, and the validity of the conclusions depend upon its acceptance. Real saving is defined as *real expenditure* on future goods, a *product of price and quantity,* or, in slightly different terms, the amount of current income voluntarily given up in purchasing future goods. This conception of real saving seems to have been that implied by Marshall and the many others who have been concerned with the effects of interest-rate changes on the behavior of individuals.

Bailey's analysis may be more favorably interpreted as being based on an alternative definition of real saving. In one place he explicitly defines saving as the demand for future goods, and by this he presumably means the *quantity of future goods* in real terms. His argument demonstrates that this quantity will always vary positively with fully compensated interest-rate changes. In this context Bailey's argument is correct, and the errors imputed to it in this note are not applicable. But the usefulness of such a definition of real saving would seem to be limited. So far as I know, future goods have never been classified as inferior, and no one has claimed the existence of a Giffen's paradox in this respect. The issue is wholly different, and Bailey's analysis, while certainly helpful, does little to remove the fundamental ambiguity. In the more widely accepted and, in my opinion, more meaningful definition, real saving still depends upon the elasticity of demand for future goods.

The Backbending Supply Curve
of Labor
An Example of Doctrinal Retrogression?

Some scientific innovations turn out, in retrospect, to have retarded rather than to have advanced our understanding of real-world phenomena. Modern demand theory may provide an example with respect to the possible negative response of labor supply to increases in wage rates. The possibly backbending portion of the supply curve of labor is now widely "explained" in basic economic theory by an apparently straightforward application of the Hicksian income-effect–substitution-effect apparatus.

My purpose in this article is first to suggest that this set of tools is wholly unnecessary; resort to income effect offsets to substitution effects is not required. The general point is elementary and is apparently familiar to scholars in international-trade theory, but its specific application to the labor-supply curve seems to have been forgotten in modern discussion. A secondary purpose is that of returning the analysis to the simple and essentially correct explanation provided by Lionel Robbins in 1930.[1] It is perhaps unfortunate that Robbins paired a demand curve for income, his first diagram, with an offer curve of total effort in a second diagram, rather than with an orthodox labor- or effort-supply schedule. Had he straightforwardly taken the course of deriving a supply schedule for effort directly from the demand for income, the whole analysis might have been clarified once and for all.

From *History of Political Economy* 3 (Fall 1971): 383–90. Reprinted by permission of the publisher.
1. Lionel Robbins, "On the Elasticity of Demand for Income in Terms of Effort," *Economica* 10 (June 1930): 123–29.

I shall first present the elementary analysis in general terms. I shall then summarize the standard discussion of the backbending labor-supply curve. Following this, I shall demonstrate that an income-effect explanation is not required. In the process, I shall suggest the specific source of the change in paradigm.

The most important key to an understanding of the phenomenon is the recognition that in any act of exchange the individual participates *both* as a demander and as a supplier. To demand one thing is to supply another. For example, consider an individual in a two-good world who is initially endowed with a quantity of one good, apples. Suppose that he is now confronted with alternative prices for the second good, oranges, these prices being designated in apple units. We can then trace out his demand schedule for oranges. The same behavior that is depicted in this demand schedule can be depicted, alternatively, in terms of a supply schedule for apples. In the latter, prices would be denoted in orange units. Hence, a high demand price for an orange, in apple units, corresponds to a low supply price for an apple, in orange units. Numerically, the prices are simply reciprocals, one for the other.

Given this construction, it should be relatively easy to see that the range over which demand for one good is price elastic corresponds to a range over which the supply response for the other good is positive. If demand is of unitary elasticity, the same quantity of the offered good is supplied regardless of price. And over the range where demand is price inelastic, the supply response is negative. If less total outlay is made as a result of the larger quantity purchased at a lower price, the quantity of the other good offered is necessarily lower at a higher price than at the lower price. In terms of our example, if the total apple outlay on oranges falls as a result of a reduced apple price of oranges, this is the same as saying that the total quantity of apples supplied is reduced as a result of a higher orange price for apples. Diagrammatically, the supply curve that depicts the same behavior as that depicted by an orthodox downsloping demand curve in the reciprocal dimension may exhibit a backbending segment.

There is nothing strange or bizarre in this. No resort to a Giffen-like paradox is required as explanation. Income-compensated demand schedules need not be price elastic over all ranges. The fundamental reciprocity between demand and supply was formally developed a century ago by Walras.[2]

2. Léon Walras, *Elements of Pure Economics,* trans. William Jaffé (Homewood, Ill.,

The specific relationship between supply response and the elasticity of reciprocal demand has long been a part of the elementary theory of international trade. Although Marshall illustrated his analysis with total offer curves rather than supply curves as such, the relationship is clearly presented in his *Money, Credit, and Commerce.*[3] In an expository paper on the theory of foreign exchange, Machlup referred to the translation of a demand relationship into its reciprocal supply relationship as a "good undergraduate exercise."[4] Elementary textbooks in international trade include diagrams that translate the demand for one currency into the supply of another.[5]

Given both the simplicity of the analysis and its familiar and long-standing usage in other applications, it is perhaps surprising that the standard textbook discussions of the backbending supply curve for labor remain so complex. Furthermore, the phenomenon is almost always referred to as "peculiar" or "perverse." The modern orthodoxy proceeds as follows. As the wage rate rises, the price of leisure (a good) goes up. The substitution effect, in isolation, prompts the individual to purchase less leisure, which means that he works more hours. However, this may be more than offset, over certain ranges, by an income effect that operates in the opposing direction. As the individual's opportunities improve, he will demand more leisure, a superior good. This effect, in isolation, will generate a reduction in hours of work supplied. The combination of these two forces may yield the backbending portion of the curve.[6]

As suggested above, Robbins' analysis was much more straightforward. He explained the possible backbending portion of the labor- (effort-) supply curve in terms of the inelasticity of the demand for income in terms of effort.

1954), 92–106. The analysis was apparently unchanged through the several editions of Walras' book, dating from the first edition in 1874.

3. Alfred Marshall, *Money, Credit, and Commerce* (London, 1923), app. J, 331–60.

4. Fritz Machlup, "The Theory of Foreign Exchanges," *Economica*, n.s. 6 (Nov. 1939): 375–97.

5. For a single example, see Delbert A. Snider, *Introduction to International Economics*, 4th ed. (Homewood, Ill., 1967), 296–97.

6. The following are examples of modern textbooks that present the analysis that I have here called the "orthodoxy." See Kenneth Boulding, *Economic Analysis*, 4th ed. (New York, 1966), 1:262–63; Milton Friedman, *Price Theory* (Chicago, 1962), 203–6; Kelvin Lancaster, *Introduction to Modern Microeconomics* (Chicago, 1969), 212–14; Richard G. Lipsey, *An Introduction to Positive Economics* (London, 1963), 283–85; William Vickrey, *Microstatics* (New York, 1964), 65–66.

It seems plausible to suggest that the change in paradigm here can be traced directly to the dramatic change in the explanations offered by J. R. Hicks in his two treatments of the phenomenon. In his *Theory of Wages*, published in 1932, Hicks fully accepted Robbins' analysis. In a footnote reference to Robbins, he explicitly recognized the simple transposition between demand and supply that was involved, along with the elasticity origins of negative supply response.[7] In 1938, when he published *Value and Capital*, Hicks explicitly introduced the modern explanation.[8] He employed labor supply as an example of a situation where an income effect might dominate the offsetting substitution effect. In his search for familiar examples with which to present his new theory of demand, Hicks perhaps inadvertently introduced a more complex explanation of an observed real-world phenomenon than was required.

By implication if not directly, the received analysis suggests that were it not for the presence of an income effect the labor-supply curve would necessarily slope upward throughout its length. Recognition of the reciprocal nature of the supply-demand relationship indicates that such an inference is erroneous. Elimination of the income effect will not guarantee the absence of the possible negative response of labor supplied to wage-rate increases. To indicate this, consider confronting an individual with an idealized compensated choice set. Assume that information is sufficient to allow precise income compensations to be computed, compensations that are such as to keep the individual, after choice, on the same utility level. As a potential demander of income (supplier of labor), he is confronted with a set of price alternatives, as in the simple orange-apple model previously discussed. For each of the price offers, however, there is an accompanying income transfer (positive or negative) just sufficient to keep the person on the same utility level. These transfers must be carried out independent of the demand choices. They must take the form of lump-sum taxes or subsidies, arranged so that the person makes no conscious connection between their magnitude or existence and his own choices for income. From this sort of conceptual experiment, we can derive a fully compensated demand curve for income.[9] Since

---

7. "The elasticity of demand for income must be positive; but this means that the elasticity of individual supply of labour must be either positive or lie between 0 and −1." See J. R. Hicks, *The Theory of Wages* (1932; reprinted New York, 1948), 98 n.

8. See J. R. Hicks, *Value and Capital*, 2d ed. (Oxford, 1946), 36–37.

9. For purposes of analysis here, any of the several means of depicting the required

this demand curve traces out the locus of successive positions of individual equilibria generated *solely by the substitution effect,* its slope must be negative throughout the range. It is incorrect to infer from this, however, that the labor-supply response represented by this *same* behavior must be consistent with an upsloping supply curve throughout its range. Such an inference would imply that all fully compensated demand curves exhibit an elasticity greater than unity in absolute value throughout their whole range. This is, of course, a far more restrictive requirement than that which dictates the downslope. There is no reason why a fully compensated demand curve may not include ranges where elasticity coefficients are less than unity.[10]

By stating that a fully compensated demand curve for income may include ranges where standard price elasticity coefficients are less than unity, we are at the same time stating that the fully compensated supply curve for labor that is represented by the same behavior includes a backbending segment. This may be clarified in Figure 1. Leisure is measured along the ordinate, and income along the abscissa. Initially, assume that the person is at E, where leisure is being exchanged for income. Now assume that the wage rate rises, as indicated by the reduced slope of LL', but that this wage increase is fully compensated. This means that the individual must be confronted with a tax, measured in units of labor (leisure) such that his new equilibrium position will allow him to reach the same level of utility as before. The required compensation is, therefore, LH, and his new equilibrium is shown at E'. Note that in this position the individual is explicitly and voluntarily *supplying* HJ units of labor (leisure) for JE' units of income. This is *less* than he was supplying in the initial equilibrium at the lower wage rate (HJ < LG). In total, of course, he is giving up more leisure rather than less, but it is improper to relate the compensating tax LH to the explicit labor-income choice that the person makes. The compensating tax may, of course, be measured in ei-

---

compensation analytically may be adopted. In the idealized version discussed, the individual is allowed only to shift among positions along a given indifference curve, reflecting a constant level of utility. Alternatively, he may be allowed to shift utility levels so long as these are constrained to the set of points on some defined production-possibility surface.

10. I made this point, in another connection, in my earlier criticism of Bailey's paper on saving and the rate of interest. I did not, at that time, see that the analysis applies equally well to the backward-bending labor-supply curve. See my "Saving and the Rate of Interest: A Comment," *Journal of Political Economy* 67 (Feb. 1959): 79–82. The paper that prompted my note was Martin J. Bailey, "Saving and the Rate of Interest," *Journal of Political Economy* 65 (Nov. 1957): 279–305.

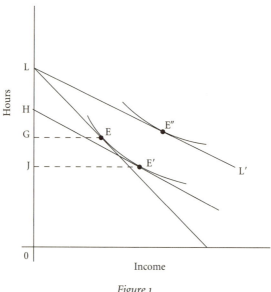

Figure 1

ther labor or in income. The tax is a conceptual device that allows us to sepa-rate the individual's behavior as a supplier of labor in response to a pure wage-rate change, and his behavior as a supplier of labor in response to an income change. In order for the device to be at all applicable, the compen-sating nature of the tax, as such, cannot be recognized by the individual. He must consider this tax to be imposed exogenously and coercively upon him quite independent of his own behavior. Hence the fact that the individual may actually give up more leisure rather than less in response to the com-bined change in wage rate and the offsetting income compensation tells us nothing. This total response reflects a behavioral combination of an adjust-ment to a wage-rate change and an adjustment to the compensating income change.

The analysis suggests only that an income effect is not *required* for an ex-planation of the backbending supply curve for labor. It does not suggest that an income effect, if present, will not operate as the standard paradigm indi-cates. If the wage increase is uncompensated, the new equilibrium is at E″, which, in this illustration, also entails a *smaller* expenditure of leisure than at E. The difference between the individual's position at E′ and at E″ can be ex-plained by the working of a pure income effect. This effect will normally operate to cause the uncompensated supply curve for labor to bend backwards more quickly and at a somewhat greater rate than the fully compensated supply curve. This is guaranteed if the income elasticity of supply of labor is negative. There may, of course, exist cases in which the fully compensated supply curve is upsloping while the uncompensated curve bends backward over the same range. Hicks cannot, therefore, be faulted for his introduction of this as a possible example.

In accepting and repeating the second Hicksian analysis as the only apparent explanation for the backbending supply curve of labor, economists may have overlooked a point that is so elementary it is subtle. In an economic act, the individual is, indeed, both a demander and a supplier. But he cannot be a demander and a supplier of the same good simultaneously. Yet this is what the standard treatment appears to imply. The labor-supply analysis is incorporated into demand theory by treating labor as the negative of leisure, a good with which the individual is endowed. Hence, when wage rates rise, the price of leisure also rises, and the apparently simple application of demand theory suggests that the substitution effect is to make the individual *demand* less leisure rather than more. When this is not observed, it seems necessary to explain the results by the presence of an income effect.

This is an issue of confusion at a very elementary level. In the relevant exchange under consideration, the individual acts as a *supplier* of leisure not as a demander. He supplies leisure (which is desired by the market in its labor form) and demands dollars of income (other goods). The behavior that is observed as we confront the individual with alternative wage bids cannot be treated both as a supply and as a demand function for leisure. The behavior can be treated as either a supply function for leisure (labor) *or* a demand function for income, as Robbins' analysis directly suggested. The individual who works fewer hours at a higher wage rate is exhibiting a demand for income that is price inelastic.[11]

11. I am indebted to Charles Goetz, Mather Lindsay, and Richard McKenzie for comments on earlier drafts of this paper. An editorial reader of this journal also provided helpful substantive and bibliographical suggestions.

The Homogenization of
Heterogeneous Inputs

James M. Buchanan and Robert D. Tollison

> The absurdity of treating land-use as a homogeneous magnitude
> has been commented upon above; regarding labor, the fallacy
> has been pointed out often enough—quite typically by writers
> who go ahead to discuss "wages in general," as if the concept had
> meaning.

> —Frank H. Knight, "The Ricardian Theory of Production and
>   Distribution," in *On the History and Method of Economics*
>   (Chicago, 1956), 76.

This paper examines the allocative effects of institutional constraints that
require purchasers to treat *heterogeneous* inputs as *homogeneous* for input
pricing. Our attention was drawn to this problem by a comparative analysis
of salary policies in academic institutions, but further exploration suggests
widespread applicability and relevance in such areas as (1) the differential allocative effects of craft and industrial unionization of the labor force; (2) the
allocative effects of "equal pay for equal work," either as an institutionally
adopted "principle of justice" in compensation, or as a result of legal prohibitions on discrimination in payment; and (3) the channelization of profit-
or rent-seeking activities, and the subsequent processes through which prof-

From *American Economic Review* 71 (March 1981): 28–38. Reprinted by permission of
the publisher.

We are grateful to Thomas Borcherding, Geoffrey Brennan, Roger Congleton, Roger
Faith, Robert Mackay, Robert McCormick, Dennis Mueller, and Gordon Tullock for
helpful comments on earlier drafts of this paper. The usual caveat applies.

its or rents are dissipated. We shall not attempt to discuss these, and possibly many other, applications of our analysis, except for purposes of illustrating the argument. We shall concentrate on the elementary analysis.

Orthodox price theory contains a well-developed analysis for the pricing of homogeneous inputs, even when at another level it is acknowledged that inputs may in many cases be unique. Standard procedure simply imposes homogeneity by abstraction, a step that has often been the focus of criticism. This theory of input pricing is not wholly consistent with the theory of the organization of production, which is usually considered to involve the combination of separate inputs synergistically, inputs that are by implication heterogeneous rather than homogeneous. Indeed, the role of the entrepreneur is widely interpreted to be that of sensing potential profits from new input *combinations*. Our analysis allows both the organization of production and the entrepreneurial role to be more readily brought within a framework analogous to that of the orthodox theory of input pricing.

I. Heterogeneity and Homogeneity

Heterogeneity and homogeneity may, of course, be defined in many different ways, and the problem is to define and to use these terms appropriately for the analytical purposes at hand. One source of common confusion lies in economists' proclivity to think of inputs (and outputs) in physical dimensions rather than in terms of valuation. Even within the valuation rubric, however, it is necessary to distinguish categorically between *internal* and *external* valuation, between the two separate sides of choice, so to speak.

In the internal evaluation of separate input units, the prospective purchaser or demander could classify units by homogeneous bundles, with homogeneity defined in terms of predictions of potential contributions to product value. Such a calculus would, presumably, be embodied in the ultimate demand for input units. Our concern here is not with the demander's *internal* evaluation of input units, save insofar as this enters the demand function. Rather our direct concern is with the *external* evaluation of inputs, which are presented to the potential purchaser as market-determined input prices. These prices reflect the opportunity costs for such input units, as perceived by the owners of the resource inputs themselves. In our context, the owner of an input foregoes value (pecuniary and nonpecuniary), measured by the amount that the unit may command in alternative uses to that which involves the sale to the prospective purchaser. The difference between the opportunity cost perceived by the owner of a resource unit and the actual price or wage received for the unit in a transaction is economic rent in the usual definition. This rent will figure prominently in the analysis that follows.

In terms of external evaluation, homogeneity and heterogeneity must be defined by the prices that the prospective purchaser or demander faces. If input *A* is available for purchase at the same price (wage) as input *B*, these two units are *homogeneous* in external value terms, regardless of their possibly differing anticipated contributions to product value for the purchaser (and hence their possible internal heterogeneity), and regardless of any similarity or difference in physically observable attributes. If, on the other hand, input unit *C* can be purchased at a price (wage) that is different from that required to purchase input unit *D*, these two units are *heterogeneous* in external value terms, regardless of their possible differences or similarities, either in internal evaluation or in physically measurable attributes.

II. A Model of Heterogeneous Input Combination

We now introduce a model that includes a profit-maximizing firm (or entrepreneur) which senses an opportunity for putting together a particular combination of input units. This combination includes capital and management inputs that are purchased competitively in ordinary markets. But it also includes a bundle of "labor inputs." By assumption, these latter units are heterogeneous in the external evaluation sense defined above. For simplicity in exposition, we assume that the prospective input combination, the "labor bundle," includes only one unit from each type or kind. The analysis could, of course, be extended to apply to the combination of several homogeneous units from several heterogeneous groups. Each unit is available at a price that is determined in a competitive market setting, and the firm has no influence over the price that it pays for any particular resource unit.

In order to simplify the exposition initially, we assume that the inputs are internally valued at the same level. The entrepreneur imputes an equal anticipated product value to each of the units in the "labor input bundle," despite the fact that he also recognizes that the separate units "do different things" and, hence, are less than perfectly substitutable one for another. Our conception of production here is that of a synergistic, team production process. Part of the process includes other inputs, such as capital, which, as noted above, are purchased competitively, and part includes the separate, heterogeneous labor inputs. All of these inputs are combined by the entrepreneur to produce an output expressed in terms of a market value. The entrepreneur must decide what market value of output to produce, and he must hire and combine the units of productive inputs to produce this output.

Armen Alchian and Harold Demsetz have analyzed the problem of monitoring and disciplining inputs in a team production process.[1] Our concern is with the analysis of the hiring of the heterogeneous labor inputs used in such processes. The production process that we analyze does not embody a fixed-coefficient production function. Within limits, entrepreneurs can substitute among categories of labor inputs. A contractor can build a house with wooden or plaster walls, with different labor inputs as well as capital, with carpenters or plasterers. If plasterers have a lower competitive supply price than carpenters, the contractor can build more houses with plaster walls. This substitution among heterogeneous labor inputs will show up in the market value of the contractor's housing output. But there is a point in this process of substitution beyond which the contractor-entrepreneur cannot go; he cannot build his houses completely out of plaster. We shall return to discuss the concept of team production with heterogeneous inputs at a later stage in the paper. Suffice it to say here that the conception of team production that we envisage for purposes of analysis is quite different than that used for the conventional analysis of the pricing of inputs, in which different units of an input are readily substitutable for one another.

In the model as postulated, we can now build up a "supply schedule" for the separate "labor" inputs that the entrepreneur will face, as depicted in Figure 1. Note that this schedule is not the same as that which is familiar in orthodox analysis, where the input units measured on the abscissa are, by definition, homogeneous in some "physical" sense. In the schedule of Figure 1, input units are arrayed along the abscissa in the order of the ascending market prices for hire. The marginal valuation or demand curve is drawn in the usual manner. The size of the input combination, and hence the rate of out-

---

1. "Production, Information Costs, and Economic Organization," *American Economic Review* 62 (December 1972): 777–95.

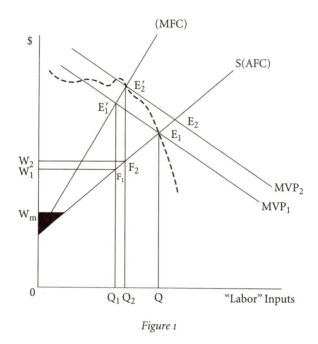

Figure 1

put production, is assumed to be variable, even though inputs undertake differing tasks. The entrepreneur will extend his purchases to Q, which is the efficient rate of input use, given his evaluations. At Q, the last unit of input hired will, of course, be paid at the E_1 rate. All other units will be paid in accordance with their market-determined prices, all lower than E_1.

We should stress the nature of the upward-sloping "supply curve" S in Figure 1. This curve differs from the standard supply relationship in the heterogeneity of units measured. The curve is, however, a genuine marginal labor input cost curve for the firm, and the equation of marginal input cost with the estimated value of product at E_1 mirrors the standard efficiency requirement. The profit-maximizing firm or entrepreneur will combine units of labor input (Q in number) out to E_1, however, only because he faces S as the marginal cost curve. This amounts to saying that he must be allowed to purchase each of the input units at the market price established externally *for each unit of input.*

This purchase "policy" appears to duplicate that which might be adopted by a monopsonist, who is somehow able to discriminate perfectly among separate suppliers of homogeneous inputs. The perfectly discriminating monopsonist will also be led to the efficient quantity of resource use.[2] What is interesting in our model, however, is the absence of *any* market power on the part of the purchasing firm. We can assume full competition in the firm's product market, along with competition in each one of the input markets that it faces. Efficiency emerges from the profit-seeking behavior of all participants in the interaction. This result is, of course, in line with the neoclassical orthodoxy.[3]

III. Institutional Homogenization

We now want to apply our analysis to examine the effects of an input pricing policy that requires equalization of payments (wages) for some or for all the heterogeneous units that are purchased by a firm.[4] In long-term equilibrium, no firm earns profits. From this condition, it follows that *any* increase in costs must generate losses, and, in consequence, some exit of firms from the competitive industry. In the context of heterogeneous input purchases, any requirement that firms pay above-opportunity-cost prices or wages increases the cost of the firm's output, generates losses, and ultimately reduces the

2. Buchanan, in a discussion of military manpower, observed that "the fact that the supply curve slopes upward indicates differential productivity in alternative employments despite the homogeneity of units in producing military services" (James M. Buchanan, *Cost and Choice* [Chicago, 1969], 90).

3. To our knowledge, aside from Buchanan's precursory discussion, the standard theory of input purchase and pricing contains little treatment of the particular implications of input heterogeneity emphasized in this paper. As the introductory quotation suggests, Knight often criticized the economic theory of input pricing for failing to come to grips with the implications of input heterogeneity, but he never expanded upon this basic criticism. Martin Bronfenbrenner's early application of monopsony theory to input pricing offers a partial exception. "Potential Monopsony in Labor Markets," *Industrial Labor Relations Review* 9 (July 1956): 577–88. The emphasis in the standard approach is typically on the purchase and pricing of homogeneous inputs under various market conditions. See, for example, the discussion in Milton Friedman, *Price Theory* (Chicago, 1976), 176–93.

4. In the context of an application of conventional monopsony theory, Thomas Borcherding suggests the importance of assumptions about equal wages for identically defined jobs. See T. E. Borcherding, "A Neglected Social Cost of a Voluntary Military," *American Economic Review* 61 (March 1971): 195–96.

number of firms in the affected industry. Industry output declines, and product price goes up. There will be some welfare loss approximated by a Harberger-type triangle underneath the demand curve and above the cost schedule for the industry's product over the relevant adjustment range. This welfare loss will be directly related to the size of the *rents* created by the homogenization in pricing.

A truncation of the lower bound to input prices (wages) may force homogenization over some range of inputs without modifying the apparent equilibrium of the firm, as depicted at E_1. For example, suppose that a minimum-wage law requires all labor to be paid a wage of W_m, generating rents as shown by the darkened triangle for the lowest opportunity cost workers. The firm will still face the marginal input cost curve S beyond the height W_m, and will attain equilibrium at E_1. But any firm at E_1 under these conditions will be one among a smaller number of firms than would have been the case without the minimum-wage restriction. Any increase in the minimum-wage restriction will increase net welfare losses, as well as the net transfer of rents to the marginal input owners who remain employed.

Our primary interest, however, lies in determining the effects of a general requirement that prices (wages) be uniform over *all* units of inputs that are hired or purchased. Suppose that such a policy comes to be enforced by a law against differentiation in compensation among labor inputs. If this policy should be forced on one firm in isolation, it could not survive under the competitive conditions postulated. We seek to examine the effects of such a policy that is enforced for all firms in the product group, all of which have comparable production functions.

Initially, we assume that the individual firm is allowed to select the level of the uniform input price it is to pay, along with the number of input units it will purchase at that price. The S-type curve of Figure 1 will no longer represent a marginal input cost curve to the firm under these conditions. This curve will now reflect a schedule of *average* input costs, the familiar construction from orthodox monopsony theory. At any point along such a curve, costs will be higher to the firm than under opportunity cost pricing by the amount measured by the triangle bounded by the S curve, the uniform price, and the ordinate. Faced with the uniform payment requirement, firms initially operating at position E_1 will seek short-term adjustment by shifting to E_1', determined by the intersection of the MVP_1 curve and the new curve of marginal input cost. The short-run price will be W_1, with Q_1 units of input employed.

Even with these short-term adjustments, however, firms will make losses because of the increased costs in rent transfers, and some firms will leave the industry. As this long-term adjustment takes place, total industry output falls further, and demand price will rise, which will in turn increase a firm's marginal value product estimates for input units. For a firm that remains in the industry, a new short-term equilibrium will be attained at some position like E_2', with an input purchase rate of Q_2. The firm will also be in long-term equilibrium with zero profits or losses.

The input price or wage W_2 defines that wage or price for which the uniform compensation requirement can be met with *minimum* welfare losses. By construction, any level below W_2 will encourage the firm to expand employment by paying differentially higher prices for extramarginal units. Any level above W_2 will satisfy uniformity only at increasing welfare costs.[5]

By looking at E_1 and E_1' (or at E_2 and E_2'), the homogenization of the heterogeneous inputs in pricing seems to have the effect of making the firm in a fully competitive setting, in both product and factor markets, behave as if it were a genuinely nondiscriminating monopsonist. In this context, note that the total welfare losses cannot be measured by the triangles ($E_1 E_1' F_1$) or ($E_2 E_2' F_2$), multiplied by the number of firms. Such a measure offers only a short-term approximation to these costs. If we think of n_1 firms in the initial competitive equilibrium depicted at E_1, welfare costs in the short term are approximated by $n_1(E_1 E_1' F_1)$. As firms leave the industry, however, total welfare costs are reduced, and if n_2 firms remain in the industry in some new

5. Our construction differs from that of familiar monopsony theory in one important respect that deserves mention at this point. In the orthodox analysis of the nondiscriminating monopsony firm, the externally imposed requirement that the firm pay some wage above that average factor price it would optimally select can result in an expansion in the employment of labor by that firm. Since, by construction, labor's marginal product in the firm exceeds that elsewhere in the economy, the increased employment is welfare improving. By contrast, in our construction, *any* increase in rents increases costs in the competitively organized industry, reduces industry output, and with normal input relationships, must *reduce* employment. The *curiosus* of orthodox monopsony theory is not applicable here.

long-term equilibrium, welfare costs of the uniformity requirement are then minimally valued at $n_2(E_2 E_2' F_2)$. In each measure, however, the number of firms is fixed, whereas any accurate measure of welfare costs must embody long-term adjustments in industry output and price, as evaluated by final consumers of the industry product.

To this point, we have explicitly assumed that the inputs in the labor bundle, defined as heterogeneous in terms of their supply prices to the firm, are homogeneous in terms of their anticipated internal productivity to the firm. The analysis fully applies to all bundles of possible inputs that can be grouped by internal valuations in this manner. The apparent restrictiveness of the internal homogeneity assumption may be relaxed, however, without destroying our results, provided we are careful to specify the side conditions that must be met. For any set of input units that might be assembled, the set of externally determined input prices provides a natural basis for arraying the separate units along the abscissa, and, hence, for the construction of the marginal cost or supply schedule. Unless we assume homogeneity among the units in terms of anticipated internal productivity, however, things become considerably more complex in deriving the demand or marginal evaluation schedule. Once we make such an assumption, we are able, of course, to devise a marginal evaluation schedule that is precisely analogous to that in orthodox input pricing theory, one in which the law of diminishing returns and the demand schedule for the product determine the single-valued relation between input usage and value. But in the absence of internal homogeneity, why should all potential inputs in team production be expected to produce equal increments to output value?

The evaluation of a specific unit of input, described by its place in the prescribed array, will reflect some combination of two quite separate elements. First, units placed first in the array will tend to generate higher increments to product value by the ordinary law of diminishing returns, considering organization and other inputs as the fixed factors. Secondly, however, units may, *ceteris paribus*, be estimated to contribute differentially to product value. The combination of these elements may be such as to introduce nonconvexities in the demand or evaluation schedule of the firm for the set of inputs as arrayed. Stability requires that the demand or marginal evaluation schedule cut the marginal cost schedule from above, but, beyond this, little can be said about particular shapes in the most general setting. If, however, we assume that the schedule is convex from below, the general conclusions reached above about the introduction of uniformity in compensation hold.

Even if we allow for nonconvexities, so long as the evaluation curve does not, at any point over the inframarginal range, fall below the profit-maximizing uniform rate of payment (W_2 in Figure 1), the conclusions continue to apply. One such schedule is depicted by the dotted curve in Figure 1. If, however, the schedule should be sufficiently "misbehaved," forced equalization of payment for inputs would result in a complete shift in the team's composition. Units of input at differing places in the initial array might be dropped, and a new array might be formed, once again in terms of external prices in the absence of forced equalization. Given such a new array, our model would again fully apply, with units of inputs at the lower end of the array receiving relatively higher rents from equalization policy.

IV. Team Production with Heterogeneous Inputs

Consider, as an example, an entrepreneur who is organizing a construction team. Suppose that the potential members of this team include, in ascending order of competitively set wage rates: a laborer, an excavator, a painter, a carpenter, a plasterer, a mason, a tile setter, an electrician, an insulator, a plumber, and a cabinet maker. Suppose that, at the prevailing competitive wage rates established separately in each occupational or skill group, all eleven of the potential members are employed. (We could, of course, allow for differing numbers from each group.) By the terms of the previous analysis, if the entrepreneur's projections are accurate, the outcome is efficient, locally and globally.

Now suppose that someone petitions for unionization of the whole team. An election is held, and suppose that at least six members of the group vote to unionize. Subsequently, suppose that the union demands, and gets, an agreement for uniformity in compensation over all members of the team, but that the firm is allowed to set the uniform wage to be paid and the number of workers to be hired. It is clear that those workers whose opportunity costs are relatively low and who remain employed will gain rents in the process. The workers with relatively high opportunity costs may secure positive but lower rents if they remain employed on the team, and they will lose only the transaction costs involved in a shift to alternative employments if they are not retained as members of the team. The team's organizer, the entrepreneur, will find his costs per unit of output increased, and will undergo short-term losses until adjustments to the new cost schedule are made. Consumers of the team's product will lose surplus in the amount of the rents gained by the inframarginal inputs, plus the excess social loss measured by the value of output lost over its true marginal cost.

If the union is allowed to set the uniform wage, to apply over all of the labor inputs hired, this wage need not be that which will be profit maximizing for the firm, given the uniformity requirement. The union-set wage may be above W_2 in Figure 1. In this setting, the firms that remain in the industry after all adjustments may each employ more than Q_2 from the bundle of heterogeneous inputs, but there will be fewer firms in the industry than under the firm-set uniform wage plan. And, since total rents are higher, total welfare losses will exceed those present when firms are allowed to select their preferred uniform levels of compensation.

Implications for the predicted effects of differing forms of unionization emerge clearly from the analysis. Suppose that, in an alternative scenario to that sketched out above, carpenters unionize across all employers and set standard rates. These rates will tend to lie above competitive levels, and the employment of carpenters will be adversely affected. But, per head, carpenters will secure higher returns than in the absence of such unionization. Generalized unionization and standard wage setting within each of the crafts or skills, within each of the heterogeneous input sets separately, need not, however, result in an elimination of the differentials in compensation rates among the different crafts, as faced by the employing entrepreneur or firm. The organizer of team production may still confront an array of input prices for the heterogeneous inputs considered as potential members of the team, and given such an array, he may be led to some admittedly second or third best optimum rate of input usage.

The familiar differences between craft and industrial unionization emerge directly from the analysis. Relatively low-skilled workers will tend to secure differentially higher gains from unionization and wage standardization across some or all heterogeneous inputs employed by a given firm, or by all firms producing a given product, provided that they expect to remain employed after unionization. Hence, we should predict that pressures for such unionization, and for the tendency toward standardization of input prices that would follow, will be greater from those workers whose skill category may be relatively low, but whose contribution to team production is estimated to be relatively higher than their higher-skilled cohorts. (Skills are defined here implicitly by relative opportunity costs in competitive labor markets, which would presumably reflect some equilibrium of supply and demand within separate input groups.) By comparison with the low-skilled workers, those in the relatively high-skilled "professions" or "occupations" may secure little if any gain from cross-input wage standardization. Members of these groups may expect to secure net rents from successful unionization across all members of each narrowly defined profession, which would presumably succeed in increasing wages above competitive levels.

As we noted, our attention was drawn to this problem by comparing alternative salary policies in academic institutions, which seem to offer excellent real-world examples of the heterogeneous input phenomena. The college or the university can be modelled as a team, one that combines heterogeneous inputs to produce some "education-research" services. Potential contributors to the team may include professors (instructors) from various academic disciplines: English literature, history, philosophy, sociology, political science, psychology, biology, chemistry, physics, economics, engineering, business, law, medicine, and so forth. As arrayed here, competitive salary levels in each of the labeled disciplines stand in some roughly ascending order. Pressures on the university toward uniformity in salary scales would have the effects traced out in the basic model of Sections II and III.[6] Faced with requirements for equalization of salaries across heterogeneous disciplines, universities will tend to drop (or fail to add) high-salary disciplines to the "academic team" that is organized to produce academic output. It also

---

6. Academic institutions tend to be nonproprietary rather than profit maximizing. This difference between these institutions and private firms makes universities more vulnerable to pressures for standardization. The welfare effects of standardization under non-profit-maximizing conditions are similar, but not identical, to those derived above for profit-maximizing firms. Geoffrey Brennan and Robert Tollison offer a more detailed examination of the academic institution's behavior and its allocative effects. See H. G. Brennan and R. D. Tollison, "Rent Seeking in Academia," in *Toward a Theory of the Rent-Seeking Society*, ed. James M. Buchanan, Robert D. Tollison, and Gordon Tullock (College Station, 1980).

follows that demand shifts will generate larger shifts in the employment of team members from high-salary than from low-salary disciplines.

V. Equal Pay for Equal Work

The examples discussed suggest that the separate inputs combined in team production are indeed heterogeneous, and not only in the narrowly defined sense introduced earlier in the paper. Painters *are* different from carpenters; historians *are* different from economists. This natural (and nonscientific) classification of inputs or factors in terms of visible, and apparently observable, physical attributes is helpful in gaining some acceptance of the analytical conclusion that any artificially contrived and enforced homogenization for pricing purposes must generate losses in allocative efficiency. In a comparable sense, however, the same natural tendency to classify inputs by physically measurable attributes or dimensions creates difficulties in securing the acceptance of the extension of the identical analytical conclusion in a setting where inputs may be heterogeneous in the external valuation sense, but where they may "seem" homogeneous in physical characteristics, and where they may also be homogeneous in internally estimated contributions to product value.

To imply that worker C, who seems identical in physical appearance to worker D, and who, furthermore, is observed to produce precisely the same physical output as worker D (both may, for illustration, be seen to operate similar machines that produce six widgets per hour), is *different* for wage payment purposes from worker D because C's opportunity cost (his external earning capacity) is different, runs immediately afoul of commonly held ethical criteria for "justice." Such criteria dictate that such apparently equal workers *should* secure equal payment. It becomes much more difficult in such a setting to convince skeptics that justice, legally secured, is gained at the expense of allocative efficiency.

In our analysis, even if separate units of input are physically identical, and even if each unit adds the same amount to product value for the firm, these inputs are *heterogeneous* if their opportunity costs differ. Any artificially enforced policy that requires firms to follow an "equal pay for equal work" guideline, therefore, must be allocatively inefficient. This is not to suggest, of course, that equal pay for equal work as a result or end state may not emerge from the normal workings of the market process under many, perhaps most, circumstances, and particularly those circumstances that are characterized by freedom of entry and exit by firms in separate product lines and by workers in separate employments. However, as a criterion for some legally enforced wage setting, equal pay for equal work cannot fail to have the effects suggested.

In terms of the efficiency norm, "equal work" is inappropriate as the criterion for "equal pay." This criterion should be "equal cost," which is, of course, that which the market will tend to meet if its operations are unimpeded. The equal work criterion will be satisfied only if there exist no equalizing differences present that will introduce differences among opportunity costs at the margins of adjustment. And, of course, there is no way of determining whether or not such differences exist, other than that of allowing the market itself to work freely.

Issues of "discrimination" easily arise here. Is it not "discriminatory" to allow employers to pay differing wage rates to workers who produce equal measured products? Again, reference to our earlier example will prove useful in clearing out tightly packed emotional cobwebs. No one would think of discrimination if he should observe a contractor paying a plumber a higher hourly wage rate than a painter. Why, then, should discrimination seem to be present when worker C is paid a lower wage rate than the equally productive worker D, if the employer can hire C at a lower opportunity cost?

Suppose that, upon examination, worker C should be found to have a strong locational preference for employment in place E where the employment is, and that he will indeed accept employment at E at some wage rate considerably lower than that required to hire worker D. Equalization of wage rates, at the level that D requires, will amount to paying C an economic rent over and above his true opportunity cost, and the necessity of paying this unnecessary rent will force the employer to reduce the rate of input purchase (and of output production) below that which is socially efficient.[7]

---

7. In the specific setting discussed here, the single employer would be interested in hiring worker D at the differentially higher wage required, only if he exhausts the supply of workers like C, given an assumption that initially the C and D workers are interchange-

VI. Input Heterogeneity in a Generalized Setting

In this section we want to examine the possible relevance of the phenomena we have analyzed in a more general setting, and specifically to examine how the results might be modified in the long run. To what extent is the input heterogeneity that is central to our analysis a short-term or disequilibrium phenomenon that will tend to disappear as resources shift into and out of alternative categories? To what extent does the input composition of team production change as adjustments might be made to the differing opportunity costs of inputs? To what extent will consumers tend to shift purchases toward products and services that embody relatively high proportions of inputs that are priced at relatively low opportunity costs?

For all practical intent, our analysis has potential policy relevance only for personal or human inputs into the productive process. Land and capital will normally be priced by the play of ordinary market forces, and any proposed forced homogenization of heterogeneous units would appear, and be, absurd. Consider, then, labor input alone, and look at the possible substitutability among heterogeneous input categories within the inclusive labor services rubric, that is, substitutability among differing occupational, skill, and professional groups. As noted previously, the competitive wage level that will emerge for any given group of homogeneous units within a single category will depend on some amalgam of both demand and supply elements.

If, from some preexisting or postulated equilibrium wage level relationship between two separate categories, say between carpenters and plumbers, there occurs an exogenous demand shift that modifies the relationship, marginal adjustments will occur. Some workers will undergo retraining to shift from the relatively lowered to the relatively increased wage occupation. New entrants will tend to enter more rapidly in the latter occupational category than the former. These long-term adjustments will tend to return the relationship between wage levels in the two occupations to their previously existing

---

able. In this setting, therefore, the firm is a monopsonist of the traditional variety. Our analysis suggests only that the discriminatory input pricing that the monopsony firm would naturally follow is required for allocative efficiency. The monopsonist need not, of course, retain the "rents" that might otherwise be gained by input owners. Competition in the product market may allow the monopsonist to survive only if he is able to discriminate in the purchase of inputs.

equilibrium. But there is nothing in such long-term adjustments that insures wage rates in the two categories will achieve ultimate equality. "Equalizing differences" may remain as between occupational categories, even with long-term adjustment, differences that may be due to differences in the intrinsic attractiveness or unattractiveness of employments, or due to natural limits on the supply of specific talents among persons. So long as such equalizing differences are acknowledged to exist in the long-term equilibrium adjustments in the supply of labor to the different occupational and professional groupings, our analysis remains unaffected.

A different sort of substitutability may take place, however, within the production function of the organizer of production. To the extent that the heterogeneous inputs are substitutable one for the other in the production function, the profit maximizer will, of course, prefer to purchase those units that can be hired at the lowest opportunity cost. This activity on the part of firms will tend to increase demand for the low opportunity cost categories, and to bring wages or prices toward equality with those for other inputs. This equalization process will continue so long as the substitution possibilities are efficient. As we stressed at the outset of our analysis, however, to the extent that there remain genuine advantages to team production, such input substitution is limited, even with long-term adjustments. Much the same conclusion holds for the long-term substitutability among final product items by ultimate consumers. There are finite limits beyond which substitution motivated by price differences becomes inefficient.

If input heterogeneity arises from differences in opportunity costs that embody no equalizing differences, and there are no advantages in team production that require some combination of differing talents or skills, "unequal pay" for "equal work" becomes a phenomenon to be observed only in short-term or disequilibrium situations. In the literal definitional sense, unequal pay for equal work is inconsistent with the conditions required for long-term competitive equilibrium. As noted earlier, equal pay for equal work tends to emerge, where it is relevant, from the working of market forces. Even in this context, however, any premature and forced homogenization of pricing for the initially heterogeneous units of input will prevent the allocative adjustments that are required to attain the end-state equalization in compensation without coercion.

Consider as an example a group of immigrant workers who initially have very low opportunity costs and who will accept employment at relatively low wages. Firms that hire workers will be observed to make differentially higher profits. Demands for the services of such workers will increase, and wages will tend toward equality with those of other groups with comparable skills. Suppose, by comparison, that all employers are forced to pay equal wages from the outset. There will now be no profit opportunities in hiring the immigrants. The rate at which members of this group are absorbed into the labor force will be retarded, and the economy will suffer a welfare loss due to resource misallocation over a longer time period.

VII. Conclusions

Orthodox theory assumes that inputs are readily classifiable into groups that internally contain units that are indistinguishable, one from another, both in opportunity costs or in contributions to value. The theory of pricing is then applied to each type or class of input separately considered. Prices are set in accordance with the values of marginal product, but there is no difference between what is sometimes called the "internal" marginal product and the "external" marginal product. No problem arises concerning the definition of heterogeneity or homogeneity among input units. As noted, the relationship among the prices for input units drawn from different classes and combined by the firm has not been analyzed directly to our knowledge, and little or no attention has been paid to the allocative effects of forced homogenization in pricing for heterogeneous input units. As our applications suggest, however, this sort of homogenization is widely observed in real-world economies, and notably in connection with labor inputs.

There are two separate but related strands of analysis in neoclassical theory that are analogous to the analysis in this paper. Constructions that seem almost identical to our own are to be found in the orthodox monopsony theory. Perhaps the most interesting feature of our model lies in the demonstration that our results emerge even if the firm operates within a fully competitive structure, with no influence on either the price of its product or the price of any of the inputs that it purchases. In this context, the firm that organizes team production among units of heterogeneous inputs behaves analogously to a perfectly discriminating monopsonist. It attains allocative efficiency in input usage (and output production) because it is able to secure the heterogeneous input units at their differing opportunity costs, measured in the competitively determined set of input prices.

The upward-sloping "supply curve" for heterogeneous inputs may be confronted by firms that remain extremely small relative to the market for either the product or for any one of the inputs purchased. The firm need not be large relative to the market for inputs for the upward-sloping cost curve to emerge, as would be the case in the standard derivation of a monopsony position. The forced homogenization has the effect of making the fully competitive firm act as if it becomes a nondiscriminating monopsonist. In both cases, welfare losses emerge. However, the ultimate policy implications are quite different in the two cases. The welfare losses of nondiscriminating monopsony can be eliminated by the introduction of competition in the markets for inputs. The welfare losses from forced input homogenization can also be eliminated by the "introduction of competition," but there it takes the form of allowing ordinary markets to operate without interference.

The second strand of analysis that is analogous, although less directly, to our analysis is found in the famous discussion of rising supply price that occupied the best minds of the profession in the 1920's and 1930's, with the debated issues finally resolved in Joan Robinson's paper.[8] Marshall and Pigou had argued that competition in industries characterized by a rising supply price tends to produce an inefficiently large output. The opponents of this view finally proved that competitive organization generated the optimal output, that rents did not constitute social losses, and that any restriction below the competitive output levels would guarantee welfare losses. In the models of rising supply price under competition, however, individual firms face parametric input prices defined over bundles of separately considered homogeneous input units. Firms do not face rising supply prices for inputs arrayed in terms of competitively established opportunity costs. While our results are broadly consistent with the conclusions reached in this great neoclassical debate, they clarify an ambiguity in demonstrating that competitive output is efficient even when the competitive firm itself faces upward-sloping input cost schedules.

---

8. "Rising Supply Price," in *Readings in Price Theory,* ed. George J. Stigler and Kenneth E. Boulding (Homewood, 1952).

Trying Again to Value a Life

James M. Buchanan and Roger L. Faith

In a fascinating—if confusing—note, John Broome tries to demonstrate that any "attempt to value life in terms of money is more or less doomed to failure."[1] Broome's argument seems to be in error on several counts, some of which we shall not discuss here. However, the central flaw in his whole argument lies in a misunderstanding of *cost*. When does any attempt to *value* life arise for an individual or for a collectivity? Only when a *choice* is confronted does a valuation process become necessary. And only when choice is confronted is opportunity cost meaningful.[2]

For purposes of argument here, let us stipulate, with Broome, that life to an ordinary person is of infinite value, hence ruling out potential suicides as well as all those who might sacrifice their own lives for others in exchange for finite monetary rewards or anything else. From this stipulation it follows that no person will choose a course of action that promises certain death. No one will play Russian roulette with all six chambers of the gun loaded.

To choose certain death, however, is not at all equivalent to choosing a "risk of death," which each and every one of us does every day. The object for choice is quite different in the two cases, and the costs are quite different, even for the person who might die in a risky venture. At the moment of choice among the alternative "possibles,"[3] a person may rationally accept a risk of death in exchange for a measurable monetary reward, the applause of the crowd, or even for a few extra minutes of time. In the more dramatic

From *Journal of Public Economics* 12 (October 1979): 245–48. Copyright 1959. Reprinted with permission from Elsevier Science.

1. John Broome, "Trying to Value Life," *Journal of Public Economics* 9 (1978): 91–100.
2. See James M. Buchanan, *Cost and Choice* (Chicago: Markham, 1969).
3. Cf. G. L. S. Shackle, *Epistemics and Economics* (Cambridge: Cambridge University Press, 1972).

instances, for skyscraper workers, race car drivers, mercenary soldiers, high-wire circus performers, and speeding motorists, such exchanges become routine.

Whenever risk or uncertainty is involved, the consequences of choice are unpredictable in a deterministic sense. These consequences may involve damages, including loss of life and, for some purposes, it may prove useful to attempt to measure the "costs" or damages of such consequences. However, these ex post "costs" are wholly irrelevant for behavior except insofar as they might provide some informational basis for other choices that might be made in future periods. To say that "costs" are infinite for the person who loses his life in the draw of a lottery in which he rationally chose to participate is to say nothing at all about the *value* that such an individual placed on life in the moment at which the choice was made. These ex post "costs" can, in no way, influence the choice behavior that created the consequences.

Broome concentrates his criticism on cost-benefit analysis, which has been largely applied to collective choices among alternative investment projects. There are two related ambiguities that may arise in such applications, and Broome may have intuitively sensed one or both of these in his rejection of this approach. The first involves the presumed objectivity of cost and, by inference, of compensation. The second involves the meaning of the Pareto criterion for social improvement.

Specifically, Broome rejects the compensation test of theoretical welfare economics, even if actual compensations are paid. In effect, he argues that compensations could never properly be computed in terms of finite values for the person whose life is lost in a particular project. No finite benefits could offset the cost; hence, a paradox exists. All projects involving loss of life should be rejected on a proper application of the cost-benefit test, despite the apparent social desirability of some subset of these. While Broome admittedly concentrates his attention on collective evaluations, an extension of his analysis to private choice implies that no decisions involving probable loss of life would ever be taken. But, of course, all decisions do carry some risk of death. Taken literally, Broome's ideal setting is indeed the stationary state![4]

---

4. Such commonplace activities as driving during rush hour (risk of accident), going to the movies (risk of contagious disease), and arguing with one's neighbor (risk of a fight) would be avoided. All rational individuals would become recluses.

Many economists, including some who work within the cost-benefit tradition, are no doubt subject to criticism for their implied definition of cost. If costs are conceived as "damages" that may be objectively measurable by external observers ex post, from which it follows that they may also be estimated or predicted ex ante, again by external observers, Broome's criticism would be apt. Measured "damages" to the person whose life is lost are infinite. Hence, if properly estimated in the initial computation, no such project could secure approval. If, however, costs are related directly to choice, and are treated as subjectively estimated barriers to choice by those persons who are to bear the consequences, costs become the value of the rejected alternatives. No paradox can possibly arise. The critical element here is that all persons who participate in a project must *agree* to such participation *in advance* of the project's implementation. Effectively, the rule must be a *property rule* as opposed to a *liability rule,* to use the convenient terms of Calabresi and Melamed.[5]

The ambiguity in the definition of opportunity cost, which may be shared by Broome and perhaps by some of those whom he criticizes,[6] is closely related to a more pervasive ambiguity in the application of the criterion for Pareto-superiority. Once again, if costs are conceived to be objectively measurable rather than subjective, these costs can be both estimated and added up by some party or parties external to those who suffer the consequences of choice either as net burden sharers or net beneficiaries. With full compensation, of course, there are supposed to be no net burden sharers; net benefits are greater than or equal to zero for all persons. If the objectivity of costs is denied, however, the *only* test for compensation is that which is indicated by observed agreement among all individuals to the terms of "exchange" implicit in the compensation. And as we have already noted, all such net "improvements" must be anticipated rather than realized, ex ante rather than ex post. Hence, mistakes must be allowed for. The only test for Pareto-superiority of one project over another lies in the expressed or revealed una-

5. G. Calabresi and D. Melamed, "Property Rules, Liability Rules, and Inalienability: One View of the Cathedral," *Harvard Law Review* 85 (1972): 1089–1128.

6. But not by E. J. Mishan, the only economist cited by Broome. Mishan, *Elements of Cost-Benefit Analysis* (London: Allen and Unwin, 1972), makes it clear that the relevant costs are subjective.

nimity of all persons affected by the alternatives. The Wicksellian unanimity test incorporates both the Pareto-superiority criterion and the cost-benefit test, when properly conceived and applied.

An understanding of the Pareto criterion has direct relevance for some of the bizarre examples suggested by Broome. There is nothing inconsistent or paradoxical in the failure of a project involving a loss of a single advance-identified life to pass the Wicksellian test while at the same time a project, yielding the same benefits, but which involves the loss of several nonidentified lives to be randomly determined secures unanimous approval. Consider the following example. It is discovered that a rare disease will, with certainty, take the lives of two hundred randomly determined individuals if gone unchecked. It is also discovered that an antidote can be manufactured from a special substance in individual A's brain, and that extraction of the substance guarantees A's death. By the Pareto criterion, A will reject any proposal to obtain the serum. Now suppose it is known that one of every one hundred individuals has the special substance in his or her brain and there is no way of knowing who these people are without destroying their brains in the process. If it is then proposed that all individuals partake in a lottery to see whose brain is to be inspected, the lottery would be unanimously accepted since the probability of dying from the search lottery is less than the probability of dying from the disease. Despite the fact that only one person must die in the first case whereas many may die in the second, the Pareto criterion yields the economically correct result in both situations.

PART FIVE

Opportunity Cost and Efficient Prices

Opportunity Costs
and Legal Institutions

The word *cost* may be used to convey several meanings. When *opportunity* is put in place as an antecedent modifier, the set of possible meanings is restricted. Opportunity suggests the presence of something of value that may or may not be chosen; the word *opportunity* connects cost to human choice. And *opportunity cost* suggests that something, a course of action, is rejected in order to achieve something else. That which might have been can, of course, never be. Hence, any realization of a foregone opportunity is a logical contradiction.

How, then, is opportunity cost measured at all? The value of that alternative that might have been chosen but that can never be becomes quantifiable only in the internal or subjective calculus of the person who makes the relevant choice, and this value exists temporally only at the moment of choice itself. Opportunity cost is, therefore, necessarily reckoned in a utility dimension that cannot be observed externally. At best, tolerably acceptable proxies for opportunity cost can be introduced under carefully specified institutional settings.[1]

Because the value of a foregone opportunity is reckoned in a utility rather than a commodity or monetary dimension, non-physical attributes of choice alternatives can readily be entered into the evaluation. The anticipated value of the course of action not chosen may include any attribute that either enhances or retards the intrinsic worth of the "thing in itself." The opportunity

From *The New Palgrave Dictionary of Economics and the Law,* vol. 2, ed. Peter Newman (London: Macmillan, 1998), 710–15. Reprinted by permission of the publisher.

1. J. M. Buchanan, *Cost and Choice: An Inquiry in Economic Theory* (Chicago: Markham, 1969).

cost of the road chosen by Robert Frost's traveller may depend on whether or not the road not chosen does or does not imply trespass on private property.

Legal institutions affect human action largely through their impact on the relative opportunity costs of alternatives faced by persons in their varying capacities or roles as choosers—whether as prospective purchasers of end-items in consumer-goods markets; as prospective sellers of resource services (including labour) in markets for inputs; as prospective investors of accumulated funds in financial markets; as prospective entrepreneurs in organizing the production of value; politically, as prospective voters-choosers, including all of the participating roles in the politics of democracy (electoral, bureaucratic, executive, legislative, judicial); and, finally, as prospective members of the continuing constitutional evaluation of the alternative sets of constraints that define the integrated legal-political-economic-social regime of interaction.

Inclusively interpreted, this essay's title is such as to allow almost anything within the umbrella rubric of comparative social structures to be discussed. If we accept the presupposition that human beings, everywhere and at any time, are described, at least in part, by general proclivities that can be operationally defined, and, further, if we eschew situationalistic explanations for everything, we are left with potential variability in political-social-legal institutions as the primary means through which betterment of the human condition may be furthered. In a persuasive paper, Mancur Olson argued that differences in observed levels of personal well-being among separate nations are to be explained by differences in the set of political-legal-social institutions that act to constrain behaviour.[2] Dispute may well arise over whether or not "the law," as it exists, has been, or should be, designed, explicitly or implicitly, to achieve economic purpose. But there is no disputing the obvious point that "the law," whether actual or potential, does indeed exert significant effects on behaviour and that these ultimately influence measured levels of economic well-being.

Human beings achieve their potential for satisfaction only in a social order that both describes and proscribes the rules within which they act, one

2. Mancur Olson, "Big Bills Left on the Sidewalk: Why Some Nations Are Rich, and Others Poor," *Journal of Economic Perspectives* 10, no. 2 (1996): 3–24.

with another, whether in one-to-one, market-like exchange transactions or in more complex, many-person interaction processes. In an inclusive definitional sense, the whole set of such rules may be summarized under the rubric of "the law," independent of any consideration of origins or means of enforcement. And, at this level of abstraction, the rules that constrain persons in their behaviour towards one another are not different, in kind, from the constraints of the natural world. It is folly to swim against the raging torrent; it is also folly to steal gold from the well-guarded treasury. In both cases, the opportunity costs of such choices are prohibitively high.

At yet another level of analysis, however, a distinction between natural and non-natural constraints emerges from the recognition that the set of rules, "the law," is, itself, artifactual, even if much of it may have evolved without conscious or explicit design aimed at the accomplishment of specific purpose. What is important here is the acknowledgement that, in prospect, law can be *made,* or reformed, at some margins of adjustment, even if evolutionary processes may successfully explain how many of the existing rules came into being. Some such acknowledgement becomes a necessary prerequisite to improvement in the human condition. When reform or change enters the discussion, the subject is almost always centred on changes in law, in rules, in legal institutions—changes that are directly translated into shifts in the relative opportunity costs of alternative behavioural options that persons confront.

Reform by Rules Change: A Classic Example

The discussion may be facilitated through usage of a familiar example, the now classic Prisoners' Dilemma, used here as a two-person metaphor for a large-number social interaction. Consider the simple two-by-two payoff matrix in Figure 1, where person *A* chooses between Rows and person *B* chooses between Columns. Ordinal payoffs in each cell are as shown, with the left number for *A,* the right for *B.* Rational choice dictates that *A* choose Row 2 and that *B* choose Column 2, generating a solution or outcome in Cell IV. Each person faces a dominant choice; no matter what action the other is predicted to take, the payoff structure dictates a singular pattern of behaviour. Note that the solution or outcome in Cell IV *emerges* from the separately made choices of *A* and *B*; this solution, as such, is not explicitly chosen by

Figure 1

either person. And, of course, it is not the most preferred position for either person, or even by the collectivity of both players. Hence, the familiar label, the dilemma, or, in a large-number setting, the "tragedy of the commons."

This interaction may be discussed specifically in opportunity-cost terminology. For person A, the foregone opportunity of choosing Row 2 is the expected value of the payoff that would emerge from a choice of Row 1—a payoff that is less than that which would emerge from a choice of Row 2. And vice versa for person B. There is no behavioural incentive for either person to initiate independent action that will allow escape from the dilemma.

Suppose, however, that both persons fully recognize the situation that they each separately confront in this interaction. Clearly there is a potential for both persons to be made better off if some agreement can be reached on arrangements that will modify the payoffs faced. Institutional reform might be of several types. Agreement might be reached on a set of penalties for behaviour deemed to be harmful and/or rewards for behaviour deemed to be beneficial. For illustration, suppose A and B agree to impose penalties on d-like behaviour (Figure 1). This change will reduce the opportunity cost for A in taking the Row 1 action and that for B in taking the Column 1 action. Sufficiently high penalties on d-like behaviour (or sufficiently high rewards for c-like behaviour) will generate an emergent solution in Cell I, where both (all) persons secure higher payoffs than in the initial Cell IV equilibrium. Indeed, in its simplest sense, the situation in Cell IV, if understood, should prompt the classic call "there ought to be a law."

Implementation of any effective set of penalties (or rewards) aimed at generating the mutually preferred (Pareto-superior) result requires agreement, or, more specifically, collectivization or politicization of the interaction. The institutional regime that allows persons separately to make independent choices among alternatives must be modified, either through some change in incentives that will cause persons to choose differently or through more explicit political selection of the behavioural combination that will produce preferred results. Instead of a system of rewards and penalties on good and bad behaviour, agreement may be reached that will, simply, declare bad behaviour "against the law." In the simple matrix of Figure 1, person *A* can no longer choose a Row 2 action; person *B* cannot choose a Column 2 action, but must choose the *c* alternative, generating the preferred Cell I solution. The off-diagonal attractors in Cells II and III no longer exist.

Privatization

Another institutional means of escaping from the dilemma—and a means that may prove more efficacious in many settings than in others—involves a change in rules that operates to remove or to reduce the payoff (utility) interdependence among persons that creates the difficulty in the first place. This approach requires that we ask the question: Why are the payoffs of one person dependent on behaviour of the other? Does the observed interdependence stem from some necessary feature of an interaction or is it amenable to elimination or reduction by a change in law?

Here the familiar "tragedy of the commons" illustration is expositionally helpful. Consider the setting in which each of several (or many) ranchers grazes steers on an open range—the commons that is freely available to all users. Overgrazing results and the valuable pasture is used up in the sense that no recognition of its value enters into the calculus of the separate users. A collective-political solution might involve some set of penalties (prices) on usage of the pasture, as in our earlier example. Instead of this scheme, however, more effective rules-change here might take the form of "privatization." Individuals—either one, several or many—might be assigned ownership rights in the valued resource that carry with them the legally enforceable authority to exclude others from usage.

Reform that establishes or reassigns property rights in valued resources may be preferred to direct political manipulation for several reasons. Efficient usage of a valued resource emerges from the rational choices of separate owners rather than from a politically determined set of prices (penalties) on usage. In any situation, choice-makers face opportunity costs that reflect anticipated value of alternatives that are not chosen. But these rejected alternatives may vary in their incidence as between the chooser and others who are in the relevant interdependence relationship.

The rancher who adds a steer to the commons foregoes only a small share of the anticipated value of the grass that the steer will eat. By comparison, under private ownership of the grazing range, the rancher who adds a steer foregoes the full amount of the anticipated value of the grass to be eaten—value that would be available if the steer is not added. Some numbers will make the illustration concrete. Suppose, in the first setting, there are 1000 steers on the commons, only 10 of which belong to the single rancher who, correctly, anticipates that an additional steer will eat $1000-worth of grass, thereby reducing the value of all other grazing animals. To the individual rancher, however, only 1/100 of this value, or $10, will be reflected in the loss in value to his own steers. Again by comparison, think of the rancher who owns a separately bounded parcel of the range land. The anticipated value of grass that might be eaten by a steer is again $1000, but this anticipated shortfall in value will all show up as reduction in value of the rancher's own herd.

The example demonstrates precisely how law and legal institutions affect allocative results indirectly through their influence on incentives that confront individual choosers. In a strict resource-using sense, adding the steer has identical effects in the two settings. A value of $1000 is somehow sacrificed or given up. But, when translated into the opportunity cost of choices faced by those persons who confront the alternatives, the two settings seem quite different. Predictably, differing allocative results will emerge.

In effect, what privatization of a valued resource accomplishes is a matching between decision or choice authority with those consequences of choice that should be reckoned in any efficiency calculus. Note, however, that efficiency emerges from, and indeed is defined by, the separate decisions of owners-users who confront opportunity costs that reflect the full value of sacrificed alternatives. In this indirect sense, the law of property does, indeed, serve the purpose of promoting economic efficiency—a principle that has been recognized at least since Aristotle.

The commons example is also helpful in introducing the critical distinction that must be made between the establishment of ownership (exclusion) rights as a means of internalizing the consequences of choices in resource usage and the particularized assignment of such rights as among persons in the relevant political community. The efficiency-enhancing purpose of the law of property is achieved under *any* assignment, subject only to the proviso that competitive conditions generally prevail. That is to say, no matter which set of persons in the community succeeds in securing rights of ownership in the valued resource, their own decision calculus, separately exercised, will ensure that efficient usage occurs. It matters not at all whether the previously open commons be assigned to ranchers *a, b, c* through *m* or to ranchers *n, o, p* through *z*. The law of property will have met its purpose upon the assignment itself; the distribution is irrelevant.

Economists will be familiar with this neutrality result; versions of it are widely discussed under the rubric of "the Coase Theorem." The important principle to be stressed is that while the particular assignment of ownership rights among persons is of little or no economic consequence, the assignment of ownership rights, as such, is the *sine qua non* for efficiency in allocation. It matters not *who* owns the valued pasture; it matters much that it be owned by *someone*, anyone.

The implementation of reform that establishes and assigns separate ownership-exclusion rights can be interpreted as a response to the plaint that "there ought to be a law," noted earlier. In this perspective, the law of property finds its *raison d'être* in the efforts of persons to improve their economic well-being. But what are the limits? If someone, anyone, owns everything that is valued, and if the law of property and contract operates with reasonable efficacy, is there more that "the law" need do?

Unfortunately, perhaps, not all that is valued can be separately and privately owned. Persons live, one with another, in many non-privatized dimensions; each person (family) does not exist in a protected bubble all her own from which she departs only to engage in reciprocal exchange (market) transactions. There are "natural" commons, so to speak, that cannot be privatized, at least in the ordinary sense. Further, there may be economies of scale in the usage of some goods, quite apart from the technology of excludability. In sum, the social order cannot be wholly privatized; interdependencies among persons remain that cannot be brought readily within the inclusive market-exchange nexus. To the extent that such non-exchange interdependencies are present, there is a mismatch between choice-making authority and the incidence of the consequences of choice. The opportunity costs that inform choices will tend to undervalue the estimated foregone alternatives that deprive all but the choosers.

Externality

Economists discuss non-exchange interdependencies under the inclusive term *externality*. If the activity of one person (or firm) generates non-compensated benefits or harms on another, the opportunity costs that inform choices may not fully incorporate the spillover or external components since these do not impact directly on the utility (wealth) of the chooser. The interdependence is not internalized as it would be in an ordinary market exchange transaction. The slight increase in the city's smog is a consequence of a freeway trip, but individuals other than the prospective driver bear the major incidence. The impact of the driver's choice on others may not be appropriately weighted in the decision calculus.

The early neoclassical welfare economics, derived from the analysis of Pigou,[3] suggested that, once an externality is identified, the generating action should be subjected to political correction, either through some collectively imposed structure of penalties (or rewards) or through direct political management. The object of the politicization, in either case, is that of bringing "private" cost into line with "social" cost. Institutional reform embodies directed changes in the opportunity costs faced by relevant choosers.

Two flaws in this seemingly straightforward Pigovian logic were exposed in the last half of this century. First, the normative structure was based on the romanticized notion that those who hold authority to make political-bureaucratic choices are themselves basically benevolent as well as omniscient. Public choice theory, sometimes called "politics without romance,"[4] carries the implication that persons who make choices, no matter under what authority, confront the opportunity costs peculiar to the choice setting; there is no basis for any presumption that a political decision maker will either be able or be motivated to choose among options in such fashion as to

3. A. C. Pigou, *The Economics of Welfare*, 4th ed. (1920; reprint, London: Macmillan, 1932).

4. J. M. Buchanan, "Politics without Romance: A Sketch of Positive Public Choice Theory and Its Normative Implications," *IHS Journal, Zeitschrift des Instituts für Höhere Studien* 3 (1979): B1–11.

reflect "social" costs, if, indeed, the whole notion has any meaning in this context. Explicitly politicized corrections for externalities may or may not result in improvements over the uncorrected market interaction, externalities and all. Pragmatic, case-by-case comparison is indicated.

A second major flaw in the Pigovian construction lies in its failure to relate the postulated economic interdependence with the legal structure—a failure that was exposed in Coase's now classic paper, which stimulated a major part of the whole law-and-economics research programme.[5] When a person or firm inflicts damage or harm to another (or others), the obvious question is whether or not that action that is observed is within or without the law, whether the person who carries out the action does so within her legal rights or goes beyond these rights to invade the rights of another (or others). If the action is not within the law, that is, if the actor invades the rights of another (or others), the primary means of corrective adjustment is effective enforcement of either criminal or tort law, or both—enforcement that will effectively prohibit the damage-causing action from taking place.

If the action that is taken is within the law, that is, if the actor imposes damages on some third party or parties while staying within her defined legal rights, the economist should ask, Why does the market fail to work here? The removal of a non-compensated harm is equivalent to the addition of an ordinary good. And, in any exchange equilibrium, goods are traded until all mutual gains are eliminated. Hence, at a genuine trading equilibrium, the observed presence of a non-compensated harm must suggest either that the externality is infra-marginal or that it is Pareto irrelevant; that is, the harm to the person or persons externally affected is not valued as highly as the benefit to the acting person or firm.[6] In either case, the observation of non-compensated harm does not imply distortion in the allocation of resources and a need for correction. Relevant opportunity costs are internalized to those charged with choice authority.

A neutrality theorem was introduced in the third section, with reference to the assignment of ownership rights. The logical equivalent of this theorem

5. R. H. Coase, "The Problem of Social Cost," *Journal of Law and Economics* 3 (1960): 1–44.

6. J. M. Buchanan and W. C. Stubblebine, "Externality," *Economica*, n.s. 29 (1962): 371–84.

emerges in the externality setting, but its validity is less apparent due to institutional differences in the two cases. Consider a particular course of action that a person (or firm) might take that will impose damages on another. Does it matter whether the actor is assigned a legal right to undertake the action? Or whether the person potentially damaged is assigned a legal right to prevent the action? Economists will recognize this setting as that in which the Coase Theorem embodying the neutrality result initially emerged.

On first consideration, the opportunity costs of taking the action in question would seem to be quite different in the two legal settings. The actor, if assigned the right to take the action, would more heavily weight the impact of the no-action alternative on her own anticipated well-being, thereby possibly neglecting the impact on the utilities of others. By contrast, the acted-on would reverse the weighting. But what this initial consideration neglects is the market or exchange process as a means through which the relative values of goods and bads among separate potential traders are adjusted towards equality. The actor who fails to take into account adequately the value of the avoidance of potential spillover damage to the acted-on may be underestimating the opportunity costs of taking the action in question. That which the acted-on would pay to avoid the damage is a part of the opportunity cost for the actor, even in the setting where there is a clearly assigned legal right to take the action in question.

Conversely, in the setting where the potentially acted-on holds the legal right to prevent the action, the opportunity cost of exercising such a right must include the payment that the actor would be willing to make for permission. When these across-exchange payments are taken into account, the neutrality theorem again applies. No matter what the assignment of rights, efficiency tends to emerge. It is the assignment of rights, as such, that matters, not the specific distribution.

As noted, however, the neutrality result is less apparent in the externality setting because the institutional structure differs from that discussed earlier. Here there is a more explicit recognition that rational behaviour on the part of participants in the nexus requires exploitation of mutually profitable exchange opportunities when these are available. Further, there is the evident presumption that the legal structure that facilitates exchange remains invariant under differing rights assignments.

Most importantly, neutrality in the externality setting requires small numbers on both sides of the interaction, precisely because the result emerges from exchanges, which can only be effectively consummated at relatively low transactions costs. Properly interpreted, Coase's neutrality theorem requires that transactions costs be low or non-existent. If either or both sides of the externality account involve large numbers of persons, transactions costs may be such as to make exchange difficult and indirectly to rehabilitate elements of the Pigovian construction. Consider a setting where one person, the actor, may impose external or spillover damage simultaneously on a large number of other people. If the actor holds a legal right to take the action at issue, she may underestimate the value of the foregone alternative to others, and she may not be in error when she fails to incorporate a value for a payment that might be secured from refraining from taking the action (or for taking action in the external economics setting). The large group of affected parties may find it difficult to organize any joint payment.

On the other hand, should the large group, collectively, hold a legal right to prevent the action, the potential actor, who might be willing to make some payment for permission, might find the required payment prohibitively high, since the members of the affected group might not readily agree on the distribution, among themselves, of shares in smaller payments.

In situations where potential trades must, in either case, be worked out by many persons, acting as a group, on one or both sides of the interaction, it seems evident that the actual allocation of resources may be quite different in separate assignments of legal authority.[7]

The neutrality result does not apply because there remains an externality or publicness relationship among members of any large group on either one or both sides of the potential "externality exchange." There remains a commons problem among parties, and incentives are such as to prevent low-cost organization of efficiency-generating transactions with acting persons or firms. We are left with the prospect of comparing possibly inefficient market outcomes, left uncorrected, and possibly inefficient politicized outcomes, under collectivized corrective institutions. In such cases, reassignment of rights may not suffice to ensure that opportunity costs are effectively internalized.

7. For extended discussion of the effects of numbers in externality relationships, see J. M. Buchanan, "The Institutional Structure of Externality," *Public Choice* 14 (1973): 69–82.

Uncertainty and Ambiguity in the Law

To this point, the discussion has been based on an implicit presumption that the legal rights to undertake particular actions are assigned with certainty and are, therefore, readily enforceable. Under this presumption, in the relevant small-number settings, the neutrality theorem applies, and the economic interdependencies between parties are effectively internalized regardless of how rights are assigned. Persons face opportunity costs that reflect the full consequences of the choices to be made.

Consider what the introduction of uncertainty and/or ambiguity in the assignment of rights does in this setting. Suppose that a person who might potentially take an action that would exert harm on another does not know whether or not she will be held liable for damages. Nor does the person who might be damaged know whether or not claims for liability can be enforced, after the action is taken. In this situation, it may seem more profitable for the potentially damaged person to plan to seek legal recourse through claims for damage than to seek to prevent the damage being imposed through some exchange-like agreement with the acting party. This pattern of action seems likely to take place when the potentially damaged party overestimates the prospects of recovering damages relative to the estimates made by the actor.

It seems clear that the extended market or exchange-like internalization that might validate the neutrality theorem loses credibility in settings of legal uncertainty. The opportunity costs that inform choices in a regime of legal uncertainty need not reflect the value of the alternatives among which choices must be made. Allocative distortions may emerge even in an imaginary regime in which the uncertainties in the law are resolved costlessly by some random device. The distortions loom much larger in any regime of legal uncertainty where disputed claims are settled through litigation that requires resource usage, as represented by the activities of lawyers, judges and courts. These outlays are deadweight losses, over and beyond the allocative or excess burden losses.

Who suffers the ultimate costs measured by the resource wastage of lawyers? And how can changes in constraints be implemented that will prove mutually beneficial? The standard externality solutions do not seem to apply.

In one interpretation, lawyers become spoilers in that they act to destroy economic value. Consider an extension of the commons example used earlier. Onto the stylized post-commons, privatized, pastorally efficient setting, let us now introduce a predator who removes the borderline fences and blurs the boundaries beyond recognition. The valued resource is neither owned-used in common, nor is it owned-used privately-separately. The range wars and territorial disputes that describe the fictionalized American West find their modern equivalents in the burgeoning litigation that saps the economy's productive potential. The tragedy of the distributional conflict reflected by the modern litigation explosion is not amenable to reform in a way comparable to the straightforward privatization of the commons. Reform must go beyond assignment of ownership rights; reform must extend to insurance of predictability of claims. Resource owners must be protected against claims for liability invented by the legal entrepreneurs, whose value product can only be negative.

Conclusions

As noted earlier, this essay might have allowed discussion of many subjects in the intersections of law, politics and political economy. Somewhat arbitrarily, perhaps, attention has been centred on the role of legal institutions, and notably those of property and contract, in creating the conditions within which choices are made by individuals, and, in particular, on the behavioural differences that might be predicted to emerge in differing legal settings.

Legal institutions determine the incidence of the consequences of choice, and an objective for legal-political-constitutional reform must be that of achieving a closer correspondence between consequences of choice and the authority to make choices. To the extent that consequences can be effectively internalized to the chooser, there need arise none of the familiar problems summarized as dilemmas, tragedies or externalities.

Internalization means that both the anticipated benefits and the opportunity costs of a prospective course of action, as faced by whoever is in a position of authority to choose, impact largely if not exclusively on the utility of the chooser, rather than on others. Individuals can be left "free to choose" because they suffer the full consequences. Legal institutions offer the structural means through which adjustments may be made so as to secure the relevant matching as far as is practically possible.

Peak Loads and Efficient Pricing
Comment

I. Introduction

In a 1957 paper, Peter O. Steiner presented a theory of peak load pricing,[1] which his major critic, Jack Hirshleifer, hailed as a "truly major contribution" which contained "essentially the correct solution."[2] An earlier French paper by M. Boiteux, and unknown to Steiner, contained an analysis that is similar in many respects.[3] My purpose in this note is to demonstrate that both Steiner's and Boiteux's analyses obscure certain complexities in the theory of peak load *service* pricing. As a result, the "solution" which they present seems more determinate than the general model warrants. Apparent determinancy is produced only by the implicit adoption of unjustified assumptions concerning the uniformity of marginal price over quantity.

In both papers, the central elements of the analysis are developed geometrically through the utilization of orthodox demand and cost curve constructions. It will be convenient to follow Steiner's treatment here, which, to use Hirshleifer's words, employs the "illuminating device of vertically add-

From *Quarterly Journal of Economics* 80 (August 1966): 463–71. Copyright 1966 by the President and Fellows of Harvard College. Reprinted by permission of MIT Press Journals.

1. Peter O. Steiner, "Peak Loads and Efficient Pricing," *Quarterly Journal of Economics* 71 (November 1957): 585–610.

2. Jack Hirshleifer, "Peak Loads and Efficient Pricing: Comment," *Quarterly Journal of Economics* 72 (August 1958): 451.

3. Boiteux's original paper appeared in 1949 under the title "La Tarification des demandes en pointe: application de la théorie de la vent au coût marginal" in *Revue générale de l'electricité.* It is contained, in slightly modified form, in translation, in J. R. Nelson (ed.), *Marginal Cost Pricing in Practice* (Englewood Cliffs, N.J.: Prentice-Hall, 1964), 59–89. This same translation appeared earlier in *Journal of Business* 33 (April 1960): 157–79.

ing the demand curves."[4] In resorting to this construction, Steiner refers to the analogous theory of public goods formally stated by Paul A. Samuelson.[5] Neither Steiner nor his critics, however, seem to have heeded Samuelson's own quite explicit warnings against the usage of precisely this geometrical device to arrive at "solutions" to the public-goods problem.[6] In a different sense and unrelated to the theory of public goods, Boiteux's failure to recognize the restrictiveness of his model is even more surprising, since, at several points in his various contributions to the Nelson volume, he makes specific reference to practical cases where marginal price varies over quantity.[7]

Figure I reproduces Steiner's shifting-peak diagram in its essential respects. A two-period model is assumed, with the demands in these two periods assumed independent of each other. D_1 represents the demand curve for the service in one period; D_2, the demand curve for the service in the second period. These curves are drawn net of operating or running cost of the facility in each period; these costs are constant at the level indicated by b, the horizontal axis in Figure I. The curve drawn horizontally from β represents the marginal cost (average cost) of supplying system capacity, which is assumed to be constant over varying output ranges. Steiner's solution is obtained by vertically summing D_1 and D_2 to get D_c, and then locating equilibrium system capacity at the indicated intersection between this curve and the cost curve.

4. Jack Hirshleifer, "Peak Loads and Efficient Pricing: A Prior Contribution," *Quarterly Journal of Economics* 73 (August 1959): 497.

It is perhaps worth noting that, strictly speaking, the vertical summation of demand curves is not necessary, even if the assumptions of the model are fully accepted. Since the whole analysis is a rather straightforward application of Marshall's theory of joint supply, the "solution" can be derived by subtracting the demand curve for one period from the capacity supply or cost curve. Such an alternative, and Marshallian, approach to the peak load problem geometry might have, also, facilitated the discussion concerning the presence or absence of "price discrimination" in the Steiner solution, the main point raised by Hirshleifer.

5. Steiner, "Peak Loads," 589n.

6. "For there is something circular and unsatisfactory about both the Bowen and Lindahl constructions: they show what the final equilibrium looks like, but by themselves they are not generally able to find the desired equilibrium." Paul A. Samuelson, "Diagrammatic Exposition of a Theory of Public Goods," *Review of Economics and Statistics* 37 (November 1955): 354.

7. For example, see Nelson, "La Tarification," 17.

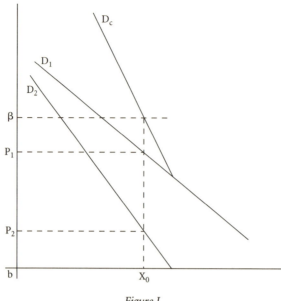

Figure I

Equilibrium capacity or quantity is shown at X_0, and the optimal prices to be charged in each period are determined by the intersection of the period demand curves with the vertical drawn from X_0. The efficient or Pareto-optimal price for period 1 is P_1, for period 2 it is P_2. As is apparent from the construction, the model lends itself readily to extension for any number of periods.

II. Uniformity in Marginal Price

The questionable feature in the analysis is the assumption of *uniformity* in marginal prices over quantities demanded in each period, by the same demander. This assumption greatly simplifies the analytical construction, but there seems to be nothing in the nature of utility-service sale to insure this sort of uniformity. If the model should be restricted to goods, and not applied to services that are consumed as purchased, then the possibility of interpersonal resale within periods might tend to insure against the possibility of "price discrimination" over quantities sold to single buyers. However, it seems plausible to expect that "price discrimination" over quantities sold to single buyers will accompany "price discrimination" among separate buyers in separate periods. With utility services such as electricity, to which the analysis has been directly applied, direct resale possibilities are not present. Hence, quantity discounts, quantity premiums, block tariffs generally, are both institutionally feasible and empirically observable.[8]

If the assumption of uniformity in marginal price is dropped, the whole geometrical construction becomes much more complex than is apparent from either the Steiner or the Boiteux paper. Unless buyers can be conceptually confronted with a set of horizontal supply curves at various prices, *no demand curves can be derived.* No single-valued relationship between quantities demanded and price exists. It becomes necessary to distinguish between marginal price and average price, and for each marginal price there may exist several quantities demanded, as the terms of the whole "price offer" are changed. Determining the optimal system capacity through a vertical summation of orthodox demand curves becomes clearly impossible.

The fundamental questions are not changed. These remain: What capacity should be constructed? How are the costs of this capacity to be shared among demanders in the separate periods? Note that, as I have phrased it here, the second question is more general than the comparable Steiner-Boiteux question, What prices are to be charged in each period?

The necessary marginal conditions that must be satisfied for Pareto optimality are the familiar ones, and these are properly stated in the analyses under discussion. Summed marginal prices must equal marginal capacity cost. The distribution of cost shares over infra-marginal ranges of demand can, however, affect the *location* of the margin both in terms of system capacity and in terms of relative marginal prices. The marginal conditions cannot be isolated from the total conditions without the introduction of arbitrarily restrictive assumptions. The variations in cost shares will influence the location of equilibrium via income-effect feedbacks on demand. The convention of uniformity in marginal price over quantity, transferred from the analysis of private-goods markets, insures a specific allocation of cost shares, both at the

8. Interestingly enough, Steiner explicitly states that the phenomenon of peak loads is "characteristically found" where the services are not storable. Steiner, "Peak Loads," 585.

margin and over infra-marginal units. But this is only one among a sub-infinity of sharing arrangements, and there is nothing sacrosanct about its usage.

The necessary conditions that must be satisfied for Pareto-optimality or efficiency do not include any requirement for marginal-price uniformity.[9] The introduction of variability in cost shares over infra-marginal quantity ranges of demand has no "welfare" or "efficiency" significance in the Pareto sense. Such variability does, of course, have distributive significance; the choice among different price-offer sets finally rests on the decision-maker's evaluation of different distributions of net consumers' surplus among separate period's demanders. The appropriate analogue is the zero-sum game. If the capacity of the system can be increased at constant marginal cost, and if the management of the enterprise seeks only to cover this cost, the introduction of a nonuniform set of marginal prices to one period's demanders must be matched in an offsetting manner by a set of offers to the second period's customers. If utility services are made available in one of the two periods at quantity discounts, these services must be made available to the second period's consumers at quantity premiums. The precise terms of an internally consistent set of price offers over all periods will determine the distribution of consumers' surplus as between these periods' demanders, but, so long as the necessary marginal conditions are satisfied, variations in these offers will not imply Pareto inefficiency.

III. Multiplicity of Price Offers

The main points here may be illustrated in the construction of Figure II, which is similar to, but in essential respects different from, that of Figure I. Given constancy in the costs of supplying system capacity, let us suppose initially that the separate price offers in the two periods take the form shown by the curves M_1 and M_2. For simplicity, think of only one demander in each period, and neglect considerations of strategic behavior. Alternatively, think

---

9. This has been noted in another connection by Yale Brozen. See his "Welfare Theory, Technological Change, and Public Utility Investment," *Land Economics* 27 (February 1951): 72ff.

Although he is never fully explicit, M. Boiteux implies that such marginal price uniformity is required for Pareto optimality. For example, see Nelson, "La Tarification," 27.

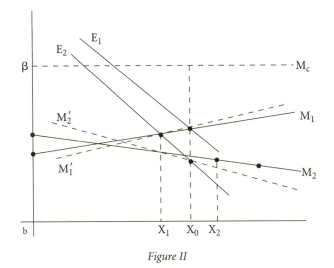

Figure II

of several demanders, each of whom is confronted by price offers as represented.[10] Note that, as constructed, $M_1 + M_2 = M_c$, at any level of quantity. The *M curves* are curves of marginal price as these are confronted by the separate demanders. In period 2, utility services are available at a quantity discount; marginal price is reduced as larger quantities are purchased. Hence, marginal price lies below average price throughout the range. In period 1, utility services are available only at a quantity premium; marginal prices increase as quantities demanded increase; marginal price exceeds average price for all quantities.[11]

10. As still a different alternative, we could imagine a pricing structure such that the curves M_1 and M_2 would represent marginal prices only for the group of demanders in each period, with each single demander being faced with a uniform marginal price. The level of the latter would, in this case, depend on the aggregate quantity demanded by the whole group. In demanding capacity under such conditions as this, each consumer would exert an external economy on all fellow consumers in the same period. Appropriately drawn rules for collective behavior could internalize these external economies, in which case the model would become equivalent to the single-demander example suggested in the text. Real-world block tariffs seem normally to apply to levels of individual or unit quantities demanded.

11. For a general discussion of variation in marginal price over quantity, see my "The Theory of Monopolistic Quantity Discounts," *Review of Economic Studies* 20 (1952–53): 199–208.

The set of price offers represented by M_1 and M_2 is consistent with the level of capacity cost, M_c, and with the constancy of marginal capacity cost over quantity. This set need not, however, be consistent with the demands that may be expressed in the separate periods as these price offers. At the price offer, M_1, a specific quantity, say, X_1, may be taken in period 1. At the price offer, M_2, a specific quantity, say, X_2, may be taken in period 2. So long as $X_1 \neq X_2$, the set of offers is not successful in matching supply and demand efficiently. By some process of trial and error, we may assume that the pricing authority arrives at some set of offers that will bring the two independent demands into consistency, while remaining within the restrictions imposed by the cost or supply side. One such set is shown by the curves, M_1' and M_2' on Figure II. Both demanders now desire to purchase the same quantity, X_0, which is an equilibrium or optimal system capacity. Note, however, that the marginal price, at equilibrium, for the demanders in period 2 remains identical to the marginal price under the previous offer set. He is now persuaded to reduce his preferred purchases to X_0 because he secures a smaller consumer's surplus over infra-marginal quantities.[12]

The levy of fixed charges along with flat-rate tariffs is a more familiar pattern of utility-service pricing than continuous variation in marginal prices over quantities. Through appropriate adjustments in the fixed charges imposed on separate-period demanders, along with correlated shifts in flat rates, this combination will, under some configurations of demand, produce fully efficient results, even in the constant-cost case.

Through any one of several schemes, a consistent and efficient pricing structure can be selected. It is important to recognize that there will be *many sets* of efficient price offers, including the one depicted by Steiner and Boiteux. There is nothing in the general model which suggests uniqueness here, and the implied uniqueness of the Steiner-Boiteux models arises wholly from the implicit assumption of uniformity in marginal price. This is indicated in Figure

12. In the construction of Figure II, continuous variation in marginal price has been assumed. However, as Gabor has demonstrated, any such schedule can be converted into a block pricing schedule so as to produce identical results, and vice versa. The analysis applies, therefore, to all systems of block pricing, systems that seem especially characteristic of utility services. For the relationship between block pricing and continuous variation, see André Gabor, "A Note on Block Tariffs," *Review of Economic Studies* 23 (1955–56): 32–41.

I, where it may be shown that there is only one set of prices that will satisfy the necessary marginal conditions for efficiency. In the construction of Figure II, by contrast, there will be many sets of offers that meet the necessary marginal requirements.

Once an efficient set of price offers has been located, and equilibrium has been established, it then becomes possible to construct marginal evaluation schedules for the demanders in the separate periods. These are shown as E_1 and E_2 in Figure II. These curves are similar to demand curves, but they are different in that their uniqueness depends on the specific price offers in being. And there will be a different set of marginal evaluation curves for each separate set of price offers. It is for this reason that marginal evaluation curves, or "demand curves," independently derived, cannot be employed to "find" equilibrium capacity or optimal marginal prices.[13]

The emendation on the standard analysis presented in this note might be considered to be of minor importance if plausible reasons can be found to insure that the same solution is produced under the alternate constructions. Variations in marginal price over quantity may have distributively important results, but so long as these do not shift the quantity of capacity indicated to be optimal, little is obscured by neglecting the imperfections of the model that have been emphasized here. It will now be useful to examine the possible means of neutralizing the effects of marginal price variation.

The effects on optimal quantity of capacity and on optimal marginal prices stem from income feedbacks on demand. If we could assume that the service in question is characterized by zero income elasticity of demand, the Steiner-Boiteux analysis can be rescued in all essential respects. Here, a single-valued relationship between marginal price and quantity demanded may be derived, and these relationships may be used, as Steiner employs demand curves, to produce a unique equilibrium solution. In such a model, variations in marginal price over infra-marginal units cannot affect the evaluation that an individual places on the marginal unit. Indifference curves for the individual are parallel along any vertical drawn from the quantity-of-service axis. This assumption of zero income elasticity removes the inde-

13. Geometrically, the marginal evaluation curve for a single individual is constructed by plotting the slopes of successive indifference curves as these cut a defined opportunity curve.

terminacy, but it seems to be acceptable only for those services that make up a relatively small proportion of consumer or purchaser outlay. This is, of course, the standard and familiar Marshallian escape route. Application of the theory to such important services as electricity can scarcely depend on such a restrictive assumption.

A second, and more plausible, escape from the apparent limitations imposed on the analysis may seem to be offered by the possibility of mutual offsets in income effects among separate demanders. As suggested, so long as the public enterprise seeks to earn no monopoly profits, and so long as capacity can be supplied at constant costs, the distribution of the consumers' surplus among separate-period demanders becomes analogous to a zero-sum game. The gain in income by one set of demanders must be offset by the loss in real income by some other set of demanders. If the income elasticity of demand for all groups can be assumed roughly the same, modifications in the distribution of costs over infra-marginal ranges would seem to wash out among all sets of demanders. Somewhat unfortunately, this elementary inference is wrong because it must be recalled that all demanders must finally adjust to the *same* system capacity. The model is essentially equivalent in this respect to the pure public-goods model where the same issue has plagued simplified construction from the outset. The point here may be shown by first assuming the existence of full equilibrium. Now impose a change that will increase the share of the consumers' surplus received by the demanders of period 1 and reduce the share received by demanders of period 2 without changing relative marginal prices. Income effects will cause the first group to increase quantity demanded, if the service is a normal one, and the second group to reduce quantity demanded. To restore equilibrium, some shift in marginal prices will be required, and, of course, there is no necessity that the new equilibrium will settle at the same quantity as before.

IV. Conclusion

The conclusion appears inescapable that, for utility-service pricing as for public-goods pricing, the allocational decision cannot be isolated from the distributional decision. Choosing a specific distribution of the total costs among the separate-period demanders will, of course, determine a specific allocation of resources and a specific set of marginal prices that must be attained if Pareto efficiency is to be achieved. On the other hand, within certain limits, choosing a specific investment in system capacity will determine the distribution of total costs along with the set of marginal prices that must be present if the Pareto conditions are to be satisfied.[14] In either case, the limits of economic analysis are reached sooner than either the Steiner or the Boiteux analysis implies.

The discussion of this note has been limited to the model where the long-run marginal costs of supplying capacity are constant, the model adopted by Steiner in his basic paper. Extensions to the increasing-cost and decreasing-cost models are, of course, possible. For the decreasing-cost case, as Brozen correctly noted, variations in marginal price over quantity offer one means of covering total costs without resort to general tax revenues. However, it is precisely the possibility of such recoupment of consumers' surplus in monopolistic public enterprises, regardless of cost relationships, that may lead to a relative overexpansion of investment in public-service facilities when the welfare "rules" are not strictly observed. As a conservative rule for management, therefore, uniformity in marginal price over quantity may be plausibly defended. As a necessary rule for efficiency in the welfare sense, it cannot be justified. As a convention to make our theoretical analysis less cumbersome, it can be adopted only if we are certain of its limitations.[15]

14. This is essentially the point emphasized by Strotz in the public-goods model. See Robert H. Strotz, "Two Propositions Related to Public Goods," *Review of Economics and Statistics* 40 (November 1958): 329–31.

15. Since the submission of this note for publication, a paper by Oliver Williamson, "Peak Load Pricing and Optimal Capacity Under Indivisibility Constraints" (mimeographed, November 1965), has come to my attention. Williamson does not, however, consider the point made in this note and he seems to accept the Steiner analysis in this respect.

The Optimality of Pure Competition in the Capacity Problem

Comment

In a recent paper,[1] Lawrence H. Officer suggests that a competitive industry will supply optimal capacity under the conditions of Peter Steiner's multi-period demand model[2] and that optimal prices for utility services in the several periods will also emerge. Steiner's solution, presented initially as a normative rule for the welfare-maximizing public-enterprise monopoly, is held to describe the equilibrium results of a decentralized competitive process.

Officer deserves credit for calling attention to a neglected area of analysis. Economists are prone to search for solutions to allocation and pricing problems which are then offered to the welfare-oriented government agency that exists only in the economist's own scheme of things. They are reluctant to examine the outcomes that emerge under the spontaneous coordination imposed by competitive market structures, whether these be perfect or imperfect. For those of us whose utility functions include centralization of decision-making as a "bad," demonstrations of the efficiency of market order in unexpected places are always heartening.

Nonetheless, the limits of the competitive models must be fully recognized. In this note I shall show that the competitive organization of supply

From *Quarterly Journal of Economics* 81 (November 1967): 703–5. Copyright 1967 by the President and Fellows of Harvard College. Reprinted by permission of MIT Press Journals.

1. Lawrence H. Officer, "The Optimality of Pure Competition in the Capacity Problem," *Quarterly Journal of Economics* 80 (November 1966): 647–51.

2. Peter Steiner, "Peak Loads and Efficient Pricing," *Quarterly Journal of Economics* 71 (November 1957): 585–610.

in the capacity problem will only produce the results claimed for it under a highly restricted set of conditions. These seem to be more confining than Officer appreciated. I shall demonstrate that his interpretation of Steiner's model is only one of several possibilities. My analysis shows that, even given all of Steiner's assumptions, the competitive organization of supply need not generate either an optimal level of capacity or an efficient set of prices.

In his analysis, Steiner sought to separate the two classical public-utility problems. His emphasis was on the problem of determining optimal capacity and efficient prices under conditions where the level of demand differs among separate time periods. He wanted to examine these issues independently from the more familiar investment and pricing problems that arise under conditions of decreasing average costs. In order to accomplish this separation, Steiner assumed both operating costs and capacity costs to be linear functions of output.[3] This insures that the welfare-maximizing rules produce no conflict with profitability rules for investment decisions.

In his note Officer interprets Steiner's constant average capacity cost assumption as one that implies "a unitary homogeneous production function."[4] From this he argues that "Such a production function under monopoly is precisely analogous to the production conditions of a purely competitive industry of identical firms."[5] If this argument is accepted, it follows that competition can effectively generate the optimal level of capacity and the optimal structure of prices, these being such as to utilize capacity fully in each period. In essence, Officer says that Steiner, by isolating the peak-load problem from the decreasing-cost problem, has removed the barrier to effective competition. Hence, while Steiner's solution is formally correct, it represents the outcome of the competitive process, not only the welfare norms for the public-enterprise monopoly.

Officer's interpretation of the Steiner model is unduly restrictive. Nowhere in Steiner's discussion, nor in that of his critics, is there specific reference to a "unitary homogeneous production function," and this need not be an implication of the explicit cost assumption that is made. Total capacity costs can remain a linear function of the number of units of capacity built

---

3. ". . . we assume throughout that operation costs are a linear function of output, and that the cost of capacity is a linear function of the number of units of capacity built." Steiner, "Peak Loads," 585.

4. Officer, "Optimality of Pure Competition," 649.

5. Ibid.

even if the production function is not of the type specified by Officer. For consistency with Steiner's model, it seems best to specify that long-run average costs of capacity are constant, but that this is the result of two separate and offsetting forces. Increasing returns to scale of facility can be precisely offset by rising supply prices of factors that are specific to the industry. The long-run average cost of expanding capacity remains constant, but competitive organization of supply becomes inefficient in this setting. Steiner's analysis here derives a set of welfare-maximizing norms for the public-enterprise monopoly that is unique to this institution. No longer does the solution depict the emergent outcome of a competitive process.

The analysis need not, of course, be limited to the situation where these two elements precisely offset each other so as to hold long-run average cost constant. Increasing supply prices of factors can more than balance off the advantages of scale. In this case, long-run average cost of capacity will rise. Competition will neither be viable nor efficient, however, because the average cost function for the monopoly will lie below the competitive supply curve by the factor of the scale advantage. Here the Steiner solution continues to define the necessary marginal conditions which must be satisfied when the optimal capacity level is attained along with the set of marginal prices.[6]

The general point deserves emphasis. Nondecreasing long-run average costs are a necessary but not a sufficient condition for the viability of competitive supply. If factor prices rise as the industry expands, nondecreasing average costs and decreasing average costs are alike incompatible with competition in the presence of economies of scale. A limited survey of textbook discussion suggests that this point is not fully appreciated.[7]

6. Strictly interpreted, the Steiner solution defines only the necessary marginal conditions for optimality in either this or the constant-cost case. Indeterminacy in prices over inframarginal ranges is present in both the constant-cost and the increasing-cost models, but may appear to be greater in the latter. Insofar as differing inframarginal prices exert income-effect feedbacks on demand, the location of the optimal capacity level is itself modified. On this point, see my note "Peak Loads and Efficient Pricing: Comment," *Quarterly Journal of Economics* 80 (August 1966): 463–71; also, see the elaboration by André Gabor, "Further Comment," ibid., 472–80.

7. See, for example, A. A. Alchian and W. R. Allen, *University Economics* (Belmont, California: Wadsworth, 1964), 412; Richard G. Lipsey, *An Introduction to Positive Economics* (London: Weidenfeld and Nicholson, 1963), 225; William S. Vickrey, *Microstatics* (New York: Harcourt Brace, 1964), 249.

Private Ownership
and Common Usage
The Road Case Re-examined

One of the most famous illustrative examples in the literature of economic theory is that of the good, narrow road and the rough, but wide, road. This example was introduced by Professor Pigou in his *Wealth and Welfare* and in the first edition of *The Economics of Welfare*[1] in an attempt to lend support to his general proposition that over-all economic efficiency could be increased by a transfer of resources away from increasing cost industries. The validity of this argument was questioned by Professor Frank Knight in his now-famous article "Fallacies in the Interpretation of Social Cost,"[2] in which he used the specific road example to show that in a regime of private ownership, prices tend normally to be so adjusted as to insure the necessary conditions for optimum resource use. The road illustration was also employed by many of the other participants in the great debate involving resource allocation among industries of differing cost characteristics.[3]

From *Southern Economic Journal* 22 (January 1956): 305–16. Reprinted by permission of the publisher.

I am indebted to Marshall Colberg, Malcolm Hoag, Richard Leftwich, Roland McKean, and Jerome Milliman for helpful suggestions at various stages of this paper.

1. A. C. Pigou, *Wealth and Welfare* (London: Macmillan and Company, 1912), 163; *The Economics of Welfare*, First Edition (London: Macmillan and Company, 1920), 194.

2. *Quarterly Journal of Economics* 38 (1924): 582–606. Reprinted in *The Ethics of Competition* (London: Allen and Unwin, 1935), 217–36. Subsequent reference will be to the latter.

3. A useful summary of the general discussion may be found in Howard S. Ellis and William Fellner, "External Economies and Diseconomies," *American Economic Review* 33 (1943): 493–511. Reprinted in *Readings in Price Theory* (Chicago: Richard D. Irwin, 1952), 242–63.

In this paper I shall be concerned with the specific analysis of the road example rather than with its generalization. This concentration will require a more complete examination of the various institutional structures which might provide a framework for the example. From this approach several interesting and complex points arise which tend to be overlooked when the purpose is that of using the road case merely to illustrate more important general principles. While the results of the analysis will not affect the consensus which has been reached by economists on the broader issues, they will modify accepted conclusions concerning utilization of facilities when common usage is present. When technological external diseconomies exist, changes in the resource ownership pattern as a means of producing efficient resource usage will be shown to be of more limited efficacy than has been generally supposed. Although the analysis applies particularly to the field of highway policy, especially when direct toll charges are imposed on users, it may readily be extended to other problems such as the common oil pool, the common fishing ground, and the common hunting preserve.

I

I shall first restate the example briefly. There are two roads, one of which is broad and poorly constructed and can handle traffic of any volume without generating congestion. The other road is narrow, and, therefore, limited in its traffic capacity, but it is smooth and fast. Original construction costs are neglected. Commercial vehicles are the only users of the roads.

Pigou showed that if there were no tolls placed on the usage of the superior road, too many vehicles would tend to travel on it. Toll charges placed on the usage of the good road would be in the social interest. On this point there was, and is, no dispute. Knight objected, however, to the extension of the Pigou argument to the general case, and he specifically stated that under a regime of private ownership the correct tolls would tend to be established without governmental interference.

Professor Knight was led to this conclusion by reasoning from the application of labor to superior and marginal land, correctly showing that under private ownership the market will tend to equalize marginal, not average, products of labor on the two types of land. He did not find it necessary to distinguish the various possible institutional arrangements through which this allocation could be achieved. It will be useful if such a distinction is made here.

The first, and most immediately suggested, arrangement is that in which the land owner hires the labor. As the owner of a unit of superior land hires additional units of labor, he is conscious of the decrement in average product, or, in other words, the marginal adjustment is internal to his decision. Labor will be allocated in such a way that its marginal product is equated on the two types of land. It is noted that this result will be forthcoming under *any* ownership pattern of the superior land provided only that the final product is competitively priced. There could exist completely centralized (single) ownership of the superior land if the total production on this land is small relative to total production in the economy.

A second institutional arrangement in which the necessary conditions for optimum resource allocation are present is one in which labor hires the land. Individual workers hire the use of discrete units of superior land. Each worker estimates the demand for land units on the basis of the familiar law of variable proportions, land to fixed labor in this case. Competition among workers will tend to equalize returns to labor on the superior and marginal land as before. But, in order to insure that the full amount of the superior land be utilized, the ownership pattern of this land must be such that the superior land units are competitively priced. If the total amount of superior land is fixed and not reproducible, completely centralized ownership may result in competitive pricing, that is, the monopolistic and competitive solutions may be equivalent.[4] This is a special case, however, and in order that competitive pricing be guaranteed, the land ownership pattern must be effectively decentralized. If the restriction of fixity is removed, and superior land is reproducible, land prices must be at marginal cost levels. Effectively decentralized ownership will always be required to produce the proper resource allocation in this situation.

If a third type of institutional arrangement is now introduced, the problem of describing the process through which the market achieves the efficient resource adjustment becomes more difficult. Assume that individual workers hire the land, not in discrete units as before, but instead they are now

---

4. In simple geometrical terms, this would be the case if the vertical supply curve should cut a straight-line demand curve to the left of its midpoint.

allowed to purchase rights to contribute to and to share equally in the total product. Workers do not hire land in separable physical units; the amount of land per worker is reduced as more shares are purchased. The individual in buying these shares will not be able to take into account the decline in the average product of others which is brought about by his own action. Interdependence among individual productivities is present, or, in more precise terms, technological external diseconomies. Workers will tend to equalize individually estimated marginal products on superior and marginal land, but this will not produce equality between social marginal products of labor on the two opportunities. If this interdependence among individual productivities is to be taken into account, it must be done through an institutional ownership pattern which will price superior land shares in such a way that the correct usage is promoted.

II

The problem having been introduced in terms of the more familiar land-labor example, the road case may be reconsidered. The analogy between the two is analytically but not institutionally complete. The essential difference is that whereas in the land-labor example real-world institutional arrangements are normally of the first or second type, in the road case the standard pattern is the third type. This difference explains why this third type of adjustment has never been carefully considered when the purpose was that of illustrating general principles. This provides the basis for Knight's statement that the illustration is "clearer if we think of the owner of the road hiring the trucks instead of their hiring the use of the road."[5] By this assumption, the road example is made equivalent to the normal, or first, land-labor case, and the market selects the desired resource adjustment through a reasonably simple allocation process. The owner of the superior road can take into account the decrease in the average product of "each" truck caused by the addition of one truck, and, therefore, he can equalize the marginal products of trucking resources on the superior and the inferior roads. Immediately following the above-cited statement, however, Professor Knight continues, "the effect is the same either way; it is still the same if some third party hires the use of

5. "Fallacies," 221.

both." In order to understand under what conditions the effect is the same, certain specific institutional assumptions will have to be closely examined.

A second institutional arrangement which will produce the required equalization of marginal products can be indicated. If there is a single large trucking firm choosing between the superior and the wide road, the services of both being free, this equalization will be effected. It is assumed that the market for the final product, freight services, remains competitive even in this case of the single large trucking firm. The conclusion that the necessary conditions for optimum resource allocation are present when road services are free holds so long as we retain the assumption of fixity and permanence in the two plants. If we consider the road plants as subject to depreciation, competitive pricing of the road services is required in order to insure that the centralized trucking firm will allocate trucking resources properly.

An institutional arrangement which would clearly not produce the desired results is one in which a single large trucking firm, large enough to make the required adjustment internally, is faced with a single owner of the superior opportunity. In this case too many resources will be devoted to the wide (free) road since any positive price placed on superior road services will cause the large trucking firm to restrict usage below the point where the marginal product of trucking resources on the wide (free) road is equated with the marginal product on the superior road. This conclusion remains true whether the market for the final product, freight services, is competitive or monopolistic.

III

The three arrangements mentioned are not, however, as interesting or as realistic as others which will be discussed here in somewhat more detail. The most interesting is provided in the case of centralized ownership of the superior road and the common usage of the road by a fully competitive trucking industry. This case should also offer more constructive suggestions concerning the proper pricing policy for highways than any of the others. Assume trucking to be a fully competitive industry, composed of a large number of firms. The superior road is owned by a single profit-maximizing firm, public or private. The road is assumed indestructible allowing the whole question of maintenance costs to be neglected; this simplification will not affect the analysis.

The trucking firm hires the use of the road, not the whole road, nor even divisible shares of road surface per unit of time, but rather rights to use the road during a particular time period along with an undetermined number of other truckers. To the individual trucking firm there are clearly external diseconomies of superior road use. The marginal product of road service (described as the right to use the road) which will enter into the firm's decision is greater than the aggregate marginal product of that road service. The individual firm's own action in purchasing a share of the highway reduces the productivity of shares to all other truckers.

There is general agreement among economists that the market does not produce the efficient allocation of economic resources when technological external diseconomies are present. The diseconomies involved in road use are obviously technological rather than pecuniary. As more trucks use the superior road, the average productivity of all trucks falls solely due to the physical effect of congestion. The production functions of the trucking firms are changed.[6]

---

6. Road usage provides a specific, and not unimportant, example of the fourth type of interdependence mentioned by Scitovsky, the only one which he characterizes as "external economies and diseconomies." The production function of the individual trucking firm depends not only on the factors utilized by the firm but also on the output of other firms. This fits Meade's precise definition of external diseconomies. (See Tibor Scitovsky, "Two Concepts of External Economies," *Journal of Political Economy* 62 [1954]: 144–45; J. E. Meade, "External Economies and Diseconomies in a Competitive Situation," *Economic Journal* 62 [1954]: 67.)

The road case has been used by many economists to illustrate the existence of external diseconomies. See, for example, Jacob Viner, "Cost Curves and Supply Curves," *Zeitschrift für Nationalökonomie* 3 (1931): 221.

Mr. R. F. Kahn was able to deny the existence of external diseconomies in the specific road case by a peculiar chain of reasoning. Having defined marginal private productivity as a change in a firm's output resulting from a change in the input of one factor, the firm's expenditure on and the total amount of the other factors remaining unchanged, and marginal social productivity as the change in the total output of the community under the same conditions, he makes the following statement: "In considering the application of all other factors, considered as one composite factor, to the factor 'road,' our definition of marginal social productivity—and by implication of external diseconomies, which are said to exist when marginal social productivity falls short of marginal private productivity—requires that the amount of road space utilized by the firm which increases its output shall remain constant. It follows that the amount of road space available to all other

The important question, and it is one which transcends the particular application to the road problem, concerns the fundamental reason why the existence of technological external diseconomies arising out of common usage prevents the market mechanism from producing the necessary conditions for the optimum allocation of resources. Is it because individual utilities or productivities are interdependent? Or is it because some resources which are commonly used are not centrally owned? Or do these two reduce to the same thing? If the absence of centralized ownership is emphasized, all that appears to be required to produce over-all efficiency is some modification in the ownership of the relevant resource, along with the profit-maximizing pricing of the resource services. Monopoly pricing which maximizes rent on the superior opportunity would seem to be the socially desirable arrangement.[7] The commonality of usage may still remain. On the other hand, if the failure of the market mechanism is held to stem from the interdependence among individual decisions, the required efficiency may be produced only by a centralization of the decision-making, or, in other words, a removal of the commonality of use. In the first case, centralized ownership of the commonly used resource is the only institutional change suggested. In the second case, centralized ownership of the resource and centralized decision-making concerning its use is recommended.

The argument that centralized ownership alone will produce the required usage may be examined first. Its validity depends on the proof that the owner of the commonly used resource, the good road, will be led by the profit motive to fix a price which will, in fact, cause individual users of the facility to

---

firms also remains constant. Their output is consequently unaltered; and marginal social productivity does not differ from marginal private productivity." Quite clearly, however, any change in output must be measured in vehicle or ton-miles per time unit and must change the amount of road space utilized by the firm under consideration as well as change the amount available to other firms. Mr. Kahn was apparently trapped by his own definition into assuming an impossible situation. (R. F. Kahn, "Some Notes on Ideal Output," *Economic Journal* 40 (1935): 18.)

7. This is explicitly stated by H. Scott Gordon in his analysis of the common fishing grounds problem. His treatment is similar to that of Professor Knight, and the fishing grounds problem is similar, in most respects, to the road problem. See H. Scott Gordon, "The Economic Theory of a Common-Property Resource: The Fishery," *Journal of Political Economy* 62 (1954): 124–42.

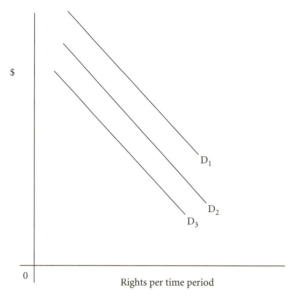

Figure 1. Demand for road inputs

produce the efficient utilization. It must be emphasized that the actual re-source adjustment must result from the actions of the individual competitive trucking firms, not from any direct action on the part of the owner of the good road.

The demand for the services of the good road must originate with the in-dividual trucking firms. As discussed in the second land-labor illustration above, there would be no serious problem of deriving a demand function if the individual trucking firms could purchase highway services in discrete and homogeneous units. The demand function for the individual firm would be derived by the application of successive units of highway services (square feet of road space per unit time) to the fixed amount of non-highway factors.[8] The law of variable proportions would be fully operative. If we leave conges-tion out of the picture, this is essentially the situation. There will be a down-sloping demand curve for highway inputs for each trucking firm. The aggre-gate demand curve for superior road services could then be derived by the normal summation of individual demand curves.

8. All non-highway inputs cannot, of course, remain fixed. Certain inputs (e.g., fuel, driving time) must covary with highway inputs.

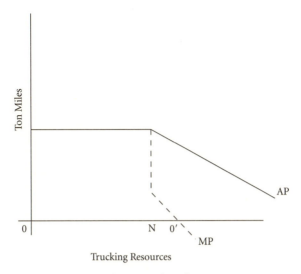

Figure 2. Productivity of trucking resources

Now congestion must be introduced. The productivity of "rights" to highway usage received by the individual firms will depend on the usage of the road by other firms. This additional factor will enter into the individual firm's purchase decisions. Individual demand functions will be shifted by expectations of traffic volume.

This may be illustrated geometrically in Figures 1 and 2. Figure 1 depicts the demand curve of the individual firm for the inputs described as rights to use the good road during a particular period of time. D_1 represents the firm's demand curve when no congestion is expected.[9] D_2 and D_3 represent lower levels of demand (marginal value product) based on expectations of traffic volume sufficient to generate congestion.

Figure 2 is drawn with the factors reversed. The road is now considered the fixed factor, and the curve AP is the average product of trucking resources as they are applied to the superior road. It should be noted that the factors are reversed for the aggregate of firms, not for the individual trucking firm. This is an important step since the definition of the appropriate dimension appears to have been the source of much of the confusion surrounding

9. Similar down-sloping demand curves, at a lower level, could be derived for the services of the free road, but these are not necessary to the argument.

this road problem. (See Footnote 6 for Kahn's denial of external diseconomies.) The declining average productivity is not due to the action of any one firm but rather to the action of all firms. If the base line is taken to represent the average (marginal) productivity of trucking resources on the free road, the proper investment of trucking resources on the good road is shown at $00'$, where marginal productivity on the two opportunities is equated.

Figure 2 is related to Figure 1 only in that the location of the demand curve for "rights" to superior road use is a function of expected traffic volume, or the amount of aggregate trucking resources applied to the fixed road. The shifting downward of the individual demand curves is due to the declining average productivity of trucking resources. If the individual trucking firm expects no congestion, that is, if it expects total usage to be less than $0N$, D_1 is the relevant demand curve. On the other hand, if it anticipates total traffic of $00'$, the demand will be D_2. The individual firm has no power of determining the operational point along AP.

The market demand curve for "rights" to use the good road during a particular time period is not derived by a simple summation of individual demand curves except when congestion is absent. Once congestion appears, the individual demands become interdependent. The road owner must take into account not only the declining individual demand curves but also the declining average productivity of trucking as total traffic increases. The interdependence among productivities requires that each firm estimate as correctly as possible the action of all other firms and base its own action upon this estimate. Mutually correct prediction of this sort by all firms is, of course, impossible. After a traffic pattern has been established, however, reasonably accurate prediction of total volume may be possible, and the road owner may be able to determine a profit-maximizing price within limits of uncertainty somewhat broader than the usual monopolist.

In either the congestion or the no-congestion case, it seems clear that the pricing policy of the single owner of the good road will result in road usage, in terms of "rights" per time period, which is not identical with that represented by $00'$ in Figure 2. The total number of toll tickets sold will produce a traffic volume on the good road smaller than that which would be necessary to equalize the marginal productivities of trucking resources on the two opportunities. The profit-maximizing pricing policy of the road owner will generate an overly restricted usage of the superior facility.

This result may be easily demonstrated in the no-congestion situation. If congestion is not present on either road, no trucks should use the poor road, and the good road should be operated as if it were a free good. But the single ownership arrangement will cause a price to be placed on its services. If the individual firm's demand curve for the services of this road is down-sloping, the existence of any positive price will tend to restrict road usage to some degree.

The result is similar, although somewhat more complicated, in the presence of congestion. The single road owner will be able to take into account the declining average productivity of trucking as traffic volume increases. The marginal adjustment will be internal to his pricing decision. Insofar as this factor alone is reflected in the price chosen, the correct usage will tend to be promoted by the single owner's action. But the owner will also take into account the down-sloping demand curves of the individual trucking firms. Insofar as he incorporates these data into his pricing decision, the usage of the road will tend to be below that which is socially efficient.

Only if the individual firm's demand curve for superior road use should be horizontal will the institutional arrangement in which the single owner sells road inputs to a fully competitive trucking industry tend to produce the efficient allocation of traffic between the good and the free roads. In this situation, the aggregate or market demand curve would tend to reflect only the declining average productivity resulting from increased traffic volume. Monopoly pricing on the superior road, subject to the special uncertainties created by the interdependence among individual decisions, would tend to promote socially desirable results under these conditions. This type of individual firm demand curve appears to have been implicitly assumed in some of the arguments which suggest that centralized ownership alone will produce the desired results. But this construction appears to have little in its support. With a fixed amount of non-road factors, e.g., trucks and terminals, a trucking firm will pay a greater price for the first few rights to travel on the road during a given time period than for the nth right. Beyond its normal capacity of operations, additional trips would require double shifts, undermaintenance of equipment, etc. In other words, rights to road use are no different from any other type of input. The law of variable proportions must be operative, at least after the initial range.

It must be concluded that single ownership of the superior opportunity along with monopoly pricing of road services will not produce the allocation of resources which is dictated by efficiency criteria. The monopoly control arises in the sale of superior road services only. Throughout the analysis we are assuming that the market for the final product, freight services, remains fully competitive.

IV

The case in which the ownership of the superior opportunity is assumed to be decentralized will now be examined. In the restricted road example, this ownership pattern is not possible, but it is interesting to determine the results as if it were. Therefore, assume that the over-all superior road is broken up into a number of smaller superior roads, the number being sufficiently large so that no single road can influence significantly the total traffic. If these good roads are physically separated, congestion will arise independently on each road. A declining demand curve will face each of the superior road firms; this will arise, not because the firm is sufficiently large to influence the total supply of road services, but because of the declining average productivity of trucking resources as they are applied to the individual road. In terms of the earlier figures, the down-sloping functions for road services facing the road owner will arise from factors which are the basis of Figure 2 alone. Insofar as each of these road firms estimates the declining average productivity of trucking resources accurately, and insofar as the various trucking firms correctly predict the amount of traffic volume on each road, the profit-maximizing pricing of the superior road services will tend to promote the correct allocation of total trucking resources among the several superior roads and between the superior roads and the free road.

This appears to be the institutional arrangement that is implicit in Professor Knight's argument. Although the arrangement is impossible in the specific road example, since there is only one good road, it indicates that there does exist an institutional pattern in the common usage case which provides the necessary conditions for optimum resource use. But several interesting features are to be noted. The area of common usage, and thus interdependence, is reduced to the size of the individual small superior road. And monopoly pricing, not competitive pricing, is the basis for the individual road firm's policy. There is an interesting combination here of competitive and monopoly elements. Competition in the market for final product is assumed throughout. Competition among individual trucking firms is also present. And there are a sufficient number of road firms to allow competitive conditions to be present. But each road firm must be a price maker. It follows a monopoly pricing policy in that it equates marginal revenue, which is less than price, with marginal cost. The firm's only control over price must arise from congestion or from the existence of the external diseconomies in road use; the monopoly arising from the control over the total supply of "rights" to superior road usage which was present in the centralized ownership case must be absent. Rent on each of the several superior roads will tend to be maximized by this arrangement, but it is to be emphasized that total rent on the superior opportunity as a whole will *not* be maximized. Mr. Kahn is, therefore, correct when he indicates that competitive ownership of the superior opportunity is required, and that monopoly ownership will lead to an overly restricted usage.[10] Both Knight and Gordon are wrong when they state that aggregate rent must be maximized on the superior opportunity.[11] The single owner could, by taking into account monopoly elements arising through his control over "rights" to road use which are independent of congestion, exact from users of the facility a higher total rent than could the aggregate of the numerous owners in the alternative case.

V

The remaining institutional arrangement which must be examined is the one in which both competitive ownership and competitive pricing of the superior opportunity is present. Assume that there are a sufficient number of superior roads to insure that no one appreciably affects the total traffic, but also assume that these roads are interconnected in such a way that congestion arises on the whole road system and not on a single road. Congestion is a function of total superior road usage, not the usage of any single superior road. This may be imagined as the case where the numerous superior roads cross each other at frequent intervals and congestion appears at the intersections. Although far-fetched in this particular application, this arrangement is

---

10. R. F. Kahn, "Some Notes," 17–18.
11. Knight, "Fallacies," 224; H. Scott Gordon, "Economic Theory," 129.

not without relevance in the real world. In fact, this is the arrangement most closely analogous to the stock examples of external diseconomies, e.g., the smoking chimneys. Each road owner will be faced with a horizontal demand curve for road services since he has no control over the total supply of superior road "rights" to be put on the market; each road owner will be a price taker since congestion is not a function of traffic on his individual road at all. Price will be established at marginal cost, which is zero in this example. An explanation of the zero price may be in order. If there were a fixed total supply of "rights" to superior road usage, there would tend to be a positive price established. This would be similar to our land-labor example where laborers hire discrete units of land from competitive land owners. The price would then be set at the market-clearing level, or, in geometrical terms, where the aggregate demand curve cuts the vertical supply curve. But in the highway problem, there is no fixed total supply of rights to use the road. Road services do not "run out" regardless of the number of users. Since additional users of a single road would impose no cost on the individual road owner, competition among such owners will tend to bid the toll charges down to zero. There will result over-usage of the superior opportunity in this sort of *competition,* which may have been assumed implicitly in Pigou's original contention. There would, of course, be costs imposed on society by the addition of users to the total superior opportunity. But since these costs arise solely from congestion they will not be borne by road owners but by other users, and, therefore, they cannot influence road supply and, through supply, price.

VI

The several possible ownership and pricing arrangements have been traced through in order to determine which of these patterns would produce the required necessary conditions for optimum resource allocation. It was found that single ownership of the superior opportunity along with monopoly pricing of the resource services would result in socially undesirable restriction on the usage of the good road whether or not congestion is present. Too many trucks would be forced into using the free road. It was shown that competitive ownership and competitive pricing of road services would result in over-utilization of the good opportunity relative to the poor one when congestion is present. This ownership and pricing pattern produces efficient results only when congestion, that is, external diseconomies, is absent. Only in the intermediate pattern in which competitive ownership prevails but monopoly pricing principles are followed are the results consistent with efficiency criteria when interdependence among user decisions is present. Only in this case will the superior road owner, when making his pricing decisions, take into account solely the decline in the average product of trucking resources which is due to congestion.

These arrangements have been examined as if they were all possible. If the analysis is limited to the original specific example of the one good road and the one free road, no private ownership pattern for the road alone will produce the necessary conditions for efficient resource use. The efficient usage may be achieved in any one of the three following ways. First, trucking operations may be centralized and all roads made free, provided that alternative transportation media are sufficiently good substitutes to keep the market for freight services fully competitive. Second, a single superior road owner may be forced to operate as well as own the road, hiring the use of trucking resources, treating them as inputs, and marketing the final product (freight services) himself in a fully competitive market. Third, the government may own the roads and price the road services at the level of marginal social cost. In application to the real-world problem of highway operation, this third alternative provides the only meaningful criterion for operational efficiency.[12]

The questions raised earlier may now be answered. The statement that individual utilities or productivities are interdependent is equivalent to saying that some resource which is commonly used is not centrally owned. But from this it does not follow that a change in ownership alone is always sufficient to produce the necessary conditions for attaining a Paretian utility frontier. The difficulty in securing the efficient resource utilization by changes in ownership alone stems from the institutional facts of life. In many cases, it is impossible to secure the centralization of ownership required to make the external diseconomies of usage internal to a single owner without *at the same time* providing the single owner with a degree of monopoly control over the total supply of resource services. Insofar as technological external disecon-

12. See my "The Pricing of Highway Services," *National Tax Journal* 5 (1952): 97–106, for a discussion of this criterion.

omies arise from an expansion in usage of a whole resource category or even a substantial part of this, it is clear that ownership changes alone will not be sufficient. Only in those cases where the extent of the commonality of usage is limited to a relatively small proportion of the total resource supply (not final product supply) can ownership arrangements be exclusively relied upon to produce desirable results.

Although this paper has been limited to an analysis of the road case under each of the several possible institutional arrangements, the conclusions reached may be readily extended to all problems where commonality of usage creates interdependence among user decisions. Familiar examples are the common oil pool, the common fishing ground, and the common hunting preserve. The analysis indicates that the centralization of ownership of the common oil pool, for example, may cause an overly restricted usage of the pool even if the market for oil remains fully competitive. If the pool possesses any advantages which make it unique as a superior resource, the single owner may sell drilling "rights" to competitive purchasers, and, by so doing, he can secure a greater rent than he could if he does all the drilling himself. Only if the individual common pool is one among many like pools will the proper rate of pumping be promoted by single pool ownership. Assuming, as has been the case throughout the analysis, that the market for the final product remains fully competitive, both the ownership and the operation of the superior facility must be centralized if the efficient utilization of resources is to be produced without direct governmental interference.

Introduction

L.S.E. Cost Theory in Retrospect

In his paper "Economics and Knowledge," included in this volume, Hayek scarcely mentioned "cost." Nonetheless he provides indirectly the strongest argument for attempting, through the publication of this collection of essays, to focus the attention of modern economists on the elementary meaning of cost. Hayek emphasized the differences, in principle, between the equilibrium position attained by a single rational decision-maker in his own behavioural adjustments, given his preference function and the constraints that he confronts, and the equilibrium potentially attainable through the interaction of many persons. To Hayek the latter "is not an equilibrium in the special sense in which equilibrium is regarded as a sort of optimum position."

Despite Hayek's warning, since the 1930s, when his essay along with some of the others in this collection was written and when the L.S.E. tradition in cost theory was developed, economists have increasingly analysed equilibrium states in terms of their optimality or non-optimality properties, defined by criteria for maximizing some objective function. It is somewhat paradoxical that Robbins, whose contributions to London cost theory cannot be questioned, should also have been at least partially responsible for the drift of modern economic theory towards the mathematics of applied maximization, variously elaborated, and away from the analysis of exchange processes. In *The Nature and Significance of Economic Science*,[1] Robbins supplied

From *L.S.E. Essays on Cost*, ed. J. M. Buchanan and G. F. Thirlby (London: London School of Economics and Political Science, 1973), 1–16. Reprinted by permission of the London School of Economics.

1. London, 1932.

the methodological paradigm within which modern micro-economics has been developed. Elementary textbooks throughout the world soon came to define "economics" in terms of "the economic problem," the allocation of scarce resources among alternative ends. So defined, the "problem" faced by the individual on the desert island, the Crusoe so familiar to us all, is, at base, quite similar to that faced by the society or the community of persons. The paradigm was somewhat differently put, but with the same effect, by Paul A. Samuelson in his influential *Foundations of Economic Analysis,* when he stated:

> They [meaningful theorems in diverse fields of economic affairs] proceed almost wholly from two types of very general hypotheses. The first is that *conditions of equilibrium are equivalent to the maximization (minimization) of some magnitude.*[2] [Italics supplied.]

The increasing conceptual quantification in economic theory was almost necessarily accompanied by increasing conceptual "objectification." Once the magnitude to be maximized is symbolically defined, attention is quite naturally diverted to the manipulation of the symbols and away from the initial leap into presumed objectivity itself. The increasing conceptual quantification need not have introduced confusion save for the simultaneous developments in theoretical welfare economics. Within what Hayek called the "Pure Logic of Choice," the formal theory of utility maximization, mathematical rigour has offered aesthetic satisfaction to the sophisticated without loss of explanatory potential. More importantly, the increasingly elegant and formalistic content of general-equilibrium theory, and notably its emphasis on existence proofs and stability conditions, yields pleasure to the talented, criteria to the critical, and convictions to some who have remained unconvinced about the overall efficacy of market order.

So long as the object for discussion, and for theorizing, is either the individual decision-maker or the interactions of separate decision-makers *in markets,* no harm is done and perhaps some good is added by conceptual

---

2. Paul A. Samuelson, *Foundations of Economic Analysis* (Cambridge, Mass., 1947), 5. Samuelson's Nobel lecture provides evidence that his own position has not substantially changed. See "Maximum Principles in Analytical Economics," *American Economic Review* 62 (June 1972): 249–62.

objectification. Confusion arises only when the properties of equilibrium, as defined for markets, are transferred as criteria of optimization in *non-market* or political settings. It is here that the critical distinction between the equilibrium of the single decision-maker and that attained through market interaction, the distinction stressed by Hayek, is absolutely essential to forestall ambiguity and analytical error. The theory of social interaction, of the mutual adjustment among the plans of separate human beings, is different in kind from the theory of planning, the maximization of some objective function by a conceptualized omniscient being. The latter is equivalent, in all respects, to the problems faced by Crusoe or by any individual decision-taker. But this is not the theory of markets, and it is artificial and basically false thinking that makes it out to be. There are properties or characteristics of equilibria in markets that seem superficially to be equivalent to those attainable by the idealized optimization carried out by the planner. But shadow prices are not market prices, and the opportunity costs that inform market decisions are not those that inform the choices of even the omniscient planner. These appear to be identical only because of the false objectification of the magnitudes in question.

This is what the great debate on socialist planning in the 1930s was all about, comment to the contrary notwithstanding. And modern economic theorists measure their own confusion by the degree to which they accept the alleged Lange victory over Mises, quite apart from the empirical record since established. The central issue in this debate should not have been the possibility or impossibility of socialist calculation. All the participants were wrong in concentrating on this. The difference in data confronted by decision-makers in different institutional settings is quite sufficient to prove that the properties of market equilibrium cannot in the nature of things be duplicated under non-market institutional structures. This is not of course to say that "efficiency," defined in a different but legitimate planning sense, cannot be defined in an ideal-type socialist model. Of course it can. But it is a wholly different "efficiency" framework that is involved here, informed by the marginal-value estimates of the planner and not by the participants in markets.

I think that it is legitimate to trace the sources of error to fundamental misconceptions in the theory of opportunity cost, misconceptions that the London (and Austrian) scholars were attempting to clarify, and which later I tried similarly to rectify with my little book *Cost and Choice* in 1969.[3] Unfortunately neither the London contribution nor my book seems to have exerted much effect on mainstream thinking in economic theory.

But I am getting ahead of my story. As I noted above, the increasing conceptual quantification, and objectification, of economic theory need not have sown confusion without the accompaniment of developments in theoretical welfare economics. Precisely at the time that methodologists were effective in formalizing economic theory within a more rigorous maximization framework, interest in "market failure" rather than "market success" was at its peak, and, with this, interest in the extension of economic theory to socialist organization became widespread. The Robbins definition of the allocation problem, with its implied emphasis on the universality of scarcity, supported such an extension. It was predictable that economists, trained professionally to analyse market equilibria, and increasingly adept at formalizing the maximization paradigm, should begin to discuss planning problems and solutions as if these required the same set of tools as those applicable to market phenomena. In retrospect it seems singularly unfortunate that the institutionalists should have lost favour precisely when their emphasis on and expertise in the functioning of organizational-institutional structures, and the impact of differing structures on behaviour of decision-makers, might have, with some intrusion of analysis, yielded their highest marginal product in effective critical scholarship. Instead the mathematically sophisticated analytics of such scholars as Hotelling were allowed to go unchallenged despite their vulnerability in this most fundamental sense. And young economists everywhere learnt to appreciate the beauty of the mathematical models of what they called "an economy." Theirs was not the role of sceptic, and to question quantification and objectification itself quickly came to be the mark of eccentricity rather than excellence.

Is it any wonder that, in the idealized fully quantifiable and fully objectifiable "economy" that commanded all attention, the market itself should come to be regarded as a "mechanism," as an "analogue computing device," to be legitimately treated as one among several alternative means of allocating resources, to be evaluated comparatively in terms of some criteria of accomplishment? And so it should be in such a world.

3. Chicago, 1969.

The quest for objectivity is eternal and perhaps praiseworthy, but what has modern scholarship to offer where the classical economists tried and failed? There seems little harm in speculating about the properties of an economy whose only scarce resource is a homogeneous glob of something (putty clay or L'il Abner's schmoos) that may be instantly convertible into any one of a large number of final goods upon which consumers place value. In this setting the cost of any one good becomes the displaced physical alternative, measurable separately in any one of the other n goods potentially available from the single homogeneous source. If a unit of good X uses up twice as much of the scarce resource as a unit of good Y, the cost of X is properly defined as 2Y, and the cost of Y as one-half X. In such a model it is meaningful to consider the planner's problem of maximizing output, defined in values or prices of goods, from the single scarce input. The norms of theoretical welfare economics can be applied directly to this purpose. The omniscient planner can solve his maximization problem quite simply by setting the prices of goods at their relative marginal costs, arbitrarily choosing one good as numeraire. As the final consumers adjust quantities demanded to the announced set of prices, the value of total output, denominated in the numeraire, will be maximized.

Nor need we limit analysis of such a conjectural economy to the planner's problems. As an alternative speculative exercise we may suppose that our homogeneous glob of scarce resource (putty clay or schmoos) is initially and arbitrarily parcelled out among persons under a private-property-rights arrangement. By assumption, the individual owners are completely indifferent as to just what set of final goods their own assigned input becomes in the transformation. These owners are motivated solely by their own desire for final goods, command over which is measured by income, denominated in some commonly agreed numeraire good. The only difference between this model and the one described earlier is that this one "works on its own," once private-property-rights are defined and protected. The scarce resource will be allocated among uses; final goods will be "produced"; prices will be set. The "market" equilibrium that emerges will in this case be equivalent in all respects to the solution of the maximization problem posed for the planner in the earlier model. Prices will equal marginal costs, not because some hidden planner has now drawn on the norms of welfare economics, but because this equality is descriptive of the end of the trading process. If this equality is not satisfied, further gains-from-trade would be possible; potentially realizable surplus would remain unexploited. Not only can we deduce the equivalence in results between these two models on some *a priori* basis. We could also *observe* such equivalence in an objectively verifiable sense.

I do not think it a caricature to describe modern economic theory as being grounded on the two conjectural models that I have briefly sketched, and on the equivalence between their "equilibrium-optimality" properties. Viewed in this simplistic perspective, however, the models paradoxically suggest that economic theory has advanced little, if at all, over that advanced almost two centuries earlier by the classical economists. In one respect at least, the classical writers were more honest in their efforts. They sought to explain relative prices by relative-input ratios of homogeneous labour. They fell short precisely because the deficiency in their common objective standard for measurement was revealed for all to see. This prompts the question as to why modern theorists have been so much more successful in concealing the fundamental flaw in their structure. "Camouflage by complexity" provides only a part of the answer here. The classical economists failed because their standard for measurement was demonstrably deficient, but also because their logical structure was not complete. One must read much into classical structure if any general-equilibrium theory of markets is to be discerned. They did not close the circle, and the lacunae in their essentially one-sided explanatory model provided the source for the familiar normative critique associated with Marx. The circle was completed by the subjective-value theorists, by the Marshallian synthesis, and, more explicitly, by the Walrasian theory of general equilibrium. These several contributions represent a major conceptual advance over classical economic analysis by criteria of logic and coherence. But the logical symmetry achieved in explaining the workings of the economic process was secured at a cost which is reflected by drainage of empirical, objective content. The classical economists offered us a positive-predictive theory of relative prices; this theory was falsified. But the neoclassical model contained no comparable predictive hypotheses; there was no externally measurable standard which allowed the scientist to make predictions from observable data. This post-classical theory described an interaction process and allowed the identification of certain properties of equilibrium positions. But there was nothing upon which the economist could have based objective predictions about relative-price formation.

This was surely sensed by Alfred Marshall as witnessed by his lingering adherence to classical models, and the desire for some restoration of predictive content offers a motivation for his time-period analysis. Frank Knight was also unwilling to disregard fully the classical precepts, and, despite his affinity with some of the Austrians, students of students of students of Knight continue to learn, and to learn well, the lessons of the deer and beaver. The reaction of the Austrians was quite different. They seemed quite willing to jettison the putative objective content of the classical hypotheses. The full implications of this may not have been recognized by the early Austrians, but in Mises and his followers economic theory is explicitly acknowledged to be wholly non-objective. Intellectual tidiness rather than empirical or explanatory content seemed to be the purpose of both earlier and latter-day Walrasians.

As I have suggested above, confusion emerged only when (1) theorists overlooked the absence of objective content in neo-classical and general-equilibrium analysis, *and* (2) when they attempted to utilize the properties of market equilibrium as norms for the optimizing solutions of problems posed in non-market institutional settings. The presence or absence of objective content assumed instrumental significance only when the planner was introduced, whether in the administration of state or public enterprises (piecemeal or *in toto*) or in levy of corrective taxes and/or subsidies on production in markets. The control or correction of allocation requires that norms be invoked, and these norms must come from somewhere. The presumption of modern economic theory that such norms are readily identifiable must be attributed to the acceptance of the paradigm one-resource model sketched above.

In any plausibly realistic market process, however, only prices have objective content. This being so, how can prices be settled by reference to "costs" or to anything else? It will be useful to discuss briefly the precise relationships between prices and "costs" in full market equilibrium. (In this treatment I shall follow closely the discussion in *Cost and Choice,* page 85.)

In full market equilibrium expected marginal benefit for each participant will be equal to marginal opportunity cost, both measured in terms of the person's subjective valuation. All persons confront uniform relative prices for goods; this is a necessary condition for the absence of further gains-from-trade. Since each participant is in full behavioural equilibrium, it follows that each person must also confront the same marginal cost. As a demander the individual adjusts his purchases to insure that marginal benefit equals price. Hence the anticipated marginal benefits of a good, again measured in the numeraire, are equal for all demanders. As a supplier, the individual adjusts his sales to insure that anticipated opportunities forgone, marginal opportunity cost, equals price. Hence marginal opportunity cost in the numeraire is equal for all suppliers.

Prices tend to equal marginal opportunity costs in market equilibrium. But costs here are fully analogous to marginal benefits. Only prices have objective, empirical content. Neither the marginal valuations of demanders nor the marginal costs of suppliers can be employed as a basis for determining or setting prices. The reason is that both are brought into equality with prices by behavioural adjustments on both sides of the market. Prices are not brought into equality with some objectively measurable phenomena on either the demand or supply side.

The implications of this basic, and in one sense, elementary fact for applying economic theory's tools to the making of control decisions for a wholly or partially socialized institutional structure have not been fully recognized, even by those who have partially escaped the dominance of the single-resource model. To an extent the blame for this lies in the failure of the London economists, and of the latter-day Austrians, to develop a full-blown "subjectivist economics" that commands intellectual respect while seeming to retain explanatory relevance. Mises and his followers have been too prone to accept the splendid isolation of arrogant eccentrics to divorce their teaching too sharply from mainstream interests, and too eager to launch into polemic: epistemological, methodological, ideological. Certain members of the London group, although profoundly influenced by the Austrians via both Hayek and Robbins, had the merit of maintaining more practical interest in business decision problems. But unfortunately their interest was too pedestrian to allow them to attempt the "grand design" that might have been produced from the cost-theory foundations which they developed.

As a result, we find Hayek (and Mises even more emphatically) talking largely to the disciples of the Austrian faith, and alongside we find Coase, Edwards, Thirlby, and Wiseman taking up the cudgels against orthodoxy in detailed and particularistic applications. In their later papers both Thirlby and Wiseman seemed to recognize the grander implications but both men were perhaps discouraged by their failure to secure acceptance of their particularistic arguments, discouraged to the extent that neither made the attempt to draft the "treatise" that seemed to be required, and which still seems to offer challenge.

Perhaps the most significant L.S.E. impact on modern economics has come through an indirect application of opportunity-cost theory rather than through an undermining of basic cost conceptions. "Marginal social cost," enthroned by Pigou as a cornerstone of applied welfare economics, was successfully challenged by R. H. Coase a quarter-century after his initial work on cost. His now-classic paper on social cost,[4] which reflects essentially the same cost theory held earlier, succeeded where the more straightforward earlier attacks on the marginal-cost pricing norm—attacks by Coase himself, by Thirlby and by Wiseman—apparently failed. Nonetheless the still-provisional success of Coase's modern challenge should be noted. As this is written, in mid-1972, the implications of Coase's attack on the Pigovian concept of social cost for the elementary textbook discussions of opportunity cost have not yet been realized. Advanced textbooks, and notably those written in what may loosely be called the "Chicago-Virginia" tradition, devote some space to the "Coase theorem," but the standard chapters on cost in these same textbooks remain as if the more fundamental critique in the Coase paper had never been published.[5]

A primary purpose of this summary of doctrinal developments has been to emphasize the general importance of the theory of opportunity cost, and the London contributions to the development of a fundamentally correct theory which has not yet come to inform mainstream thinking in economics. The significance may, I fear, be hidden from those who glance only at the volume's title, *L.S.E. Essays on Cost,* and whose subjective image of "cost" calls up carefully specified algebraic functions, sharply etched geometrical

4. R. H. Coase, "The Problem of Social Cost," *Journal of Law and Economics* 3 (October 1960): 1–44.

5. This summary of the impact of the London cost theory should include mention of G. L. S. Shackle. Although Shackle does not specifically present his ideas in opportunity-cost terms, his whole approach to decision is fully consistent with that developed by the London theorists. Shackle was both directly and indirectly associated closely with the London group. For Shackle's most appropriate treatment of decision, see his *Decision, Order, and Time in Human Affairs* (Cambridge, 1961).

figures or actual numbers carried to at least two decimal points in account-
ants' worksheets. Such an image may unfortunately be reinforced by a su-
perficial survey of titles of some of the independent essays included here.
Coase, Edwards, and Thirlby, in some of the papers reprinted here, were interested in practical problems faced by business decision-makers in business
administration as such. They were attempting to use economic theory in this
severely practical setting, to apply opportunity-cost notions to the problems
faced in everyday economic choices. In this effort the London economists
did not themselves fully appreciate the uniqueness and originality of their
approach. To an extent they looked on themselves as writing down, in the
context of practical-problem situations, what "everyone knew" about cost,
at least everyone around L.S.E. during the period in question.

As the norms drawn from the description of competitive equilibrium
came to be presented more and more as "rules" for socialist planners, and
"marginal-cost pricing" was elevated into a paradigm for the management
of public enterprise, the significance of getting the elementary confusions
identified, and with this the relative importance and uniqueness of the London approach, came to be recognized. Both Thirlby and Wiseman, in the
most recently published papers in this volume, recognized the depth of
mainstream intellectual error, but their plaints were largely ignored. One
reason perhaps lies in the fact that the critique of orthodoxy is too fundamental; to accept fully the implications of the theory of opportunity cost that
is implicit in these essays requires the modern economist to throw overboard
too much of his invested intellectual capital. How can we write the elementary textbooks and teach the elementary course if we cannot draw the standard cost curves? How can we carry out benefit-cost analysis and pretend
that we are assisting in social decision-making? How can we say anything at
all about managing nationalized public enterprises?

What is so "revolutionary" in the theory of opportunity cost that threat-
ens the very foundations of modern applied economics? This introductory
essay is not designed to summarize the papers reprinted in the volume, and
I do not propose to develop my own interpretation and application of the
theory. I have done the latter in *Cost and Choice*. But brief elaboration of the
central argument may offer some support to my assertions about significance. The basic idea is at once extremely simple and profound. *Cost* is in-

herently linked to *choice*. This notion did not of course originate with the economists associated with the L.S.E. in the 1930s or before or since. As students of Frank Knight learnt, elements of the correct theory of opportunity cost are found in Adam Smith's deer-and-beaver model. Even before the subjective-value revolution, Francesco Ferrara in Italy was sharply critical of classical theory on opportunity-cost grounds.[6] The opportunity-cost conception was explicitly developed by the Austrians, by the American H. J. Davenport, and the principle could scarcely have occupied a more central place than it assumed in P. H. Wicksteed's *Common Sense of Political Economy*.[7] This book was independently influential at L.S.E., and it properly deserves mention here.

At the L.S.E. there was the beginning and the widening recognition of the implications of elementary opportunity-cost theory for applications of economics. Herein lies the contribution of the economists who are represented in this volume. Almost all professional economists, old and new, can provide a rough working definition of opportunity cost that is tolerably acceptable for pedagogic purposes. But very few economists, new or old, have been consistent. Almost none of them beyond the London-Austrian axis has recognized just what his own definition suggests for the application of his discipline.

Simply considered, cost is the obstacle or barrier to choice, that which must be got over before choice is made. Cost is the underside of the coin, so to speak, cost is the displaced alternative, the rejected opportunity. Cost is that which the decision-maker sacrifices or gives up when he selects one alternative rather than another. Cost consists therefore in his own evaluation of the enjoyment or utility that he anticipates having to forgo as a result of choice itself. There are specific implications to be drawn from this choice-bound definition of opportunity cost:

1. Cost must be borne exclusively by the person who makes decisions; it is not possible for this cost to be shifted to or imposed on others.

---

6. See my *Fiscal Theory and Political Economy* (Chapel Hill, North Carolina, 1960), 27–30 for a summary treatment. One of my own unfinished projects is a critical analysis of Ferrara's work, with a view towards making his contribution more widely known to English-language readers.

7. London, 1910.

2. Cost is subjective; it exists only in the mind of the decision-maker or chooser.

3. Cost is based on anticipations; it is necessarily a forward-looking or *ex ante* concept.

4. Cost can never be realized because of the fact that choice is made; the alternative which is rejected can never itself be enjoyed.

5. Cost cannot be measured by someone other than the chooser since there is no way that subjective mental experience can be directly observed.

6. Cost can be dated at the moment of final decision or choice.[8]

In any general theory of choice cost must be reckoned in a *utility* rather than in a *commodity* dimension. From this it follows that the opportunity cost involved in choice cannot be observed and objectified and, more importantly, it cannot be measured in such a way as to allow comparisons over wholly different choice settings. The cost faced by the utility-maximizing owner of a firm, the value that he anticipates having to forgo in choosing to produce an increment to current output, is not the cost faced by the utility-maximizing bureaucrat who manages a publicly owned firm, even if the physical aspects of the two firms are in all respects identical. As the London economists stressed, cost is that which might be avoided by not making choice. In our example the private owner could avoid the explicit incremental outlay *and* the incremental profit opportunity should he fail to produce the output increment. The socialist manager, by our assumptions, could avoid the same objective consequences by taking the same course of action. These consequences could be measured in monetary terms. But the opportunity cost relevant to choice-making must be translated into a utility dimension through a subjective and personal evaluation. The private owner may evaluate the objectively measurable consequences of choice quite differently from the bureaucrat, although both are utility-maximizers.

I am not suggesting that the contributors to the London tradition in cost theory fully appreciated and understood all the implications of their own conception, nor that even now they would endorse my interpretation of this conception. I suggest only that their several papers mark a beginning of such

8. For a detailed discussion of each of these attributes of opportunity cost see my *Cost and Choice*, chapter 3.

appreciation, that they reflect an early critical questioning of aspects of modern economic theory, a questioning that is more urgently needed in the 1970s than it was when they wrote.

While the contribution of the L.S.E. group of economists should be emphasized, the constructive content of their work should not be exaggerated. Taken as a whole, the London effort is largely negative in its impact. Properly interpreted, it demonstrates major flaws in the applications and extensions of economic theory. But there is little in this work which assists us in marrying "subjectivist" and "objectivist" economic theory. Few modern economists would be willing to go all the way with the latter-day Austrians and convert economics into a purely logical exercise. Most of us want to retain, and rightly so, positive and predictive content in the discipline, to hold fast to the genuine "science" that seems possible. To accomplish this, however, *Homo economicus* must be returned to scientific respectability, and economists must learn to accept that hypotheses may be falsified. Finally, and more importantly, we must try to construct meaningful, if limited, norms for decision-making in non-market institutional structures. In competitive markets prices tend to equal marginal costs, but do we want to *make* prices equal "marginal costs" in non-market settings, when we fully realize that marginal costs can only be objectified by the arbitrary selection of some artificially homogenized measure? Do we really want to make one beaver exchange for only two deer when poisonous snakes abound near the beaver dams? Of course not! But how do we know that the snakes are there? Because the beaver hunters think they are?[9]

9. I am indebted to my colleagues Thomas Borcherding and Gordon Tullock for helpful comments.

PART SIX

Increasing Returns and the Work Ethic

Economic Interdependence
and the Work Ethic

I commence with a confession of sorts. I have been unable to release myself, intellectually, from a determination to unravel, at least to my own satisfaction, the relationship between the simple choice of an individual, any individual, to work more or less, and the well-being of other persons who interact with the chooser in an extended production-exchange network. I entered this inquiry with a strongly held intuitive hypothesis to the effect that a choice made by anyone to work more, to add value to the economic nexus, generates benefits to others in the interaction, or, to put the hypothesis differently, and more generally, that there is *economic* content in the work *ethic,* that, in this respect as in others, we are ethically as well as economically interdependent.

I have not abandoned my hypothesis, but I have not fully resolved the question in all of its ramifications, even at the minimal levels of meeting my own internal requirements. But I am now able to state my hypothesis more clearly, and to embed it in a plausible analytical account. This chapter presents the argument nonformally, in part to avoid the distraction from the general implications of the hypothesis that formalization might involve.

I shall proceed as follows. In section 1, I shall "purify the model," so to speak, by listing, and describing briefly, the economic-institutional settings within which the ethical interdependence hypothesis clearly holds. Although these settings are intrinsically of some interest and, also, contain implications of important policy relevance, they do not embody my primary concerns. These settings are, therefore, noted in order to get onto the central issues.

From *The Economics and the Ethics of Constitutional Order* (Ann Arbor: University of Michigan Press, 1991), 159–78. Copyright 1991 by The University of Michigan. Reprinted by permission of the publisher.

Section 2 presents these issues full face, in the context of an apparent contradiction, the resolution of which has spurred my interest from the outset. Section 3 represents my best attempt to put the opposition's case, the argument that my hypothesis is simply in error, that there is no economic content in the work ethic under the standard assumptions of economic theory. Section 4 advances my own provisional attempt to modify the received theory to allow my hypothesis to be valid, based on my continuing refusal to bow before the forces of analytic convention. Section 5 extends the analysis, especially as it relates to other elements in the theory of competitive equilibrium. In section 6, the welfare implications of the analysis are examined, with an emphasis on the internalization of externalities through the introduction of ethical constraints. The summary evaluation and extension in section 7 concludes the chapter.

1. Fiscal Interdependence and Team Production

As announced, my purpose in this section is to "cleanse" the analysis, to describe briefly those settings in which the work ethic hypothesis is obviously valid, at least in some respects, but to do so in order to eliminate interference with the later examination of the more interesting question. The first such setting also serves to illustrate, in elementary fashion, the general issues that are to be addressed.

Consider an economy that is organized, and effectively operates, competitively. Rigorous description of the properties of equilibrium is not required at this stage. A public, or collectivized, sector of this economy exists through which collective consumption of public goods and services are financed from revenues collected from a tax that differentially impacts on measured income, as opposed to a benchmark tax on full income. In this regime, *fiscal interdependence* is such as to insure that the work-leisure choice made by any work supplier (or income earner) exerts Pareto relevant external effects, at the margin, on all other persons in the nexus.[1] By a decision to work an extra hour, day, or week, a person increases the effective base of tax which will, in turn, allow others in the nexus to enjoy higher rates of public goods benefits and/or lower tax rates. From the initial position of independent adjustment

1. For an early analysis see James M. Buchanan, "Externality in Tax Response," *Southern Economic Journal* 33 (July 1966): 35–42.

equilibrium, an agreement (including compensations where required) among all participants that involves input suppliers offering more inputs to the economic nexus must, over some range, promise benefits to everyone. In such a setting, the existence, maintenance, and promotion of an ethical constraint that discourages the consumption of leisure can provide a partial substitute for a potential utility-enhancing general agreement.

I shall neglect further discussion of this sort of fiscal interdependence, although full recognition of the relationship does, indeed, carry obvious implications for the organization of the tax structure. In what follows here, I shall simply assume that any taxes are levied on individuals in such fashion that liabilities for tax (and hence the tax base) cannot be modified by individual behavioral choices.

A second setting in which the validity of the hypothesis cannot be challenged embodies production under conditions where there are genuine advantages from the joint supply of effort by all members of a team. Since, by construction, individuals produce more when they participate jointly than when they produce separately, there exist genuine technological externalities at the individual work-leisure choice margins under decentralized and non-integrated competitive adjustment. If, however, the presence of team production or joint supply advantages extends over relatively limited subsets of the total work supply population, entrepreneurs would be predicted to emerge to internalize the relevant externalities among individual members of production teams. If the extent of jointness efficiencies is sufficiently limited to allow these advantages to be internalized within less than industry-sized firms, there need remain no Pareto relevant external effects in full competitive equilibrium.[2]

2. Economic Interdependence and Ethical Independence

The formal model of competitive economic interaction, cleansed of those features that could generate apparent Pareto relevant externalities at the in-

---

2. My colleague Roger Congleton, with whom I have worked jointly on several aspects of the analysis of the work ethic, has examined the importance and relevance of team production more fully in a draft paper, "The Economics of the Work Ethic" (Center for Study of Public Choice, George Mason University, 1988).

dividually defined choice margins between work supply and leisure, is descriptively interesting in its fundamental ethical implications. Despite the acknowledged benefits secured by all participants in an extended network of economic interdependence, there seems to exist no discernible generalized ethical interdependence, at least along the quantitative work-leisure dimension that remains my exclusive concern in this chapter. There is no apparent economic interest, as reflected in expected utility gains and losses, on the part of any one participant in the work-leisure choices made by others in the nexus.

The person who chooses to add a unit of input, who works an extra hour, day, or week, receives a payment (per time unit) that is the precise equivalent to the increment in product value that is generated by the incremental unit of input. Total product value increases by the same amount that the measured income of the person who supplies the incremental input increases. The incomes (and utilities) of others remain unaltered. From this characteristic of competitive equilibrium, it follows that others remain unaffected by, and hence remain uninterested in, the supply of work effort put on the market by the person in question, or indeed, of anyone else. In the formal model of competitive adjustment in equilibrium, individuals do not affect each other. To employ, in a somewhat different sense, the characterization used by David Gauthier, the competitive market in equilibrium is a "morally free zone."[3]

This result seems to be in apparent and blatant contradiction to the elementary principle that is stressed in every economics primer, the principle that there exist mutual gains from trade, and that all participants gain from the specialization that becomes possible only as trade occurs. How is this apparent contradiction to be reconciled? How is the positive relationship between the utility secured by an individual participant and the size of the inclusive production-exchange nexus ("the market") to be made consistent with the apparent absence of any relationship between any individual's work effort and the utility of others with whom he or she interacts? If an individual's utility does, indeed, depend on the size or the extent of the market, then it would seem to follow that any increase in this size, such as that embodied in the supply of an additional unit of input by any person, must be utility

3. David Gauthier, *Morals by Agreement* (Oxford: Oxford University Press, 1985).

enhancing to others, at least in some potential sense. In this case, however, there must then exist some economic interest on the part of any one participant in the work-leisure choices made by others. Ethical content seems to be restored, despite the implication that is drawn from the conventional model of competitive adjustment.

The intellectual-analytical challenge is evident. What is wrong with the standard model of general equilibrium in an idealized competitive economy that allows the implication of total ethical independence to be derived?

3. The Ethical Irrelevance of Work-Leisure Choice

In this section, I shall present the "opposition's" case. I shall outline, in a nonrigorous way, the formal theory of competitive equilibrium to demonstrate that, under the standard assumptions, there is no ethical content in the work-leisure choices made by individual participants in such an idealized economic interaction setting.

In equilibrium, team production advantages of the ordinary sort are internalized within firms, each one of which operates in the range of constant returns to scale. Entry, actual or potential, insures that no firm receives pure profit. Each firm is small, relative to the industry producing its product, and each firm is a price taker, both as a supplier of product and as a demander of inputs. Each input supplier is also a price taker and freely adjusts quantities supplied to the parametric input price, as dictated by the relative evaluation of earning and nonearning alternatives (work and leisure). Each consumer of final product, or demander, is also a price taker in all markets and freely adjusts quantities purchased in accordance with relative evaluations placed on the different goods that are available. All demanders of final product, all suppliers of inputs, and all decision makers for firms are in positions of optimal adjustment. The necessary conditions for Pareto optimality are satisfied, and, more restrictively, the solution is in the core. There is no economic incentive for any individual, or any coalition of individuals including the all-inclusive coalition, to modify behavior to depart from the equilibrium position as defined.

Let us postulate that this equilibrium is, now, shocked by a single change in behavior. One worker or input supplier, for any reason, increases by one unit the rate of input supplied to the market. This worker supplies one additional hour-per-day, day-per-week, or week-per-year to the production-exchange nexus, which is now larger by precisely the value added by the additional unit of input.

The analytical exercise may be limited to pure comparative statics. We may describe the properties of the ultimate postchange equilibrium and identify the differences between this position and the prechange equilibrium. There will, of course, be transitional shifts in values of the relevant variables, and these shifts will affect utility levels attained by differing groups of market participants during transition periods. These short-run or intermediate-run effects are not of central concern here. I am interested only in the long-run or permanent effects that remain after the idealized system of interaction settles down, conceptually, to its full postchange equilibrium.

Initially it will be expositionally convenient to present the analysis in a single-factor model. We may assume that labor is the only input, or, alternatively, that, as subject to choice by the supplier, "labor" embodies some complementary factor, "capital" in fixed proportions.[4] In this setting, the property that captures my attention here is the identity of both the product price and input price vectors in the prechange and postchange equilibria. And, because these price vectors are not modified, the potential utility levels attained by persons other than the individual who initiated the parametric shift are not changed. Persons do not, therefore, have a long-term economic interest in the supply of inputs put on the market by others. The increase in product value between the two equilibrium positions is precisely measured by the wage, or input price, paid to and received by the individual whose preference shift generated the change in the system.

This result depends, admittedly, on the absence of input specialization, at least over the relevant range of change generated by the shift, in input supply and subsequent output mix. Some units of input must, at the margin, be capable of generating equal increments to value in all uses, although remaining inputs may be allowed to earn genuine rents in specialized uses.

It is perhaps worth noting here that the world of competitive adjustment described in the standard models, at least as I have described it, is in all re-

---

4. In this respect the model is similar to that used by Martin Weitzman, "Increasing Returns and the Foundations of Unemployment Theory," *Economic Journal* 92 (December 1982): 787–804.

spects equivalent to the world of classical economics and, indeed, can be conceived as only an extension of Adam Smith's deer-beaver model in which relative costs of production determine relative prices to the exclusion of any demand-side or utility influence. Under the defined assumptions of the standard model, any shift in demand, generated by a change in preferences among final products, will, of course, generate shifts in relative supplies, but, unless there exist specialized inputs over the range relevant to the demand shifts, there will be no change in the vector of relative prices.

Dependence of relative prices on demands may, of course, be introduced through some presumption of input specificity, even after full adjustment. But this step would require some relaxation of the standard assumptions of the competitive model, specifically that which embodies constant returns to scale. I do not propose to depart from the input specificity conditions here.[5]

4. Return to Relevance

My hypothesis states that the idealized competitive equilibrium under all of the assumptions embodied in the standard model may *not* be Pareto optimal, which amounts to stating that there may exist nonexploited "gains from trade" remaining to be captured from some potential agreement among all participants. Specifically, my hypothesis is that all participants, as suppliers of inputs and users of outputs, can move to higher levels of utility by modifying behavior to generate an increased supply of work effort to the exchange nexus. I suggest that the error in the received analysis is to be located in an

5. The general results are not modified if we drop the single-factor assumption, although there will be net gainers and net losers in the shift between the two competitive equilibria. The postulated increase in the supply of *labor* inputs by the single person will increase the returns to suppliers of the complementary input, "capital," and at the same time reduce returns to suppliers of substitute inputs, "labor." These changes in the input price vector may, in turn, generate changes in the output price vector as differing outputs reflect differing factor proportions.

The relevant result, for my purpose, is that, despite the generated changes in input and output prices, the external beneficiaries of the increase in the supply of the one input cannot, in net, compensate the external losers while retaining gains sufficient to compensate the single-input supplier to modify his or her preferred behavior. In other words, the multifactor model does, indeed, introduce externalities into the choice of any input supplier, but under the standard conditions of competitive equilibrium adjustment, these externalities remain pecuniary and, hence, Pareto irrelevant.

oversight of the full implications of the principle of the division of labor, or, more generally, of specialization. As noted earlier, this principle is recognized generally in the acceptance of Adam Smith's proposition that "division of labor is limited by the extent of the market," but the implications of this familiar proposition for the optimality properties of competitive equilibrium seem to have escaped critical notice, with only few exceptions.

Clearly, any increase in the quantity of any input supplied to the nexus extends the market. Hence, by the Smithean principle, an increased division of labor is made possible. But the defined formal conditions for competitive equilibrium insure that all gains from specialization have been fully exhausted; hence, there are no welfare effects that emerge from the extension in market size. I suggest that this result is artificially produced by the assumptions imposed on the particular model that has come to dominate the neoclassical research program, and that a more acceptable model can be developed that will remove this contradiction. Both models are, of course, analytical idealizations, and neither is designed to reflect reality in any directly descriptive sense.

Let me return to the simple exercise in comparative statics. The economy is in its idealized competitive equilibrium; a single person now works an additional unit of time, reflecting a shift in revealed preference between supplying input to the market and supplying "input" (time) to the production of the person's *own* consumption of leisure. In the latter internalized "exchange," units of time yield utility flows directly; added leisure increases utility, at least over the ranges of choice relevant for analysis. In the external exchange between the person and the market, the converse relationship holds; units of time supplied in exchange for wages reduce utility. It is only indirectly that such exchanges become part of a utility-enhancing behavioral strategy. As the income is spent on the purchase of any valued product, the utility loss incurred in the sacrifice of leisure is offset by the utility gain in product value. Put simply, in the standard model, persons supply inputs to the market nexus for the purpose of being able to purchase output from this nexus. Suppliers are motivated by the prospects of becoming demanders. Say's law is surely valid at this juncture of the analysis. Supply emerges only because it enables its own demand to become possible.

How does this excursion into the elementary behavioral logic of choice in markets relate to my proposed reformulation of the model of competitive equilibrium? The person who supplies the additional unit of work to the nexus receives a wage or income for that unit. This income is returned to the market as an increase in demand for final product. This increase in demand, which is matched by the initiating increase in supply that made it possible, will create the potential for the exploitation of further specialization, *in some production*, that remained just below the margin of economic viability in the prechange equilibrium. The real cost of production (measured in minimally necessary quantities of inputs required for producing given outputs) in the affected industry (or industries) falls. The vector of output prices changes to reflect lower relative prices for the product (or products) now produced at reduced real costs. The vector of input prices will not change, if measured in relative terms, provided that units of input are not product specific over relevant ranges. If measured in terms of an output price index or numéraire, however, the value of inputs increase. For any given quantity of input supplied to the market, the income earned from the sale of that quantity will enable the supplier to purchase a higher index-valued bundle of product value than before the change. For any individual supplier who purchases a product bundle that includes the reduced-cost-price good, there is an increase in utility. The increase in the supply of work by the single person generates external or spillover benefits on all persons in the market nexus who purchase that particular good (or goods), the production costs, and price, of which are reduced due to the exploitation of specialization that is made possible by the market's extension.

5. Competitive Equilibrium, Increasing Returns, and Externalities

The general framework for my argument has been sketched out, but there remains the task of filling in the analytical details. My model violates the generalized constant returns condition imposed for the standard derivation of competitive equilibria. In order for any extension in the size of the production-exchange nexus to generate utility or welfare-enhancing effects, constant returns must be absent in *at least one industry* in the economy. For this industry (or industries), the increase in the demand for product calls forth a supply response that embodies a lowered real cost of producing. For this industry (or industries), the long-run supply-curve slopes downward.

The good (or goods) in question is/are produced under conditions of *increasing* returns to size of output for the industry.

This condition need not be inconsistent with competitive organization. Increasing returns to industry output need not imply increasing returns to the output of any single firm within the industry under unchanged conditions of demand. Each single firm may be informed about returns to industry output, but any attempted expansion in isolation would reduce the equilibrium outputs of other firms, making the single firm unable to capture the scale advantages. These gains can be captured only with an increase in demand for the industry's product, which does take place here with the addition of purchasing power to the nexus. For at least one industry, the increment to demand that takes place makes possible a reduction in the average cost of production, thereby generating utility gains to all participants in the nexus who consume the product so affected.

If the industry (or industries) that might be adjusted to take advantage of further specialization could be identified in advance, either by some ideally omniscient centralized economic planner or by decision makers in some idealized collective process, then arrangements might be worked out through subsidization to insure the capture of the potential offered by the new technologies. But, lacking such omniscience and also recognizing the realities of politics, how can the potential advantages of increasing returns be secured?

If the identity of the industry (or industries) that might be the location of the increasing returns is unknown, any reduction in outlay on any industry required to finance the subsidization of other industries might reduce, rather than enhance, the productivity of the economy. There remains, however, one end use of capacity that cannot qualify for the increasing returns characterization due to an extension of specialization. This "industry" is that which is necessarily nonspecialized, namely, that which produces the own-consumption of each person in the economic nexus. From this fact follows the conclusion that any means of reducing the production of a nonmarketable product, mainly leisure, must extend the size of the market for other industries, which must, thereby, include at least some extension of the demand for that industry or industries subject to increasing returns.[6] It is in this sense that the ex-

6. Only the classic paper on increasing returns by Allyn Young seems to recognize the

ternality discussed here is peculiarly present with the work-leisure margin for individual choice.

In a larger sense, the whole issue of the existence of a competitive equilibrium or some quasi-competitive equilibrium in an industry that operates under increasing returns remains outside my direct interest or concern. Even if the industry (or industries) so described must be organized monopolistically, or, alternatively, if effective competition among firms requires the presence of firm-specific demands thereby generating a monopolistically competitive industry structure, the "externality" stemming from the work-leisure choice will remain.[7]

My emphasis is exclusively microeconomic, but there are analytical affinities between the argument sketched out here and that developed by Martin Weitzman, whose interests and emphases are exclusively macroeconomic.[8] His argument suggests that generalized increasing returns can offer plausible microeconomic foundations for understanding the emergence of quasi-competitive unemployment equilibria. In particular, Weitzman does note the contradiction between the Smithean emphasis on the division of labor as related to market size and the constant returns condition in standard competitive theory. Earlier, N. Kaldor stressed the same point in the context of a generalized critique of equilibrium theory.[9]

I have repeatedly referred to the "externality" involved in the behavioral adjustment made by individuals in choosing between work supply to the market and the supply of leisure to themselves. The peculiar nature of this externality warrants more detailed discussion. Note, first of all, that the externality need not be identified by any such attributes as location, occupation, or industry classification. The behavioral margin of relevance involves

---

critical point here; see "Increasing Returns and Economic Progress," *Economic Journal* 38 (1928): 527–42.

7. A general summary-survey of the whole set of familiar increasing returns controversies, along with appropriate references to the relevant literature, is found in S. Vassilakis, "Increasing Returns to Scale," *The New Palgrave Dictionary of Economics*, ed. J. Eatwell, M. Milgate and P. Newman (London: Macmillan, 1987), 2:761–65.

8. Martin Weitzman, "Increasing Returns and the Foundations of Unemployment Theory."

9. N. Kaldor, "The Irrelevance of Equilibrium Economics," *Economic Journal* 82 (1972): 1237–55.

the supply of productive effort to the production-exchange nexus at any point and at any level of productivity. In particular, note that the operating characteristics of the industry within which the work-leisure choice is made are totally irrelevant. The externality applies to all work-leisure choice margins, whether in increasing, constant, or decreasing returns industries. The increase in value to the overall nexus exerts its external effect only as and when the input supplier returns the added value earned to the market as a consumer-purchaser, thereby generating an increase in effective demand. If the extent of the market limits the potential for deriving the advantages of specialization, at least one industry in the totality that describes the production-exchange nexus must exhibit increasing returns. And the beneficiaries of the externality, stemming from the increase in effective demand initially generated by the person who spends the income from his increased work effort, are those persons who include in their consumption portfolio the good (or goods) produced under conditions of increasing returns. The effects are, of course, reversible; a choice made by an individual to reduce the supply of work to the nexus, with the subsequent decrease in effective demand, will generate a negative externality or diseconomy on all persons who consume the product of the increasing returns industry (or industries).

The externality identified here differs from those that are more often treated in welfare or applied economics and in at least two basic characteristics. There need be no relation of contiguity, locational or otherwise, between the generator of the external effect and the recipients of benefit (or harm). In comparison, consider a few familiar examples. The pollution in the river reduces the fishing and boating opportunities for those who live downriver. The resident who maintains a fine flower garden increases the utility of this neighbors on the street; Coasian cattle invade the land of the neighboring farmers; Marshallian firms are in the same industry. On the other hand, and by contrast, the work-choice externality is potentially economywide, or beyond if the economy is defined to be smaller than the trading nexus.

The individual who supplies additional work in the industry that produces x_i, among the set of final goods denominated: $x_1, x_2, \ldots x_n$, generates value to all persons who consume-purchase x_j, the good produced under increasing returns, who may be "far away" from both producers and consumers of x_i in any and all dimensions.

A second difference between the work-supply externality and others that are more familiar lies in the way in which the benefits (or harms) enter the utility functions of the persons affected externally. In the notation above, the externality affects the utility of the consumer-purchaser of good x_j that is produced under increasing returns through a reduction in the price of x_j. There is no effect on the utility function analogous to the addition of floral splendor by the gardener along the street or on the production function analogous to the pollination of the apple orchard by the neighbor's bees. The consumer-purchaser of the good produced under increasing returns, x_j, finds his or her budget constraint modified by a lowered price for x_j. And this price effect is not, in this case, offset by a compensating price increase elsewhere in the economy, as faced by this or any other consumer-purchaser. The effect emerges as a pure price change made possible by the increase in the aggregate supply of economic value to the economic nexus. The analyst must resist the temptation to disregard the externality because it enters the utility function through price. In the traditional terminology, the externality is "technological," and, hence, Pareto relevant, because it expands the choice-set of some persons in the nexus, without fully offsetting restrictions in the choice-sets of other persons.

Two emendations to the conventional externality analysis can be helpful in facilitating an understanding of the work-supply effect. If we assume that consumption is generalized, in the sense that all final goods are included in each participant's preferred consumption bundle, then every participant in the economic nexus, in his or her role as a final user of the good produced under conditions of increasing returns, becomes a beneficiary of the increase in the work supply of any worker in the whole nexus. If we introduce a model of household production, where Beckerian Z goods are "produced" with the appropriate set of x goods directly purchased from the market, then any reduction in the price of an x good (in this case x_j) modifies the production function for some Z good, making the externality appear analogous to those that are more familiar in orthodox analysis.

6. The Ethical Internalization of Economic Externalities

The precise description of the work-supply externality is helpful in the consideration of possible internalization or correction. In this section, I shall examine four alternatives: (1) intraexchange bargaining, (2) institutional evolution, (3) politicized correction, and (4) ethical norms. I shall try to support the second part of my hypothesis to the effect that, within limits, a culture may internalize the relevant work-supply externality through instillation of a work ethic.

The presence or possible presence of an identified externality suggests directly that "gains from trade" remain to be exploited in some all-inclusive, or economywide, sense. And the recognition of this point provides a precautionary warning to economists who would base their diagnosis of market failure on direct observation by parties external to the potential exchanges or trades that may emerge, or may have emerged, to internalize any relevant externality. This lesson taught by Coase and his followers has been learned.[10] The first question to be asked, therefore, after my putative identification of the work-supply externality, concerns the prospects that this alleged market failure might be or might have been internalized by appropriate intraexchange bargains, agreements, contracts, or trades.

Reference to the Coase literature suggests immediate attention to numbers involved in the relevant interactions. As noted earlier, genuine advantages of team production in the ordinary joint supply sense will tend to be captured through the organization of firms. But for the economywide externality that the work-supply choice embodies, the answer to the question is surely negative. Intraexchange bargains among parties who interact outside ordinary markets can be predicted to emerge in small-number settings, or even in large-number settings if and when affected subsets can be represented as having well-identified joint interests.[11] As the descriptive analysis of section 5 makes clear, however, bargained internalization of the work-supply externality seems beyond the plausible. Consumers, as a group, are beneficiaries of increased work supply, but within the inclusive consumer set there are differentially arrayed benefits depending on relative preferences identified only through conditions of production of goods. It is difficult even to

---

10. R. H. Coase, "The Problem of Social Cost," *Journal of Law and Economics* 3 (1960): 1–44.

11. James M. Buchanan, "The Institutional Structure of Externality," *Public Choice* 14 (Spring 1973): 69–82.

design some imaginary scheme of compensations and payments that could command general agreement.

A second means of internalization that warrants mention is that classified as institutional evolution. As we analyze their workings, markets are idealized, and the institutions that we observe do not seem descriptively close to the analytical idealizations. It may seem plausible to suggest that the institutionalized departures from the analytical idealizations may have evolved and remain viable precisely because they effectively internalize relevant externalities. Examinations of those institutions that seem to affect work supply most directly yield ambiguous results, with perhaps some weighing toward a negative evaluation. Conventions and arrangements, both formal and informal, have emerged over time to place minimal limits on the supply of work, such as the minimal forty-hour week, along with the introduction of differentially higher time rates for overtime work supplied—these arrangements could be rationalized on some implicit "as if" recognition of work-supply externalities. But there exist other developments that seem to reflect adverse effects on work effort. Historically, the length of the workweek has been substantially reduced; the years of working life have been cut, sometimes dramatically, by social retirement programs, some of which are compulsory; there has been almost continuous increase in the number of days of holiday and sickness leave—all of these developments seem opposed to any institutionalized embodiment of directional correction for the external economy in work supply.

In the theoretical welfare economics of midcentury, the mere identification of an externality offered an apparent normative basis for the implementation of politicized correction. The impact of public choice theory has been to destroy this rather simplistic and unexamined argument. Politics, like markets, sometimes fails, and prospects for effective political correction for externalities can be assessed in the same fashion as those for intraexchange corrections discussed briefly above. Even if the importance and relevance of the work supply externality should come to be acknowledged by all economists who proffer advice to practicing politicians, could we predict corrective measures to be taken in the interplay of interest-driven, constituency-based politics?

Reference to the record of political action on the structure of taxation should place an immediate damper on hope for politicized internalization here. The setting of fiscal interdependence sketched out in section 1 is descriptive of real-world fiscal reality in the United States and elsewhere. Fiscal externalities that serve to exacerbate the work supply effects that would remain in a world of fiscal neutrality remain uncorrected. Fiscal examples aside, however, it is not easy to create a model of modern democratic politics that would yield approval for a tax on consumption designed to yield revenues for the payment of generalized wage subsidies, which might be one possible shape of politicized internalization.

We are left with the fourth alternative, that which might internalize the work-supply externality through the instillation, maintenance, and transmission of an ethical precept or set of precepts. Before discussing this alternative directly, however, it is necessary to address a possible critical challenge to my whole analysis here, and especially to its welfare implications. If the incentives offered to individual participants who are free to make any sort of contractual agreements they choose, whether through markets, politics, or otherwise, are not sufficient to generate satisfactory internalization, are there justifiable grounds for the claim that the noncorrected solution is nonoptimal in any meaningful sense of the term? If some analogue to transaction costs emerges to prevent the implementation of an enforceable agreement, contract, or trade that will internalize the externality, is not the noncorrected solution optimal, despite the existence of spillover benefits? Is the work-supply externality identified in the analysis of this paper Pareto relevant?[12]

In this case, we might acknowledge that there do, indeed, exist external effects from the work-leisure choices made by individuals and that these effects modify the attainable levels of utility by those in the nexus who consume the final products of increasing returns industries in the economy, while, at the same time, we could abandon efforts to construct arrangements that would modify incentives to secure increases in work offered to the market. A policy norm of noninterference or laissez-faire with reference to individualized work-leisure choices would seem to be dictated in this setting.

There is much to be said for this position, and especially if prospects for corrective internalization are limited to the alternatives considered to this point. (If binding contracts are possible, and persons who seem to be caught

12. James M. Buchanan and W. C. Stubblebine, "Externality," *Economica* 29 (November 1962): 371–84.

in apparent Prisoners' Dilemma settings are then observed not to make such contracts, then, through their own behavior, they reveal that the diagnosis of the dilemma was in error.)[13] The very exercise of diagnosis is useful, however, even if, when advanced as hypothesis, it is falsified by an absence of agreement. And it is important at this point to recognize that the impossibility of securing viable and stable agreements through institutional arrangements that rely on the self-interested behavior of individuals tells us little about the prospects for corrective internalization through the introduction of ethical principles.

It is difficult to introduce ethical or moral constraints into the analytical apparatus of the economic theory of choice. The person who supplies work to the market nexus appears simply to adjust quantities to the parametric wage per time unit that he or she confronts. There would seem to be no operational way to determine the extent to which the work-leisure choice actually made embodies the influence of an ethical norm, including the very existence of any such norm. It is possible, however, to depict the constraining force of an ethical standard analytically, provided that we resort to a construction that incorporates internal as well as external constraints on individual choice.

Figure 14.1 illustrates. The indifference contours reflect the relative evaluation of money income and leisure, both of which are "goods." The lines drawn from M, the position of maximal leisure, depict the external constraint imposed by the market situation, with the slope of these lines measuring the wage rates per unit time (assumed here to be uniform). In the absence of any internal constraint, and with a wage rate shown by the slope of MY', the position of individual equilibrium is reached at E.

We may incorporate a work ethic by treating its presence as an *internal* constraint. If the person locates at M, an internal cost is now assumed to be experienced, a cost that may be evaluated in terms of the money numéraire, and represented in figure 14.1 by the distance MK. As units of work are supplied to the economic nexus, this internal cost (of loafing) is progressively reduced. Note that, as depicted, the individual who faces the wage rate indicated by the slope of MY, and who is also constrained internally over the

13. James M. Buchanan, "Positive Economics, Welfare Economics, and Political Economy," *Journal of Law and Economics* 2 (October 1959): 124–38.

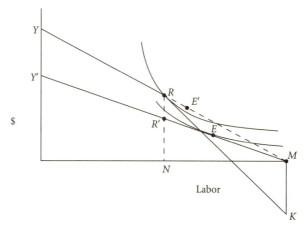

Figure 14.1

range *NM*, will locate at *R*, which is a corner solution. The segment *RM* is simply unavailable to the chooser in this modified construction.

Note, however, that the position at *R* is not attainable by the individual's own effort from the alternative equilibrium at *E*. The individual is, indeed, "better off" at *R* than at *E*, as depicted in figure 14.1. But for the individual located at *E*, a private decision to work more would simply produce a shift to *R'* where he or she becomes worse off. It is the presence of a *generalized* work ethic among all or large numbers of participants in the economic nexus, combined with the presence of increasing returns somewhere in the system, that generates the increase in the wage rate. And with the increase in the wage rate, the position attained in the presence of the internal constraint is preferred to that position attainable under the lower wage rate in the absence of the internal constraint.[14]

The construction sketched out above, and depicted in figure 14.1, is misleading, however, because it presumes that the individual who chooses is psychologically aware that the ethical constraint prevents the attainment of what would seem to be an otherwise preferred position (at *E'*). It seems surely to be more descriptive to suggest that the individual may not be conscious of

---

14. David Levy has used a related construction to indicate the possible relevance of moral constraints for another purpose. See David Levy, "Utility Enhancing Consumption Constraints," *Economics and Philosophy* 4 (1988): 69–88.

the ethical norms that guide the choices made in everyday market dealings.[15] As choices are made, the individual senses no constraining influence at all. As felt internally, the individual moves to a most preferred position within the economically feasible set on the utility function that is revealed by his or her choice behavior.

This feature alone suggests that internalization through ethical norms may be more readily accomplished than through any bargained or politicized alternative. In a bargained internalization, those persons and groups that expect to secure benefits must compensate those whose behavior exerts the external benefit or harm. And even if politicization need not encompass the all-inclusive set of participants in an "exchange," there remains a necessity of securing agreement among competing interests, which may also require that expected beneficiaries pay, in some fashion, for the utility gains consequent on the modifications in behavior of those whose choices are to be changed. In comparison and contrast, the ethical constraint, if operative and influential, acts unilaterally on the behavior of the supplier of input to the nexus. The beneficiaries get a "pure play"; they find levels of well-being increased without any necessity of making payment. Bargains, trades, agreements, political compromises—these remain outside the whole calculus.

This nonreciprocal feature of ethical internalization suggests, in turn, two additional, and derivative, aspects that deserve notice. The first relates to the central meaning of Pareto relevance in the theory of externality. An externality is defined to be Pareto relevant if the potential gains (harms) to those who expect to be benefited (harmed) exceed in value the expected losses (gains) that the indicated change in behavior (at the margin or in total) will impose on those who make the change. The classification of externality relationships into Pareto relevant and Pareto irrelevant sets requires a benefit-loss comparison, both by the economist observer who makes some initial diagnosis and, finally, by the affected parties on the two sides of the relationship. And the set of externalities that remain Pareto irrelevant is by no

---

15. F. A. Hayek, especially, has stressed the adherence to codes of conduct in the market that are below the level of individual consciousness. See F. A. Hayek, *Law, Legislation, and Liberty,* vol. 3, *The Political Order of a Free People* (Chicago: University of Chicago Press, 1979).

means empty; when transaction costs are reckoned, this set may be large indeed. Note that the utility interdependence remains, however. The Pareto irrelevant classification refers only to the prospects for *economic* internalization.

When we consider internalization through ethical constraints, there is no meaning to the relevant and irrelevant classification scheme, because there is no requirement that the benefits to some potentially affected parties be measured against losses to others. In other words, so long as utility interdependence remains, a potential for ethical internalization is present. For those externality relationships that are Pareto irrelevant, the only means of correction lies in the prospect for some ethically generated modification in choice behavior.

A second characteristic that stems from the nonreciprocality of ethical internalization involves the relative importance of generalization in participation among the whole set of affected parties on one side of the externality relationship. This aspect is closely related to, but seems conceptually separate from, the importance of transaction costs in determining the Pareto relevance or irrelevance of an externality. Consider, again, the work-leisure margin for a single input supplier to the economic nexus. The additional value that might be added to the nexus through an additional time unit generates benefits to all persons who may consume the goods produced under conditions of increasing returns. The input supplier produces a genuine "public good" for members of the consuming group because no single member of this group can secure utility gains separately from others in the set. There is no means, therefore, through which particular benefited parties may effectuate factored down, small-number "trades" with any single-input supplier, or even with all input suppliers treated jointly.

The "publicness" characteristic of increases in input supply does not change under ethical internalization. But because the benefited parties, singly or in total, are not required to "finance" the "public good" that supply increases embody, there is no threshold barrier akin to that imposed by the difficulties of overcoming free riding. Since the "public good" is produced by any increase in input supply, so long as one person modifies his or her behavior due to the presence of a work ethic, some correction for the externality takes place.

7. Work as Benevolent Self-Interest

Perhaps the most familiar statement in *The Wealth of Nations* is that which tells us that "it is not from the benevolence of the butcher, the brewer, or the baker, that we expect our dinner, but from their regard to their own interest."[16] We understand Adam Smith's argument here, but if we take the conventional theory of distribution in the competitive economy seriously, we immediately sense an apparent contradiction. If the butcher, and everyone else, takes from the economy precisely the equivalent of the value added to the economy by his efforts, how do we benefit from individuals' self-interested behavior?

Suppose that the butcher decides to retire early and go fishing, and that he does so out of strict self-interest. How will this change in his behavior affect the rest of us? Not at all in the long-term sense, if we accept the marginal productivity theory of distribution and assume that the economy is effectively competitive. The size of the market will become a mite smaller upon the butcher's retirement, but after other butchers expand their scales of operation, prices will return to the same levels that existed before the butcher ceased to butch.

I have argued that the conventional theory of competitive adjustment must surely be in error in this inference, and that we must look for ways to modify conventional reasoning to allow an accommodation of Smith's central theorem concerning the gains from trade that extended division of labor facilitates. I have sought to show that, in order for the utilities of other participants in the network to be affected by a change in the size of the economic nexus, some relaxation of the constant returns to scale condition for idealized competitive equilibrium must be effected. There must exist increasing returns (decreasing costs) in at least one industry in the all-inclusive production-exchange nexus.

Fortunately for my purposes, I am not required to enter directly into the controversial areas of analysis involving the consistency between increasing returns and competitive equilibrium which, in turn, produce divergent models of industrial organization. Nor is it necessary for me to specify, even concep-

16. Adam Smith, *The Wealth of Nations* (Indianapolis: Liberty Fund, 1981), 26–27.

tually, the relative share of total production that emerges from increasing returns operation, or to distinguish these industries from others (as, for example, between manufacturing, service, and agricultural sectors). For my purposes, I require only that increasing returns characterize operations in at least one industry, which need not be identified. For expositional simplicity, I have tried to present the analysis to minimize the differences with the conventional competitive models. Hence, I developed the argument in the context of an industry characterized by Marshallian external economies, where the advantages of scale cannot be captured by individual firms. But the results are in no way restricted to that setting.

I have tried to show that the characteristics of the work-supply externality are such that there are severe barriers to either intramarket or politicized correction, leaving the burden of internalization to the possible embodiment of ethical norms in the work choice. To the extent that a work ethic enters the choice calculus of input suppliers, whether or not this be conscious, consumers somewhere in the economy secure spillover benefits. There is economic content in the ethic of work. And because there is this economic content, there is justification for both individualized and collective efforts to promulgate, maintain, and transmit this ethic throughout the culture as well as intergenerationally.

The butcher whose benevolent self-interest dictates work does "good" for others that is lost when he goes fishing. The antiwork ethic of the 1960s summarized in the admonition "take the time to smell the flowers" involves an explicit invitation to destroy economic value for others than the addressee. And, of course, the size of the external effects is directly related to the market value of the input potentially supplied. The radiologist who loafs harms others much more than does comparable behavior by a fast-food employee.

I have deliberately limited discussion in this chapter to the work-leisure choice margin, measured along a time-unit dimension, as the potential source of expansion and contraction in the size of the economic-exchange nexus. The analysis is obviously applicable to qualitative as well as quantitative changes in the values of inputs supplied. The central analysis is, also, readily extendible to sources of change in market size that do not involve behavior of individual input suppliers, *at least directly.* Perhaps the most obvious margin of relevance is that determined by the political-legal constraints that delineate, along several dimensions, the area within which persons are allowed to carry out voluntary exchanges. And specialists in trade theory have long recognized that extensions in the size of the trading network allow for further exploitation of gains from specialization, and increasing returns models have been introduced.

In this literature, however, there seems to have been relatively little attention paid to the inconsistency between nonexhausted gains from specialization and the standard analysis of competitive equilibria. But my suggestion that the work-supply externality is analogous to the "trade extension" externality would surely not be surprising to trade theorists.[17]

The analysis has implications for many other policy areas such as population control, immigration, women's entry into the labor force, work requirements for welfare, and retirement programs, along with those for tax structure already noted. My central concern is, however, not with the derivation of specific policy implications in these areas. My emphasis is limited to an attempt to define the economic basis for an ethic of work. And, if my aim must be generalized, it is to convince fellow economists that we remain ethically as well as economically interdependent, along the work-leisure margin of choice as along so many others. If we, as economists, continue to neglect these ethical interdependencies, even as they embody relevant and important economic content, we stand vulnerable to the accusation that our sometime esoteric analyses become the modern equivalent of the medieval debates about angels dancing on pins.

17. See W. J. Ethier for a useful analysis that also contains references to the trade literature, "National and International Returns to Scale in the Modern Theory of Institutional Trade," *American Economic Review* 72 (June 1982): 389–405.

The Economics and the Ethics
of Idleness

I. Introduction

In this chapter, I want to concentrate attention on idleness in the use of potentially productive resources, particularly on the ethical aspects of individuals' choices concerning the margins of productive employment. This subject matter has been neglected in modern microeconomic analysis, which has embodied the presumption that potentially productive resources will be employed optimally, within the constraints faced by individual resource owners, so long as the choice of employment is voluntary. The whole Keynesian macroeconomic emphasis, which came to occupy the attention of economists in midcentury and did have profound political impact, was centered on involuntary unemployment, or, to use my terminology in this chapter, on idleness that is not chosen to be preferred by resource owners. Furthermore, the modern emphasis of economists, to the extent that they have concerned themselves at all with idleness in resource use, has been almost exclusively confined to labor; little or no attention has been given to possible idleness in the utilization of nonlabor resources, the primary subject matter here.

It is necessary first to define idleness, which I do in section II. I then proceed, in section III, to show that there are ethical implications of individual choices in resource utilization. Initially, I develop the analysis in application

From *Ethics and Economic Progress* (Norman: University of Oklahoma Press, 1994), 112–28. Copyright 1994 by the University of Oklahoma, Norman, Publishing Division of the University. All rights reserved. Reprinted by permission of the University of Oklahoma, publisher.

A somewhat different version of this chapter was initially presented as the Henry George Lecture at St. John's University in November 1990.

to labor or work input, an application that was developed in chapter I. In section IV, I briefly sketch the outlines of an argument to the effect that voluntary choices made by resource owners need not be such as to generate economic efficiency in the standard sense, an argument that directly counters the conventional wisdom in economic theory. In section V, attention is shifted from labor to nonlabor resources. Finally, in section VI, some interesting policy implications are suggested that seem to follow from the whole exercise.

II. Idleness Defined

Precisely what do we mean when we say that a resource, or resource unit, remains "idle"? We define idleness by its opposite; a resource is idle when it is not "at work," when it is not "employed." More generally, we can say that a resource is idle when it is not being used to produce value that it might otherwise produce. Such generalized understandings are satisfactory for most purposes, but they are not sufficiently specific for my purposes here.

Note, in particular, that the definition suggested could be used in application to the activities of Robinson Crusoe, all alone on his island and totally outside any nexus of interaction, economic, political, or social, with other human beings. Crusoe may, of course, work hard and employ his own talents and time to produce something of value to himself. In some descriptive sense, we could measure Crusoe's idleness as distinguished from his work. But his choices in this respect could not carry ethical content since there are no others who could possibly be affected. And Crusoe might, for example, spend his time and energy, his "work," building sand castles that are swept away by each evening's tides.

I want to introduce a more useful meaning of idleness by opposing this use of resources to "work in an interactive relationship with others" or "employment in producing value for others." In this more restricted but more useful definition, a person is idle when and to the extent that he or she withholds work effort from the market, even if, on some "private island," nonmarketable sand castles are constructed. A resource, or resource unit, that can produce value when placed on the market but that is withheld from the market or from production for own use by the owner, which allows consumption purchases on the market to be replaced, is *idle*. The subjective value that may be produced for the resource owner is irrelevant.

I also want to rule out of consideration any nonvoluntary idleness in the use of resources. Involuntary idleness may be important in many settings, but this sort of idleness is not my concern here. For the analysis and discussion that follows, I shall presume that all owners of resources may, if they choose to do so, place such resources in employment by way of sale on the market. There exists a parametric price per unit of resource supplied to the market, and the owner-supplier may adjust amounts to this price, from zero to some employment maximum (or idleness minimum).

As noted, I initially develop the argument in application to labor, but I do not restrict the analysis, as such. Idleness can characterize the utilization of any resource, labor or nonlabor, no matter how classified. I shall make the appropriate extensions as required. There are differences between labor and nonlabor resource units that are worthy of notice, however, differences that offer some explanation of economists' concentration on labor. The presumption is that for any nonlabor resource, under the assumption that resource owners face parametric prices in the market, voluntary choices will always lead to maximum resource utilization, or, stated conversely, to minimum idleness. I demonstrate that this conclusion does not follow if we are careful to remain with the definition of idleness stated above.

III. Is It Unethical to Loaf?

Consider a simple example, in which we initially neglect the fiscal interdependence considerations treated in chapter 4. There is a highly trained, professionally competent radiologist who is, at age forty-five, at the height of his career. He can secure an income of $200,000 annually. In January 1994, this person chooses, voluntarily, to work no more. He opts for the life of leisure; he "retires"; he lives off his accumulated savings, plays golf and tennis, and enjoys society. He undertakes no further productive effort. Henceforth, he remains idle.

How would this choice be evaluated by the modern economist? The forgone payment of $200,000 would have reflected, in some rough-and-ready sense, the net contribution to value in the economy that was made by the radiologist. The value of the national economic product will fall by this total on the radiologist's choice to retire. But the economist would also note that the $200,000 also measures the preretirement income received by the radiologist. Hence, the person who makes the choice between productive work and idleness bears the full burden of payment. No one else in the national economy is affected, at least in any directly measurable economic sense. The choice made by the radiologist is the same as if he were, indeed, a Robinson Crusoe on his private island. There seems to be no ethical content in this choice, no ethical implications that result, because others find themselves in the same positions whether or not the radiologist chooses work or leisure.

There are some necessary qualifications to this conclusion. First, as the discussion in chapter 4 makes clear, if taxes are levied on measured money income, then the choice made by anyone to earn less income and to take more leisure will reduce public goods benefits and/or increase taxes on others in the fiscal system. I shall simply acknowledge the effects of this fiscal interdependence here; I shall neglect further discussion because I do not want to base my central argument on this point. Second, if resources are specialized, as is always the case for transitional periods, the change in relative prices will generate gains for some groups and losses for others. In some long-run sense, however, these effects disappear, and, under the conditions presumed necessary for a workably competitive economy, the primary conclusion seems to stand up. There seems to be no important spillover effect on others that stems from the choice made by one income earner, even a high-income earner, to loaf rather than to continue to supply productive effort to the economic nexus.

This apparent result squarely contradicts one of the first principles of economics, a principle first enunciated clearly by Adam Smith in 1776. There exist mutual gains-from-trade; all parties gain from exchange, and these gains increase with extension in the size of the trading network. As the network of exchange expands, increasing advantage emerges from the increased specialization that is made possible. What has happened when the radiologist in our example decides to work less is that the market has been reduced in size. There will be less prospect of fully utilizing the advantages of division of labor, at least for some area of production in the economy. There will be permanent changes in the price vector for outputs; inputs will earn less than before; the purchasing power of an input in terms of potentially purchasable output will fall. If this hypothesis holds, then the choice made by the radiologist in the example does, indeed, exert spillover effects on others in the whole system of interaction. This choice on the part of one person will necessarily harm others in the system. And if harm to others is the criterion for unethical or immoral behavior, the choice to loaf rather than to continue to offer productive work to the economic nexus can legitimately be classified as unethical or immoral.

IV. Increasing Returns

Here as well as in earlier chapters, I have exposed what I consider to be a rather glaring contradiction between two parts of the conventional wisdom in modern economics, a contradiction that seems to have been largely, if not completely, overlooked. The tone of my discussion in the preceding section, as well as earlier in this book, conveys my own analytical preferences, so to speak. I want to argue in support of the basic principle that all members of the inclusive production-exchange-consumption nexus tend to secure gains as the effective size of this nexus expands and that these gains are inexhaustible. That is to say, increases in specialization are always possible as markets are extended, producing, in turn, increases in economic well-being for participants.

But acceptance of this principle requires that the standard conditions for the attainment of equilibrium in a competitive economy be modified in some way. The vulnerable assumption in the model of competitive adjustment is that which postulates that, at equilibrium, firms operate everywhere in the range of constant returns to scale of operation. Note what happens under this postulate. In our simple example, the radiologist chooses to work no more. The competitive adjustment process ensures that, after a transitional period, the price of radiology services will return to the same level as that prevailing prior to the decision made by the single supplier to cease productive effort. The services previously provided by the man who chooses to smell the flowers will now be generated by some expansion in the scale of operation of other radiologists or by the entry of newly trained professionals. In either case, after the gains and losses over the transitional period are damped and a new equilibrium established in the industry, the first result identified emerges. The choice between idleness and productive effort on the part of any input supplier does not permanently affect the economic well-being of others.

To generate a result consistent with the inexhaustible gains-from-trade story, we must allow for the presence of increasing returns (decreasing costs) to the size of the economy. In our example, the size of the measured nexus is lower by $200,000 annually compared with what it was before the shift in preferences on the part of the person in question. Somewhere in the system, at some or all locations, in some or all industries, there are now specialist producers or suppliers, of some inputs or some outputs, who find that the market faced is no longer sufficient to allow previously established patterns of trade to remain viable. Production is forced into a higher-cost mode of operation because the market will no longer support the specialization attained under the extended market. There will be an increase in the real price of the products or services that are ultimately produced. The shrinkage in the size of the economy will have required resort to an "inferior" technology, relative to that which was supportable before the change.

V. The Idleness of Nonlabor Resources

To this point in my argument I have introduced analysis and material that I have discussed differently and in somewhat more detail in earlier chapters. I now propose to enter uncharted territory, to extend the same analysis to apply to nonlabor resources. It is relatively straightforward to discuss the choice between idleness and productive effort in application to labor. The picture becomes cloudy when nonlabor resources are treated. In my radiologist example, it is meaningful to think about the shift in preferences that caused the person to cease supplying productive effort to the marketplace and to supply, instead, hours of leisure to himself. There is nothing incoherent about a utility function that shifts in such a way as to make this choice take place. Leisure, or the uses to which leisure may be put, yields utility values to the individual, values that must, in all cases, be compared with those that emerge from the ultimate purchasing power over consumable goods and services that income received from the sale of productive work effort makes possible.

But what is the equivalent to the utility value of leisure for nonhuman resource units? Recall that we must always remain within an individualistic calculus of choice here. Resource units do not, in themselves, take on characteristics that allow us to attribute values directly to them. We must remain with the utility calculus of those persons who own and control the utilization of nonhuman resource units. But why should an individual, as owner-supplier of a nonhuman resource unit, secure any potential utility value from withholding this unit from the market nexus?

It is relatively straightforward to understand why the owner of a resource unit would place such a unit on the market. The resource unit, if it is productive, yields a market price that provides the owner with income that may be used for the purchase of desired goods and services from other markets. But why should such an owner ever choose to withhold or to withdraw a unit from the marketplace?

For this result to occur, idleness in resource use must yield direct utility to the owner, analogously to that yielded by leisure to the supplier of potential work effort. Again, consider an example. A person accumulates under his personal ownership and control several thousand acres of marginally productive agricultural land. This land is leased or rented to farmers who produce and market crops. The lease or rental value to the owner is $10,000 annually, which is approximately the value of the increment to product attributable to the land itself. The owner receives the $10,000 in annual rental value and returns this value to the income stream in either consumption goods purchases or indirect investment in capital goods.

Let us now assume that the owner of the land experiences a shift in preferences concerning the usage of the land. He chooses voluntarily to withdraw the land from active production of crops and to utilize this resource in its natural state, say, as a hunting preserve. The land becomes idle, in my usage of terms here. To the owner, the choice can be fully rational; the owner withdraws the land from production for the market in the full knowledge that he or she is sacrificing $10,000 annually in rental or market value. The utility value now placed on the idleness of the land must be anticipated to yield more than the utility yielded by $10,000.

The example seems in all respects analogous to the labor-supply example of the radiologist discussed earlier. The inclusive economic nexus is made smaller by the decision of the landowner to withdraw the resource from production for the market. A market value of $10,000 could be produced with the resource, but this value is now replaced with a utility yield that is enjoyed exclusively by the owner of the resource. Other persons in the production-exchange-trading nexus are placed in a less-preferred position due to the shrinkage in the size of the market. The smaller economy will be unable to allow for the full exploitation of the scale advantages that the potentially larger market might make possible. Some of the benefits of specialization will be lost.

If work is praiseworthy and loafing is blameworthy; if there is positive economic content in an ethic of work, as I have argued in chapter 1 and elsewhere, then there must also be comparable normative implications for the employment of nonlabor resources. If nonlabor resources are capable of producing value on the market, or value that is a direct substitute for goods that would otherwise be purchased from the market, there are external or spillover effects of decisions made by resource owners concerning the way in which these resources are used.

Note that the emphasis here is not explicitly distributional, although distributional implications may be derived indirectly. In our example, the owner of the land does not exert a negative externality on others in the polity because he has extensive holdings. The negative externality stems exclusively from the owner's use of the holdings, from the withholding of potentially productive resources from the market nexus. Indeed, it is the owner's decision to forgo measured money income, the rental value of the land, that imposes the costs on others. Because the owner does not earn this income and return it to the economy's circular flow as effective demand, the gains-from-trade that might otherwise be possible are not exploited.

VI. Implications

Recognition of the ethical content present in choices between placing resource units on the market and withholding them in idleness does not imply that there need be some all-or-none commitment. Recognition that the radiologist, in the first example, does indeed provide spillover benefits to others in the economy as he produces value that he, in turn, spends for his own purposes, does not allow us to infer that the radiologist is immoral if he supplies anything less than the physically determined maximum number of hours of work. Additional work supply involves disutility to the supplier, and this decrement to value must be measured against (1) the utility value of the income earned to the radiologist, plus (2) the spillover value to others in the nexus. Beyond some point, the disutility of additional work surely offsets the value, both internal and external, of this work, even in some idealized felicific calculus. The point of my whole discussion here is to stress that there should be some recognition given to the value to others than the work supplier in the choice made between productive effort and idleness.

Much the same logic applies to the landowner's choice in the second example. The landowner does indeed impose costs on others in the economy as he withdraws land from the production of marketable value. But there need be no normative inference to the effect that land, or any other nonhuman resource, should always be utilized so as to yield maximal marketable product value. The hunting preserve presumably yields utility to the owner, and this utility (like leisure to the worker) should not be left out of account. Again, the point to be noted is only that the effects on others than the choice maker, the landowner in this example, should not be overlooked.

I have argued that it would be extremely difficult, if not impossible, to internalize or correct for resource use externalities by ordinary economic or political adjustments. I suggested that such internalization that exists enters the calculus of choice makers by way of ethical constraints, which may or may not be conscious to the choosers. The radiologist may feel guilty when he does not work, and the landowner may feel a guilt of sorts when he converts the land into a hunting preserve.

Recognition of the interdependencies discussed can, however, lead to agreement on institutional changes that will, at the least, remove perverse incentives. The potentially useful changes are perhaps most evident in tax policy. The radiologist who chooses to forgo income for leisure should be required to pay *more,* not less, in taxes. Yet, as we realize, most tax systems that are based on income would allow the radiologist's tax liability to be reduced as the income earned in the market falls. In this respect alone, the substitution of a consumption or expenditure base for an income base of tax would represent a major welfare-enhancing step. The landowner of our second example, who withdraws land from productive use to a purely private use, should be required to pay higher, not lower, taxes in any fiscal system that embodies a conceptually agreed on structure of incentives.

As we move beyond fiscal incentives, perhaps the most serious distortions in incentives are to be located in the failure of effective decision makers on resource use to be confronted with relevant opportunity costs, even to the extent faced by genuine resource owners in our two examples. At the very least, both the radiologist and the landowner make choices to withdraw resources from the market in the full knowledge that they will, privately and personally, suffer the loss of measured product value. In many cases, however, and especially in the modern economy-polity, resource use decisions are made by political agents, presumably acting on behalf of citizens. And these agents do not face the incentives of the marketplace at all. The coalition in the legislature that approves the withdrawal of productive land for preservation of "wilderness areas" or "wildlife habitats" loses neither the direct opportunity cost of lost market value nor the spillover harms generated by the necessary reduction in the size of the inclusive trading nexus along with the effects of the lowered tax base. If public policy analysts could incorporate the elementary principle that "resource use matters" for the ultimate size of the market, some corrective offset to the modern prejudice against the production of market value might be introduced.

Let me end with a private, personal story. In May 1989, I visited Prudhoe Bay, on the Alaskan North Slope, where I toured the oil-producing facilities. Let me state categorically that there could be no place more desolate than this North Slope in the absence of facilities—a barren, frozen, uninhabitable desert. There exists another section of the North Slope that is anticipated to yield oil, but development has been prevented because of the misguided and confused judgment that such pristine wilderness should be preserved. This judgment is, to my mind, grossly immoral and especially so in that those who pronounce such judgment, and who do, indeed, exert political influence, do not stand to suffer any of the adverse consequences of the smaller economy that must result as we fail to take advantages of our resource-using opportunities.

The main thrust of my argument has been that the market, as it operates, does not fully take into account the advantages of production for the market because some share of these advantages accrue to other than those who make choices directly. But the argument is strengthened manyfold in application to politics, where those who make ultimate resource-using decisions share almost none of the costs of the sacrifice of opportunities that are forgone.

Idleness for private aesthetic purposes comes at a cost that even the hard-nosed economists have not properly reckoned. Should we be surprised at all by the relative decline in the productive record of the U.S. economy after the flower children of the 1960s came to work and the romantic environmentalists mounted their efforts to make us return to a natural state? Idleness is idleness is idleness, no matter what the dross.

The Simple Economics of the Menial Servant

I. Introduction

Adam Smith made much of the distinction between productive and unproductive labor, and the ratio between these categories of employment was a central determinant of the wealth of a nation. This ratio provided a rough measure of the extent of the market, which, in turn, set limits on the potential for the division of labor. And, as Helen Boss notes, "Adam Smith's Scottish soul is particularly troubled by the 'unproductiveness' of menial servants."[1] Neoclassical economics does not incorporate the productive-unproductive labor distinction, and the conventional wisdom attributes analytical error to Smith in this aspect of his general argument.

My purpose here is to suggest that perhaps it is neoclassical economists generally who are in error and that Smith's argument may be made coherent on careful and critical reinterpretation. I shall demonstrate that, under conditions to be specified, the participants in an economy may be "better off" in terms of their own revealed preferences in settings where they collectively discourage the purchase of personal services of others, in the capacities of menial servitude. My analysis is limited here to what we may call the "welfare economics" of menial servitude rather than the more familiar relationship

From *Ethics and Economic Progress* (Norman: University of Oklahoma Press, 1994), 129–45. Copyright 1994 by the University of Oklahoma, Norman, Publishing Division of the University. All rights reserved. Reprinted by permission of the University of Oklahoma, publisher.

The central argument of this chapter was initially presented at a seminar at George Mason University in February 1991, and it was again presented at the Southern Economic Association meeting in Nashville in November 1991.

1. Helen Boss, *Theories of Surplus and Transfer* (Boston: Unwin Hyman, 1990), 47.

between the productive-unproductive labor ratio and classical theories of economic growth.

II. The Extent of the Market

Smith's distinction between productive and nonproductive labor must be analyzed within the context of his overreaching principle to the effect that the division of labor is limited by the extent of the market. Modern economists, with a small but rapidly growing number of exceptions, have by and large paid lip service to the central Smithean proposition here, while proceeding to ignore its implications almost completely in their analysis. The Smithean principle suggests, quite simply, that any extension or expansion in the size of the market or production-exchange nexus will necessarily allow for an increase in specialization, which must, in turn, increase the overall productivity of the resource inputs that are devoted to generating outputs for such nexus. By inference, there is no upper limit to this potential for specialization.

Economists have been able to ignore the implications of the Smithean proposition here because they have postulated, either explicitly or implicitly, that the quantity of resources is exogenously fixed. That is to say, the "size of the market" is not within the choice set of participants in an economy, either individually or collectively. Given such a postulate, it is not surprising to find that Smith's principle has been more fully discussed and understood by those economists who analyze problems in international trade.

But, of course, the postulate of resource fixity is absurd. The quantity of input supplied to the market or production-exchange nexus is a choice variable, within the choice set of individuals, either as they adjust privately and independently to the constraints they face or as they participate variously in collective decisions for the group, as they may or may not impose constraints that will be faced jointly by all or some participants. To postulate fixity in the supply of the most important input, labor, to the market is to carry forward the exploitation thesis that workers are required by subsistence limits always to maximize the hours of employment and/or to accept the more sophisticated utilitarian fallacy that classifies nonwork (leisure) as a "good" that is analytically equivalent to market input.

Clearly, the extent of the market can be expanded endogenously by choices made by participants to supply more inputs to the market and fewer inputs to themselves, in nonmarket uses. As individuals supply more inputs to the market nexus, specialization is increased, and the productivity of inputs increases. The quantity of outputs, appropriately measured, that is purchasable from any given input is increased.

From this straightforward analysis, it follows that the supply of inputs that will be forthcoming under individualized adjustment to input prices (wages) as if these prices are parameters will be suboptimal. There will exist an external economy in input supply, at the work-leisure choice margin, an externality that will not be exploited. All persons in the economy can be made "better off," by their own evaluations, by some modification in the constraint set that will offer incentives for an enhanced input supply.

I have discussed this labor supply externality more fully in chapter 1, and I shall not elaborate earlier arguments here. But a different formulation of the work-supply externality analysis will be helpful in moving toward the central argument of this chapter with reference to the unproductiveness of menial servitude.

III. A Simple Model of Labor Supply When the Extent of the Market Matters

Consider an economy in which all persons are identical, both in their preferences and in their capacities or endowments. In this setting, there would be no trade under the standard neoclassical assumption of constant returns of scale of production for each good. Trade will prove beneficial only if there are increasing returns to specialization, which I assume to be present. Further, I assume that the gains to specialization are not exhaustible, no matter what the extent of the market.

Specialization takes the form of the replacement of general purpose or multipurpose inputs by newly specialized inputs that enter into the production of final goods.[2] There are many goods in the economy, produced with

---

2. In this respect, the model is similar to that introduced by W. J. Ethier, "National and International Returns to Scale in the Modern Theory of International Trade," *American Economic Review* 72 (June 1982): 389–405.

many inputs. The valued bundle of goods that is produced and marketed may be measured in units of an all-purpose numeraire consumable unit, X.

Smith's principle states that X is produced under increasing returns from the supply of inputs. For simplicity, assume that labor is the only input and that the amount of labor supplied to the market is Z. Then X, the all-purpose consumable, is produced under increasing returns to Z.

Persons have available a fixed number of potential labor inputs, measured by total time available (24 hours per day). Since, by assumption, all persons are identical, if all behave in the same way, each person would confront a nonconvex production possibility set. Such a production possibility frontier is depicted by the curve P in figure 1, where hours (Z) are measured on the abscissa and income (X) along the ordinate. The individual will not, however, be aware of the generalized increasing returns present in the economy. If the economy operates competitively, each person will confront an apparent transformation set that reflects a fixed wage rate, which is determined independent of the individual's choice. The competitive equilibrium adjust-

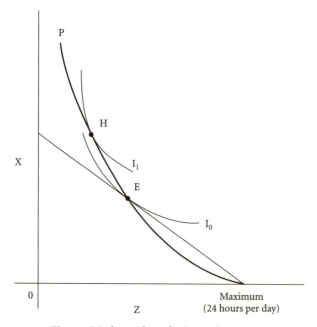

Figure 1. Work supply under increasing returns

ment is shown at E, where the individual's (all individuals') marginal rate of substitution between labor supplied to the market and income (through the wage rate) is equal to the apparent possibility constraint and where the solution falls somewhere on the real set of production possibilities.

It is clear from the construction in figure 1 that E, the competitive equilibrium, is nonoptimal. The individual (all individuals) may be placed in a position of higher utility if the solution could, somehow, be shifted to H, where the marginal rate of substitution between work supply and the wage is equal to the real rather than the apparent marginal rate of transformation. (This result can be easily understood if we think of a setting where a single individual, in a one-person economy, faces the situation depicted. Utility maximization would dictate a location of equilibrium at H, not at E.) In the competitive adjustment equilibrium, there is a suboptimal supply of labor to the market nexus and a supraoptimal supply of labor to the nonmarket uses, including leisure.

This result is derived independent of any prospect for defining, in advance, the good or goods in the market that are produced under increasing returns of the standard sort. The result suggests that the supply of labor input is suboptimal so long as the basic Smithean principle concerning the extent of the market is accepted, that is, so long as the gains from further specialization remain unexhausted. The result emerges exclusively from the elementary fact that specialization, hence increasing returns, cannot be extended by the supply of inputs to nonmarket uses, that is, to the "production" of nontradable "goods." Once the use of potential labor market input for nonmarket purposes is recognized and the necessary absence of gains from specialization in "producing" for such purposes is acknowledged (specialization could not conceivably extend beyond each person's use of his own leisure), the nonoptimality of individualized parametric adjustment to exogenously determined wage rates is evident.

Note that the construction indicates that the range of suboptimality in the supply of market input is limited. In chapter 1, I have suggested that one means of internalizing the externality here is through the inculcation of a work ethic, which operates as a constraint of preferences. Note that such an ethic that might expand work effort beyond that point depicted at H in figure 1 would, in itself, be overly constraining.

IV. Identification of "Goods" That Cannot Be Produced under Increasing Returns

The analytical conclusion of the previous section hinges on the identification of input use that cannot give rise to increasing returns; this procedure is the reverse of that which characterizes much of modern welfare economics, where the attempt is made specifically to identify input uses that generate increasing returns. And the approach here seems more in keeping with the Smithean emphasis, especially with the emphasis of Allyn Young,[3] who, in his seminal paper, associated economic growth with increasing returns but made no attempt to identify, in advance, the industries where specialization would generate relatively greater benefits.

If leisure, or own-consumption use of inputs, can be identified as a utility-enhancing "good" that cannot possibly generate increasing returns and, indeed, may generate the opposing effect through reducing the overall size of the market or exchange nexus, some further search for other valued "goods" that might be comparable in this respect to own-consumption uses of own inputs might be suggested. And it is only here that I return to the economics of menial servitude, the primary subject matter of the chapter.

Consider, now, the same simple model as previously analyzed, but assume that one of the valued goods in the X bundle is personal service. Persons in the economy have preferences such that services provided by others enter as arguments in utility functions, again assumed identical for all persons in the economy. Personal services differ from nonwork or leisure, however, in that these services are directly tradable; they are marketable "goods" that persons sell and purchase through the market or price system.

As before, we incorporate acceptance of the basic Smithean principle concerning the effects of extending the market. We postulate that there are increasing returns, generally, as measured in units of X, with increases in the supply of Z. The composite consumable, X, is, however, now made up of two categories of "goods," personal services, X_s, and all other "goods," X_{ns}. Can we now argue that inputs used to produce X_s cannot give rise to increasing returns, comparable to the results applied to leisure or nonwork earlier?

---

3. Allyn Young, "Increasing Returns and Economic Progress," *Economic Journal* 38 (1928): 527–42.

V. Personal Services as Such

It seems evident that if care is taken to specify precisely what personal service or menial servitude means in the context of the model analyzed here, we can indeed add such service to the putative listing of "nonproductive" labor, which we have essentially redefined as that labor which cannot possibly generate increasing returns. At least two qualifications must be placed on the type of personal services that fall under the classification suggested here. First of all, the use of inputs for personal service may substitute for own-service in nonmarket purposes and, in the process, provide scope for extension in the effective size of the market. A household example is familiar. A person may, through the purchase of the personal services of someone else (e.g., services for care of children), have more time available for supply of his or her own inputs to the market nexus, inputs that are valued more highly than those replaced by taking the services supplied by the employee from the productive nexus. A second qualification involves the possibility that personal services may be supplied only in a package with other inputs that may, indeed, generate increasing returns and, in the process, give rise to a reduction in the personal service component of the final consumable. Haircuts may offer an example here. Barbering services are required to supply haircuts, but these personal services are supplied jointly with other technical equipment services. As the market for haircuts increases, increasing resort to the technical equipment components (e.g., electric clippers) in the jointly supplied "good" may increase the productivity of the complementary personal inputs of the barber. The result may be that the time spent per haircut is reduced, indicating the presence of generalized increasing rather than constant returns.

I suggest, however, that these are qualifications on the general Smithean claim and that they do not seriously undermine the validity of the proposition. To the extent that labor inputs are used to provide personalized services, as such, to others, even as fully valued and paid for on competitive markets, these inputs are used unproductively relative to those uses that might give rise to increasing returns consequent on specialization. If I purchase, for a full market wage, the services of a menial servant, whose work for me in no way makes me a more productive input supplier to the marketplace and whose work is not supplied jointly with some nonpersonal input components, I am, in taking this choice, reducing the relevant extent of the market, as measured in terms of its potential exploitation of gains from specialization. Clearly, the extreme limits of specialization are reached when one person does nothing other than provide personal services for another. The productivity of this sort of input cannot possibly be enhanced by any widening of the market nexus.

The construction of figure 2 is structurally identical to that in figure 1, but here the trade-off depicted is that between X_s, personal services, and other goods, X_{ns}. Since we have postulated that there must be increasing returns to Z, the input of labor services to the whole economic nexus, as measured in X, the numeraire consumable, there must be a nonconvex real possibility frontier between personal services and other goods, as shown by P' in figure 2. The individual who faces exogenously determined competitive prices will, however, be unaware of the generalized trade-off and will adjust to the solution shown at E'. The solution is suboptimal in that the preferred solution at H' remains within the possible. Conceptually, all persons could be

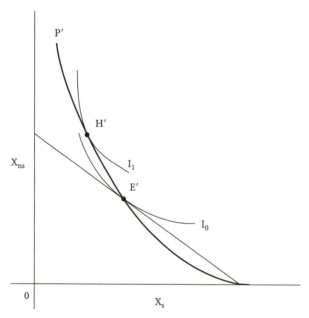

Figure 2. Increasing returns to goods other than menial service

brought into agreement on the imposition of institutional constraints that would cause the solution to shift toward H' and away from E'.

We may conclude, I think, that something more than Adam Smith's "Scottish soul," as named by Helen Boss, led him to classify menial service as relatively unproductive. His particular argument here may have been, instead, based on very solid economic analysis, even if he could not fully articulate his basic intuitions.

Note precisely what is being argued here. In earlier chapters, I have tried to establish the following proposition: If we accept the basic Smithean theorem that relates the division of labor and, hence, productivity gains from specialization to the extent or size of the market, and if, further, we acknowledge that the effective size of the market, as measured by the quantity of inputs supplied, is endogenously chosen by participants, then it follows that individuals will not, in full competitive adjustment, offer optimal input supplies to the market at a level that will generate overall efficiency in resource use. The argument of this chapter is a direct extension of the earlier proposition but with an important difference. If we can identify valued uses of inputs that are intrinsically limited in their potential for allowing any exploitation of further gains from specialization, then acceptance of the Smithean theorem implies that a shift of demand from such "relatively unproductive" uses to other uses that might possibly allow for some exploitation of increasing returns will be welfare improving, quite independent of any overall adjustment in the supply of inputs to the market.

Note that the external diseconomy identified here is imposed by the person who uses income to purchase or demand the personal services of another person. The particular choice of a person to supply personal services is not, in this setting, different from a choice to work for a wage in producing goods. Again, as Smith noted, the shift of demand away from the services of personal servants or retainers and toward the purchase of goods became one of the means through which economic growth was made possible.

VI. Baumol's Unbalanced Growth Model Revisited

To this point, I have restricted discussion to a single input use, the provision of personal services, as such, by some persons to others, even in a fully reciprocal and voluntary set of market exchanges. My concentration on this input use is prompted by a desire to evaluate Smith's particular attribution of relative unproductivity to this employment of labor. If my central argument is accepted, Smith's treatment is, in a sense, validated, despite the dominance of opposing arguments in the conventional wisdom of modern economists. But if the argument is accepted, even provisionally, the restriction of analysis to menial or personal service becomes arbitrary. An extension of effort to examine other input uses, including but not limited to Smith's listing, that may be classified to fall within the relatively unproductive category is clearly in order.

Perhaps surprisingly, given the apparent attitude of most modern economists toward the productive-unproductive labor distinction, we find that such an extended classification has been made but in quite another context and not explicitly related to Smith's extent-of-market theorem. I refer here to William J. Baumol's seminal paper "Macroeconomics of Unbalanced Growth."[4] In his model, Baumol divided the economy into two sectors, distinguished by predicted rates of growth in labor productivity. The sector characterized by constant or low growth in productivity was defined to include those activities where "for all practical purposes the labor is itself the end product" (416). Examples were teaching, chamber music and orchestral performance, theatrical presentation, and fine cooking.

Baumol did not, however, relate his analysis to Smith's distinction between productive and unproductive uses of labor, although it would have represented a simple step for him to assign those input uses described in terms of low productivity into a "relatively unproductive" category. Further, Baumol did not connect his analysis with the increasing returns sources of potential economic growth that Young had tried to initiate several decades earlier. Baumol's focus seemed to be primarily on the temporal dimension of productivity growth in his two sectors of the economy rather than on any quantitative dimension that might be measured by the relative sizes of the two sectors.

It now seems even more interesting that Baumol, himself a distinguished welfare economist, failed to draw any welfare inferences from his model.

---

4. William J. Baumol, "Macroeconomics of Unbalanced Growth," *American Economic Review* 57 (June 1967): 415–26.

From the perspective of a quarter century later, it becomes possible to interpret Baumol's failure here in terms of the mind-set of neoclassical economics of the 1960s. The rate of economic growth was attributed to exogenous technological change that Baumol did, indeed, identify with particular sectors of the economy but that was not deemed to be dependent on the allocation of resources as between sectors. All productive activities were assumed to be characterized by constant returns to scale, and Smith's central theorem was relegated to the elementary textbooks. Operating from within this mind-set, Baumol's insights simply did not allow him to recognize that welfare-improving shifts from his relatively unproductive to relatively productive uses of resources were within the possible.

As we move now into the mid-1990s, the possibilities of economy-wide increasing returns are being reexamined and not only in international trade theory;[5] classical theories of economic growth are being revived and reinterpreted;[6] theories of endogenous growth are on the frontier of economic analysis.[7]

Formalized definitions and existence proofs of the static allocative efficiency of competitive equilibrium occupy decreasing attention. Developments both in analysis and in observed reality force economists to recognize the interdependence among the economic, ethical, and political environments within which persons interact. During the last two decades, economists, generally, have learned that institutions matter. They must increasingly come to learn that ethics also matter. In both respects, we are returning to the classical tradition of Adam Smith after the Walrasian diversions of more than a half-century.

5. Nicholas Kaldor, *Economics without Equilibrium* (New York: Sharpe, 1985); James M. Buchanan and Yong J. Yoon, eds., *The Return to Increasing Returns* (Ann Arbor: University of Michigan Press, forthcoming).

6. Walter Eltis, *The Classical Theory of Economic Growth* (London: Macmillan, 1984); Gavin Reid, *Classical Economic Growth* (Oxford: Blackwell, 1989).

7. See, in particular, the several important papers by Paul M. Romer ("Increasing Returns, Specialization, and External Economies: Growth as Described by Allyn Young," University of Rochester, Rochester Center for Economic Research, Working Paper no. 64, December 1986; "Growth Based on Increasing Returns Due to Specialization," *American Economic Review* 77 [May 1987]: 56–62; "Endogenous Technological Change," *Journal of Political Economy* 98 [October 1990]: S71–102).

Constitutional Implications of Alternative Models of Increasing Returns

James M. Buchanan and Yong J. Yoon

1. Introduction

Our recently published volume, *The Return to Increasing Returns* (1994), was titled to suggest the shift of attention of modern economists toward increasing-returns phenomena. This change of emphasis is both stressed and exemplified in the book by Brian Arthur under review.[1] It is descriptively accurate to suggest that modern economists are breaking away from and out of restricted confines imposed by constant- and decreasing-returns models and, hence, necessarily toward acceptance of increasing-returns phenomena.

But it would be wrong to infer that the models of increasing returns that are introduced as alternative constructions are identical either in their conceptual foundations or in the implications that may be derived for the constitution of economic policy. We propose to use this occasion for reviewing Arthur's book to elaborate some of the distinctions among the alternative models of increasing returns and to suggest the correspondent implications.

From *Constitutional Political Economy* 6 (Summer 1995): 191–96. Reprinted by permission of the publisher, Kluwer Academic Publishers.

1. W. Brian Arthur, *Increasing Returns and Path Dependence in the Economy* (Ann Arbor: University of Michigan Press, 1994).

2. Taxonomy

In this section we discuss each category of the increasing-returns concepts, concluding with that of Brian Arthur.

Consider, first, the implicit definition of increasing returns in *neoclassical general equilibrium models.* Production and preference functions for well-defined goods exist, and these are readily identifiable. Increasing returns are present when, for some production function, output increases dispropor-tionately with inputs. Competitive organization of the production-supply of the increasing-returns goods is not viable. The nonpoliticized market equi-librium embodies monopoly, with consequent allocative inefficiency. Aggre-gate welfare may be increased by a shift of resources toward the production-supply of goods that exhibit increasing returns.

In conventional welfare theory, such market failure offers a basis for ar-gument in support of politicized correction. More sophisticated normative discourse, postpublic choice,[2] suggests that the acknowledged inefficiencies of market adjustments should be compared, pragmatically, with predicted inefficiencies of attempted political correction.

Mathematical formulation. Consider an economy with positively valued commodities y_1 and y_2. These commodities are produced by $y_1 = f(x_1)$ and $y_2 = g(x_2)$, where x_1 and x_2 are input vectors. Note that the economywide inputs $x_1 + x_2$ are fixed. Commodity y_1 is produced by constant returns to scale if $f(\lambda x_1) = \lambda f(x_1)$ for any positive λ; and commodity y_2 is produced by increasing returns if $g(\lambda x_2) > \lambda g(x_2)$.

Consider, second, the meaning of increasing returns in the *Marshallian external economies model,* which reappears in a modern variant in the endogenous-growth models developed by Paul Romer and others.[3] Increas-ing returns (economies of scale) do not describe the production functions of the separate producing units (firms). But the productive activity of each firm, over a whole sector of the economy, generates external economies for

2. See J. M. Buchanan, R. D. Tollison, and G. Tullock, eds., *Toward a Theory of the Rent-Seeking Society* (College Station: Texas A&M University Press, 1980).

3. P. Romer, "Growth Based on Increasing Returns Due to Specialization," *American Economic Review* 77 (May 1987): 56–62; "Endogenous Technological Change," *Journal of Political Economy* 98 [October 1990]: S71–107.

other producing units, thereby increasing the ratio of valued outputs to inputs with sectoral expansion.

Nonpoliticized market adjustment need not, in this setting, generate incentives for the formation of monopoly. But the equilibrium attained in the market remains allocatively inefficient because of the presence of the non-internalized externality. Aggregate welfare can be increased and economic growth enhanced by a shift of resources toward the sectors of the economy that exhibit external economies. As in the other model, however, politicized attempts at correction must be examined for their comparative efficiency enhancing properties.

For Marshall, external economies were located in industrial sectors of the economy as opposed to the constant- or decreasing-returns agricultural sectors. For Paul Romer, the external economies, which take on public goods attributes, are present in the generalized production of knowledge, an inclusive sector of the economy that has grown to be much more significant after the communication-information revolution.[4]

Mathematical formulation. An individual firm faces a production function $F(A, x)$, where A is parametric for the firm, but variable with the industry size. We may interpret A as a nonrival input such as technical knowledge. The production exhibits constant returns with respect to input x, $F(A, \lambda x) = \lambda F(A, x)$; but for the industry, $F(\lambda A, \lambda X) > \lambda F(A, X)$.

Consider, third, a model of *monopolistic competition.* In this setting, firms attain profit-maximizing equilibrium at outputs where production functions exhibit increasing returns to scale, internal to the firms themselves. Freedom of entry ensures the absence of positive profits in industrywide or economy wide equilibrium. The desirability of variety, as expressed by the distinct preferences of demanders for the differentiated outputs of the separate firms, prevents the exploitation of internal scale economies. There need be no external economies of the Marshallian type; production functions need not be interdependent.

If monopolistic competition describes only some sectors of an otherwise competitive economy, the equilibrium attained in full-market adjustment re-

---

4. A. Marshall, *Principles of Economics* (1890; 9th [variorum] edition, ed. C. W. Guillebaud, London: Macmillan, 1961); Romer, "Endogenous Technological Change."

mains allocatively inefficient in the sense that all demanders of the goods produced under monopolistic competition generate, at the margin, external economies on other persons in the economy. Stylized correction would require an increase in demand for all products produced in the monopolistically competitive sectors at the expense of some decrease in the demand for products in remaining sectors of the economy.

If a somewhat more modest stance is taken here, and it is assumed either that monopolistic competition may describe the operation of the whole economy or that there is no means of empirically classifying separate sectors into those that may and may not be monopolistically competitive, no implications for efficiency-enhancing reallocations of resources follow, even in some idealized conception of political action.

On the other hand, and importantly, this model yields direct normative implications concerning policy toward the extension of market size. The widening of the effective trading nexus (for example, by lowering barriers to exchange with units from other economies) has the effect of increasing demand for all differentiated products with the subsequent exploitation of the economies of scale. And these implications follow without any necessity to identify particular sectors of the economy that might be classified to be monopolistically competitive.

Mathematical formulation. Among potential products, commodities x_1 through x_n are produced. All commodities are produced with the same cost function: $l_i(x_i) = \alpha + \beta x_i$, where l_i is input, say labor, required to produce output x_i; α is fixed cost and β is marginal cost. The equilibrium is characterized by the Chamberlinian tangency conditions: marginal revenue equals marginal cost and average revenue equals average cost. That is, (1) $p(1 - 1/\epsilon) = \beta w$; and (2) $px - (\alpha + \beta x)w = 0$, where p is the price and ϵ is the elasticity of demand for the commodity, and w is the wage. Given the total input L, the number of different goods produced is, $n = L/(\alpha + \beta x)$. The aggregate input L can be increased by increased work effort of individuals or by widening the trading nexus.

Fourth, consider a model that embodies *generalized* or *economywide increasing returns* due strictly to the specialization of labor or resource inputs. Such an economy need not exhibit increasing returns in a manner similar to those treated in the preceding three subsections. There need be no production that, as such, exhibits scale economies over an extended range; no external economies in production need be present; and there need be no differential demands for products of particular firms. Increasing returns here emerge solely and exclusively due to the relationship between market size and possible specialization, as recognized by Adam Smith.[5]

At any size of the exchange nexus, at the margin there exists a specialization that is only marginally viable in the sense that any reduction in the size of the nexus would make such specialization noneconomic. Conversely, any increase in the size of the nexus will make some specialization economically viable that could not be so at any smaller limit. For such marginally viable specializations, production may take place under conditions analogous to those faced by producing firms in monopolistic competition; the marginal specialization faces falling unit cost. But the generalized setting treated here differs from that of monopolistic competition in the fact that it is the potential for specialization in resource use rather than specialization in preferences that generates the departure from the idealized conditions of competitive equilibrium.

In this model, increasing returns are an emergent property of specialization in response to the increased size of the production-exchange nexus. Increases in valued output per unit of valued input emerge as a result of the extended specialization that is recognized and exploited by those who are in localized positions to take advantage of opportunities. There need be no prior identification of such prospects, even conceptually. There is, in this sense, no allocative inefficiency, as such, under the standard parameteric assumptions. Existing resources in current production cannot be reallocated so as to generate a higher valued product.

On the other hand, generalized efficiency can be enhanced by any outward extension of the size of the market nexus, either externally by expanded trade with others (units) beyond the boundaries of the (national) economy or internally by a shift from nonmarket to market end uses of inputs.[6]

---

5. J. M. Buchanan, "Order Defined in the Process of Its Emergence," *Literature of Liberty* 5 (Winter 1982): 5; A. Smith, *An Inquiry into the Nature and Causes of the Wealth of Nations* (1776; reprint, ed. R. H. Campbell and A. S. Skinner [vol. 1], Oxford: Oxford University Press, 1976).

6. J. M. Buchanan, *Ethics and Economic Progress* (Norman: University of Oklahoma

In its constitutional implications (that is, the structure of the rules that defines the parameters within which economic interaction takes place), this model of generalized increasing returns resembles that of the monopolistic competition model discussed earlier, provided that the latter is interpreted in the modest or nonomniscient sense that denies the possibility of classifying separate sectors of the economy.[7] Both models offer analytical bases for normative argument in support of market extensions, which may be accomplished externally or internally.

Mathematical formulation. Individual firms face constant returns. But the economywide production $Y = F(X)$ has the property that $F(\lambda X) > \lambda F(X)$, where Y is the output vector and X is the input vector in the exchange nexus.

Consider, finally, increasing returns in the *positive feedback models* that exclusively occupy the attention of Brian Arthur. Semantically, *positive feedback* may seem to be little more than an alternative term for *increasing returns,* although attention is directly focused on the formal mathematical properties of the phenomena, perhaps at some cost of neglect of the economic, and choice-related, elements. In Arthur's paradigm, however, the ubiquity of positive feedbacks, along with basic resource scarcity, creates a critical dependence between the allocative choices, initially made, and the relative attraction exerted by the various possible avenues for resource investment.

In dramatic contrast with the (neoclassical) general equilibrium models, a contrast that Arthur stresses, there is no unique equilibrium outcome of market process, given a set of endowments and preferences. Nor is there a uniquely determinate optimal allocation. Instead allocative outcomes depend on the paths through which these outcomes come to be generated. History matters, and changes in initial conditions may operate to determine how the economy arrived at where it is observed to be in any descriptive sense. Increasing returns, either at the level of the single producing unit or at the level of some agglomeration of units, arise whenever significant positive feedbacks occur, and these may arise from any of several sources:

Press, 1994); J. M. Buchanan and Y. J. Yoon, eds., *The Return to Increasing Returns* (Ann Arbor: University of Michigan Press, 1994).

7. J. M. Buchanan, "The Domain of Constitutional Economics," *Constitutional Political Economy* 1 (Winter 1990): 1–18.

learning by doing, network interactions between and among suppliers and demanders,[8] locational externalities akin to the Marshallian, informational contagion, and others.

The acknowledged presence of increasing returns does not, however, suggest resource misallocation, as such. There are, indeed, many "might have beens," but these alternative possibilities no longer exist, having been forever precluded by the particularized choices that were, in fact, made and implemented. And there is no clearly discernible means of changing the choice-making rules so as to ensure that development paths not yet traveled will generate "better" allocative futures.

There are no direct implications for the size of the economic nexus in Arthur's model. Rather, the focus is on the critical importance of choosing the "right" technology. Even if one technology is eventually superior to the other, it is possible that in present value terms, or due to myopic expectations, the choice of inferior technology can be preferable.

Mathematical formulation. Consider two technologies, A and B, competing for adoption by a number of customers. The payoff to adoption depends on the number of persons, $n_A(n_B)$, who lock themselves in by adopting $A(B)$. Suppose the payoffs are $10 + n_A$ for technology A; and $5 + 2n_B$ for technology B. Then, even though technology B is superior if enough people adopt it, it may never be adopted because at an early stage, the payoff of technology A is more attractive.

3. Conclusions

In this review essay, we have presented a taxonomy of modern increasing-returns models in an effort to locate the contribution of Brian Arthur relative to that of other economists who have joined with him rejecting the conventional constant- or decreasing-returns framework for analysis. We do not suggest that particular economists can be fully identified as working exclusively within one or the other of the separate classifications listed in Section 2. For example, Ethier combines elements of the monopolistic competition and generalized increasing-returns models, while Krugman's work seems

8. M. L. Katz and C. Shapiro, "Network Externalities, Competition, and Compatibility," *American Economic Review* 75 (June 1985): 424–40.

to incorporate the external economies, monopolistic competition models, along with some attention to the positive feedbacks stressed by Arthur. Paul Romer's work is amalgam, of sorts, of Marshallian external economies and Arthur's positive feedbacks. We do not suggest that the taxonomy is one that contains mutually exclusive categories; neither do we suggest that the models are specific, or differentiated, enough conceptually to treat them as separate. This is particularly so because both Ethier and Romer use the Dixit and Stiglitz formulation for their intermediate input markets.[9]

To us, it is somewhat easier to classify Brian Arthur's work than that of many others. His emphasis and interest is focused on the formal properties of positive feedbacks, whether these are manifested for the individual productive unit or for the undefined units of agglomeration. In the latter setting, the positive feedbacks are related to the external economies model, but Arthur's concern is with explanation and understanding of how existing results have come into being rather than with how "better" results might have been achieved. Properly interpreted, Arthur's model does not generate a settled normative conviction as to the relative efficacy of market entrepreneurship and politicized direction in making the critical initial selections of paths that determine the course of future economic progress.

Arthur's work is analytically more distant than those of the other modern economists considered here from the traditional normative focus of political economists, who have sought always to use their analyses to improve what is, either at the level of specific allocational change or reform in constitutional rules.

Finally, the alternative models of increasing returns may be compared in terms of their normative implications for regimes that may or may not embody encouragement for an extension of the production-exchange nexus. Clearly, both the monopolistic competition and the generalized (increasing-returns) models offer direct linkage to arguments for extended market size

---

9. W. J. Ethier, "National and International Returns to Scale in the Modern Theory of International Trade," *American Economic Review* 72 (June 1982): 389–405; P. R. Krugman, "Increasing Returns, Monopolistic Competition, and International Trade," *Journal of International Economics* 9 (November 1979): 469–79; Romer, "Growth Based on Increasing Returns," and "Endogenous Technological Change"; A. K. Dixit and J. E. Stiglitz, "Monopolistic Competition and Optimum Product Diversity," *American Economic Review* 67 (June 1977): 297–308.

but not for detailed intervention. The general equilibrium and the external economies models offer normative support for extended market size only if the range of increased returns remains nonexhausted after internal corrections for market failures. Only the positive feedback model seems to be normatively silent in this respect. Would world well-being have been improved or worsened by the imagined but not experienced integration of separated economies, each of which, alternatively, developed their own technological history? Will the imagined integrated Europe of 2050 be more or less productive of value than a Europe of separately exclusive national economies?

Who Cares Whether the Commons
Are Privatized?

Neoclassical welfare economics contains precise definitions of the necessary conditions that must be satisfied in order to meet the criteria of efficiency or optimality in the allocation and use of scarce resources. Failure to satisfy any of these conditions implies a shortfall in economic value below that which might be produced, with value being measured by the ultimate evaluations of the individual participants in the whole economic nexus. From this elementary base, economists, generally, have inferred that overall value maximization, that is, efficiency or optimality, is an appropriate welfare objective, in the sense that it allows for appropriately qualified normative judgements in the comparisons among alternative institutional structures. The Pareto construction, and perhaps especially as this is amended to incorporate Wicksellian agreement as the necessary epistemological test, allows economists to translate the whole neoclassical exercise into meaningful hypotheses about individual expressions of support for institutional changes.[1]

Individuals in their roles as generalized consumers are presumed to be interested in the satisfaction of the efficiency norm, since this result ensures that the most highly valued bundle of end-items for final use is made available from any given expenditure of resources. From this interest, it is presumed that individuals, as consumers, will positively support reforms that aim at maximizing total product value in some aggregate sense. Some neo-

From *Post-Socialist Political Economy: Selected Essays* (Cheltenham, U.K.: Edward Elgar, 1997), 160–67. Reprinted by permission of the publisher.

1. See James M. Buchanan, "Positive Economics, Welfare Economics, and Political Economy," *Journal of Law and Economics* 2 (1959): 124–38, and "The Relevance of Pareto Optimality," *Journal of Conflict Resolution* 6 (1962): 341–54.

classical economists have elevated the presumed welfare of the nonspecialized consumer to independent criterial significance in the evaluation of policy proposals.[2]

Especially since the development of public-choice theory, economists have recognized that individuals' interests as consumers need not track their interests as producers, and that, due to the presumed greater specialization among persons in their producer roles, generalized support for efficiency in resource use may not find expression in politicized decision structures. That is to say, politically expressed preferences may not suggest to legislators that economic efficiency, as such, finds much constituency support.

In this chapter, I shall challenge a basic presupposition in this familiar chain of neoclassical and public-choice, welfare logic—a challenge which, if accepted, will weaken still further the presumption that aggregative efficiency in resource use is a politically viable objective alternative to the more obvious separated interests of producer groups. I shall suggest here that within the neoclassical analytical framework such aggregative efficiency is not necessarily an economic interest to individuals, *even in their roles as generalized consumers-producers*, quite apart from differential interests in market restrictions. That is to say, even if we could supervene or otherwise neglect the revealed preferences of persons who act in furtherance of their specialized roles as producers, there may remain situations which observing economists classify to be demonstrably inefficient but which do not, in any sense, provoke the reform interests of persons as generalized consumers-producers. The second section presents these results through the use of a familiar and highly simplified set of examples of commons overusage.

If the results can be generalized to apply to relevant barriers to allocative efficiency over and beyond those that are normally discussed under the "tragedy of the commons" rubric, the analysis would seem to suggest that generalized individual interest in, and support for, efficiency-enhancing schemes for reform may require the satisfaction of specific distributional criteria. The third section examines these issues. The central proposition that efficiency as a normative objective for reform will not secure widespread support in the

---

2. See William H. Hutt, *Economists and the Public: A Study of Competition and Opinion* (London: Jonathan Cape, 1936).

absence of these distributional requirements, depends critically, however, on acceptance of the analytical framework of neoclassical economic theory. The fourth section relates the whole exercise to the relevant underlying presuppositions of neoclassical theory and demonstrates that a particular change in these presuppositions may restore the efficiency support inferences that economists tend to draw from their constructions.

Back to Basics: Some Deer-Beaver Analytics

We can scarcely do better than return to Adam Smith and to examine his model of the deer-beaver economy with the purpose of assessing support for efficiency as a policy norm.[3] Let us suppose that the long-run equilibrium or natural price ratio is two deer for one beaver, which reflects relative input costs: one day's labour to kill a deer, two day's labour to kill a beaver. Persons are homogeneous, both in endowments and in preferences, and labour is the only factor. The input-output relationships are assumed to be invariant over the relevant margins of production. They do not rule out, however, the presence of commons phenomena over certain areas of the forest. Assume that persons (who are equally adept as deer or beaver hunters, although there is clear advantage to specialization) are allowed to choose freely between the two productive activities. And further assume that the whole forest remains open to all hunters, whether of deer or beaver. There is no ownership of the forest, or any part thereof. But suppose now that there exists a relatively small glen, within the larger forest, where deer abound, and that hunting deer in this part of the forest is much more productive, over some initial ranges of use, than elsewhere. Deer hunters will rationally exploit the opportunities of the glen so long as the net returns from their outlay exceeds that attainable from other parts of the forest. In familiar terms, the productive glen is a scarce resource, and if it is treated as if it is not, usage will be extended to the point at which its total value is dissipated. We have here a classic example of the tragedy of the commons imbedded inframarginally within Smith's classic illustration.

Aggregate value in this simple economy can be increased by privatizing

---

3. Adam Smith, *The Wealth of Nations* (1776; reprint, Modern Library edition, New York: Random House, 1937).

the ownership of the glen. Suppose, now, that some person, anyone, claims an ownership right, encloses the glen and charges fees for hunting deer. Overall efficiency in the economy increases; a resource that was valueless as used earlier now produces value.[4]

But who gains from the enhanced efficiency with which resources are now utilized? Note particularly that consumers, as such, do not gain, since the price vector does not change. One beaver still exchanges for two deer; both absolute and relative prices are unchanged by the efficiency-enhancing privatization. Individuals, in their roles as producers, neither gain nor lose. In the commons equilibrium, the overexploitation of the glen was such that the returns were equalized on the more productive and the less productive parts of the forest. The gains from privatization accrue solely and exclusively to the person or persons who are successful in seizing, or otherwise securing, the ownership rights. The owner or owners secure the full value produced by the efficient usage of the scarce resource. No other persons in the economy, regardless of their roles as consumers and/or producers, gain. But it is important to recognize also that, if we neglect short-run adjustments, no one loses either. Consumers or producers neither lose nor gain from the privatization. Basically, the stance of persons who fully understand, articulate and express their economic interest, strictly speaking, should be one of indifference towards proposals to privatize the commons.

Even within the confines of this extremely simplified model, the analysis suggests that support for institutional change that takes the form of privatization of resources previously used in common may be very narrowly limited, although opposition to such change may also not be widespread. If, however, persons are less than fully informed about the workings of the economy, if personal envy affects individual attitudes or if there should exist elements of human capital specialized to the use of the commons, we should expect that these modifications in the model would find expression in opposition to rather than support for privatization.

Widespread or general support in favour of privatization as an institutional reform would seem to be forthcoming only if large numbers of persons could somehow be brought within the group that shares the benefits of

4. See Frank H. Knight, "Fallacies in the Interpretation of Social Cost," *Quarterly Journal of Economics* 38 (1924): 582–606.

ownership, as these might be capitalized upon the act of establishing such ownership. I shall return to this point later.

Economists will perhaps criticize the restrictiveness of the elementary Smithean model. The privatization of marginally irrelevant commons may be acknowledged to generate little if any generalized interests on the part of consumers and/or producers, despite the efficiency-enhancing results of such privatization. But, say the economists, values are set at the margins, and the whole analysis may be inapplicable to privatization in settings where margins are affected.

We may readily modify the Smithean setting to examine the efficacy of this possible criticism. Under the same general assumptions, let us now suppose that, as before, a beaver can be produced upon the outlay of two days' labour, and that this input-output relationship remains constant over all possible ranges of supply. Suppose, however, that a comparable production relationship does not characterize deer production. From the outset of production, assume that deer are produced under increasing costs. As more units are produced, the outlay per unit, measured in labour time, increases.

In this case, the whole forest becomes the overly exploited commons for the hunting of deer while it remains without value for the hunting of beaver. If there is no ownership, deer hunters will enter into production so long as the net return per day's labour exceeds or equals that in the production of beaver. A day's labour in deer must, therefore, yield the value equivalent of one-half a beaver in equilibrium. In orthodox efficiency terms, in the commons solution there will be too many persons hunting deer relative to beaver. Upon privatization of the forest for deer production, the rational owner (owners) will commence to charge fees for deer-hunting permits. Fewer persons will produce deer; the quantity of deer produced may decrease, stay the same or increase, depending on the location of the pre- and post-privatization equilibria on the production frontier. In the post-privatization equilibrium, the relative price of deer may increase, stay the same or decrease.[5]

---

5. The indeterminacy here stems from the shift in the production frontier that privatization, and subsequent optimal usage of the now valued resource, represents. For a general discussion, even if on a somewhat different point, see Charles J. Goetz and James M. Buchanan, "External Diseconomies in Competitive Supply," *American Economic Review* 61 (1971): 883–90.

In this model, the determinacy of the equilibrium price ratio is, of course, no longer present. We cannot predict how many deer will exchange for one beaver either before or after ownership is established; the price ratio, in either case, will depend on both the relative demands and the relative costs of the two goods. Privatization, of course, will increase aggregative value; the previously nonvalued resource will be optimally combined with complementary inputs in production; the newly established owner (owners) of the scarce resource will secure the full value of its addition to the economy's total product.

But what can we say about support for efficiency-enhancing privatization in this setting? It is no longer so easy to separate consumer and producer roles, especially when we recognize that there is a second productive resource—land for deer production—that affects valuation at the relevant margins of adjustment. The presence of constant input costs in production of one of the goods provides a base that anchors the productivity of this input, labour. Under the assumptions of the model, a day's labour can never be valued (in equilibrium) more highly than one-half a beaver, whether employed in deer or beaver production, so long as both goods are demanded in the final equilibrium. But privatization will reduce inputs into deer production and may increase, leave unchanged or even decrease the relative price of deer. At issue is whether the deer-beaver bundle that is purchased by the worker-consumer, who is not an owner, will be valued at a higher or lower total than the bundle purchased before privatization.

We know, of course, that the economy, considered as a whole, is more efficient after privatization, and that a larger value of goods is produced. Ratios between marginal rates of substitution in production are brought into equality with ratios between marginal rates of substitution in consumption, and the production possibility frontier for the whole economy is shifted outward by the change. But the economy cannot be considered as a unit for purposes of my exercise in this chapter. Disaggregation is necessary, and particularly as between the owner (owners) of the valuable resource (land in deer production) that is privatized and others who remain strictly as workers-consumers.

I suggest that the results attained from analysis of the first model carry over to this model, although formal proof might be difficult to present. In any case, I leave such proof (or disproof) to others. The intuitively convincing logic is, however, straightforward. Workers-consumers who do not share in the newly created value of ownership are faced with an incentive structure, which takes the form of rental prices for use of the land for deer production, that guarantees efficient allocation of labour as between the two goods. The rental value of the land in deer production will be equal to its marginal product, evaluated in the post-privatization equilibrium price ratio. Workers, in either deer or beaver production, will earn their marginal product, and payment of land rentals and wages will exhaust total value produced in the economy. The latter result holds so long as we maintain the neoclassical postulate of constant returns to scale. And there is nothing within the example here to suggest departure from this postulate.[6]

But will the worker-consumer who does not share in the newly created ownership value be better or worse off than before privatization? The marginal value product of a day's labour will, of course, be higher. But the relevant comparison is that between marginal value product, evaluated at the post-privatization equilibrium ratio of prices, and the *average value product*, evaluated at the pre-privatization equilibrium ratio. And there seems no way, *a priori*, to make this comparison, since, as noted earlier, the price ratio may move in either direction or remain unchanged. The possible effects on the economic position of the worker-consumer who does not share in the value of land ownership would seem, in any case, to be of the second order of smalls and would not be sufficiently important to motivate expressions of support or opposition. Nonowners, therefore, will tend to be relatively indifferent as to privatization when proposed as an institutional reform, although, as noted with reference to the first model, they will perhaps tilt towards opposition as we depart from presumptions of full information, no specificity and complete rationality.[7]

Distributional Constraints in Efficiency Gains

The criteria for allocative efficiency are not affected, of course, by the simple point that the examples are designed to demonstrate. Since aggregate eco-

---

6. In this setting, the constant-returns postulate would seem to be "innocuous" in the sense noted in Edward C. Prescott and Rajnish Mehra, "Recursive Competitive Equilibrium: The Case of Homogeneous Households," *Econometrica* 48 (1980): 1365–67, especially p. 1367.

7. Implicitly, I have assumed that a resource-using public sector does not exist. If public goods are collectively supplied and collectively financed, or if collective transfers are present, the results will be modified.

nomic value is increased by any removal of barriers to efficient resource use, there must exist some structure of institutional reform that will increase the well-being of some members of the relevant community while damaging no one. The efficiency-enhancing privatization of the commons may not benefit nonowners, generally, but neither does it cause them harm. The net beneficiaries are those who secure the ownership rights, regardless of how these rights are assigned. And, in the examples, there is a once-and-for-all increase in present value attributable to the attainment of ownership of the value-producing resource, which carries the authority to control usage.

Those persons who apply their resources to the use of the commons before privatization may neither gain nor lose from the shift to private ownership (save in the short run), despite the fact that, post-ownership, they face rental fees for usage. By construction, in equilibrium these users earn competitive rates of returns on their outlay either before or after the establishment of private ownership. In one sense, no one in the community bears or suffers the incidence of the inefficiency that the absence of private ownership creates. The loss is to be reckoned here only in terms of foregone opportunities rather than consciously sensed damages or harms. On the other hand, the restriction of the usage of a facility, through pricing or otherwise, that was previously available on some unrestricted basis, may be opposed, in part, irrationally, especially if users consider that the rights have been arbitrarily assigned. In this setting, in particular, envy may emerge to tilt the balance towards maintenance of the *status quo* tragedy of the commons. Such a prospect, which may well loom large in real situations, suggests that some Wicksellian test should be incorporated into early considerations of institutional change, and that users of the relevant resource to be privatized be assigned at least some share in the value created by privatization.

The analysis prompts an interesting question: Who "owns" the commons? Who has an ethical claim to the value that the scarce resource could produce but which is not being produced? All members of the community, as politically organized? The state, as such? All who participate in the production-exchange-consumption nexus? Users of the commons? Consumers of the goods produced on the commons? A more relevant question might be, how can privatization of the commons take place at all? The ownership rights have value, and anyone who has the authority to assign these rights has the means to capture this value.[8] And will not the prospect of securing such authority itself set off rent-seeking investment that may, in some limiting cases, dissipate in advance the net efficiency gains from the establishment of ownership rights?

The whole analysis suggests that the standard economists' concentration on the efficiency-enhancing properties of privatization is not sufficient independently to carry much weight in discussions of institutional reform. The distribution of the value of the ownership rights to be created becomes important in generating the required political support for any efficiency-enhancing proposal. Efficiency *per se* must be replaced by efficiency "for whom." Some of the implications are clear. Proposals to privatize scarce facilities through auction, with funds collected from successful bidders to be used either to reduce taxes or to expand public programme benefits, tend to ensure wide sharing in the value created by the reform. Proposals to assign ownership rights directly to users may or may not succeed in stimulating sufficiently broad support for effective privatization. Proposals to assign newly created ownership rights to the "managers," to that small set of persons who have acted in supervisory roles in the collective enterprise that has been described to contain elements of the commons tragedy, will almost surely fail to find support beyond a very narrow constituency, despite the promised efficiency gains. Distribution as well as allocation matters.

Restoring Efficiency as a Supportable Policy Norm

If we restrict analyses of economies to the limits imposed by the presuppositions of neoclassical theory, efficiency, as such, seems to have quite limited authority, on its own and independent of distributional considerations. But it is important to recognize that we need not be bound by the conventional limits of neoclassical theory, and that efficiency may emerge as a broadly supportable policy norm, quite independent of distributional constraints, under some modifications in the presuppositions of this theory. In particular, I refer to the constant-returns postulate that is required to prove the allocative efficiency of competitive equilibrium. If we substitute the postulate

---

8. See James M. Buchanan, "The Coase Theorem and the Theory of the State," *Natural Resources Journal* 13 (1973): 579–94 for an elaboration of this argument.

of economy-wide and generalized increasing returns for that of constant returns, we can derive a logic of generalized support for the efficiency gains that privatization of the commons creates, quite apart from distributional limits, even if, at the same time, we must perforce abandon the central theorems of neoclassical welfare economics, as these are normally discussed.

The establishment of ownership rights adds to value in the economy and, in the orthodox logic, the increment to value accrues primarily, if not solely, to those who secure these rights. But suppose we depart from the constant-returns postulate and consider a many-good economy that is described by economy-wide and generalized increasing returns; a larger production-exchange nexus ensures that the value of output produced per unit of input increases as the economy expands. In this case, all persons in the economy, and not only newly established owners of valued resources previously used as commons, will secure some indirect gain consequent on the expansion in the size of the economy that the value of the resource represents. Even if they secure no direct share in the ownership, and hence in the imputed value therefrom, persons will find that, in the larger economy that emerges as resources are more effectively utilized, input-output ratios move in their favour. There will exist a generalized interest in economic efficiency in the large—an interest which should translate ultimately into politically expressed support.

The whole exercise suggests that orthodox treatment of the whole set of related issues that can be brought under the tragedy of the commons dilemma, along with the efficiency gains promised by privatization, may have been flawed by an unquestioned adherence to the postulates of neoclassical economic theory. In this, as in other areas of current relevance and importance, modern economists need to examine some of the implications of these neoclassical postulates.[9] When and if they do so, they may find it necessary to rethink, and possibly to reconstruct, some of the foundations of their discipline.

---

9. In my own case, it was my stubborn refusal to accept the neoclassical implications that the quantity of effort supplied by others exerts no effect on my own welfare that eventually led me into the necessary abandonment of the constant-returns postulate. See James M. Buchanan and Yong J. Yoon, eds., *The Return to Increasing Returns* (Ann Arbor: University of Michigan Press, 1994), which contains all of the important contributions in the increasing-returns tradition, from Adam Smith through to modern theories of endogenous growth.

PART SEVEN

Economic Theory in a Postsocialist World

Asymmetrical Reciprocity in Market Exchange
Implications for Economies in Transition

I. Introduction

Western visitors to those parts of the world that before 1991 were politically organized as the Soviet Union have been impressed by the attitudes of persons toward behavior in ordinary exchanges, attitudes that seem to be so different from those in Western economies. The essential elements of an "exchange culture" seem to be missing, and this absence, in itself, may be central to the effective functioning of market economies.[1] Individual participants in ordinary exchange relationships in Western economies act as if they understand the simplest of all economic principles, namely, that there are mutual gains from trade, that the benefits are reciprocal, that exchange is a positive-sum game. This "as if" understanding, which remains perhaps below our level of consciousness in the West, is largely missing from the public attitudes of citizens of the former Soviet Union, who behave as if the gains from trade do not exist, or at least are one-sided rather than mutual.

There is a familiar story that illustrates the thesis: "In the Soviet Union, both parties to an exchange lose; one party loses the goods; the other party

From *Social Philosophy and Policy* 10 (Summer 1993): 51–64. Reprinted by permission of the publisher.

I am indebted to my colleague Roger Congleton for helpful discussions.

1. See James M. Buchanan, "Tacit Presuppositions of Political Economy: Implications for Societies in Transition" (George Mason University, Fairfax, Va.: Center for Study of Public Choice, 1991, mimeographed). The present essay builds on, extends, and modifies the arguments of this earlier paper.

loses the money." This statement may offer a concise, if exaggerated, summary of the general attitude toward exchange that seems to describe the behavior of many (of course, not all) persons in the republics that were formerly parts of the Soviet Union.

In this essay, I propose to offer an *economic* explanation for some of the differences in behavioral attitudes that we observe, as between Western economies and those of the Eurasian republics. In the West, with developed market systems, economists concentrate initial attention on the mutuality of trading gains and on the *reciprocity* in any exchange relationship. And a recognition of this reciprocity seems to inform public participation in markets. What is often overlooked is the asymmetry in the reciprocal relationship between buyer and seller in developed money economies. The buyer of goods and/or services who offers, or "sells," money in exchange possesses a bargaining advantage that is often overlooked. The central-command economy reverses the direction of advantage, even when exchange dealings are permitted. The differences in the incentives that confront participants in the two organizational settings generate predictable differences in observed behavior and in behavioral attitudes.

I should stress at the outset that my focus is exclusively on the economic, as opposed to the ideological, sources of explanation of observed behavior in the exchange process. The ideological denigration of market exchange, as a general system of organizing economic relationships, may have exerted influences on individual behavior over and beyond those analyzed here. And, of course, at some higher system level where organizational-institutional decisions on structure were made, ideological motivation may explain why persons were confronted with the circumstances that contain divergent economic incentives.

In Section II, I introduce the formal analysis by reference to the workings of an idealized model of a barter economy in the absence of transactions costs. This model is introduced solely for the purpose of comparison with the workings of a money economy, still idealized, but as made minimally necessary by the presence of transactions costs. This second model is examined in Section III. In Section IV, I identify the asymmetry in the reciprocal exchange relationship, even in the idealized money economy, and I indicate observable features of Western economies that do not falsify the hypothesis that such an asymmetry exists. Section V takes the obvious next step and extends the analysis to the command economy that does not allow full scope for the operation of the institutions of market exchange. The results suggest that the behavioral roles of participants in such economies may become quite different from those in market cultures. In Section VI, I discuss some of the implications of the analysis for problems of transition from a command to a market structure.

II. Idealized Exchange—A Pure Barter Economy

Consider a setting in which the exchange process operates ideally, in the analytical-conceptual sense and beyond any feasibility limits imposed by the limits to human capacities. Persons enter into exchange dealings, one with another, in the full knowledge of all potential trading opportunities. Further, the exchange network, the economy, is sufficiently large such that, for each and every buyer or seller in the market for each and every good or service, input or output, there exist large numbers of sellers or buyers, among whom any single buyer or seller may choose. Finally, there are no costs incurred by any buyer or seller in shifting custom from one alternative to another.

Note that in such an idealized, zero-transactions-cost setting no person, whether buyer or seller, in any exchange relationship secures any differential gain from exchanging with the single seller or buyer with whom a particular exchange is effectuated. Neither party's action, in making the particular cross-market transfer, generates benefits for the other, for the simple reason that alternative buyers or sellers, to whom trade may be shifted, are available at no cost. Gain emerges, of course, to any person, whether buyer or seller, from the availability of or access to "the market," without which grossly inefficient self-production would be necessary.

For my purpose, the noteworthy feature of this idealized model is the implied behavioral indifference that each participant in the exchange network will exhibit toward those with whom exchanges are made. In such a setting, nothing that might be called an "exchange culture" would have meaning. Each participant may, if he or she chooses, behave as if he or she exists in total independence of others, despite the complete interdependence among all persons who participate in the inclusive network. No buyer need invest any effort in persuading, cajoling, or convincing any seller to offer goods and services, and no seller, similarly, will find it rational to try to persuade any buyer to take his wares off the shelf. The reason is straightforward: there exists a sufficiently large number of alternative sellers or buyers to insure that, if one person does not trade, a replacement immediately appears to whom trade can be shifted and at no differential cost.

III. Idealized Exchange with Money

I now propose to modify the idealized exchange model described in Section II in only one respect. Assume, as before, that there are no costs of making exchanges, and that all participants have full knowledge about the qualities of goods. Further, assume, again as before, that the economy is large, and that there are many sellers and many buyers in the market for each good and service. Assume now, however, that there are limits to the knowledge that any participant has about the location of those persons in the economy who seek to purchase precisely the same good he or she seeks to sell, and vice versa. That is to say, direct barter is costly in the sense that each participant in a potential trade must undergo some search effort in locating the desired matching trading partner.

Recognition of the costs of search that make direct barter inefficient provides an economic explanation for the emergence of money, either in the form of some good that comes to be widely accepted as a medium of general exchange through some process of cultural evolution, or in the form of some good or some symbolic representation, the value of which is guaranteed by the collective body that protects private property, that is, by the state. The existence of money allows sellers to eliminate costly searches for other persons who are themselves sellers of goods that are desired in exchange. Similarly, money allows buyers to purchase goods that they desire without the necessity of searching for persons who seek to buy precisely that which they offer in exchange as sellers. The familiar metaphor that refers to money as the lubricant of the exchange system is helpfully explanatory.

Under the severely restrictive conditions assumed to exist, however, the behaviorally relevant conclusions reached above with reference to the idealized exchange economy seem to continue to hold. Since there are many buyers and many sellers in the markets for any good or service, any input or output, the individual participant need not be at all concerned about the person with whom an exchange is effectuated. The seller of red shoes need not invest in efforts to convince potential buyers to purchase his stocks since, by definition, there exist alternative buyers who will purchase the stocks and with no cost to the seller. Similarly, the buyer of red apples need not invest in attempts to persuade any single apple seller to offer his wares, since, again by definition, there exist many alternative apple sellers to whom the apple buyer may turn and without cost. There is no economic basis for the emergence of any attitude other than behavioral indifference toward specifically identified cross-exchange partners.

IV. Asymmetrical Reciprocity

The summary analysis of the preceding paragraph is, I submit, incorrect at worst and misleading at best. The introduction of money, even under idealized settings for the operation of an exchange economy, modifies the presumed anonymity, and consequent symmetry, in the pairwise buyer-seller relationship; and this modification has important behavioral implications.

Consider, again, the working properties of an idealized money economy. Figure 1 reproduces the familiar "wheel of income" diagram from introductory textbooks in economics. The individual at *A*, who either possesses or produces a good or service (perhaps an input into some process) that is not desired for his own or internal use, enters one market as a seller of that good or service, which we may call *X*. If we ignore sequencing here, we can say that this individual simultaneously enters another market as a buyer of that good or service (or bundle of goods and services) that is desired for final end use; say this good or service is *Y*. The individual in question is a supplier of *X* and a demander of *Y*, in the two separated markets.

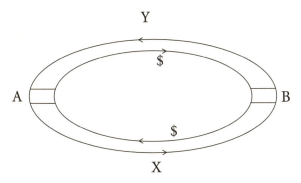

Figure 1. Wheel of income

A person cannot, however, enter unilaterally in any market. The reciprocity relationship requires that each participant in an exchange enter simultaneously as buyer and seller. The individual identified above as the seller-supplier of X and the buyer-demander of Y enters the market for X and the market for Y in the necessary reciprocal positions as a buyer-demander of money (\$) in the X market, and a seller-supplier of money in the Y market. The generalized or fully fungible good, money, becomes the intermediate instrument of value that allows the individual entry into the two markets of his ultimate interest.

The asymmetry enters when we recognize that the money side of any exchange has an inherent "transactions costs" advantage, which in turn improves the "bargaining" power of the person who takes such a role. Consider, once again, a pure barter economy without money, but with some limits on knowledge. Clearly, the person who possesses or produces a good that is, relatively, more generally desired than others will find it less costly to effectuate exchanges for whatever good he ultimately desires. Money becomes the limiting case of a good that is generally desired by all participants in the exchange network, even if not intrinsically but instrumentally. The trader who accepts money for units of any nonmoney good or service secures a nonspecific medium of value that facilitates reentry into any market. The ideal fungibility of money gives the supplier-seller of money an asymmetrical claim to the gains from exchange. By the very definition of what money is, the possessor, and hence potential supplier, of money faces lower transactions costs in completing any exchange than the possessor, and potential supplier, of any nonmoney good or service. The fungibility of money provides the possessor with enhanced power to "walk away" from any exchange for goods and services, a power that the possessor of any nonmoney good or service simply does not have.

The basic asymmetry in the money-goods exchange is obscured by the proclivity of economic theorists to "define away" the features of the exchange process that are sometimes of most interest. As noted, if transactions costs were, literally, defined away, there would be no need for money at all; the pure barter economy would operate with ideal efficiency. When the rigorous assumptions required for the working of a pure barter economy are modified, however, and money is recognized to be an efficiency-enhancing institution, attempts are made to idealize the operations of the money economy by postulating that each and every buyer and seller, whether of goods or money, faces a sufficiently large number of cross-exchange options to guarantee that no person has market or exchange power, in the differential sense instanced above. Once transactions costs are introduced at all, however, there seems to be no plausibly acceptable logic for refusing to acknowledge differentials in "bargaining" advantages as between those persons who enter markets as suppliers-sellers of money and those who enter as demanders-buyers. To put the same proposition conversely, it is the demanders-buyers of goods and services that have an asymmetrical advantage over the suppliers-sellers, and in all markets.

As we move away from the abstracted models for the working of a production-exchange economy and toward a more descriptively satisfying appreciation of the economy as it actually seems to function, the basic asymmetry identified here may become painfully obvious, and my whole discussion may be taken to represent trituration. I suggest, however, that the money-goods asymmetry assists in an understanding of much of the behavior that we observe in developed economies, both historically and currently. The institutions of market exchange, as we know them, incorporate a recognition of this asymmetry, even to the extent that their familiarity breeds analytical oversight.

In markets as we know them, sellers of goods and services peddle their wares, advertise, create attractive displays, adopt attitudes of deferential demeanor toward potential buyers, and behave, generally, as if their customers' interests are their own. "We aim to please"—this slogan describes the attitudes of those traders on the goods-and-services side of the goods-money exchanges, rather than vice versa. And we should find ourselves surprised if this behavior were absent. We do not observe buyers of goods and services setting up their own market stalls with signs that read "we buy apples," except in unusual circumstances. In product markets, we see some, but not much, buyer advertising. Potential buyers of goods and services apparently feel under no compulsion to act as if the interests of a seller are of relevance. Such buyers remain behaviorally indifferent toward the interests of any identified seller.[2]

---

2. Labor markets may seem to offer an exception to the generalizations suggested here. Sellers of labor (a service) sometimes advertise their availability, but more often it is buyers of labor (employers) who advertise to attract sellers. The absence of homogeneity

The distinction between the two sides of the money-goods exchange stressed here does not depend on the pricing institutions that are in place. In developed economies, sellers tend to offer their wares to potential buyers at quasi-fixed prices, and the latter remain free to purchase varying quantities. In many developing economies, by contrast, sellers do not fix prices in advance, save as some preliminary move in what becomes a complex bargaining game with buyers. In both sets of pricing arrangements, however, we observe sellers-suppliers in the active roles of seekers for potential buyers and investors in efforts at persuasion, rather than the opposite.

The asymmetry stressed here is, of course, implicitly recognized in the usage of the term "consumers' sovereignty" to describe the exchange economy. This term, which might be better replaced by "buyers' sovereignty," suggests that sellers of goods and services, or suppliers, are and must be responsive to the interests of buyers, and, hence, that the latter are the ultimate sources of evaluation. Conventional discussion of the consumers'-sovereignty feature of market economies does not, however, take much note of the relevant behavioral implications.

An alternative way of discussing the asymmetry in the money-goods exchange relationship is to introduce the differential specificity of valued assets, as held by each party prior to exchange. Whether we analyze a pure exchange economy, in which persons commence with determinate endowments of goods, or a production-exchange economy, in which persons commence with endowments of talents that may be organized to produce goods, the potential supplier in any exchange for money is, by definition, locked in, relatively, by the specificity of the valued asset in possession, pre-exchange, and, for this reason, is more vulnerable to terms-of-trade manipulation than the potential cross-exchange demander, whose pre-exchange valued asset takes the form of money.[3]

---

among separate units demanded (that is, the variation in skills and qualifications among potential employees) may offset, or even reverse, the direction of effect emphasized here generally.

3. The relationship between differential asset specificity as between parties to contract, and the vulnerability to opportunistic behavior, has been discussed by Armen Alchian and Susan Woodward, "Reflections on the Theory of the Firm," *Journal of Institutional Theoretical Economics* (*Z. Ges. Staatswiss*) 143, no. 1 (1987): 110–37.

V. Asymmetry Inversion in Command Economies

How would it be possible to remove or even to reverse the asymmetry in the basic exchange relationship in an economy? Reversion to a system of barter through some prohibition of a generalized money medium could remove the asymmetry here, but only at the expense of gross inefficiencies occasioned by the costs of search. In such an economy—one without money but with transactions costs—each market participant is both a buyer and a seller of goods (services), and there is no generalized advantage to either side of an exchange. As noted earlier, there would be a particularized advantage to either the buyer or seller of the goods that are in relatively wider usage in the economy.

Let us consider, now, an economy in which money has been introduced, but where money is not, in itself, a sufficient medium to insure the effectuation of an exchange. Such an economy would be described by money prices for goods, but accompanied by some set of complementary nonmonetary "prices," or arrangements, that would be required to complete a transaction. The nominal money prices for goods and services would be politically established—and at a level below those prices that would clear markets, that would equate demand and supply. Straightforward public-choice analysis of the incentives of persons in bureaucratic authority to set money prices suggests that such prices will remain always below market-clearing levels.[4] Bureaucrats lose any rationing authority if prices are set at market-clearing levels, and such authority is desired both for its own sake and as a source for the extraction of favors (rents). There will tend to exist excess demands for the supplies of goods brought forth in all markets. Each seller will tend to face more demanders for his product than can possibly be satisfied.

In such a setting, any reason that a seller-supplier might have for acting as if he is motivated by the interests of buyers is absent. Sellers will be behav-

---

More generally, economists have analyzed the effects of asymmetric information in the operation of exchange. The pioneer in these efforts was George Akerlof, "The Market for 'Lemons': Quality Uncertainty and the Market Mechanism," *Quarterly Journal of Economics* 84 (August 1970): 488–500.

4. David Levy, "The Bias in Centrally Planned Prices," *Public Choice* 67, no. 3 (December 1990): 213–26.

iorally indifferent toward each and all potential buyers; they will have no incentive to please particular buyers, not even to the extent of providing quality merchandise, since there will always be buyers ready and willing to purchase whatever is made available to them.

Consider, by contrast, the behavioral stance of the participant who enters the exchange relationship as a potential buyer, who possesses a stock of money in the hope of securing goods and services. Each person in such a role will face the frustration experienced in an inability to get the goods in the quantities desired, and of the quality standards wanted. Buyers, with money, become the residual claimants to the gains from exchange, a role that is directly contrary to that which buyers occupy in the well-functioning money economy, as analyzed earlier. "Buyers' sovereignty," which was mentioned earlier as a shorthand description of the central feature of the exchange economy, is replaced by "sellers' sovereignty," provided we are careful to include within the "sellers" category those persons who hold bureaucratic authority to establish arrangements for nonprice rationing among demanders of goods and services.

In the command economy, as sketched out in capsule here, buyers of goods and services become the supplicants, who must curry favor with the sellers and their agents, who must, somehow, "aim to please," over and beyond some mere offer of generalized purchasing power in the form of money. Sellers remain indifferent to the pleas of buyers, and not only because of the excess number of demanders. Sellers also realize that if they exchange goods for money, they, too, must return to other markets, as buyers, who must, in turn, expect to encounter the frustrations of buyers throughout the system.

The chronic "shortage" of goods that describes the workings of the command economy stems directly from the imposed politicization of money prices, as does the generalized supplication of buyers toward sellers-suppliers, including the relevant members of the bureaucratic apparatus. The institution of money, as such, is not allowed to serve its standard efficiency-enhancing function. The nonprice rationing arrangements, which emerge as supplementary to money prices, become analogous, in their economic effects, to the search costs that barter involves in the absence of money.

The command economy, with politicized money prices, along with supplementary rationing arrangements, will be characterized by a "money overhang," that is, by a supply of money that is in excess of that which is needed in exchange transactions, at the politically set money prices. Indeed, without such "money overhang" the authority that is exercised by the whole price central regime loses its "bite." Unless potential consumers-buyers are provided with more money (through wage payments) than they can spend on products, at the controlled prices, the authority of bureaucrats to ration scarce supplies becomes unnecessary. This excess money supply, in its turn, sets up additional incentives for the emergence of exchange transactions that are outside the boundaries of legitimacy in some formal sense. Black, shadow, or underground markets will emerge more readily when persons are unable to satisfy their demands for goods through standard exchange channels and when they have available, at the same time, unused and unusable stocks of money. As this shadow sector increases in size over time, as measured either by the volume of transactions or by the number of participants, the behavioral norms that describe the operation of the whole legal order must be undermined.

The fact that money is not allowed fully to perform its efficiency-enhancing role in the economy must also set in motion evolutionary pressures toward the emergence of some good that will secure general acceptability as "real money," quite distinct from the money issued by the state monopoly. In Russia, and in other former socialist economies, the currency of developed nations (dollars, marks, Swiss francs) has emerged to fill this role, at least in part. And, in the shadow exchanges between these monies and goods, the asymmetry observed in Western economies is partially restored. Sellers of goods do, indeed, seek out and court potential buyers who are thought to possess hard currencies.

This transitional stage aside, however, the point to be emphasized is that, in the command economy, as it traditionally functions, the whole economic culture is dramatically different from that which we observe in Western market economies. The near-total absence of seller-supplier efforts to attract custom and to please potential buyers shocks Western observers who visit the territories of the former Soviet Union. The paucity of billboards in the Moscow of 1990 was not primarily attributable to regulatory prohibition. This result emerged directly from the fact that no seller-supplier of any good or service felt any economic pressure to respond to customer interests or to expand the demands for products. The sales clerk at the kiosk, as a selling agent, behaved very differently from her Western counterpart, but not because of ethnic origins; she behaved differently because in the Russian mind-set that permeates the citizenry generally, the seller-purveyor of goods need not be concerned about customers.

The Russian visitor to the United States is equally surprised when the behavior of sellers-suppliers is observed, both directly and indirectly. Such a visitor is overwhelmed by the neon blazes, the multicolored billboards, the slick magazine pages, and the TV commercials, as well as behaviorally by the stance of those persons who act as agents for suppliers for almost all goods and services. Coming out of an economic culture where buyers are the universal supplicants, the Russian visitor stands aghast at the supplication of sellers and their agents. Neither this Russian visitor nor his American counterpart in Moscow understands that the dramatic differences in the two cultures can be explained, at least in large part, by variations in the incentive structures. The American setting allows the asymmetry in the money-goods exchange relationship to be played out fully in the development and operation of its market institutions. The Soviet Union, by contrast, attempted, throughout its existence, to counter this asymmetry by the politicization of money prices, with an acknowledged major increase in the costs of making transactions, but also with the unrecognized impetus given to the emergence and operation of an economic culture that must be subversive in any effort to move toward the market structure.

VI. Implications for the Transition from a Command to a Market Economy

This essay is not presented as a contribution to the explanation of how economies operate—either exchange (market) economies or command (socialized) economies. My emphasis is on and my interest is in the behavioral differences that the separate systems tend to motivate and to accentuate, differences that are readily observable, and on the implications of these differences for the problems of transition from a command to a market economy—the transition that the countries of Central and Eastern Europe now face.

In an earlier essay (see footnote 1), I concentrated attention on the apparent failure of participants in the socialist economy to recognize the reciprocal nature of the exchange relationship and the presence of mutuality of gain to all parties. I did not, of course, suggest that participants in the developed market economies of the West explicitly understand even this most elementary principle of economics and that a comparable understanding was missing in the command economies. I did suggest, however, that the basic principle of reciprocal exchange had come to inform the consciousness of many persons in Western economies, even if there seems to be little or no articulation of such a principle within the range of ordinary competence.

In that essay, which was advanced only in an exploratory fashion, as is this one, I attributed the absence of such an "exchange mentality" or mindset to the conjectural history that persons accept as descriptive of their social development. I suggested that in Western societies, and especially in the United States, the central notion of gains from trade emerges naturally from a historical imagination that traces economic and social development from family independence and self-sufficiency (the frontier homestead) through stages of increasing interdependence as specialization proceeds, always accompanied by increasing standards of living. In this imagined history, however, the exit option, the potential for withdrawal into independence, remains at the back edge of understanding and interpretation, thereby insuring that the expansion of trade and exchange must enhance well-being for all members of the society.

I suggested that participants in the former Soviet economy carried with them no such historical imagination of economic development, and that there was no comparable conjectural history of self-sufficient independence from which the economy emerged. Instead, cooperation was always imagined, not as achievement of mutual gains through exchange, but as taking place within a collective-community enterprise. Individual cooperative behavior, even as idealized, was modeled exclusively as the fulfilling of tasks assigned in a collective endeavor, assigned by some command authority. When I sketched the elements of my analysis to a Russian intellectual, he aptly described, and accepted, the thesis as, "the Russians are natural slaves; the Yankees are natural traders."

I see no reason to back off from or to withdraw the arguments made in my earlier essay; I remain convinced that the analysis contributes to an understanding of some of the difficulties in making the transition from a command to a market economy. I now think, however, that the arguments advanced in this essay supplement and extend those of the earlier essay usefully, and allow me to offer an economic explanation of some of the apparent differences in mindsets that need not be so critically dependent on a presumed divergence in historical imaginations. The importance of historical imagination may have been exerted at a more fundamental level than that discussed in the earlier essay. An imagination that is grounded on the liberty and independence of individual families might have proved a formidable barrier against collectivization of the economy. A "socialized United States" may never have been within the realm of the possible. History, and the historical imagination that it shapes, matters. And different national experiences may affect the feasibility of adaptation to different organizational structures. In the view of many observers, Poland's role in the revolution against the Communist regime was due, in part, to the historical position of the Catholic Church.

The possible oversight of the earlier treatment lay in my failure to appreciate that the "exchange mentality" that I took to be descriptive of Western attitudes toward markets generally, is manifested largely, even if not exclusively, in the observed activities of those who find themselves in roles as sellers-suppliers (or their agents) of goods and services, and that their behavior finds its origins, at least in part, in the asymmetry of the goods-money exchange. Conversely, I generalized the behavioral indifference of sellers or selling agents in the former Soviet Union to the whole culture, without noting that the structure within which exchanges take place removes incentives for sellers to behave in ways comparable to their Western counterparts.

Entrepreneurial or leadership roles in implementing exchanges-transfers of valued goods among persons and units in the command-control economies have been taken by those persons who possess differential access to nonmoney means of influencing choices, through personalized relationships, through extra-market barter arrangements, through sublegal bribes, payoffs, and kickbacks. In other words, the entrepreneurial talents that have been rewarded in the command economy, as it operated, were those of the "fixers" rather than those which might have represented some differential ability to recognize latent demand in nonexisting goods and to design and organize the production of such goods in response to such demand. In other words, there was little or no supply-side entrepreneurship, as such—in dramatic contrast with Western-style capitalist economies, where, at least in principle, such entrepreneurship should remain a dominant feature.

The entrepreneurship manifested in the activities of the "fixers" is not, of course, absent from Western economies, especially as these economies have developed to include large and rapidly growing socialized or public sectors. As governments have grown, in all dimensions, over the course of the century, there has been the developing recognition that private profits may be located in the exploitation of public as well as private opportunities.[5] Entrepreneurs who seek to capture the rents created by the artificially contrived scarcities stemming from politicized economic regulation, sometimes called "rent-seekers," are behaviorally similar to those that emerge in the more pervasive regulatory structure of command economies. We need only point to the thousands of lawyer-lobbyists whose activity consists exclusively in exploiting loopholes in the complexities of tax law and in seeking the creation of still further loopholes through new legislative changes.

The unanswered empirical question is whether or not the scarce set of entrepreneurial talents are generalizable over the two quite distinct roles. And the answer here will be critical for the problems of transition. Is a successful rent-seeker, who has demonstrated an adeptness at implementing value transfers in a regulated-politicized setting, likely to be equally successful when, as, and if the incentive structure shifts and success requires that attention be paid to organizing production to meet demands of consumers? Or do the distinct entrepreneurial roles require quite divergent talents? These questions stand as a challenge to my economist peers who place their primary reliance on direct empirical results.

My own intuition-interpretation suggests that the experience of the command economy, in which there has been little or no differential reward offered for supply-side creativity, will exert relatively long-lasting effects, and that the transition to a market economy will be made more difficult because of this absence of an entrepreneurial tradition. Those persons who have been skillful in responding to the disequilibria of the command structure may find the switch to the new role beyond their limits.

Entrepreneurs are, of course, emerging in the transition economies. Both

---

5. For a generalized discussion, see James M. Buchanan, Robert D. Tollison, and Gordon Tullock, eds., *Toward a Theory of the Rent-Seeking Society* (College Station: Texas A&M University Press, 1980), and especially my introductory paper, "Rent Seeking and Profit Seeking," pp. 3–15.

those who were and might have been the "fixers" and those who held positions of bureaucratic authority are moving to take advantage of the opportunities opened up by institutional changes. The question is not so much whether entrepreneurship will emerge as whether that which does emerge will prove sufficiently creative to stimulate the impoverished and sluggish economies in ways that may prove necessary to insure that the revolution's ultimate result will be positive.

A useful distinction may be made at this point between the Kirznerian and the Schumpeterian definitions of entrepreneurship, a distinction that has been the source of longstanding debates within the subdiscipline of Austrian economics. Israel Kirzner, who has long stressed the importance of the entrepreneurial function in an economy, models the entrepreneur as responding to disequilibria, essentially as an arbitrageur, who locates and exploits disparities in potential exchange values as among separate locations, persons, and production opportunities.[6] In this conceptualization of the entrepreneurial role, there should be relatively little difficulty encountered in transforming the "fixer" of the command economy into the equilibrating supply-side organizer of production and distribution in the operative market economy. By contrast, Joseph Schumpeter models the entrepreneur as a disequilibrating force, as a creator of destruction to established ways of doing things, as a disrupter of existing and predicted channels of exchange.[7] In this conceptualization, the supply-side entrepreneur acts quite differently from the arbitrageur, even if the latter is defined in the broadest possible terms. The entrepreneur creates that which does not exist independent of his or her action. To the extent that the ongoing market or capitalist economy is understood to be progressively created by Schumpeterian entrepreneurs, there can be no easy transition from the command system, quite independent of the institutional reforms that may be put in place.

Both types of entrepreneur can coexist as highly productive contributors to the successful transition toward market economies and to the growth of such

6. Israel Kirzner, *Competition and Entrepreneurship* (Chicago: University of Chicago Press, 1973).

7. Joseph A. Schumpeter, *Theorie der wirtschaftlichen Entwicklung* (Leipzig, 1912); English translation, *Theory of Economic Development* (Cambridge: Harvard University Press, 1934).

economies, once established. In my own view, the supply-side or Schumpeterian entrepreneur is unlikely to become dominant in the economies that are now in transition. And, indeed, such entrepreneurs may have almost disappeared in Western economies. In this perspective, while successful transition to a market economy is possible for the former command systems, there will be no *Wirtschaftswunder* (economic miracle) in the near term, East or West.

Economic Science and
Cultural Diversity

1. Introduction

My assignment is to offer an outsider's response to the question, "Is There a European Economics?" I propose to broaden the issue by asking, "Does the Scientific Content of Economics Depend on Cultural Parameters?"[1] This reformulation of the question recalls the central issue of the nineteenth century *Methodenstreit* between members of the German historical school and the early Austrian economists, notably Carl Menger, as well as the early twentieth-century disputes between the American institutionalists and their neoclassical peers.

My response is predictably ambivalent. There is, indeed, a universalizable science of Economics, made up of a core set of propositions that apply to human behavior in any and all environments, transcending boundaries of time and space. There is also, however, a more inclusive Economics that allows the derivation of propositions about the workings of organizational alternatives that are meaningful only within particular historical and cultural settings. The answer to the question need not be a categorical "No" or "Yes."[2]

From *Kyklos* 48, Fasc. 2 (1995): 193–200. Copyright by Helbing and Lichtenhahn. Reprinted by permission of the publisher.

1. When I mentioned the initially assigned question to three colleagues, separately, each of them responded with immediate reference to "Economics," as produced by the academic-scientific establishment and noted the possible influence of incentives operative within the European establishment. Interestingly, this interpretation of the question did not occur to me at all.

2. In an interesting recent paper, Michael D. White, "Bridging the Natural and the Social: Science and Character in Jevons's Political Economy," *Economic Inquiry* 32 (1994): 429–44, examines the position of Jevons on the relevance of cultural determinants in economic science.

II. Behavior within Constraints

Economics is a science of human behavior, a behavior that is more complex than that of nonhuman animals. Genetic determinants remain central to any explanatory enterprise, but human behavior is also influenced by norms that act as internal constraints. And such constraints may differ as among separate interaction environments that may be temporally, geographically, culturally and institutionally classified. Behavior is, of course, also influenced directly by external constraints that may operate on basic propensities to act that may be uniform over all members of the species, quite independent of time and space. The distinction between internal and external constraints on behavior is not at all easy to make, but it remains central to any resolution of the question concerning the provinciality of Economics as a scientific enterprise.

How is Economics, a science of human behavior, different from a science of the behavior of another animal species, or subspecies, say, smooth-haired fox terriers? In the second of these undertakings, the practicing scientist would recognize that any observed experimental results depend on the constraints imposed on behavior, including those that may be informally programmed by prior training. However, under uniform conditions that may be objectively specified, the scientist would predict that similar patterns of behavior would emerge among all members of the subspecies. All else equal, European fox terriers in the 1990s would not be predicted to behave differently from Asian fox terriers of the nineteenth century.

How is the first undertaking different? How is Economics, defined as a human behavioral science, to be methodologically distinguished from that applicable to any animal species? To be sure, the constraints within which behavior takes place may be observed to vary systematically with geographical location due to the territorial dimensionality of political organization, but would it not remain appropriate to hypothesize that uniform constraints generate uniform patterns of behavior?

Many economists may be unwilling to extend the claims of their science so far. They will recognize the difficulties involved in separating, even as a conceptual exercise, behavior that may be observed from the institutional setting within which such behavior takes place. Observed behavior reflects the presence of both internal and external constraints, and, to the extent that internal constraints influence choices at all, there are historical, geographical and cultural dimensions to be placed on the derivation of a scientific proposition.[3]

Several developments in Economics, inclusively defined, over the half-century following World War II may be summarized in the statement that "institutions matter."[4] But the "institutions matter" claim may be narrowly interpreted as nothing more than a call for economists to examine more carefully the structural constraints within which behavior takes place, constraints that are implicitly assumed to be subject to exogenous change. Such an interpretation prompts ideas to the effect that reform limited to modifications in formal institutional structures may be all that is required to insure progress toward the achievement of agreed upon end-state objectives. (In this attitude, we may locate some of the early post-1992 expectations that the introduction of formal legal reforms facilitating the emergence of markets would, in itself, insure economic growth and stability in former communist regimes.)

The economist who does not extend his scientific claims so far, and who acknowledges the influence of internal constraints on behavior may, nonetheless, agree on the directional efficiency of institutional reform. But any claim for the efficacy of such reform may be placed squarely within a temporal and spatial dimension.

III. Cultural Evolution and the Universalities of Economic Science

If the reality of cultural evolution as an influence on human behavior is acknowledged, it follows that differences in cultural history must exert behavioral consequences. Even if uniformity in basic genetic characteristics is postulated for all members of the human species, independent of time and place, any particular person or group whose behavior may be isolated for examination is described extragenetically by a cultural history that cannot be

---

3. James M. Buchanan, "Choosing What to Choose," *Journal of Institutional and Theoretical Economics* 150 (1994): 123–44.

4. Such research programs as law-and-economics, the new economic history, public choice, property rights economics, constitutional economics and the new political economy deserve mention.

stripped away to reveal some common behavioral generator within. The technology of modern science is unable to show us "the naked ape" as an analytical tool in any operationally useful sense. But to say that behavior cannot be fully explained by postulated genetic uniformities is not, of course, the same as saying that genetic determinants are absent altogether or even that they remain unimportant relative to nongenetic elements.

As noted earlier, there is a universalizable scientific economics, even if limited in scope, an economics that allows for the derivation of some falsifiable hypotheses that may be tested quite independent of historical and cultural context. The resolution of any apparent paradox here lies in the distinction that must be made among separate levels and directions of inquiry, defined in terms of the specificity of the predictions sought. There are propositions in Economics that transcend history and culture. Persons seek their own betterment, a state that can be objectively identified in measures of the availability of commonly valued "goods." With respect to these basic propositions, there is no "European" or "Twentieth-Century" Economics, as such. As we move much beyond these basic propositions, however, and as we try to predict behavioral responses to constraint changes more specifically, the influence of history and culture becomes increasingly relevant.

Adam Smith's understanding and explanation of a market order was conditioned by the parameters that described the "laws and institutions" of eighteenth-century Scotland, which included the morality of the traders he observed. Much of what Smith said was generalizable, as indeed the timeless and spaceless repute of *The Wealth of Nations* attests.[5] But economists have perhaps been careless in their relative neglect of the cultural provinciality of the behavior that Smith implicitly postulated. The butcher acts in his own self-interest when he supplies meat for purchase, but the butcher is presumed to act within the moral norms that impose internal limits on opportunistic cheating.

The "discipline of continuous dealings" may, of course, be invoked to explain why norms for behavior that seem internal may be externally imposed. But, as Hayek has stressed, the achievement of the extended market order must have depended, historically, on the evolution of codes of personal con-

5. Adam Smith, *The Wealth of Nations* (1776; Modern Library edition, New York: Random House, 1937).

duct that restrict opportunistic behavior even in dealings with strangers.[6] These aspects of behavior are culturally determined, and they cannot be universalized so as to apply comparably in settings described by categorically divergent temporal and spatial dimensions.[7]

If the object of inquiry is sufficiently specific to require predictions as to the efficacy of self-enforcing norms in constraining the opportunistic behavior of market participants, predictions that would, of course, be needed if alternative political-collective rules are considered, the cultural environment must be relevant. And, in such a context there is surely a "Western" Economics, even if not specifically "European," that must be different from "Non-Western" Economics.

IV. The Limits of Market and Politics

Let me return to Adam Smith. He used the eighteenth-century postulate that persons uniformly seek their own advantages to construct his analysis of the efficiency of the simple system of natural liberty, and, finally, to demonstrate that the wealth of the citizens of nations is furthered by removing political controls on market behavior. In its largest sense, Smith's message can be interpreted as telling us that there are mutual gains from trade, and that these gains will be exploited if persons are allowed voluntarily to enter into and exit from exchange relationships. From this seminal source, the normative argument for *laissez faire* seems to follow directly. Why should personal behavior be restricted in any way if, left unrestricted, it operates to the general advantage of all parties?

The enthusiasts for *laissez faire*, early and late, failed to recognize that there are two distinct parts to Smith's message. (1) There are mutual gains from trade, and (2) these gains will tend to be exploited by voluntary behavior of the prospective traders. The validity of the first proposition depends only on the identification of "goods" and the existence of differences in preferences and/or endowments (capacities) among potential traders. There is

6. F. A. Hayek, *Law, Legislation and Liberty*, vol. 2, *The Mirage of Social Justice* (Chicago: University of Chicago Press, 1976).

7. James M. Buchanan, "Profit Maximization As a Survival Strategy: Some Normative Speculations," Comments, Alchian Session, Western Economic Association Meeting, Vancouver, British Columbia, Canada, July 1994.

	B		
	C	D	
A C	3,3	1,4	
D	4,1	2,2	

Figure 1. PD matrix

no direct behavioral content. The second proposition, by contrast, implies that potential traders are predicted to behave so as to secure the *mutual* gains guaranteed by the validity of the first statement. Note, in particular, the relationship of the second proposition to the more general hypothesis that persons seek to maximize the satisfaction of their own preferences. The two hypotheses correspond only if trade or exchange is the unique behavioral alternative to the *status quo* or pretrade status of either of the two traders, in the finally factored down two-party exchange confrontation.

The familiar PD matrix *(fig. 1)*, with ordinal payoffs is illustrative.[8] Consider the options that face each of the two players, A and B. Each may cooperate (C) by reciprocally entering into the exchange relationship, and may defect (D) by attempting to exploit differentially the trading opportunity that exists. Each player secures higher payoffs in the solution CC than DD. But note that, as depicted, one or the other of the two players secures the differentially highest payoff in the off-diagonal cells. To hypothesize that mutual gains from exchange will be exploited is to suggest that either (1) the PD setting does not describe the pretrade situation, or (2) the players are internally constrained from maximizing the objectively defined ordinal payoffs. (If payoffs are defined as utility or expected utility indicators, the exercise becomes tautological.) Economists who claim universality for the basic behavioral propositions of their science and who seek to ground normative inferences strictly on these propositions may fall back on the first of these two escape routes. That is to say, the claim may be that the properly estimated expected payoffs are not such as to place players in the dominance setting

---

8. See Dennis C. Mueller, *Public Choice* (Cambridge: Cambridge University Press, 1979).

indicated. In practical terms, potential traders must always and everywhere confront penalties (in expected value terms) for unilateral efforts to capture differential advantages. Stealing, cheating, default, defraud and breach are never privately advantageous.

This generalized argument advanced in support of the *laissez faire* norm seems illegitimate. It is surely more convincing to argue that internal constraints may modify behavior in certain cultural temporal environments so as to cause potential traders to shun patterns of behavior that involve the seeking of differential advantage at the explicit expense of trading partners. But the obverse possibility must also be reckoned with. In some cultural settings, such internal constraints may not be present, in which case Smith's second proposition concerning the exploitation of the mutuality of gains may not be valid. In this case, the normative defense of *laissez faire* does not carry through, at least at the initial stage of discourse. Market organization, characterized by freedom of entry into and exit from exchange, will not necessarily insure "the wealth of nations," at least in the sense of the achievement of the economic value that the resource potential might ideally make possible.

Recognition of the limits of *laissez faire* as the normative principle for organizing the economy of a society owing to the possible absence of operative internal constraints does not, however, carry the twentieth-century romantic inference that political or collective organization is necessarily more effective. In the absence of internal behavioral constraints that limit personal behavior in seeking differential advantage, markets do not work well. But neither do the political correctives that the romantic model of "public interest" motivation seems to generate. As the modern theory of public choice has demonstrated, politics fail, along with markets, when observed results are set alongside ideally attainable alternatives.

V. Economics and Moral Philosophy

My discussion has already digressed too much toward political philosophy and away from the central focus of the paper which is aimed at answering the question about the universalizability of economic science in the face of temporal-cultural diversity. Nonetheless, the primary result seems clear. If the propositions of economic science are to be useful in drawing normative inferences concerning the constitutional-organizational structure of society, cultural parameters that describe the behavioral attitudes of participants must be taken into account. In this sense, there is indeed an Economics that must be culture bound. But if, by contrast, the propositions of economic science are limited exclusively to the derivation of empirically testable hypotheses about the effects of changes in externally imposed constraints, there need be no cultural identification. Demand curves do slope downward, independent of time, place and culture, although particular response patterns may be quite divergent in different settings.

As suggested earlier, there are important political implications to be drawn from a recognition that cultural differences can affect economic behavior. Although his particular identification of its sources may have been empirically and historically inaccurate, at least in part, Max Weber's emphasis on "the spirit of capitalism," as related to an underlying ethos was surely relevant to any understanding of economic development in Western Europe.[9] Transferences of formalized institutional structures, including the privatization of property, to environments with substantially different ethical standards in the expectation of *Wirtschaftswunder* were foredoomed to disappoint such hope.

Even more significant may be the cumulative changes in the ethos of the West. The overreaching of the modern welfare state has exerted dual effects on the taxing and spending sides of the ethical as well as the fiscal account. In the large-number settings of Western nation-states, ethical norms for voluntary tax compliance necessarily erode as revenue exactions increase. Similarly, the moral acceptability of dependency status is enhanced as increasing numbers of citizens qualify for transfers. The widely observable features of modern society cannot fail to exert indirect influences on the behavioral attitudes of persons engaged in market interactions. How long can tax cheaters remain honest traders? And how long can persons supply "honest days' work" when take-home wages move ever closer to the levels of nonreciprocated welfare payments?

9. Max Weber, *The Protestant Ethic and the Spirit of Capitalism* (London: Allen and Unwin, 1930).

It is coming increasingly to be recognized that the welfare economics of the 2000s will not be the welfare economics of the 1950s. The nongenetic behavioral uniformities of the members of the species will have been modified. Perhaps economists should stick to their lasts and continue to use their universalizable propositions to assist in the formulation of institutional-constitutional change that will at least be directionally efficacious. But they must do so in the full knowledge that economic prosperity and social tranquility may require reconstructive change in the ethical-moral constitutions within which behavior is also constrained.

Structure-Induced Behaviour in Markets and in Politics

Perhaps the most salient difference between political and market institutions is measured by distance along an exit dimension. In an idealized competitive setting, in each market, each participant as buyer (seller) confronts another as seller (buyer), and either party can exit from the interaction at zero cost. By contrast, in the stylized case of an inclusive democratic polity, each participant confronts all others in every collective interaction, from which no participant can exit. The presence or absence of the exit option, or, more generally, the costs of exercising such an option, should affect the behaviour of persons who engage in continuing sequences of interaction, whether in markets or in politics. Effects should be expected to emerge from the intertemporal feedbacks that serve to constrain behaviour differently in the two institutional settings. "That which is rational" in sequential market interactions may seem to embody a different "morality" than "that which is rational" in sequential political interactions.[1]

From *Post-Socialist Political Economy: Selected Essays* (Cheltenham, U.K.: Edward Elgar, 1997), 136–50. Reprinted by permission of the publisher.

1. The specific origins of this paper, along with the central argument, owes much to the important analysis developed by Roger Congleton and Viktor Vanberg, "Rationality, Morality, and Exit," *American Political Science Review* 86, no. 2 (1992): 418–31. For earlier analyses that are precursory, see James M. Buchanan, "Individual Choice in Voting and the Market," *Journal of Political Economy* 62 (1954): 334–43; Anthony Downs, *An Economic Theory of Democracy* (New York: Harper, 1957); Gordon Tullock, *Towards a Mathematics of Politics* (Ann Arbor: University of Michigan Press, 1967); Albert O. Hirschman, *Exit, Voice, and Loyalty: Responses to Decline in Firms, Organizations, and States* (Cambridge: Harvard University Press, 1970). For preliminary statements of some of the argument, see James M. Buchanan, "Political Ethics as a Criterion for Constitutional Design" (Fairfax, Va., Center for Study of Public Choice, 1992, working paper).

Critics of rational choice models of behaviour, as such models are conventionally interpreted, may acknowledge that institutional structure can influence criteria for rational choice. Such critics may, however, fail to appreciate that departures from the dictates of rationality, as may be motivated by presumed ethical-moral norms, may be quite differently "penalized" in separate institutional settings. That is to say, the opportunity costs of "other-regardingness" may vary as between market and political structures, in which case, the survivability or sustainability of character traits summarized under "morality" may be critically linked to descriptive features of the interaction process itself.

My aim in this chapter is to analyse the differential influences of market and political structures on the sustainability of behavioural patterns. I shall argue that because of the presence of an operative exit option individual behaviour in market relationships is more constrained, externally, than in political interaction. At the same time (and interestingly), the individual may act in furtherance of moral rules that violate canons of rationality with lower opportunity costs in market than in political relationships. Individuals who exhibit "other-regardingness" survive relatively better in the selective, evolution-like process of continuing market exchange than in the comparable sequence described in the operation of unconstrained majoritarian democracy. The participant in such politics is more or less forced, by elementary criteria of survivability, to choose and to act in furtherance of narrow or differential interest, at least to an extent that need not be paralleled in markets.

This comparative result may, in part, be mitigated by explicit constitutional constraints on the operations of politics. Such constraints can take three forms. First, politics can be modified to allow for and to incorporate some of the market's exit features. The constitutional establishment and enforcement of a federal structure of governance allows individuals, within limits, access to potential exit, thereby indirectly limiting resort to exploitative efforts to further special interests. Second, majoritarian democracy may be replaced, at least in part, by consensual democracy that requires general agreement on political actions. Third, the range for politicization may at least conceivably be constitutionally restricted to actions that are generalizable in effects over the inclusive membership of the polity, in which case differential interests, as such, are nonexistent. Discussion here is concentrated on the third type of constitutional constraints.

The organization of the chapter is as follows. The second section presents a model of stylized market choice to demonstrate that when embedded in a temporal sequence participants are severely restricted in their opportunistic departures from the behaviour that exhibits the standard "morality of the marketplace." Such behaviour does not, in commonplace discourse, depart from self-interest, institutionally defined, but the analysis does suggest that participants who do, indeed, choose to behave in accordance with norms for "other-regardingness" may sustain such behaviour within plausibly broad limits. The third section presents models of stylized political choice in a constitutional setting of unlimited majoritarian democracy. As again embedded in a temporal sequence, the analysis is designed to demonstrate that the participant, first, faces no direct constraint against possibly opportunistic behaviour and, second, is required to act in terms of differential self-interest in order to survive at all in the evolution-like processes of political selection. Finally, and as a part of the same analysis, any attempt by an individual to adhere to an other-regardingness motivation can be shown to be short-lived, at least relative to its market analogue. The fourth section modifies the analysis to consider models of constitutionally constrained political interactions. I do not, explicitly, discuss either the introduction of operative exit options through schemes of federalism, subsidiary and the like or the replacement of majority rule by a rule of unanimity. I concentrate attention on the effects of constitutional restrictions on the range of political action. The fifth section contains a discussion of applications and implications, and the final section concludes the chapter.

Models of Markets

In the highly abstracted and limiting model of competitive market exchange, no participant possesses power over another, in any sense of being able to affect another's well-being, either positively or negatively. An exchange or trade between two parties is instantaneous, and each party is able to observe accurately the descriptive qualities of the goods entered into trade—goods that are presumed to be physically homogeneous over varying quantities.

Further, each party confronts a sufficiently large number of alternative traders from whom the same goods may be purchased (to whom the same goods may be sold) on identical terms. And there is no cost involved in switching custom as among alternative traders.

Consideration of the properties of the exchange or market relationship in this highly abstracted setting for generalized competitive equilibrium led David Gauthier to characterize the market as a "morally free zone."[2] Any attempt on the part of any participant in exchange to secure opportunistic advantage must, in the model, close off any prospect for trade. No potential trading partner would enter into an exchange relationship with anyone who seeks to take undue advantage. And the generalized failure to enter exchange is, of course, equivalent to a generalized exit from exchange.

Gauthier was criticized for his "morals free" characterization of the market on the grounds that his treatment seems to transform properties of an idealized model into the descriptive reality of institutional operation.[3] In any real exchange each trader can, through his or her own behaviour, exert at least some effect on the well-being of the person on the other side of the prospective bargain. Few exchanges are instantaneous; goods are not homogeneous; quality is not readily observable. Fraud, deceit and default are always possible. Further, there are costs involved both in securing information about alternative sellers and buyers and in switching custom from one to another.[4]

Recognition of any or all of these departures from the model's idealization requires an acknowledgement that opportunistic behaviour can occur in the market relationship, that any trader may attempt to take advantage of a trading partner without immediate rejection from consummation of an exchange transaction. To the extent that opportunities for "cheating" are present, the market exchange relationship is "morally laden" rather than "morally free." And the efficacy of the relationship depends critically on the generalized adherence of participants to what may be called the "morality of the market," that is, to behavioural standards that do not extend to include generalized

---

2. David Gauthier, *Morals by Agreement* (Oxford: Oxford University Press, 1985).

3. James M. Buchanan, "The Gauthier Enterprise," in *The Economics and the Ethics of Constitutional Order* (Ann Arbor: University of Michigan Press, 1991), 195–213.

4. Dennis C. Mueller, *Public Choice II* (Cambridge: Cambridge University Press, 1989).

opportunistic exploitation of particular trading situations. Adam Smith's butcher offers meat for sale in furtherance of his own self-interest; such behaviour lies within the morality of the marketplace. But it is also in the butcher's self-interest, strictly measured at the day of sale, to put his hand heavily on the scales—a behavioural pattern that would be adjudged to violate the market's implied morality.

Economists have tended to neglect the morality of market behaviour because the presence of the exit option acts to place external limits on the extent to which opportunistic exploitation can take place in operating market structures. Even when we recognize that information concerning market alternatives is costly to obtain, and, further, that any shift of custom creates transactions costs, the potential exercise of exit (and entry) places severe limits on departures from ordinary and accepted standards for market conduct. And this aspect or feature of market relationships, generally, can best be appreciated if a temporal dimension is introduced so that any particular act of exchange may be treated as one in a possible continuing sequence over several periods. An individual who, by contrast, enters a one-time trading relationship may expect to be subjected to opportunistic exploitation, since, by definition, there is little or no expectation that the particular pairing will recur. Examples are familiar: the tout at the travelling show, the taxi driver in a large city and especially as first encountered at an airport by foreign visitors. But if and to the extent that repeated or continuing custom in an ongoing relationship is a part of the overall exchange process, the potential for exit will surely constrain resort to opportunistic behaviour. A trader who is exploited may shift custom to another, and new trading partners may enter to offer trade on nonexploitative terms. Adam Smith's butcher who does, indeed, defraud by weight faces little or no return custom. The "discipline of continuous dealings" moves the exchange process much further towards the abstracted idealization used by Gauthier than straightforward examination of isolated trades might suggest or than many economists themselves appreciate.

My purpose here is neither to array differing market-like institutions in terms of their tendencies to promote nonopportunistic behaviour nor to evaluate the relative importance of an operative exit option in ensuring that the market order, generally, works reasonably well. My point is simply that the prospect for exit from particular exchange pairings over a temporal sequence restricts the pursuit of opportunistic self-interest by traders, whether or not such traders may ultimately be guided by a generalized inner morality that would exclude such opportunism.[5] That is to say, traders are forced, by the success-survival criteria of the institutional process, to behave as if they seek to further their own interest in a nonexploitative fashion, to behave in accordance with what we may call the "morality of the market," quite independent of inner motivation.

To this point, I have allowed participants in exchange processes to have available only two behavioural alternatives, both of which may be grounded in the axioms of rational choice. I have presumed, implicitly, that traders are motivated by measured economic interest, which may or may not be constrained by the exit option as it operates in a temporal sequence of interactions. For my general aim in this chapter, I do not want to limit analysis and discussion to rational choice models of the standard sort. I want to examine prospects for individual market behaviour that is motivated by genuine "other-regardingness." Consider, then, a trader who enters into an exchange with the interests of others elevated to a status equal to his or her own. Are there elements in market relationships, as constrained by pressures of an exit option, that prevent departure from market morality in this direction akin to those elements that limit exploitative behaviour in the other direction?

Somewhat interestingly perhaps, the exit option itself provides an insurance policy, of sorts, that allows other-regarding behaviour to survive, within limits. Consider a person who has in hand a stock of goods, the potential market value for which is in excess of the anticipated cost of reproduction, but who has no desire or interest to return more than such cost from sale. The goods may be offered to buyers who will be able to realize net rental values. Such buyers will not, of course, choose to exit from such favourable terms of exchange. But the seller, also, retains an exit option, and he or she will not market goods below those values that ensure his or her survival as a participant in the process. In this setting, the seller may remain a viable economic unit despite the exhibition of altruism in his or her trading stance. (If we look at market relationships in this way, it is not surprising that the behaviour described as "pricing at cost" should have been singled out for atten-

---

5. Congleton and Vanberg work within the repeated PD game paradigm to demonstrate that an "exit if other defects" strategy tends to be successful, even against the tit-for-tat strategy.

tion by those medieval scholastics who did concern themselves directly with the morality of exchange.)

My emphasis here is upon the behavioural traits that tend to be encouraged in the evolution of market exchange relationships over extended temporal sequences. As noted, opportunistic attempts to exploit differential advantages may take place. But such behaviour reduces the prospect that practitioners will survive over the long run. The potential for exit by those who are subjected to the exploitation offers the societal feedback mechanism that ensures the ultimate demise of the trader or trading firm that deceives, defrauds, defaults or otherwise seeks to gain differentially advantageous terms of trade. To the extent that "codes of conduct" come to be established in some process of cultural evolution, as stressed by Hayek,[6] we should not expect such codes to incorporate opportunistic advantage-seeking through trade. And while the selection process that takes place within markets does not actively encourage the evolution of behaviour that reflects norms of "other-regardingness," there is no feedback generated from potential exit that will discourage the evolution of such behaviour so long as the tripwire exit at cost-price terms remains available. The market will, of course, operate to ensure that persons who extend altruism to the extreme limit of disregard for their own survival will not, in fact, survive. St. Francis has nothing to offer after the one-time dissipation of goods.

Models of Politics

In the earlier discussion of exit as a feature of market interaction, attention was concentrated on the ability of any trader (buyer or seller) to withdraw from a specific exchange relationship and to shift to a comparable relationship with another trading partner. A more fundamental possibility for market exit tends to be overlooked in this preliminary overview. An individual may, presumably, withdraw altogether from the market or exchange nexus even if the costs of so doing are high. That is to say, entry into any market network is itself voluntary. The individual retains the option of withdrawing from the market "game" itself.

6. F. A. Hayek, *Law, Legislation and Liberty,* vol. 3, *The Political Order of a Free People* (Chicago: University of Chicago Press, 1979).

Politics is different at this basic level of comparison. An individual is a member of a politically organized community; he or she does not voluntarily choose to enter the political relationship, at least in the stylized model that excludes prospects for in or out migration. Even within a political relationship, however, there is no exit option potentially to be exercised as among alternative trading sets. Persons cannot choose among collectivities, except in federal-like structures that may allow for Tiebout-type adjustments. Individuals are "locked in" to the political nexus, independent of their own active participation or the absence thereof.

The political relationship is "morally laden," even in the most stylized of models. Regardless of what person or group may be assigned the authority to make choices for the polity, the nonexcludability from effects ensures that the well-being of others than the chooser(s) may be modified, positively or negatively, by any choice that is made.

Political interaction is inherently more complex than market interaction, and any effort to model politics abstractly seems to involve dramatic departures from any semblance of observable reality. In its most general sense, politics is a process of complex exchange among all members of a polity—an exchange in which each participant gives up value through taxes and secures a reciprocal return of value through programme benefits. The "exchange" terms stipulate the shares in taxes and benefits assigned to each party to the inclusive transaction.

This basic political exchange among citizens tends to be obscured in much analysis because of the intrusion of a second, and quite distinct, "exchange" between each person and "government" or "the state" in which taxes are paid to such an entity in apparent "exchange" for programme benefits. The introduction of this second exchange between the individual and the government prompts inquiry into processes through which agents of governance are selected and monitored. I do not propose to examine the set of problems raised by this second exchange here.[7] I shall restrict analysis to a stylized model of the complex exchange among all members of a polity, thereby abstracting from all questions that involve the institutionalization of government as a means of effectuating the ultimate exchange among citi-

---

7. See James M. Buchanan, *Post-Socialist Political Economy: Selected Essays* (Cheltenham, U.K.: Edward Elgar, 1997), chapter 17, for a discussion and comparison of the two exchanges.

zens. I want to model politics "as if" collective decisions emerge from an inclusive town meeting in which all members of the polity participate.

Even in this highly abstract model, it is necessary to specify the rules under which political-collective decisions are made. I shall limit analysis to simple models of majority voting. Agreement among a number of voters sufficient to make up a majority is required to implement collective action, regardless of the attitudes or positions of members of a minority.

In the stylized model to be considered first, there are no constitutional limits on the range and scope for political-collective action. A majority coalition may impose taxes differentially on members of a minority with revenues then used either to finance public goods that yield generalized benefits to all citizens or to finance transfers differentially paid out to members of the majority coalition. In this setting, the dominant majority strategy will tend to be that which involves taxes on persons in a minority and transfers to persons in a majority.[8] In a large electorate, the minimal winning coalition will find it advantageous to implement such a straightforward differential tax-differential transfer regime unless the prospective aggregate benefits of a public good, assumed to be uniformly distributed, are at least double the aggregate tax costs.

Consider an expectational setting in which each member of a polity considers membership in a minimally winning majority coalition to be equally likely with membership in a losing minority coalition. The winning coalition is empowered to implement collective action without constraints as to either the type of action or the distribution of costs and benefits. The only constitutional guarantee is that no majority can set collective action for more than the current period. A new electoral process, with possibly a new majority, takes place in each period.

In this abstracted setting, with some heroic simplifications, we are able to model the politics of any period as a simple two-person matrix relationship between the individual who is a member of the majority and the individual who is a member of the minority. Collective action in providing a public good is available that will yield a net surplus over costs. The ordinal payoff structure is that depicted in Figure 14.1. Note that the effective majority,

8. Marilyn R. Flowers and Patricia M. Danzon, "Separation of the Redistributive and Allocative Functions of Government: A Public Choice Perspective," *Journal of Public Economics* 24, no. 3 (1984): 373–80.

B

	Pays net tax	Pays no tax and receives transfer
A Pays net tax	I 1/2, 1/2	II −1, 2
Pays no tax and receives transfer	III 2, −1	IV (0, 0)

Figure 14.1

whether this be the *A*s or *B*s, can choose among three separate solutions or outcomes, each one of which specifies the projected payoffs to each player. The fourth solution, Cell IV, is not possible by the logic of the structure, as described.

If an individual becomes a member of the *A*s, and these persons make up the minimally winning coalition, the solution will be that shown in Cell III; in which members of the coalition of *A*s exploit members of the minority, the *B*s. The majority will not choose the Cell I outcome that involves the sharing of tax costs for the purchase of the public good. The situation is, of course, reversed if the *B*s make up the winning coalition, in which case the solution is in Cell II, with the *A*s being subjected to collective exploitation.

Consider what might happen if and when a majority of voters, say the *A*s, attempts to act in "the public interest." Rather than impose taxes on the members of the *B* coalition, with transfers to the *A*s, the fiscal scheme chosen involves generalized tax financing of a public good that benefits all persons. This behaviour becomes fully analogous to the honest trader in the market who does not cheat on terms. The majority achieves the preferred Cell I solution in the period considered. But note that this majority remains highly vulnerable to defection by some of its members to a different, and less "honest," majority that might be formed during the next period. The salutary effects of the behaviour during the first period may be dissipated quickly by the formation of the new, and exploiting, majority. There is no way that members of the majority who choose to "play fair," to behave nonopportunistically, can exit from their political relationship with all other members of the inclusive polity. In recognition of this structure of interaction, participants in the political game, as modelled here, must play the exploiting strategy if they are to survive. They cannot avoid being played for a sucker, and repeatedly, unless they, too, seek to place others in the role of suckers when the opportunity warrants.

The absence of exit guarantees that the individual remains vulnerable to the "mining" of whatever value he or she may possess or produce. In the market, at each and every level of interaction, "voluntariness" remains a characteristic feature because the individual may walk away from the game, no matter how inclusively it may be defined. In majoritarian politics, by dramatic contrast, the individual can, at best, try to get "his or her share," not in the net surplus that collective action makes possible, but in the aggregate total of value possessed or produced by all members of the polity.

Towards Constitutional Reform

The model of unconstrained majoritarian politics sketched out in the previous section is extreme, but it does, nonetheless, draw attention directly to the structural features that generate the undesirable results, measured both in the failures to achieve the potential cooperative surpluses from collective action and in the failures of the incentive system to facilitate the survival of nonopportunistic individual behaviour. Unconstrained majoritarian politics produces the "churning state," to employ Anthony de Jasay's accurately descriptive term.[9]

The simplified analytical construction in the previous section is helpful because it points to the two separate, but indirectly related, avenues for constitutional or structural reform within a single polity, either one of which might mitigate, even if not eliminate, failures along both of the dimensions noted. Clearly, the nonsymmetrical or off-diagonal majoritarian solutions, as shown in Cells II and III in Figure 14.1, are achievable only through the coerced imposition of the effective majority on the minority. As Wicksell recognized, the replacement of majority rule by an effective rule of unanimity

---

9. Anthony de Jasay, *The State* (Oxford: Basil Blackwell, 1985).

would guarantee that such off-diagonal results could never be attained.[10] Persons engaged in collective choice processes would, in this case, be forced to consider only those schemes that exclude exploitation, that is, those schemes that involve some sharing of cooperative surplus over and beyond that *status quo* position. I shall not discuss the Wicksellian thrust for constitutional reform here, in part because I have analysed it at some length in earlier works.[11] I shall, instead, concentrate on a second, and different, direction for constitutional reform, which builds upon a provisional acceptance of majority rule as a central feature of democratic politics.

The matrix illustration in Figure 14.1 suggests immediately that direct conflicts between sets of participants, in this case between members of majority and minority coalitions, arise only because there exist potential solutions or outcomes that can only be attained without the agreement or acquiescence of one or more of the parties to the interaction. To generate any of the nonvoluntary outcomes, the separate players or participants must be placed in nonsymmetrical roles or positions, defined either in terms of actions taken or effects externally imposed. That is to say, *differences* between the participants must be introduced, whether these differences take the form of action or the effects of action. And these differences produce differentials in payoffs, allowing for a classification of participants as between winners and losers, between positive and negative payoffs, in absolute as well as relative terms, by comparison with some conceptualized exit benchmark.

The prospect of "winning" by imposing net costs upon "losers" becomes the attractor for the choice of participants, and it is this prospect that distracts-diverts attention from the potential opportunities for mutuality of gain through symmetrical sharing for common purpose. Constitutional reform may eliminate the *off-diagonal* solutions that embody differences between participants in action or effect that lie beyond the limits of possible voluntariness. If those outcomes (Cells II and III) that emerge only because the

---

10. Knut Wicksell, *Finanztheoretische Untersuchungen* (Jena: Gustav Fischer, 1896).

11. See, in particular, James M. Buchanan and Gordon Tullock, *The Calculus of Consent: Logical Foundations of Constitutional Democracy* (Ann Arbor: University of Michigan Press, 1962).

participants are made to be different by the coerciveness of the decision rule are placed constitutionally beyond the limits of politics, the decision rule itself may be retained.

In the highly simplified construction of Figure 14.1, it is evident that if the off-diagonal solutions are prohibited, then *any* decision rule will produce the Pareto-preferred outcome of Cell I. In this setting, whether the As or the Bs make up a majority, or whether some effective unanimity rule requires agreement among all the As and Bs, this result is invariant. In such a rarified setting, there is no basis for discussion about possible definitions of what is "in the public interest," and no difference between self-regarding and other-regarding action, at least as observable in choice behaviour.

Any move towards descriptive reality must allow for the existence of a multiplicity of potential political outcomes, all within the Pareto-preferred set and Pareto superior to the conceptualized exit outcome in Cell IV of Figure 14.1. That is to say, there may be many nonexploitative political alternatives, each one of which involves collective action aimed at generating some mutually advantageous sharing of a potential surplus, but which differ, among themselves, in the distributional consequences. Consider the set of payoff alternatives: $(.9, .1)$, $(.8, .2)$, $(.7, .3)$, $(.1, .9)$. Each one of these sets of payoffs dominates the $(0, 0)$ result, but neither of them imposes coerced loss on either party. Distributional results may motivate choice, and a majority made up of As may select the $(.9, .1)$ outcome, whereas a majority made up of the Bs may select the $(.2, .9)$ alternative. But the generalized political "discussion" here seems logically equivalent to that present in exchange when traders bicker over terms, with full recognition of the omnipresent exit option. In one sense, the game remains one of distributional politics, but it is distributional politics constrained by constitutional limits on the off-diagonals.

The participant in such constrained politics, whether in a role as a voter in a potential majority coalition, or as an elected agent for others, may behave in furtherance of a personalized definition of "the public interest" without expecting to suffer the penalty of subsequent exploitation. The "sucker's payoff" is excluded from the set of allowable results and with feedbacks on political behaviour generally. The political rhetoric of "public interest" takes on some meaning in such constrained majoritarian politics, as contrasted with the absurdities in the pronouncements that often accompany the discussion of pork-barrel politics.

Analytic construction tends to objectify the subjective reality of social interaction, and the exercise in this paper is no exception. Implicitly, the model of the majoritarian political game incorporates the assumption that participants can identify political actions that are exploitative and distinguish these actions from those that embody a mutually advantageous sharing of potential collective surplus. This assumption, as stated, can be accepted to be psychologically descriptive, but its acceptance does not allow the inference that such subjective evaluations by the affected parties need correspond with any attempted objectification by the analyst. In this context, it would perhaps have been more accurate to have left off any labels for the rows and columns of Figure 14.1 and to use the matrix of interaction only to indicate the presence of the payoff alternatives, as subjectively perceived by the participants, however these might be identified and classified. Note particularly that in such a reconstruction the payoff alternatives may not be classified similarly by the separate participants. Action considered to be exploitative by members of a coerced minority may not be considered as such by members of the majority.

Problems raised by the inherent subjectivity of the evaluation of political alternatives may be illustrated by the fact that, clearly, some tax financing of net transfers to some members of the polity is considered to be generative of a collective surplus beneficial to those who are the net taxpayers, even by the latter. In this instance, the analytical construction of the model raises questions as to the extent and the limit of such net transfers—questions that will be partially addressed in the following section.

Applications, Extensions, Implications

The whole discussion in the two previous sections may be criticized for its implied presumption that majoritarian politics, as it has historically evolved and as it operates, contains within its existing rules or constitutional structure none of the constraints that the analysis suggested to be necessary to ensure against the mutual exploitation suffered by rotating minorities. Such criticism, as might be advanced by a staunch defender of majoritarian politics, could point to the formal constitutional prohibitions against discriminatory treatment among members of the polity—prohibitions that find their traditional origins in the rule of law, in the precept that all persons be subjected to equal treatment under the law.

To an extent, the existence of such precepts in application to the operation of majoritarian politics must be acknowledged, *and appreciated.* There are constitutional limits that prevent majorities from denying the voting franchise to particular persons; there are limits placed on the deliberately discriminatory treatment of persons or groups in respect to some forms of political regulation; there are limits beyond which politically driven discrimination in taxation might not go. And, indeed, it is the existence of such constitutional limits, and the traditional understanding of these limits in constitutional law, that have prevented the most overt forms of exploitation by politics from taking place. The purpose of my discussion becomes, in this sense, both precautionary and definitional. The importance of generality in the applicability of law, as interpreted by judges, has been extended to wide areas of human interaction. But the equal importance of such generality in the applicability to politically driven action has not been adequately recognized, and notably in this century's transformation of majoritarian politics into the regulatory and transfer state.

Any effort on the part of a legislative majority to tax, subsidize or regulate differentially a group of persons classified by personal characteristics, such as gender, race, ethnicity, religion or geography would be judged unconstitutional. By dramatic contrast, almost any action by a legislative majority to tax, subsidize or regulate differentially a group of persons classified by economic characteristics, such as amount and type of wealth and income, occupational status, profession, industry, product category, form of organization and size of association, would be left constitutionally unchallenged.

With reference to the simplified construction in the two previous sections, application to the politics of the United States in the 1990s suggests that some off-diagonals are beyond recognized constitutional boundaries. But it is also emphatically clear that many possible off-diagonal solutions are both constitutionally permissible and become increasingly characteristic of modern democratic politics.

Consider restrictive trade policy, whether in the form of tariffs or quotas on imports, negotiated agreements, internal subsidies, "dumping" legislation or "fairness" requirements. Representatives of a sufficiently inclusive coalition of industries may succeed in securing legislative enactment of a set of such policies to be applied *differentially* only to the industries so designated.[12] Such legislative action would take place with little or no argument to the effect that, if protection is extended to one industry or product category, the precept of equal treatment or generality would suggest extension of like or similar protection to all industries. And, indeed, as either elementary economics or our simple matrix illustration makes clear, if such a straightforward extension of constitutional law should be made, if the off-diagonal solutions that necessarily incorporate differential treatment should be eliminated, any and all support for politically enforced restrictions on trade would vanish.

It is instructive to think of the position of the legislative agent, perhaps an economist by training, who participates in trade policy debates, out of which a majority coalition is formed and a policy stance emerges. The agent may understand and appreciate that a regime of universalizable free trade is genuinely "in the public interest" and should be preferred to a regime of trade restriction, either partial or total. Such an agent cannot, however, act in furtherance of the general "good" and hope to survive electorally. The agent will be forced, by the structure of the political game, to seek differential protection for the industry concentrated in his or her constituency, to seek membership in the successful majority coalition, even at the recognized expense of both those outside the coalition and the inclusive "public," as measured in some aggregate welfare index. By comparison, think of this same agent involved in a discussion of the alternatives: universalizable free trade and universalizable restriction. In this setting, both alternatives lie along the diagonal, and the agent who understands simple economics can, indeed, mount an argument and act in furtherance of "the public interest." There is no structurally induced pressure on the agent to depart from the moral precept of generality.

Constitutional reform aimed at eliminating differential treatment—at removing the off-diagonals—seems relatively straightforward, at least at the level of discussion here, in application to politically imposed economic regulation, as in the trade policy illustration. Comparable reform is much more difficult to discuss in application to transfer politics, in which majority coa-

---

12. James M. Buchanan and Dwight R. Lee, "Cartels, Coalitions, and Constitutional Politics," *Constitutional Political Economy* 2, no. 2 (1991): 139–69.

litions include persons who, quite explicitly, seek monetary payoffs at the expense of those outside the coalition.

On one interpretation of the argument that I have advanced, full application of the precept for generality of treatment would require that all persons be subjected to equal-per-head taxes and be eligible for equal-per-head transfers. Such a regime would, of course, eliminate off-diagonal solutions, but, at the same time, it would not allow any net fiscal transfers to be implemented. And, as noted earlier, some redistributional role for the fisc seems to be broadly acceptable, even among those persons who must be placed in positions of net taxpayers rather than potential recipients of transfers. There is a categorical difference, however, between the collective "purchase" of distributional adjustments that might conceptually be utility enhancing for all parties and majoritarian imposition of taxes to finance transfers beyond such limits. Even if explicit generality, defined as measurable equality, becomes contradictory in any scheme of collective transfers, steps in the direction of greater generality can do much to reduce the felt sense of fiscal exploitation.

A first and obvious step is that which would make all taxation general through the elimination of special tax treatment of identified sources. The argument for generality here lends support to schemes like the flat tax, with the same rate being applied to all income and over all persons. Such a scheme, if coupled with equal-per-head transfers, or demogrants, to all persons, would go far towards extending generality norms to fiscal action even in the operation of the transfer state. Differing persons would, of course, be differentially affected, but in their roles both as taxpayers and recipients, there is a sense in which all would seem to be treated equally. In terms of the metaphorical PD construction earlier, the flat tax–demogrant scheme might be considered to be quasi-diagonal.

An important by-product effect of any move towards generality in political treatment has not been mentioned. The promised opportunity to secure differentially favoured treatment, through shared membership in a successful majority coalition, provides incentives for rent-seeking investment that wastes economic value over and beyond any direct transfer between winner and loser in the political game. A special tax exemption will, indeed, allow those exempted to secure pecuniary gain at the expense of those who are provided no such treatment. But this gain-loss calculus may be matched or even exceeded by investment in efforts at persuading political agents to provide such discriminatory treatment in the first place. To the extent that constitutional rules prohibit discriminatory treatment through the political process, the incentives for rent-seeking are correspondingly reduced.

Conclusion

The discussion in the two previous sections may have seemed to depart from the main argument, as summarized in the title "Structure-Induced Behaviour in Markets and in Politics." The implications of the absence of the exit option in political interaction for the behaviour of participants seem clear enough. There is no feedback loop that works to impose penalties on those who behave opportunistically in majoritarian politics, and the rewards promised from such behaviour are such as to ensure its survival in the ongoing evolutionary process. Participants must play distributional politics if such play is allowed by the rules. The discussion in the two previous sections was aimed to demonstrate how the rules might be changed so as to restrict alternatives within the political choice set to those that might be chosen by a majority but yet remain meaningfully classifiable as "within the public interest."

The analysis suggests that much of the familiar criticism of market organization that is based on its underlying morality of "greed" or "unconstrained pursuit of self-interest" is wrongly conceived and applied. The standard question "relative to what?" must be raised. To the extent that the exit option eliminates or reduces opportunistic behaviour (the off-diagonals), the structure of markets induces behaviour that exhibits a morality of fairness, quite independent of an underlying motivation. If "greed" is defined as the seeking of gain at the expense of trading partners, this behaviour is precisely that sort which will not survive as a personal characteristic in an ongoing market order. On the other hand, and by contrast, this pattern of behaviour will find its reward in the play of distributional politics.

The widespread dissatisfaction with modern majoritarian politics stems from a hazy recognition that the "politics of greed" guarantees a mutuality of opportunity loss for all citizens. Escape from the genuine dilemma requires that some constitutional means be found that will effectively change the constraints within which political behaviour takes place. Politics must be restricted to the discussion and implementation of actions that are properly classified as alternative "public goods" that promise benefits to all members of the polity.

We Should Save More in Our Own
Economic Interest

I. Introduction

In several recent efforts, I have argued that the economic well-being of anyone by his or her own standards of evaluation depends in part on willingness
of others in the economy to supply work effort to the market.[1] I have suggested that we do, to some extent, internalize this particular externality
through a work ethic. My purpose here is to extend and to apply essentially
the same argument to saving and to an ethic of saving.[2]

It will be useful first to summarize briefly the work supply analysis since
this may facilitate understanding of the application to saving. Work, defined
as the supply of labor input to the market, is a means through which the size
of the production-exchange nexus, the market itself, may be quantitatively
determined. And the supply of more work by participants in the economy
implies a larger economy, a larger market which, in turn, implies that the
advantages of division and specialization of labor can be exploited more fully
than in a smaller economy. And each of us, in our role as user or consumer

From *Justice Across Generations: What Does It Mean?* ed. Lee M. Cohen (Washington,
D.C.: AARP, 1993), 269–82. Reprinted by permission of AARP.

1. James M. Buchanan, "On the Work Ethic," in *Essays on the Political Economy* (Ho-
nolulu: University of Hawai'i Press, 1989), 47–51; "Economic Interdependence and the
Work Ethic," in *The Economics and Ethics of Constitutional Order* (Ann Arbor: University
of Michigan Press, 1991), 159–78; Buchanan and Yong J. Yoon, "Increasing Returns, Parametric Work-Supply Adjustment and the Work Ethic" (Fairfax, Va., Center for Study of
Public Choice, George Mason University, 1991, mimeographed).

2. I have developed the argument in a somewhat modified format in the second lecture of a three-lecture series, "Ethics and Economic Progress," presented at the University
of Oklahoma, October 1991.

of final goods, prefers to live in an economy where more economic value rather than less is available in exchange for any given amount of input effort. We want "more bang for the buck," no matter how many "bucks" we may have accumulated or how many we may earn.

For those among you who are economic sophisticates, the extension of the argument to saving and capital formation may be straightforward. But since even my argument on the effects of the work ethic may not be wholly accepted, especially by my professional economist peers, some variation of the analysis in application to saving may not be out of order here. And again let us keep in mind the statement made by Herbert Spencer in the preface to his book *The Principles of Ethics*, "Only by varied reiteration can alien conceptions be forced on reluctant minds."[3]

There are, however, important differences between the supply of work and the supply of saving, and in the accompanying ethical norms that may affect individual attitudes toward these margins of choice. My decision to increase the number of hours worked per week is different from my decision to increase the rate of saving out of my current income, both in terms of my own sense of utility or satisfaction and in the ultimate economic effects on others than myself. These differences require examination in some detail.

In Section II, I shall review, very briefly, the origins of the widespread public and professional dissatisfaction with current rates of saving in the United States, and the accompanying normative agreement that saving rates are too low and should be increased. Those who share this view will be initially prejudiced to accept my argument although the ultimate grounding of the norm may remain quite different from that which I shall develop. My own argument that savings may be too low is grounded upon an evaluative judgment of the welfare analytics of individuals' choices rather than on any presumed knowledge of appropriate macroaggregate objectives.

I shall also examine, again briefly, the view that current saving rates are too low, but only because various governmental policies, notably those that involve spending and taxing, discriminate against savings, with the implication that if governmental actions could, in fact, be made neutral between

3. Herbert Spencer, *The Principles of Ethics* (New York: D. Appleton and Company, 1892).

savings and other uses of income, the normative argument in favor of more savings would vanish.

In Section III, it will be necessary to place the whole argument in an appropriately qualified macroeconomic setting. Many of us remain partially trapped in the Keynesian-inspired delusion that fails to make the proper separation between macromonetary institutional structures and the choices between current and future uses of income. It is this set of Keynesian ideas that is at least partially responsible for the change in attitudes toward saving that has been descriptive of the middle and last decades of this century.

In Section IV, I shall distinguish categorically between the argument that I advance here and that argument which introduces a normative or evaluative judgment concerning our generalized obligations, or lack thereof, to future generations of persons, to posterity as it were. The whole set of issues raised under the rubric of our obligations to the future is both important and intellectually fascinating. But intergenerational ethics is not my subject matter. My argument is advanced in support of the proposition that we should all save more, not for our children's or our grandchildren's sake at all, but in our own multiperiod economic interest. We may, essentially, finesse the intergenerational ethics issues altogether by postulating that the analysis applies to persons with multiperiod time horizons.

Sections II, III, and IV are all preliminary to the central argument, which is explicitly introduced only in Section V. By necessity, the first step in the analysis involves definitional clarification. Just what is saving? And what presuppositions of the analytical models are required to equate an increase in saving with an increase in the size of the market nexus? An elementary excursus into the intricacies of capital theory is dictated. Section VI introduces a summary comparison of the effects of increases in savings and increases in work effort. Section VII examines the internalization of the externality involved in saving choices through ethical constraints. Section VIII looks at alternative means for correction and concludes the paper.

II. How Much "Should" Be Saved?

Much of the current policy discussion about the low rate of aggregate savings in the United States seems to accept, with little critical examination, the notion that there are ways of determining how much we should save in the aggregate. And, by inference, economists-experts can tell us whether current practice meets the exogenously settled standard. Note that in my argument I do not need to be able to say just how much "should" be saved in the aggregate, despite the assertion in my title that we "should" save more than we do. My stance in this respect will seem paradoxical only to those who do not understand or who do not appreciate the individualistic evaluative framework that I try consistently to adopt. I can suggest that individuals, acting strictly in their own interest, should save more than they do when each person acts as if there were no interdependency among separate saving choices. I can advance this argument while at the same time refusing to be drawn into a position that involves evoking some external criterion for deciding what an optimal rate of saving might be. My own methodological paradigm will, perhaps, be more fully evident as the analysis proceeds. For now, I want to examine briefly the claims advanced by those who are quite willing to adjudge the existing savings rate to be lower than some ideal standard that must, presumably, offer the objective for policy.

By almost any measure, aggregate savings in the United States in 1992 are relatively low, both by comparison with savings in other developed countries and with savings in earlier periods of our history. Dispute continually rages among quantitatively inclined economists and econometricians concerning the appropriate procedures for measuring what is desired to be measured when rates of savings are discussed. What items should and should not be included? I do not have either the competence or the interest to take part in such disputes, even indirectly and at second hand.

With reference to the international league tables, and no matter how we measure what it is that we measure, the rate of savings out of current income in the United States falls well below that of other developed countries. Net national savings as a share of total product lies somewhere within the range between 2½ and 5 percent, whereas in Japan this ratio is three to four times as large, roughly in the range of 15 to 18 percent. Developed countries in Europe exhibit aggregate savings rates that fall between these limits. And, historically, the savings rate in the United States has been falling through recent years, except for a possible reversal during 1990 and 1991.

Those who evaluate the macroeconomic performance of whole "national economies" are influenced both by the international comparisons and the historical record. Economies that exhibit low rates of saving do not grow rapidly, and rates of growth, as measured, are widely accepted to be appropriate criteria for national success or failure. But who is to specify whether the savings rate in the United States is "too low" or the savings rate in Japan is "too high"? Some of the confusion on this point is exemplified in the amusing suggestions of American politicians to the effect that the Japanese should be required to relax and go on spending sprees. Stripped to its essentials, the criticism of U.S. savings habits based on vague macroeconomic performance criteria does not seem convincing despite its widespread popularity.

A somewhat more defensible position is that which adjudges the aggregate savings rate to be too low, but only because of governmental policies that discriminate against the savings behavior of individuals and institutions. The inference is that aggregate savings would increase, and perhaps substantially, if politics did not intervene in the workings of the economy.

This charge is clearly on target to the extent that the net dissaving of the federal government, in the form of its large and persistent budgetary deficits, does, indeed, make up a substantial negative item in the accounts. This item, alone, goes far toward explaining the shortfall in current savings rates below historical trends in the United States. If by some magic the budget deficit could be eliminated, the net savings rate would be substantially higher than it now is. Much the same inference would be drawn, at least by some observers, with reference to the discrimination against savings choices that describe the tax structure, at all levels of government in the United States. On the other hand and as pointed out by still other observers, there are features of the legal-institutional environment in the United States that differentially favor savings and capital formation, as witnessed by limited liability for corporate investment and relatively favorable treatment of intergenerational transfers of wealth.

In any case, it is not necessary that I examine in detail either of the familiar arguments for policy measures designed to increase the aggregate rate of saving. I have noted the existence of such arguments in this section solely for the purpose of suggesting that my central proposition to the effect that we should save more may find acceptance based on reasons that are quite different from those that I advance.

III. The Great Keynesian Delusion

I shall now digress from the main line of discussion in order to forestall possible confusion and misunderstanding that may arise. This misunderstanding may stem from what I shall here call "the great Keynesian delusion" that exerted a significant influence on public, scientific, and political attitudes during several decades of this century. The delusion is named after Lord Keynes, who offered the intellectual-analytical formulation that exerted such major effects on the thinking of economists and policymakers and continues to affect attitudes toward saving behavior even in this last decade of the century.

The central Keynesian proposition was often presented, particularly in elementary economics textbooks, as "the paradox of thrift" or "the paradox of saving." The argument suggested that the efforts of income earners to save more, to save larger shares of current income, might backfire and that, in the net, aggregate savings might fall if too many persons tried to save, due to the feedbacks on the flow of incomes. The so-called fallacy of composition was introduced to explain why individualized choices, separately made, might generate results that may be contrary to those desired by all persons in the nexus.

In order to get some sense of the appeal of the Keynesian proposition here, it is useful to recall the economic-political-institutional environment during the time that the proposition was first articulated. The 1930s were the years of the Great Depression. Almost one-fourth of the American labor force was unemployed during the worst of those years, and the problem was widely interpreted to be a breakdown of the market or capitalist economy and, more specifically, as a failure of this economy to generate a demand for its production sufficiently large to take potential supplies off the market. That is to say, the diagnosis was one that attributed failure to *underconsumption.* Hence the remedy was to be found in *spending,* whether this be private or public.

In this model, the act of saving, which represents a withdrawal from the circular flow of income or an abstinence from spending, exerts negative or undesired effects at the macroeconomic level. Business spending on plant, equipment, inventories, and labor is directly responsive to observed rates of spending on goods and services by individuals, firms, and governments. The

Keynesian diagnosis was that saving was excessive rather than deficient; public policies were advocated that would expand rates of spending. Public opinion was urged to shift toward generalized praise for expressed willingness to spend.

This diagnosis and subsequent prescription for the macroeconomic illness of the Great Depression were characterized by a tragic failure to recognize the importance of the political-institutional framework, both in providing the environmental setting appropriate for satisfactory macroeconomic performance and in offering corrective offsets to changes in individual propensities to hoard. In the early 1930s the aggregate rate of spending was, indeed, depressed, and desperate measures were needed in order to increase that rate. But the fundamental source of the trouble was wrongly identified in the Keynesian analysis. The source was squarely located in the failure of the monetary authority, the Federal Reserve System, which allowed the supply of money to fall dramatically as the banking-financial crisis deepened, whereas, as we now know, the proper action should have been just the opposite. We now know that almost any policy action would have dictated that the monetary authority maintain stability or even growth in the monetary aggregates. And had this result been ensured, there would have been no Great Depression, as such. The macroeconomy of the United States would have absorbed any temporary shock, including that which originated in the banking structure. The jerry-built Keynesian analysis, which ignored institutional failures, need not have emerged at all.

And, importantly for my purpose here, individual participants in the economy need not have been misled into an acceptance of attitudes that attribute some praiseworthy social status to consumption spending while placing a social stigma of sorts on saving. The whole set of problems that involves monetary-macroeconomic-institutional performance, along with the criteria for success and failure, need not have become mixed up and confused with individuals' choices to spend or to save.

I need not, of course, use this occasion to defend my own analysis and interpretation of either the Great Depression or my criticism of the confusion in the intellectual-analytical responses. I have included this summary section only for the purpose of holding off possible misunderstanding of my enterprise. When I suggest that we should save more, and do so in our own general interest, I am assuming that the institutional framework is such as to allow the effects of private choices to be separated from macroeconomic stability.

IV. Obligations to Future Generations

I need to clear away one more set of extraneous notions before getting to the meat of this paper's theme. To the extent that is possible, I need to divorce my argument from apparently related normative principles that invoke considerations of intergenerational ethics, principles that base saving norms in intergenerational justice, that defend saving behavior and propositions to increase savings in terms of obligations to those who live after that time in which savings decisions are made—that is, future generations. I consider the whole range of questions that concern our obligations to the future, privately or collectively, to be of great importance, and I do not think that moral-ethical philosophers (and economists) have devoted enough attention to such questions. The difficulty of getting analytical "handles" on the problems involved should not be allowed to inhibit intellectual effort.

Within the limits of my enterprise, however, I do not need to resort to the treatment of future generations to justify my argument in support of increasing rates of personal saving beyond those that emerge from the independent choices of persons. To the extent that such intergenerational arguments can be adduced to supplement and support those that I advance, and in particular if such arguments serve to bolster the force of a saving ethic, they become welcome additions to practical efforts to implement my analysis. But the normative distinction between the two sets of arguments must be kept clearly in mind. Arguments that suggest we should save more because we have obligations to future generations that are not fully reflected in current choices to save necessarily introduce interpersonal and intergenerational comparisons of utilities, comparisons that my argument avoids, as later discussion will indicate.

Consider an individual who makes an independent and wholly voluntary choice to save, say, five dollars out of each one hundred dollars of income earned. In the standard theory of choice, we should say that, at the margin between spending and saving, this person secures an anticipated utility from a dollar's worth of saving that is equal to that anticipated from a dollar's worth of spending. To say that such a person should save more because by so doing the utility of those who may come along later, the children or grand-children of the individual who saves or those of others, will be increased is to presume somehow that the interests of these future members are not accu-rately taken into account in current savings choices. But who is to judge and on what criteria? How are the utilities of those in the future to be measured and put up against the utilities of the individual who makes the current choices?

A crude utilitarian calculus may even be adduced to suggest that, rather than saving more, persons who are now living should actually save less if the economy is expected to continue to grow through time, and for exogenous reasons, income levels per person promise to be higher in future periods than those levels now observed. Hence, naive utilitarianism might suggest that, on simple egalitarian or redistributive norms, persons now living should, to the extent possible, receive transfers from those who will live later, rather than the reverse. Hence, some downward adjustment in freely chosen rates of sav-ings might be contemplated, including the dissaving represented by the gov-ernment's budget deficits.

This last argument may seem bizarre, but I introduce it here only to in-dicate that any effort to justify increased rates of saving out of current in-come because of concern for future generations may backfire. Intergenera-tional ethics should concern us. But if we can construct an argument for more saving without resorting to intergenerational comparisons, we remain that much ahead of a very complex game.

V. Saving, Capital, and the Extent of the Market

I am now at the point where I can begin to develop my central proposition. But first let me summarize what I have already said here: I have disengaged the discussion from the macroeconomic policy debates about the alleged low rates of savings; I have warned against mixing the savings choices made by individuals and the overall performance characteristics of macromonetary institutions; and I have suggested that concerns about obligations to future generations are irrelevant to my argument.

What, then, is my argument all about? In one sense, the proposition is very simple, but in another sense it is quite complex. Simply put, the prop-osition states that the act of saving allows for a release of resources into the production of capital rather than of consumer goods. This increase in capital inputs into the market operates in essentially the same fashion as an increase in the supply of labor inputs. The increase in capital expands the size of the economy, and this, in turn, allows for an increased exploitation of the division and specialization of resources. The economic value of output per unit of input expands, and this result ensures that all persons in the economic nexus, whether they be workers, savers, or consumers, are made better off and on their own terms.

This summary statement of the proposition is accurate, but it does slide by several subsidiary steps in the analysis that must be clarified. When considered at an individual level, just what is involved in an act of saving? To save is not to spend. The flow of income received by an individual allows for voluntary disposition into two composite categories: (1) spending on purchases of final or end-items of consumption and (2) saving. In a real sense, savings are a residual; they measure the amount of income left over after spending on goods and services. But what form does this savings take? The individual does not simply withdraw purchasing power from the circular income flow of the economy. The funds saved are allowed to return to the circular flow by being made available to those persons and institutions who utilize them to purchase *capital goods.*

(In the simplest model, we could think of the same person acting in both the saving and the investing roles here. Robinson Crusoe saves by foregoing the gathering of coconuts long enough to build the fishing net, a capital good. As we know, however, much of the whole Keynesian analysis was based on the recognition that the act of saving is not equivalent to the act of investment and that different persons may play different roles. It seems best, therefore, to think initially in terms of the institutional arrangements that allow funds saved by an individual to become available to those who actually carry out the purchases of capital goods separately. If the macromonetary framework is in place, and if these institutions function properly, an act of saving will find its accompaniment in an act of capital goods purchase. A dollar of new saving, a dollar not spent on purchasing final goods and services, allows for a dollar's purchase of capital goods.)

At first pass, there might seem to be no effect on the inclusive size of the economic nexus in a switch from the purchase of a consumption good to the purchase of a capital good. There would, of course, be a change in the composition of production as the allocation of resources responds to the shift in demands. If persons increase their rates of saving from current income, with offsetting reductions in consumption spending, the economy responds by generating expanded quantities of capital goods and reduced quantities of consumption goods. The aggregate size of the production-exchange nexus would not seem to be modified in the process. The shift to more saving does not seem, at first pass, to be at all analogous to the shift from nonwork to work, which does, and directly, expand the size of the economic or market nexus at the expense of the nonmarket sector.

This first pass account, however, overlooks a fundamental feature of economic life, the *productivity of capital.* If that which is purchased as a result of the release of funds from the outlay on consumption goods and services should be nothing more than storable quantities of the latter, there would be no net increase in the size of the economy as a result of the behavioral change. But capital goods are not properly modeled as consumption goods in stored form. Capital goods are instruments, or tools, that are used ultimately in the production of final goods. Capital goods are inputs into the production processes.

The essential characteristic of capital, as an abstract notion, is that it is *productive.* The precise meaning of the word "productive" in the sense used here must be clarified, especially since its application to capital goods has been the source of much confusion in the history of economic ideas. Loosely speaking, any input that is transformed into valued output is "productive"; the input is employed to a valued purpose. But this general usage is not what is meant by the term "productive" in the sense required for the analysis here. To say that capital is "productive" is to say that the value produced by the employment of capital is greater than the value that is given up or sacrificed in the production or acquisition of capital. That is to say, capital goods produce a *surplus,* over and beyond their cost of production. This productive surplus is, however, generated only in *time.* (The immediate transformation of a purchased capital good into current consumption goods would not, of course, yield any surplus at all.) This productivity through time, and only through time, has caused many economists to attribute the net productivity to time itself rather than to the attributes of capital, with undue intellectual confusion in the process. The elementary fact is that, if used through time, capital goods yield a surplus over and above the return required to amortize fully the initial value of the outlay. The investment of a dollar today yields a productive return of say, 5 percent, over a year's time for a gross return of $1.05.

This simple numerical example makes my point. The economy, one year hence, is larger by five cents than the economy today, when the decision is made to save and to invest the additional dollar, to withdraw this dollar from the spending on consumption goods. And, when the economy next year increases in size, there can be increased prospects for specialization in resource use, with the resultant effects traced out in the earlier lecture.

It may, nonetheless, be useful to trace out these effects in specific application to savings choices. Return to the numerical example above. The person who chooses to save the extra dollar today does so in the full expectation that he or she will receive $1.05 a year from today. One motivation for the saving in the first place is surely the knowledge of the opportunity to secure a larger value in the future than the value that must be given up today, as measured in the sacrifice currently of consumption goods and services. But how do *others* in the economy benefit from the saving decision of that person who does, today, withdraw the additional dollar from the stream of consumption spending? In terms of the example, it would seem that the person who saves, and this person alone, gets the full return on the investment that the saving makes possible, the full surplus generated by the productivity of capital over time. The 5 percent return over the initial outlay is owed to, and paid to, the person who sets aside the dollar, who abstains from consuming in exchange for the opportunity to increase his or her income next year.

As with the work supply externality, however, there exist spillover benefits from the saving decision. As noted, the economy as measured by the total value of product becomes larger by the size of the increment to value reflected in the net product of the capital investment that the initial act of saving makes possible. To be sure, the additional sources available for spending, on both consumer and capital goods, in the second year must come from the person who first saves and later receives this net return. But this person, in the second year, is able to return $1.05 to the consumption spending or the capital spending stream or both, which becomes the demand for goods and services produced in the economy. And an economy that is larger, if even by five cents, is able to exploit more fully the advantages of specialization in resource usage. Put the one additional savings dollar together with others that reflect like decisions on the part of many persons, and somewhere a technology that was just on the margin of economic viability may be pushed beyond the threshold of survivability.

The analysis of saving is on all fours with that which I have discussed in application to the supply of additional labor, in the form of harder work. Individual participants in an economy, through their own choices of work-versus-leisure in the one case and spending-versus-saving in the other, can increase their own economic well-being by acting in such fashion as to incorporate in their own behavior the interdependencies among their separately made choices in supplying both labor and saving inputs to the market.

VI. A Dollar Saved Is a Dollar Earned: A Quantitative Comparison

A dollar's saving represents an initial withdrawal from the consumption spending stream, which makes possible a dollar's addition to the demand for and purchase of capital goods. The increase in the measured size of the economy occurs only because capital is productive. In the next period, the economy is larger by the amount of the net product of capital, that is the return over and above full depreciation. This simple analysis seems to suggest that a new dollar of savings is much less effective in generating an increase in the size of the economy than a new dollar earned as a result of an expansion in the quantity of hours worked. The latter expands the size of the production-exchange nexus by a full dollar's worth, whereas a new dollar of savings expands the nexus in the next period by only, say, five cents.

The simple analysis in this respect is, however, quite misleading because it overlooks the fact that capital, once created, is *permanent*, in an economic value sense. A dollar of new savings, today, makes possible an increase in investment in productive capital that will yield a return over and above full depreciation, not only in the first period after the initial increment to saving-investment, but in *all* future periods. Hence, the present discounted value of the increase in the size of the economic nexus that is generated by a new dollar of savings is a dollar (assuming that the investment yields the average rate of return, and that this rate of return is also the rate of interest at which yields are discounted). In present value terms, therefore, the dollar of new savings is in effect quantitatively the same as the dollar of new earnings from an increase in work supplied to the market.

VII. Internalization Through an Ethic of Saving

My enterprise is primarily positive in the scientific meaning of this term. My purpose is that of demonstrating that an ethic of saving, a basic component of that set of attitudes often summarized under the rubric "Puritan ethics," retains economic content, even in this last decade of the century. That is to say, to the extent that these ethical constraints exist and continue to influence individual choice behavior, we are better off than we would be in their total absence. And, in this summary statement, as elsewhere, I use the term "better off" strictly with reference to individuals' own evaluations rather than my own or any other set of standards.

In the parlance of modern (Paretian) welfare economics, we *internalize* the externality of or the interdependency among our separate decisions to save through the presence in our psyche of a set of ethical constraints that dictate that we save more than our "naked preferences" might indicate to us. The strengths of these ethical constraints, and hence the degree to which they actually influence choice behavior will, of course, vary from one person to another, among differing social environments and also will not remain constant over time. I have suggested elsewhere that I sense some erosion in the strength of the work ethic, with predictable consequences.

In this respect, my concern with an erosion of the saving ethic is even more acute. Among large numbers of the American labor force, despite some erosion, a work ethic remains strong. But the observed decline in the aggregate rate of net national savings in the United States cannot be denied. And, once again, the consequences for our own well-being should be clear. We must become poorer; in our own terms, as we save less, our economy fails to grow as fast as higher rates of savings might make possible. And this verdict applies to everyone in the economy, quite independent of where a person is located in the intergenerational chain described by positive and negative bequests.

It is relatively easy to identify several sources of erosion in the strength of the saving ethic. I have already discussed briefly the Keynesian interpretation of the events of the 1930s, a diagnosis that elevated the "paradox of thrift" to center stage in the attention of economists, and that surely, with some time lag, influenced the behavior of politicians in their institutional treatment of incentives. In addition, the social stigma attached to saving behavior has presumably exerted some effect, however slight, on personal spending habits. Financial innovations that have made it easier to spend, especially from income not yet earned, have allowed persons to dissave more readily, thereby making it harder for positive saving to offset negative entries on national balance sheets.

A somewhat related, but largely independent, development has modified the structure of savings incentives, quite apart from any direct operation of ethical constraints. I refer to the emergence of the welfare-transfer state during the course of this century. A shorthand description might classify this development as the politicization or collectivization of that element in saving that had previously been motivated both by life-cycle and intergenerational bequest consideration. Politicized schemes for social insurance against income loss during retirement years are the institutional embodiments of these changes. As experience suggests, governments have proved willing to issue promises to ensure retirement income support, but they have generally been unwilling to levy taxes for the purpose of accumulating earning assets sufficient to cover future costs. In effect, the Social Security system, the system for meeting retirement income needs, has been financed from current income flows rather than from productive capital investment.

As a participant in the politicized system, the individual is motivated to reduce those savings that might have otherwise been set aside to secure income flows during retirement years. This result need not accompany politicization of a retirement or pension scheme. But such a neutral effect on aggregate savings would be produced only if the collectivized scheme is, itself, maintained on some actuarially sound basis. The failure of democratically elected legislatures to take steps to accumulate fund balances sufficient to meet pension obligations has been characteristic of the American system since its inception in the 1930s.

In a more general sense, and beyond any politicization of what might be called the organization of individualized accounts, the dramatic increase in the transfer sector of the economy has undermined incentives to save and to invest. To the extent that persons are led to expect that governmental transfer payments will be available to them as members of this or that group who qualify for eligibility as a consequence of this or that event or circumstance, their planning against many contingencies need not occur. The "cradle to grave" security promised in the idealized slogan of the welfare-transfer state stands as an open invitation to the individual to live "hand to mouth," almost as a direct complement to the politicization of transfers.

Superimposed on the emergence of the welfare-transfer state in this century was the experience of inflation, especially during the 1970s. Even for those persons who desire to carry out individualized savings plans for life-cycle, bequest, or other motives, inflationary expectations make real saving difficult. Monetary instruments carry no assurance of maintaining real value through time, and precepts of rational choice behavior dictate shifts of demand to real goods, with a clear bias toward items of consumption, current or durable. And consumer durables, although they yield benefits over time, do not qualify as productive capital in the analysis sketched out earlier.

The family, as a cohesive unit that extends beyond the lives of its individual members and which becomes the institutional base for intergenerational transmission of accumulated wealth (capital value), has become less important in our whole scheme of social interaction. Even the limited ethical constraint that sometimes instructed members of wealthy families not to "eat up the capital" has lost much of its influence.

The list of causes for shifts in behavior toward consumption spending and away from saving could be extended. But the analysis here is limited largely to a partial explanation of the effects of the shifts rather than of the causes.

VIII. Alternatives to Restoring a Saving Ethic

In the United States of 1992, it is probably not fully rational for the individual, or the family unit, to save more than a somewhat limited share of income, a share sufficient to meet personal contingencies that do not, as yet, qualify for subsidization under welfare-transfer programs. If residues of an old-fashioned, Puritan-style ethic cause persons to save more than the objective elements in their individualized choice settings dictate to be rational in some strict sense, we all benefit by way of the external effects traced out earlier. But it should be clear that the force of any such ethical norm will continue to erode further in the face of continuing, and possibly still accelerating, shifts in incentive structures. "The state will take care of you"—this is the hymn of modernity. Why should we expect, from an ethics or any other standpoint, individuals to save much at all?

The interesting feature of the political environment of the early 1990s is that there seems to be a developing recognition of the effects of the low savings rate on economic growth and also an acknowledgment that the incentive structure of the tax-transfer system (along with the budget deficit) is a relevant causal factor. It is not out of the range of plausible prediction to suggest that sometime during the 1990s we may observe attempts at *political internalization* of the interdependencies among individual saving choices. This political alternative to ethical correction could not be predicted with respect to the work supply externality. Hence, in this respect at least, an *ethic* of work continues to be more important than an ethic of saving. But, in one sense, political action aimed at restoring incentives to save and invest, although not taking the form of imposing ethical constraints on individual choice at all, may reflect at least an indirect recognition of the economic interdependencies stressed here.

Another way of making this same point is to say that the whole nest of concerns about the low rates of aggregate savings, by international or historical standards of comparison, that seem to be grounded in criteria of macroeconomic performance, such as measured rates of growth, may ultimately be grounded in some implicit and inarticulated acceptance of the analysis that I have tried to outline here. Or, as perhaps is more likely, we may get political action designed to increase rates of savings for reasons that are unrelated to the arguments here advanced, reasons that may be based on incorrect analytical foundations. Be that as it may, any effective measures to increase saving may, within limits, be analytically grounded on considerations of our own interests, and efforts to elaborate our understanding of the economic interdependencies among our separated saving choices can proceed in tandem with practical steps toward reform in the incentive structures.

Economic Theory in the
Postrevolutionary Moment
of the 1990s

Abstract

Why did economists, generally, fail to predict socialism's failure? This chapter suggests that such failure is due to economists' acceptance of a maximizing paradigm as applicable to "the economy" as a whole, when the alternative conceptualization of "the economy" as a spontaneous order would have been scientifically superior. The approach derived from the theory of games should have been helpful but was dominated for three decades by the maximizing paradigm.

Introduction

Economic theory offers an explanation of the relationships between the interactive behavior of persons and patterns of social outcomes on the presupposition that individual action is motivated by economically meaningful and conceptually measurable self-interest. Economic theory, as such, does not embody the behavioral hypothesis that persons do, in empirical reality, act so as to further measurable self-interest. To the extent that they do so, economics offers the source of hypotheses that often withstand the falsifiability test. But such falsification, if it occurs, should not be interpreted as refutation of the underlying theoretical construction, although it would suggest limits of practical usefulness.

From *The Role of Economic Theory*, ed. Philip A. Klein (Boston/Dordrecht/London: Kluwer Academic Publishers, 1994), 47–60. Reprinted by permission of the publisher.

In this elementary sense, economic theory has been vindicated by the events of this century, culminating in the revolution that has signaled the failure of the great socialist experiments. Socialism, as an inclusive system of organizing economic activity, did not achieve the objectives that its advocates defined at its inception. Socialism did not produce the goods, defined as the economic values that can emerge ultimately only from the preferences of individual participants. Economic theory explains the failure of socialism through its focus of attention on incentive structures, on informational requirements, and on the necessary uncertainties in the linkage between choices and consequences. The ex post explanation does not, however, excuse economists, generally, from their apparent failure to predict the consequences that did, in fact, occur. Why did the revolutions that marked socialism's death take place before more than a tiny minority of practicing, professional economic theorists made predictions of systemic failure?

I suggest that this woeful record of economists' performance stems from a set of scientific errors that must be put right before economic theory can begin to exert a productive influence on the hard problems of transition from socialism to alternative structures. We know, of course, that these scientific errors were, in part, driven by the ideological bias that economists shared with intellectuals generally. But the errors in scientific understanding can be divorced from the ideological setting. It is possible to discuss the role of economic theory, as such: first, in its failure to predict socialism's demise; second, in its widely accepted explanation for the antisocialist revolution, ex post; and third, in its potential contribution to problems of transition in the postrevolutionary moment of the 1990s.

It first is necessary to lay out the general domain for discussion. I define my own understanding of economic theory in the sense used in this chapter and sketch out familiar territory in the history of ideas, with emphasis on the eighteenth-century discovery of the spontaneous order of market interaction, the discovery that sparked the genuine intellectual excitement of the classical political economists. Then I discuss, briefly, the classical economists' presuppositions for the constitutional framework necessary for an effective functioning of economic order and trace out the collapse of the classical-neoclassical understanding of the working of an economy, a collapse that was influenced by the challenge of Marxian socialism, by the implicit acceptance of political idealism and by the loss of systemic evaluation and analysis. I note the emergence of the maximization or allocationist paradigm, as aided and abetted by the particular mathematics of the calculus, and at the expense of emphasis on the catallactic subject matter of market organization, and the effect of game theory as a complement to a catallactic approach. Finally, I examine the elementary, but essential, contribution that economic theory can bring to participants, academic and lay alike, who have not experienced the history of market institutions. The genuine "miracle of the market" that did, indeed, excite the classical economists can offer a basis for an enthusiastic public philosophy in postrevolutionary societies, a philosophy that the cynical, jaded, and intellectually soft citizens in Western nations may have lost forever. As economists in the West, we, too, must recover our *raison d'être* as political economists-cum-political philosophers and not as social engineers. Our science has much to answer for but also much to contribute.

The Relevant Domain

As the definition in the first sentence of the introduction implies, the subject matter of economic theory is a set of relationships between choosing and acting persons and the patterns of results or outcomes that these relationships generate. An alternative way of placing the emphasis here is to say that economics offers a theory of organizational-institutional *order*. The theory tells in a generalized and pattern predictive sense "what will tend to emerge" under this and that set of circumstances, conditions, and constraints. We use economic theory in precisely the same way that we use much other knowledge. We explain why there is tropical fruit—say, bananas—on the supermarket shelves a thousand miles from the location where the fruit is grown. We use economic theory here just as we use physics to tell us why water runs down hill. We do not, of course, claim that theory enables us, in advance, to predict that bananas, as identified, will be on the market's shelves. Nor would we use physics to predict that the liquid substance to run down that ravine will be water. Economics allows us to predict that whatever people want to purchase will be available for purchase. Economic value will tend to be created in the form that people prefer, as driven by the same persons in their dual role as producers. The grower, the shipper, the distributor, the market manager, the shelf stocker, the cashier—all these put bananas on the shelves because they expect that, in so doing, they can exchange bananas for money,

which will, in turn, allow for their own purchases of the goods that they desire, goods that will, in further turn, be put on the store shelves by those of
us who purchase the bananas.

My purpose here is not to bore you with a summary of first-week elementary economics. But I should insist that those of us who are professionals in
the discipline often neglect these elementary principles at our peril, and especially when we recognize that only a very small minority of nonprofession-
als possesses even a generalized understanding of how the economic order
works.

If my summary seems perhaps too elementary as well as too conventional, let me contrast my definition of the subject matter with more familiar claims. Economics or economic theory is *not* about "the allocation of
scarce means among alternative ends."[1] This familiar means-end formulation draws attention, first, away from the creation of value as opposed to
some allocation or utilization of value that is presumed to be in existence,
and, second, from the interactive relationships between persons that define
the order of an economy. Biblical mythology is helpful with reference to the
first point. After the expulsion from the Garden, the lot of humans requires
that they create economic value if they are to survive at all. Absent such creation, or production, there are no resources, no means, to allocate among
ends or purposes. And if humans move beyond self-subsistent existence,
production as a means of securing ultimate consumption must involve the
establishment of exchange relationships with others. Economics allows us to
construct a generalized understanding of the complex set of exchange relationships.

As noted earlier, economic theory in its essential respects is no different
from other scientific knowledge, within the appropriate limits of its enterprise. These limits are transgressed, however, when attempts are made to
move outside the constraints imposed by the human subject matter and to
objectify economic reality on some presupposition that values can be divorced from the subjective consciousness of participants in the order. To recall Gertrude Stein's comment about Oakland, "there is no there there," in
the sense of an objectifiable economic universe that lends itself to scientific

1. Lionel Robbins, *The Nature and Significance of Economic Science* (London: Macmillan, 1932).

observation and evaluation, a universe that exists separately and apart from the interlinked set of human choices and actions that bring "the economy" into being. At best, therefore, the economist as scientist is restricted to potential explanation of patterns of results, and especially when noneconomic motivations for human actors are necessarily incorporated in what may be observed.

The enterprise of economics is, however, sufficiently open-ended to allow the potential for genuinely exciting scientific advances, which will be influenced, in part, by the events of history. The unexpected and dramatic collapse of communist totalitarian regimes has renewed and reinforced the attention of economists in incentive compatibility in varying institutional structures, in the informational characteristics of choices made under uncertainty.

Order without Direction

Economic theory, as such, was born with the scientific discovery of the spontaneous coordination that emerges from the separated, locally directed, and self-interested actions of participants in a nexus of exchanges. Prior to this breakthrough in the eighteenth century, there could scarcely have existed an "economic science," properly understood, since there was no reasoned understanding of the observed patterns of the order that resulted from human behavior directed toward economic purpose. Production, exchange, and consumption could, of course, be observed, but there was no integrating vision that allowed the separated actions to be related.

At this point, we confront etymological confusion that has plagued the discipline from its beginnings, a confusion that is not, to my knowledge, matched in any other science. *Economics*, as a term, finds its origins in Greek and refers to management or to economizing, yes, to the utilization of scarce means *by a decision-making unit*. In this accurately derived etymological use of the term, economics was, of course, always with us, and there were preclassical theories of economic management in which the direction of the national household by the king, the prince, the bishop, or some other sovereign became the subject matter for learned discourse. German cameralism provided a set of precepts for the prince to follow in arranging the economic affairs of the principality, and the economizing on the use of scarce resources was central to any such exercise. Although *mercantilism*, as a descriptive term applicable to systems, was coined by Adam Smith, we find this term useful to refer to those sets of policy directed principles that offered guidance to those who "managed" the national economy, who established specific objectives such as national accumulation of treasure, national rates of growth, and national levels of employment.

It is not surprising that Keynes found the mercantilist writers to be kindred souls, since in his attempt to shift the emphasis of economics back to macroaggregative management, Keynes necessarily moved away from the central thrust of the whole explanatory enterprise. The macroeconomic theory of midcentury was strictly within the management tradition and consistent with the etymological origins of *economics* as a term.

Adam Smith himself perhaps added to the ultimate confusion by the selection of the title for his treatise.[2] *The Wealth of Nations*, read descriptively from the title's words alone, suggests that nations are the units that are wealthy or poor, and, by inference, that increases in nations' wealth are desirable. Smith did not, of course, have such a reading of his title in mind, since the whole thrust of his argument is that individuals, not nations, are the relevant units and that wealth consists in whatever it is that individuals desire. And Adam Smith's work was the channel through which economic theory in the sense used in this chapter was established, a theory of the spontaneous coordination achievable through an interlinked network of market exchanges and a theory that demonstrates the inefficacy of attempted economic management for a whole society.

Throughout the two and a quarter centuries of its history, economics, as a theoretical science, has been burdened with its two-track and mutually contradictory analytical cores. More than mere bifurcation is involved here. The approaches required for analysis in the two research programs are categorically different. A theory that offers an explanation or understanding of the coordinating properties of an exchange network cannot be harnessed into "economizing" service in any strict managerial sense, although, of course, such a theory becomes an essential component in any design and construction of the framework of rules like constitutions within which economic interaction is allowed to operate.

2. Adam Smith, *The Wealth of Nations* (New York: Random House, 1937).

My own resolution of the confusion in economics is clear from my discussion. Economic theory, properly defined, is limited to the domain of exchange relationships, and the behavior within those relationships, along with the institutional structures that emerge or are constructed to constrain those who are participants. If progress is to be made, economics must, once and for all, throw off its etymologically influenced interpretation. Ideally, we should replace the very name; *catallaxy* or *catallactics* is etymologically descriptive.[3]

The Constitutional Framework

As people in the Soviet republics are finding out in 1992, the free market does not accomplish the coordination promised by some of its naive advocates in the absence of a set of constraints that may be considered to be the rules or the constitution for the market game. The classical discoverers of the coordinating properties of markets did not sufficiently emphasize the necessary presence of such rules or institutions. If no such rules exist, the chaos that the nonsophisticate in economics more or less naturally imagines may, indeed, become descriptive of reality.

The elements of the constitutional framework are familiar, and these need not be discussed in any detail here, but a summary statement is required in order to ensure that there are some common bounds for subsequent analysis. The political-legal order must embody security of person and property, and the basic rights that define such security cannot, in themselves, emerge from an exchange-like process, despite the pronouncements of the libertarian anarchists. Without some prior agreement on or acknowledgement of what is mine and thine, how could you and I even commence a trading or exchange relationship?[4] Once we are secure in rights of ownership, we are free to make exchanges in rights, in the expectation that those received in trade will themselves be genuinely owned, once possessed. A regime in which rights are severally assigned, mutually acknowledged, and legally protected

3. See James M. Buchanan, *What Should Economists Do?* (Indianapolis: Liberty Fund, 1979).

4. See James M. Buchanan, *The Limits of Liberty: Between Anarchy and Leviathan* (Chicago: University of Chicago Press, 1975).

defines the broad boundaries of the playing field for the inclusive economic interaction process.

A corollary of the ownership and control of person and possession is the enforcement of voluntary contracts of exchange, once made. The political-legal order must operate so as to ensure that individual contractors abide by the terms of agreed-on, but not fully implemented, exchanges of rights. And, as with the initial assignments, we could scarcely expect effective contract enforcement to emerge, itself, from contractual foundations, although the libertarian argument here is somewhat more persuasive than in the former case.

There are additional, and supplementary, elements in a constitutional framework that allow a market order of an economy to function effectively. These elements, some of which remain subject to ongoing scientific debate (for example, monetary arrangements), need not be treated in this summary. My point here is to emphasize only that it is the constitutional framework (the laws and institutions, the constraint set) that becomes the appropriate focus for those who seek to reform or to improve the operation of the social process in its economic aspects.

The eighteenth-century discovery of the ordering properties of market exchange was a discovery of such properties *within* rather than independent of the political-legal structure. And classical political economy, the emerging science that elaborated this discovery, at least in early form, was interpreted as a challenge to the whole enterprise of economic management. Laissez-faire—to leave alone—applied negatively to politicized effort to interfere with, and to improve on, the workings of markets. It should never have been extended to the criticism of the necessary political effort aimed at establishing and maintaining the constitutional framework. The categorical distinction between these two levels or stages of politicization was never clearly articulated, and this ambiguity compounded that discussed earlier that involved the meaning of terms.

The Loss of Wisdom

What happened to economics after the fourth decade of the nineteenth century? We know that the excitement of scientific discovery that characterized classical political economy did not survive. Somehow the basic theoretical understanding of market order seemed to slip away, at least partially, and we observed a peculiar melange of scientific progress and scientific retrogression.

Several sources of difficulty can be identified. The classical economists' understanding of market coordination was seriously incomplete. There was no plausibly acceptable theory for the pricing of productive inputs. The cost-of-production theory for the pricing of outputs offered the basis for the Ricardian-Marxian backward extension to input pricing and notably to labor. The theory of surplus value, allegedly produced by but not fully received by labor, was used effectively by Marx to undermine the efficacy of markets, even within the attitudes that embodied the earlier discoveries. The distributional implications of market coordination were moved to center stage, providing grounds for revolutionary political proposals that were well beyond any mercantilist schemes for political management of national economies. The Marxist argument tended to weaken economists' normative evaluation of their whole scientific enterprise.

In this respect, it is singularly unfortunate that the theory of input pricing that emerged as a consequence of the 1870s marginalist revolution in economic theory could not have been developed a mere half century earlier. Such a time shift might have forestalled the Marxist critique, which was clearly based on straightforward scientific error, and the consequences that we all know might not have occurred at all.

Quite apart from the Marxist extension of classical principles that indirectly caused economists to lose confidence in their own *raison d'être*, developments in moral philosophy were also of major importance. Influenced by the ideas of Hegel, philosophers lost the eighteenth-century skepticism about the operations of political-collective institutions, a skepticism that we can interpret to have been squarely based on both analytical and empirical hypotheses. As a substitute, there emerged a romantic model of the state, a model that came to be increasingly dominant, an idealist vision of an omniscient and benevolent collective entity. Both common-sense observation and theoretical understanding were lost. Alongside idealism in political philosophy, and especially in Great Britain, classical utilitarianism provided the framework for normative evaluation of alternative policy propositions, with the effect of drawing attention away from problems of implementation through the realities of politics.

Political idealism and utilitarianism are important because, even in those societies that were not so directly influenced by the Marxian challenges, the romantic model of the state became the source for totally unwarranted comparisons between the market order, as observed in operation, and the state, as idealized. Developments in economic theory did identify and classify institutional and operational failures in the workings of markets, as against the laissez-faire idealizations, but no comparable failures of politicized corrections were brought within the canon of political science until the public-choice revolution of the last half of this century.

Maximization, Mathematization, and the Theory of Games

Genuine scientific progress has been made in economic theory since the moment of its eighteenth-century origins in discovery. The marginalist revolution, and particularly the theory of input pricing that emerged in consequence, tended to complete, in broad basic outline, the theory of market coordination. Even in this respect, however, the contributions of axiomatic general equilibrium theory midway through this century were necessary to round off the whole enterprise. But, as I also noted, the management or economizing conception of subject matter, and applied at the level of the national economy, has never been absent from economists' professional tool kit.

The potential for intellectual confusion was enhanced by some of the methodological implications of the marginalist revolution itself. In voluntary market choices made by participating individuals, values are determined at the relevant margins of adjustment, and the very idea of marginal comparison of values stems from mathematics, the central logic of the calculus. It is not then at all surprising that economic theory, as developed throughout this century, should have use of more and more sophisticated mathematical tools. And, as applied to the decision making of individuals, the calculus of utility maximization is helpfully explanatory. But the availability of the applied mathematics surely generated a bias toward artificially forced and unwarranted extension beyond individual choice to collectivities, to macrounits, to society, to the economy. Social engineering became one of the several postmarginalist versions of mercantilist economic management. As also noted, the Depression inspired shift of attention to movement among economywide macroaggregates, a shift that Keynes and the Keynesians provided with quasi-scientific status, added powerful complementary force to economic management as the ultimate motive impulse for the formulation of economic theory itself.

Even without macroeconomics, however, the increasingly rigorous efforts to define the hard core of economic theory would have ensured an emerging economizing framework, as readily mathematized through the maximization paradigm. Post-Marshall economics became the theory of allocation of scarce resources or means among competing ends, a formulation that lends itself more or less directly to a marginalizing calculus. Emphasis was shifted away from the coordinating properties of interlinked markets, in which the separate participants may, indeed, be modeled as utility maximizers, and toward properties of markets conceptualized as if they were alternatives to or substitutes for economic management schemes for inclusively defined aggregations.

A major change of direction in economic theory may have occurred in midcentury when the theory of games provided an alternative mathematics to the marginalist calculus, a mathematics that carries important implications for the very way that economists conceive what their enterprise is all about.[5] In the theory of games, attention is immediately focused on the interaction process, as such, with participants modeled as taking separate actions within specified rules (the constitution), and out of which some solution emerges that is chosen by no one, either individually or collectively. During the second third of the century, the ongoing dominance of the maximization paradigm tended to obscure the potential contribution that game theory's elegance can make toward restoring, indirectly as it were, the catallactic focus of economic theory, a focus that was never totally absent. Only within the last three decades of the century did game theory's economic emphasis shift from the choices of strategies of separate players to the search for solutions and to properties of alternative solutions and then, by inference, to the effects of alternative sets of rules on solutions, the domain of constitutional economics.

5. J. von Neumann and O. Morgenstern, *Theory of Games and Economic Behavior* (Princeton: Princeton University Press, 1944).

The Miracle of the Market

I have found it useful to organize this chapter as a history-of-ideas narrative of the development of economic theory, as personalized through my own definition of the science as stated at the outset. In one sense, therefore, the whole discussion to this point becomes prefatory to the main purpose of the assignment, as suggested in the title of the chapter itself. What role can economic theory play in those societies that have experienced genuine revolutions, in which socialist organizational structures have been explicitly rejected, both in practice and in idea, but in which market-like institutions have not emerged, at least in forms similar to those observed in Western mixed economies? What role should economic theory play in the necessary transition from socialism? The 1990s are properly classified as a postrevolutionary moment in history. Will economic theory be of value in this moment?

I suggest that we can look for an answer in the historical epoch that describes economic theory's finest hours, the few decades that span the turn between the eighteenth and the nineteenth centuries, the period of classical political economy. The ideas of Adam Smith may or may not have themselves influenced events directly as initiating causes of political changes. (I do not engage George Stigler on this point here.) But we cannot deny the role that these ideas played in the undermining of the intellectual foundations, the putative legitimacy, of the eroding mercantilist structure of national economic management. The economists were effective in convincing political leaders, and a sufficiently large number of citizens, that an economic order without politicized direction could not only be imagined but could also be expected to increase the well-being of the economy's participants generally. The central role played by economic theory during this whole epoch seems clear enough. Persons had to be, and were, convinced that a market economy would work, and work with tolerable efficiency, before they would begin to feel comfortable in unstrapping the complex harness of politically controlled economic management.

The eighteenth-century skepticism about the motivation as well as the predicted efficacy of political-collective action in furthering the interests of citizens provided fertile ground for the acceptance of the economists' ideas. The potential constitutional function of market arrangements was for the first time understood, separate and apart from any concern with any prospect for efficiency in generating valued product. In retrospect, we can understand why the classical economists, along with their media and lay supporters, were so enthusiastic about the potential value of the newly emergent science of political economy.

The setting in the postrevolutionary societies in the 1990s is in many respects similar to that of the emerging industrial economies in the late eighteenth and early nineteenth centuries, at least similar enough to warrant speculation about the positive role that might be played by the more sophisticated, and more complete, modern theory or science of economic order. To the citizenry generally, to the intelligentsia, to newly enfranchised political leaders, all of whose history has dispelled any and all of the romance that collectivism-politicization might once have held, the miracle of the market, warts and all, offers promise. The observable consequences of socialism leave little space for the motivation of strictly distributional criticisms of market capitalism.

The timing seems ripe for an emergent and newfound enthusiasm for a Central and Eastern European *Wirtschaftwunder,* an enthusiasm that can be jointly grounded in a loss of faith in politicized economic management and a generalized understanding of economic theory in its most basic, and elementary, sense. The highly sophisticated analyses of potential market failures, as evaluated against nonattainable perfection, can be put on the shelf for those who understand the current relevance of the hard-core principles. To citizens in this postrevolutionary moment, simple analyses of market successes offer the essential components of attainable dreams. Vaclav Klaus, minister of finance in Czechoslovakia, is reported to have called for a "market without adjectives," and it is perhaps only in a postsocialist setting that we might have expected such comment from a highly successful political leader. Can we even imagine his United States counterpart, Secretary of Treasury Bentsen, making such a statement?

As noted, economic theory can provide postrevolutionary intellectuals with a much more sophisticated understanding and explanation of a market order than that which effectively energized the followers of classical political economy two centuries ago. And the body of doctrine incorporated in modern economic theory is sufficiently inclusive to offer continuing challenge to those scientists attracted by the aesthetics of new ideas. The hard core can excite the intelligentsia, while the several research programs around the periphery offer promise to the practicing scientists.

For those who seek to use economic theory for more specific reform purposes, the critical distinction between adjustments in the constitutional framework, the constraints within which economic activity takes place, and attempted politicized interferences with market results remain of critical importance. The postrevolutionary institutional settings are in flux; rights have not been fully assigned and acknowledged; legal rules and norms of behavior have not been fully established; contracts among traders have not evolved through a commercial history. And, significantly, a culture of reciprocal exchange is not descriptive of social reality, a culture that is embedded in our subconscious in Western economies.[6] The most elementary of all economic principles—there exist mutual gains from trade—remains to be absorbed by people in postsocialist societies. The teaching of economics becomes socially productive in these societies in ways that we can scarcely appreciate in Western cultures.

In my definitional introduction to this chapter, I stated that economic theory, as such, is not itself an empirical science but that it does provide the source for hypotheses that may be subjected to falsifiability tests. The dramatic events that have taken place, and others that will follow, in postrevolutionary economics must surely offer empirically minded economists wonderful opportunities for examining the implications of simple hypotheses. Never in history have economists been offered such near-laboratory conditions and on so enormous a scale. Almost regardless of methodological preferences, the economist who concentrates on postrevolutionary societies must be excited about his or her scientific enterprise.

I should acknowledge that my interpretation and prediction of the role that economics and economic theory will play in the postrevolutionary moment are tinged with hope. My response is really to the question "What role *can* economic theory play?" rather than to the more neutral question "What role *will* economic theory play?"

The management-economizing conception of economics, and especially

---

6. See James M. Buchanan, "Tacit Presuppositions of Political Economy: Implications for Societies in Transition" (Fairfax, Va., Center for Study of Public Choice, George Mason University, 1991, mimeographed).

as extended normatively to policy prescription, may not have been sufficiently exorcised, and I am concerned that economists in postrevolutionary societies will import many of the wrong or misguided research thrusts of Western economics rather than select carefully for potentially helpful research directions. Without attempts to be exhaustive here, I can list (alphabetically) several research programs that would seem to offer productive insights to professionals in the new postrevolutionary economies: Austrian economics, catallaxy, constitutional economics, experimental economics, game theory, general equilibrium theory, law and economics, new institutional economics, property rights economics, public choice. By comparison and by contrast, the following programs would seem to offer little or no promise and, indeed, may be distracting elements: input-output analysis, industrial policy, linear and quadratic programming, optimal control theory, optimal growth theory, optimal taxation, social choice theory, social welfare functions, theories of planning.

Economic Theory in the West

As an end note to the chapter, it is appropriate to ask the question "What is the role for economic theory in the mixed economics of Western countries that have not experienced revolutionary changes in institutional structures?" I am much less sanguine here than in response to the same question posed earlier for postrevolutionary societies. Western economists, as practicing scientists, tend to take the elementary principles of their discipline too much for granted, and they devote far too much effort, interesting though it may be, to esoteric intellectual puzzles that often have little relevant content, even in some remote sense. (The exception, as noted, may be in modern game theory, where the intricacies of the analytics may be required to force belated recognition of the foundational shift in approach to economic process.)

Economists forget that, quite unlike the other sciences where professionally agreed-on principles command authority beyond the scientific community boundaries, economics must be made convincing to the public and its political leaders, a task that requires continued teaching of the elementary verities. "Every man his own economist" is a plague that has been with economics since its inception as an independent body of thought. As a result, the failure of the theory's professionals to renew the principles allows interest-driven politicization to intrude continuously into the operations of the market order.

We observe little enthusiasm for the principles of markets based on a widening understanding of the market's efficacy in producing and delivering valued product. And, despite the effect of modern public-choice theory in offering a partial explanation or understanding of political failures, we do not observe an intellectual rejection of "socialism in the small" that is anywhere remotely comparable to the near universal rejection of "socialism in the large" in the postrevolutionary settings.

The relatively pessimistic conclusion is that the future role of economics and economic theory lies with the postrevolutionary societies rather than in the sometimes tired science that is academically established in the West, and, merely by way of such establishment itself, will devote resources to the maintenance of whatever role serves its own interests.

Acknowledgment

I am indebted to my colleague Viktor Vanberg for helpful comments.

Name Index

Akerlof, George, 417n. 3
Alchian, Armen A., 7n. 4, 129, 263, 310n. 7,
  416n. 3
Allen W. R., 7n. 4, 129, 310n. 7
Amacher, Ryan, 104n. 9
Arrow, Kenneth, 143n. 3
Arthur, W. Brian, 488, 393–95
Aumann, Robert J., 145n. 4

Bailey, Martin J., 68n. 3, 245–47, 249–52,
  257n. 10
Bain, Joe, 191n. 1, 195n. 5, 204n. 20
Baumol, William J., 385–87
Becker, Gary S., 219–20
Binmore, Ken, 39n. 4
Boiteux, M., 298–99, 302n. 9, 307
Borcherding, Thomas E., 265n. 4
Boss, Helen, 391
Boulding, Kenneth, 63–65, 67n. 1, 191n. 1,
  195n. 5, 255n. 6
Brennan, Geoffrey, 85n. 12, 105n. 10,
  271n. 6
Bronfenbrenner, Martin, 200n. 16, 265n. 3
Broome, John, 278–81
Brozen, Yale, 302n. 9, 307
Brunner, Karl, 30–31, 42

Calabresi, Guido, 170–71, 175, 280
Cannan, Edwin, 58n. 6
Casson, Mark, 111n. 2
Coase, Ronald H., 68n. 3, 169–70, 293–95,
  335, 336

Congleton, Roger, 345n. 2, 435n. 1,
  440n. 5
Cowling, Keith, 95n. 4

Danzon, Patricia M., 443n. 8
Davenport, H. J., 337
de Finetti, Bruno, 149n. 7
de Jasay, Anthony, 445
Demsetz, Harold, 263
Dickinson, Henry, 26
Dixit, Avinash, 395
Downs, Anthony, 104n. 9, 435n. 1

Ellis, Howard S., 311n. 3
Eltis, Walter, 387n. 6
Ethier, Wilfred J., 365n. 17, 379n. 2,
  394–95

Faith, Roger, 172n. 8, 183n. 21
Fellner, William, 200n. 16, 311n. 3
Ferguson, James, 212n. 3
Ferrera, Francesco, 337
Fishkin, James, 185
Flowers, Marilyn R., 443n. 8
Frech, H. E. III, 170n. 3, 174n. 9
Friedman, David, 75n. 6
Friedman, Milton, 265n. 6; interpretation
  of Marshallian demand curve, 54–55,
  198–99, 200–3, 245; objection to
  Austrian-subjectivist approach, 28
Frisch, Ragnar, 31
Fukuyama, Francis, 43

487

Subject Index

abstraction: *Homo economicus* as, 71, 73–77; necessity of, 70–71

arbitrageurs: entrepreneurs as, 151–52, 164–67, 424

bargaining: intraexchange, 356; under property and liability rules, 171

barter economy: exchange in, 411–12; inefficiencies in, 412

behavior: distinction between economic and noneconomic, 132; *Homo economicus* model, 87–89; in Prisoners' Dilemma game, 132–33. *See also* choice; economic behavior; individual choice behavior

benefits, present-value: with elimination of monopoly restrictions, 212–13

black markets: in command economy, 419

buyers: adjustment to price change, 219–20; in barter economy, 411–12; in command economy, 417–20; demand for final products, 192–95; expectations of monopolist's price, 232–33; exploitation in quantity discount mechanism, 204–5; income transfer in quantity discount transactions from, 200–202; under marginal evaluation curve, 197–200; in money-goods exchange, 412–14. *See also* consumer behavior; consumers

capital: permanence of, 465; productivity through time of, 463

capital goods: surplus produced by, 463–64

capitalism: Knight's ethical criticism of, 127

catallactic perspective: difference from maximizing perspective, 115–16; focus on exchange, 116–17; Knight's criticisms of economic order in, 117–23; relevant externalities in, 121

certainty, cognitive: individual choice in structures of, 145–49; structures of, 144–45

ceteris paribus: data in pound of, 53; equivalent to using, 56; in macro-economic analysis, 59–65; misuse of, 56–58, 61; partial equilibrium variables in, 53–54; as restriction on variables, 53–55; use of (Boulding), 64

choice: among alternatives, 26–27, 114; to be idle, 368–70; under cognitive certainty, 145–49; in context of risk and uncertainty, 279; in idea of opportunity cost, 285; influencing extension of market size, 378–79; link to uncertainty (Shackle), 143; logic in game of derivation of policy norms, 14–18; made in context of legal uncertainty, 296; non-economic elements in, 12–21;

This book is set in Minion, a typeface designed by Robert Slimbach specifically for digital typesetting. Released by Adobe in 1989, it is a versatile neohumanist face that shows the influence of Slimbach's own calligraphy.

This book is printed on paper that is acid-free and meets the requirements of the American National Standard for Permanence of Paper for Printed Library Materials, z39.48-1992. ♾

Book design by Louise OFarrell, Gainesville, Fla.
Typography by Impressions Book and Journal Services, Inc., Madison, Wisc.
Printed and bound by Worzalla Publishing Company, Stevens Point, Wisc.